[*Samuel Bailey*]

A

CRITICAL DISSERTATION

ON THE

NATURE, MEASURE AND CAUSES

OF

VALUE

[1825]

To Which Is Added

A Review Of It [Sometimes Attributed To James Mill]
Westminster Review January 1826

And Also By Bailey

A Letter To A Political Economist Occasioned by An Article in
The *Westminster Review* On The Subject Of Value [1826]

Observations On Certain Verbal Disputes In Political Economy
Particularly Relating To Value And To
Demand And Supply [1821]

An Inquiry Into Those Principles Respecting The Nature Of
Demand And The Necessity Of Consumption Lately
Advocated By Mr. Malthus [1821]

REPRINTS OF ECONOMIC CLASSICS

AUGUSTUS M. KELLEY · PUBLISHERS
NEW YORK · 1967

A CRITICAL DISSERTATION First Published 1825

(London: R. Hunter, *St. Paul's Churchyard*, 1825)

Reprinted 1967 by
Augustus M. Kelley · Publishers

PRINTED IN THE UNITED STATES OF AMERICA
by SENTRY PRESS, NEW YORK, N. Y. 10019

A

CRITICAL DISSERTATION

ON

THE NATURE, MEASURES, AND CAUSES

OF

VALUE;

CHIEFLY IN REFERENCE TO THE WRITINGS

OF

MR. RICARDO AND HIS FOLLOWERS.

BY

THE AUTHOR OF ESSAYS

ON THE

FORMATION AND PUBLICATION OF OPINIONS,

&c. &c.

LONDON:

PRINTED FOR R. HUNTER,

ST. PAUL'S CHURCHYARD.

MDCCCXXV.

PREFACE.

THE subject of the following Dissertation is generally allowed to be one, both of high importance and of great difficulty.

" From no source," says Mr. Ricardo, " do so many errors, and so much difference of opinion in the science of political economy proceed, as from the vague ideas which are attached to the word value." And the same eminent writer, in the preface to the third edition of the Principles of Political Economy and Taxation, emphatically terms it a difficult subject. " In this edition," says he, " I have endeavoured to explain more fully than in the last, my opinion on the difficult subject of VALUE."

It is remarked by another author, that " he who is fully master of the subject of Value is already a good political economist." " Even for its own sake," he adds, " the subject is a matter of curious speculation : but in relation to Political Economy it is all in all : for most of the errors (and, what is much worse than errors, most of the perplexity) prevailing in this science take their rise from this source*."

Although much has been written and many efforts have been made to overcome the obstacles, which present themselves in this part of economical science, it may be affirmed with little risk of contradiction, that the success has not been in proportion to the labour bestowed. There appears to have been too little circumspection at the outset. The ground-work of the subject has not been examined

* The Templars' Dialogues on Political Economy, in the London Magazine for April, 1824, pages 341 and 342.

with that minuteness and closeness of attention which are due to its importance. Writers on political economy have generally contented themselves with a short definition of the term value, and a distinction of the property denoted by it into several kinds, and have then proceeded to employ the word with various degrees of laxity. Not one of them has brought into distinct view and discussion the nature of the idea represented by this term, or the inferences which a full perception of its meaning immediately suggests; and the neglect of this preliminary labour has created differences of opinion and perplexities of thought, which otherwise could never have existed.

There has been still more laxity, both of thought and expression, regarding the measurement of value. The vague manner in which the word measure, necessarily of frequent occurrence in the pages of the political

economist, is constantly employed, would surprise even the metaphysician, who is well aware
of the extensive prevalence and unbounded influence of the chameleon-like properties of
language. No writer (as far as the author of the
following pages is acquainted with works on
economical science) has ever taken the trouble to
analyse the meaning involved in the phrase. To
measure value is an expression apparently so
simple, so precise, so free from obscurity, that
it seems superfluous to bestow a single inquiry
on its import. The consequence has been
what it generally proves on such occasions:
the term has been used without any clear perception of a definite sense; several ideas
have been unconsciously and indiscriminately
interchanged, and analogies, which had merely
an imaginary existence, have been assumed as
incontrovertible premises or universally conceded postulates.

The causes of value have been also too negligently passed over. Little inquiry has been made into the nature of these causes, or their mode of operation, and to this slightness of examination may be attributed several important errors, manifested in attempts at undue generalization, in perversions of language, and in the rejection of circumstances which have a real and permanent effect.

A singular confusion has also prevailed with regard to the ideas of measuring and causing value, and in the language employed to express them. The perpetual shifting from one notion to the other, the use of common terms for both ideas, and the consequent ambiguity, vacillation, and perplexity, exhibit a remarkable picture of the difficulty of thinking with closeness, as well as of the defects of language as an instrument of reasoning.

The confusion and obscurity, which mark the

works of some of the most celebrated writers on
these momentous topics, are sufficient to make
the student abandon his inquiries on the very
threshold of the science. Words used without
determinate ideas, terms introduced without
proper explanations, definitions abandoned almost as soon as enunciated, principles assumed
without first being examined, verbal instead of
real simplifications — such are the obstacles
which everywhere meet him.

That defects of this kind disfigure the science
of political economy, no one acquainted with
the most recent works on the subject will probably deny, although a difference of opinion
may exist regarding the extent to which they
prevail.   It would be presumptuous in the
author of the following treatise to suppose, that
he had completely removed them from that
part of the science which he has attempted to
examine.   He trusts, nevertheless, that he has

done something, if not towards directly effecting
that object, at least towards opening the way
for subsequent endeavours. If he has not succeeded in putting all his propositions in a clear
light, and finally settling the various contro-
verted questions which he brings under review,
yet he may hope that he has introduced them
in such a manner as will excite in others the
interest and attention requisite for their ultimate determination. Free, on his own part,
from particular attachment to any of the positions which he has maintained, although im-
pressed with that clear conviction of their
soundness, without which it would be absurd
to intrude them on public notice; and sensible
of the thousand ways in which error imposes
itself on the understanding in the character of
truth, he will be glad of an opportunity of re-
considering his opinions, under the guidance of
a mind which has reached a higher point of

view than his own; nor will it greatly surprise him to discover, that he has fallen into errors and misconceptions as deep and as radical as any of those which he has found or fancied in the speculations of others.

From the defects here imputed to the science, it is evident that in any work, which professes to examine and remove them, the points discussed must be questions as to the use of terms, the distinction of ideas, the logical dependence of arguments, rather than questions of fact or evidence, and that its character will be essentially critical, and even polemic. In endeavouring to define the nature of ideas, to fix the meaning of terms, to investigate first principles, and to determine the real objects and results of inquiry, it was impossible, it would have been worse than useless, not to advert to the works of preceding writers, although at the expense perhaps of that neatness and elegance of deduction, of which the subject is susceptible; and certainly at the risk of incurring, if not hostility, at least the utmost severity of examination from the talents and acumen, which such a course necessarily puts on the defensive. In the present state of political economy, however, a critical reference to the doctrines of preceding and contemporary economists cannot be avoided, and ought not to be avoided if it could. A mere direct expository treatise would be of far inferior utility. However true a doctrine may be, it is of little service until its relation to other doctrines, and its connection with knowledge already extant, has been shown. Embarrassed as the science is with difficulties on which opinion is divided, it is of the utmost importance for its future progress, not only to explain and establish correct principles, but to expose the de-

lusion which has formerly misled, to trace
the process of error, to mark the particular
point where inquiry departed from the right
path, or where the unperceived fallacy, which
has vitiated a train of reasoning, first insinuated
itself into the argument. The science cannot
yet be exhibited as a regular and perfect
structure. The rubbish must be removed, the
ground cleared, the scaffolding taken down,
and all unnecessary and cumbrous appendages
must be discarded, before the building can rise
upon the eye in that simple beauty in which it
is destined hereafter to appear.

The writer, on whose doctrines the following
treatise principally animadverts, is generally
regarded as the ablest economist of his day.
It has been unfortunate, perhaps, for Mr. Ricardo's ultimate reputation, and certainly for
the science which he cultivated, that his admirers have extolled him beyond the sobriety

of truth. Strong powers of mind he unquestionably possessed; otherwise, he could
neither have produced the works which have
associated his name with the political measures
of the age, nor could he have inspired those
sentiments of admiration and deference, which
have been so warmly manifested by men, themselves of no common talents. It is probable,
however, that the excess of their admiration
has blinded them to his defects; that they have
been too much occupied with the excellence of
his speculations to note the errors by which
they are disfigured. It would be difficult, on
any other supposition, to account for the extravagant praises which have been heaped on
his Principles of Political Economy and Taxation. One of our most distinguished living
economists designates it as a " work rivalling
the ' Wealth of Nations' in importance, and
excelling it in profoundness and originality*."

* A Disc. on Pol. Econ., by J. R. M'Culloch, Esq., p. 65.

" The powers of mind," says the same writer,
" displayed in these investigations — the dexterity with which the most abstruse and difficult questions are unravelled — the unerring sagacity with which the operation of general and
fixed principles is investigated — the skill with
which they are separated and disentangled
from such as are of a secondary and accidental
nature — and the penetration with which their
remotest consequences are perceived and estimated — have never been surpassed; and will
for ever secure the name of Ricardo a high
and conspicuous place in the list of those, who
have done most to unfold the complex mechanism of society, and to carry this science to
perfection."

Conceding that Mr. Ricardo has displayed
considerable originality and power of intellect,
we may yet be permitted to doubt, whether this
splendid eulogium is not far beyond his real de-
serts. It is not easy to conceive by what process

a superiority above Adam Smith, as a profound
and original thinker, can be inferred from their
respective works. To raise the science from
the condition in which it was found by the latter, to that state of dignity and importance in
which it appeared in the Wealth of Nations,
seems to an ordinary view to have required a
far more comprehensive mind, and greater
powers of skilful disquisition, than to discover
and to follow out to their consequences the original truths, few or many, which distinguish the
pages of the Principles of Political Economy and
Taxation. The praise, too, of dexterity in unra-
velling difficult questions is surely misapplied.
The obscurity which is almost universally felt,
and felt even by readers accustomed to closeness of reasoning, and not sparing of vigorous
attention, in many of Mr. Ricardo's discussions,
incontestably proves, even on the supposition of
their perfect accuracy, a want of skill in the ma-

nagement of his materials, a defect either in
the disposition of his ideas or the employment
of his terms. It is the triumph of dexterity in
dissertation to present every proposition in
such due order and such perspicuous language,
as to lead the reader to imagine, that he should
himself have expressed the meaning nearly in
the same manner and in the same words. There
is scarcely a single train of thought in the
Wealth of Nations, which a mere tyro would
feel it difficult to follow, and of which the aim
and connection with the subject would not be
perfectly intelligible : but there are many observations in the writings of Mr. Ricardo, which
it requires the effort of a vigorous mind to
connect with the other propositions amongst
which they stand.   His ideas are often
imperfectly developed, and his reasoning appears elliptical and disjointed ; defects, indeed, which have possibly elevated rather

than lowered his standing in general estimation. The

" omne ignotum pro magnifico"

is not without its exemplifications in the field of science, and the reputation of an author for profundity is sometimes enhanced by an intermixture of the unintelligible, many readers tacitly ascribing unusual sagacity to one, who is able to understand what is incomprehensible to themselves ; while a lucid arrangement of ideas, a manifest dependence of arguments, and a perspicuity of language, such as mark a complete mastery of the subject, appear too easy and natural to infuse the slightest suspicion of the depth and vigour of intellect from which they proceed, and of which they are the surest indications.

The occasional obscurity, which clouds Mr. Ricardo's writings, has sometimes been attributed to his style, and sometimes to his ambition of paradox. But if by style we are to understand the selection of words, and the mode of combining them into sentences, the former solution is incorrect, for his language is uncommonly precise and perspicuous, and the construction of his periods is simple and compact. The latter explication is, if possible, still more unfounded, there being an evident simplicity of aim and steady pursuit after truth in his writings, such as are natural to a mind of any originality, and which exclude the idea that he indulged the contemptible ambition of perplexing his readers. The defect had a deeper source, and is to be traced, as the following pages will show, to an original perplexity and confusion in some fundamental ideas, from which he was never able to extricate himself. Although Mr. Ricardo possessed remarkable logical powers, he seems to have been less gifted with analytical subtilty; and hence his writings furnish an instance of what the observer of the

human mind must have frequently seen exem-
plified, that the strongest powers of reasoning
are an insufficient security against gross error,
if unaccompanied by that incessant analysis of
terms and propositions, and that intense consciousness of intellectual operations, which
are the properties of a metaphysical genius.
Of this cast of intellect, the most striking
instance perhaps which our own times afford is to be found in the writings of the late
Professor of Moral Philosophy in the univer-
sity of Edinburgh, Dr. Thomas Brown; a man
who possessed, in an almost unrivalled degree,
the capacity of looking into the mechanism of
his own mind, and seeing the impalpable phenomena of thought and feeling, as well as the
power of flinging to a distance the embarrassing
influence of words, and fixing his eye with
keen penetration on the things which they represented, stripped of the covering of language,

and freed from every tinge of feeling and asso-
ciation *.

To judge from his writings, Mr. Ricardo
possessed little of this faculty; little consciousness of the nature of the operations in which
he excelled, and little familiarity with the analysis of terms. His was a sort of natural vigour
of reasoning, exerting itself without the advantages of discipline, without much acquaint-

---

* The author feels a pleasure in paying this passing
tribute to the talents of a philosopher, who has taken
a giant-stride in the science to which he devoted himself, and who will be hereafter considered as one of the
most remarkable men of a period prolific in great names.
The reputation of writings like his, far in advance of the
age in which they appear, making no appeals to the senses,
and having no obvious connection with the immediate and
palpable affairs of life, is necessarily of slow growth, but
it will flourish when hundreds of names, which fill more of
the public ear, have passed to that oblivion which certainly
awaits them.

ance with the instruments employed, or much thought regarding the methods of applying them : and although his logical powers kept him in general to the employment of a term in one uniform sense when he clearly discerned it, yet, in cases where he happened unconsciously to change the meaning, or to be unaware of an ambiguity, his inaptness at analysis precluded all chance of his subsequently correcting any deviation, and the very strictness of his deductions, only led him further into error. Starting from a given proposition, he would reason from it with admirable closeness, but he seems never to have been sent back, by the strangeness of the results at which he arrived, to a reconsideration of the principle from which he set out, nor to have been roused to a suspicion of some lurking ambiguity in his terms. Hence it might have been predicted, that he would commit oversights in his premises and assumptions, for which no subsequent severity of logic could compensate.

Perhaps these remarks will serve to explain how it is, that Mr. Ricardo has been eulogized for his inexorable consistency in the use of words, and particularly for his sternly insisting on the true sense of the word value, and on using it only in one sense*. If the author of the following pages has been at all successful, in establishing the justness of the strictures which he has hazarded, this praise must be allowed to be unfounded; for it will be seen, that in the case of the word value he has almost perpetually forsaken his own definition: yet an inconsistency of this sort is by no means incompatible with a general strictness in the employment of terms. If the preceding observations are correct, a writer may be rigorously consistent in

* Templars' Dialogues, Introduction.

the use of his terms through a long train of reasoning, while the whole of his conclusions may be vitiated by an unperceived transition from one meaning to another in the original adjustment of his premises, or in the first steps of his argument.

Besides Mr. Ricardo, the only writers on whom there are any strictures worthy of notice in the following work, are Mr. Malthus, Mr. Mill, and the author of the Templars' Dialogues on Political Economy, published in the London Magazine; of whom the two latter may be considered as having adopted the doctrines of Mr. Ricardo with little variation.

Mr. Malthus and Mr. Mill are too well known to the students of political economy, to render it necessary to say any thing in this place as to their general merits, and it can excite no surprise that the writings of either should be subjects of examination in a treatise

of this nature. With the Templars' Dialogues
on Political Economy, probably fewer are acquainted, from the form in which they came before the public; and on this account, as well as
from their state of incompleteness, they would
not have occupied so many of the ensuing pages,
had not the writer of the present work regarded
them as an exposition of several of Mr. Ricardo's principles, peculiarly adapted to try their
validity.

Adopting Mr. Ricardo's doctrines, the author
of the Dialogues traces them fearlessly to their
legitimate consequences, with a directness of
logical deduction which nothing diverts; with
great copiousness and felicity of illustration,
great dexterity in putting forward the different
parts of his theme, and an occasional humour,
which even on a subject of this kind is irresis-
tible. It must be obvious that a work of this
character, pressing intrepidly forward from the

premises to the conclusion, and flinching from no consequences at which it arrives, forms a sort of *experimentum crucis,* by which the truth or falsity of the principles maintained will be rendered manifest, and is the very kind of exposition which an examiner of their correctness would desire.

It was in fact the clear, able, and uncompromising manner in which the author of the Dialogues explained the principles of Mr. Ricardo, together with the startling and (the present writer must be permitted to say) the extravagant consequences to which he pushed them, that first suggested the following treatise, the author of which takes this opportunity of expressing his regret (a regret shared by many others), that discussions so valuable for either confirming or disproving the doctrines which they enforced, should not have been conducted to their proper and their promised termination.

CONTENTS.

	Page
CHAPTER I.	
ON THE NATURE OF VALUE......	1
CHAPTER II.	
ON REAL AND NOMINAL VALUE......	37
CHAPTER III.	
ON THE VALUE OF LABOUR	46
CHAPTER IV.	
ON PROFITS	62
CHAPTER V.	
ON COMPARING COMMODITIES AT DIFFERENT PERIODS.	71
CHAPTER VI.	
ON MEASURES OF VALUE......	94
CHAPTER VII.	
ON THE MEASURE OF VALUE PROPOSED BY MR. MALTHUS	139

CHAPTER VIII.

ON METHODS OF ESTIMATING VALUE.................... 152

CHAPTER IX.

ON THE DISTINCTION BETWEEN VALUE AND RICHES. 162

CHAPTER X.

ON THE DIFFERENCE BETWEEN A MEASURE AND A

CAUSE OF VALUE 170

CHAPTER XI.

ON THE CAUSES OF VALUE 179

CHAPTER I.

ON THE NATURE OF VALUE.

VALUE, in its ultimate sense, appears to mean
the esteem in which any object is held. It denotes, strictly speaking, an effect produced on the
mind; but as we are accustomed in other cases
to give a common name to a feeling and to
the cause which has excited it, and to blend
them together in our thoughts, so in this case
we regard value as a quality of external objects. Colour and fragrance, for example, are
words which designate both the cause and the
effect, both the material quality which produces
the feeling in the mind, and the feeling produced. The philosopher, however, is the only
one who discerns the distinction, and colour
and fragrance are never thought of by the ge-

nerality of men, but as qualities of external objects.

It is precisely in the same way, that value is regarded as a quality belonging to the objects around us. We lose sight of the feeling of the mind, and consider only the power which the object possesses of exciting it, as something external and independent.

It is not, however, a simple feeling of esteem, to which the name of value, as used by the political economist, can be given. When we consider objects in themselves, without reference to each other; the emotion of pleasure or satisfaction, with which we regard their utility or beauty, can scarcely take the appellation of value. It is only when objects are considered together as subjects of preference or exchange, that the specific feeling of value can arise. When they are so considered, our esteem for one object, or our wish to possess it, may be equal to, or greater, or less than our esteem for another: it may, for instance, be doubly as great, or, in other words, we would give one

of the former for two of the latter. So long
as we regarded objects singly, we might feel
a great degree of admiration or fondness for
them, but we could not express our emotions in
any definite manner. When, however, we regard
two objects as subjects of choice or exchange,
we appear to acquire the power of expressing
our feelings with precision, we say, for instance,
that one A is, in our estimation, equal to two
B. But this is not the expression of positive,
but of relative esteem; or, more correctly, of
the relation in which A and B stand to each
other in our estimation. This relation can be
denoted only by quantity. The value of A is
expressed by the quantity of B for which it will
exchange, and the value of B is in the same
way expressed by the quantity of A. Hence the
value of A may be termed the power which it
possesses or confers of purchasing B, or commanding B in exchange. If, from any consideration, or any number of considerations, men
esteem one A as highly as two B, and are willing to exchange the two commodities in that

ratio, it may be correctly said, that A has the power of commanding two B, or that B has the power of commanding half of A.

The definition of Adam Smith, therefore, that the value of an object " expresses the power of purchasing other goods, which the possession of that object conveys," is substantially correct; and as it is plain and intelligible, it may be taken as the basis of our subsequent reasonings, without any farther metaphysical investigation.

According to this definition, it is essential to value, that there should be two objects brought into comparison*. It cannot be predicated of one thing considered alone, and without reference to another thing. If the value of an object is its power of purchasing, there must be something to purchase. Value denotes consequently nothing positive or intrinsic, but

* " We cannot express value, or a variation of value, without a comparison of two commodities." Inquiry into the Nature and Origin of Public Wealth, by the Earl of Lauderdale, p. 19, second edition.

merely the relation in which two objects stand to each other as exchangeable commodities.

In the circumstance, that it denotes a relation between two objects, and cannot be predicated of any commodity without an express or implied reference to some other commodity, value bears a resemblance to distance. As we cannot speak of the distance of any object without implying some other object, between which and the former this relation exists, so we cannot speak of the value of a commodity but in reference to another commodity compared with it. A thing cannot be valuable in itself without reference to another thing, any more than a thing can be distant in itself without reference to another thing.

It follows from this view of value as a relation, that it cannot alter as to one of the objects compared, without altering as to the other. It would be an absurdity to suppose, that the value of A to B could alter, and not the value of B to A; that A could rise in value to B, and B remain stationary in value to A; an absurdity of much the same kind as supposing, that the distance of the earth from the sun could be altered, while the distance of the sun from the earth remained as before.

Suppose that at some former period, when the value of commodities was determined by the quantity of labour required to produce them, A and B were the only exchangeable commodities in existence, and that they were of equal value. If, from any circumstances, A should, at a subsequent period, require double the quantity of labour for its production, while B continued to require only the same, A would become of double value to B; or, in other words, one A would exchange for two B. But although B continued to be produced by the same labour, it would not continue of the same value, for it would exchange for only half the quantity of A, the only commodity, by the supposition, with which it could be compared.

It may be objected to this representation of the relative nature of value, that when we say the value of A is equal to the value of B, the expression implies a quality intrinsic and absolute in each ; for otherwise, how could we affirm that an equality existed between these two values ? If the term value denotes merely a relation between A and B, would it not be absurd to talk of the equality of their values, just as it would be absurd in speaking of the distance between the sun and the earth, to talk of an equality of their distances from each other ?

In reply to this objection, if we examine the real import of our expression, when we affirm the value of A to be equal to the value of B, we shall find tto mean neither more nor less than this, tha 1A will exchange for B. This simple proposition contains the whole amount of meaning co.iched under the phrase, and it obviously expresses or includes no intrinsic or absolute quality in either commodity, but merely states a relation in which they stand to each other.

The phrase, the value of A is equal to the value of B, is in this view of the subject not altogether accurate ; that is to say, if we speak only of two objects, without reference to any others. But it will be found, that, in speaking of the value of A being equal to the value of B, we are led to use the expression by the constant reference which we unavoidably make to the relations of these commodities to other commodities, particularly to money, and the import of our language, in its whole extent, is, that A and B bear an equal relation to a third commodity, or to commodities in general.

It is from this circumstance of constant reference to other commodities, or to money, when we are speaking of the relation between any two commodities, that the notion of value, as something intrinsic and absolute, has arisen. When we compare objects with each other as exchangeable commodities, two relations necessarily mix themselves in our comparison — the mutual relation of the objects, and their relations to other objects; and it is these latter which occasion the semblance of absolute value, because they seem independent of the former, which is the immediate object of our attention. Indeed, it is generally by their relation to a third commodity, that we can at all ascertain the mutual relation of two commodities which we are desirous of comparing. If we wish to know whether A and B are equal in value, we shall in most cases be under the necessity of finding the value of each in C; and when we affirm that the value of A is equal to the value of B, we mean only that the ratio of A to C is equal to the ratio of B to C.

The relative nature of value has not, it appears to me, been distinctly seen or uniformly kept in view by our best writers on the subject. Mr. Ricardo, for instance, who agrees with Dr. Smith in his definition of value, asserts, that if any one commodity could be found, which now and at all times required precisely the same quantity of labour to produce it, that commodity would be of an unvarying value*.

* Principles of Pol. Econ. p. 10, 2d ed. Mr. Ricardo has withdrawn this sentence in his 3d edition, and presented his readers with a new section, in which his doctrines are considerably modified. The alterations, however, do not, as will be shown immediately, at all affect the justness of the strictures in the text. And it may also

If value, however, denotes merely a relation, this proposition cannot be true. We may ask, to what would this commodity bear an invariable value? What is the correlative? Would it bear the same value to all other commodities? It might do so, it is true, but certainly not in consequence of being produced by an unvarying quantity of labour: for while the labour, in this instance, remained a fixed quantity, yet if the labour in other commodities were increased or diminished, the relations of value between this one commodity, and all others, would, on Mr. Ricardo's own principle, be instantly altered.

If corn, for example, always required precisely the same quantity of labour to produce it, but all other commodities whatever came to

be remarked, that notwithstanding the suppression of the sentence above cited, he retains another but slightly different in expression. " That commodity," says he (chap. xx, on Value and Riches), " is alone invariable, which at all times requires the same sacrifice of toil and labour to produce it."

be produced by half the labour formerly expended upon them, the value of corn could in
no sense be said to remain the same. In proof
of this, take Mr. Ricardo's own definition of
value, " the power of purchasing other goods,
which the possession of an object conveys."
To say that a commodity is of unvarying value,
is, according to this definition, equivalent to
saying that its power of purchasing other goods
remains constantly uniform; or, to vary the
language, that the quantity of other goods for
which it will exchange never alters. But, in
the example we have adduced, the same quantity of corn would exchange for an increased
quantity of any other commodity; and consequently, by Mr. Ricardo's own definition, would
have risen in value.

It may possibly be alleged, that it is not the
corn, but other commodities which have varied
in value, and therefore Mr. Ricardo's language
is correct. If value were a positive or intrinsic
quality, this might be true; but since it denotes
a mere relation between two objects, to suppose
any alteration could take place in this relation

as to one and not as to the other; to suppose
that the value of A to B could be altered, and
not the value of B to A, would, as I have already remarked, be as absurd, as supposing
that the distance of the sun from the earth
could be increased or decreased, while the distance of the earth from the sun remained as
before.

The truth intended to be conveyed by saying
that B remains of the same value is, that the
cause of the altered relation between A and B
is in the former, and not in the latter; and to
determine where the change originated is in
fact the whole object of those who endeavour
to show what commodities have remained
stationary in value, and what have varied.

It is so important to bear in mind, in these
cases of rising and falling, that as A rises, B
necessarily falls; or, to speak with greater precision, that the value of A cannot increase in
relation to B, without the value of B decreasing
in relation to A, that I may be pardoned for
still further showing the impropriety, or at least
the danger, of using the terms rise and fall in

a way which implies, that when A rises or falls, B remains stationary. If A, in consequence of additional labour expended upon it, or any other cause, were to increase in value relatively to the mass of commodities, which may be represented under the letters B C D, it would be said, by most economists, that B C D had not fallen, but remained stationary; although they would evidently have fallen, or become of less value, in relation to A. The assertion of their remaining stationary, can mean only stationary to each other; and in this sense it is perfectly correct, but the correctness of the language as to B, C, or D individually, evidently depends on the existence of some other commodity to which its relation remains undisturbed. Were there only two commodities in question, the phrase " remaining stationary " would be altogether erroneous; and when there are more than two, when there are a number of commodities concerned, some of which have varied in the circumstances of their production, while others have undergone no change, this phraseology becomes destitute of all precision, and leads either to vague and nugatory propositions, or to positive error.

An illustration of these remarks may be found in a passage of Mr. Ricardo's work, where he maintains, in opposition to M. Say, that if, in consequence of increased facility in producing other commodities, cloth should exchange for a double quantity of them, compared to what it did before, we ought to say, that *cloth retained its former value*, and that the commodities, compared with it, had fallen to half their former value.* This language,

---

* " According to M. Say, if the difficulty of producing cloth were to double, and consequently cloth was to exchange for double the quantity of the commodities for which it exchanged before, it would be doubled in value, to which I give my fullest assent ; but if there were any peculiar facility in producing the commodities, and no increased difficulty in producing cloth, and cloth should in consequence exchange as before for double the quantity of commodities, M. Say would still say that cloth had doubled in value ; whereas, according to my view of the subject, he should say, that *cloth retained its former value*, and those particular commodities had fallen to half their former value."—Principles of Political Economy, chap. xx, p. 328, 3d edit.

however, would be evidently incorrect, unless the value of an object were something intrinsic, and independent of other commodities; but since value, as I have shown, is essentially relative, if any commodities had fallen in relation to cloth, cloth must have acquired additional value, or have risen in relation to those commodities.

Mr. Ricardo's proposition might, indeed, be true, if he meant by other commodities only a certain number of other commodities. These, for convenience, may be termed Class 1, and all commodities not included in Class 1 may be referred to Class 2. Now if Mr. Ricardo meant, that when Class 1 came to be produced with increased facility, so as to exchange for half the quantity of cloth, while Class 2, in point of facility of production, remained as before, cloth would retain its former value in relation to Class 2, he would be perfectly correct; but if this had been his meaning, there could have been no point of dispute between him and the author on whose language he is animadverting; and that it was not what he intended, the connection and tenour of the whole passage sufficiently evince.

The contradiction involved in affirming the stationary or invariable value of any object amidst the variations of other things, is so direct and palpable, that it may be instructive to point out the way in which a writer of such powers of reasoning, as Mr. Ricardo unquestionably possessed, has been led into so strange and manifest an error.

Since value denotes a relation between two objects, no arguments are required to prove, that it cannot arise from causes affecting only one of the objects, but must proceed from two causes, or two sets of causes respectively operating on the objects between which the relation exists*. If A is equal in value to B,

* Value implying, as I have before shown, a mental affection, and consequently all causes of value being, in reality, circumstances affecting the mind, it might be more correct to speak of the causes operating on the mind with regard to an object, than of the causes operating on the object itself; but the latter is a shorter mode of expression, sufficiently intelligible, and not likely to lead into error.

this must be owing not only to causes operating on A, but also to causes operating on B. The fact of a pound of gold exchanging for fifteen times the quantity of corn that can be obtained for a pound of silver, cannot be referred to causes operating on the corn, but to a difference in the causes operating on gold and silver. Hence, how constant or uniform soever a cause affecting one commodity may be, it cannot make that object of constant value, without the concurrence of other invariable causes acting upon the commodity with which it is compared.

It is precisely this essential circumstance, which has escaped the notice of Mr. Ricardo. When he asserts, that a commodity would be of invariable value, if it were always produced by the same quantity of labour, he overlooks one half of the causes concerned in the determination of value; for a moment's consideration will teach us, that such a commodity could be of invariable value, in relation to those commodities alone, of which the producing labour had also remained a constant quantity. Not adverting to this, Mr. Ricardo appears to have reasoned, that because the quantity of labour (according to his doctrine) is the cause of value, if the cause in any one commodity remains the same, the effect must necessarily be the same.   But granting his doctrine, that the quantity of labour determines value, it must be the quantity requisite for the production of each commodity compared, and not the quantity requisite for that of only one.   The value of both, or their relation to each other, must necessarily vary with every change in the quantity of producing labour required for either.

To assert indeed, that the value of an object, or its relation to another object, was invariable, because whatever alteration had taken place in the latter object, the former had undergone no change in the conditions of its production, would be as absurd as to assert the unvarying likeness of a portrait to the original, because, however the man had altered in feature, the portrait itself had retained precisely the same lineaments.   The relation of value, as well as the resemblance between two objects, depends upon both, and changes with a change in either of them.

Mr. Ricardo's modifications of his doctrine of the invariable value of a commodity produced by the same quantity of labour, make no difference in the force and applicability of the preceding remarks. For he still asserts, that a commodity produced by a uniform quantity of labour, would be of invariable value in relation to commodities produced under the same circumstances as itself*, as to the proportions of fixed and circulating capital, the durability of the fixed capital, and the time required to bring the commodity to market. If a commodity, for instance, were produced solely by labour, and always required the same quantity to produce it, it would be of invariable value in regard to such commodities as were produced by labour alone. Mr. Ricardo, indeed, so far agrees with the view here taken, as to maintain the impossibility of finding any commodity of invariable value.

* Principles of Pol. Econ. p. 43, third edit.

His reason for this opinion is not, however, that
the value of this commodity would necessarily
vary with the value of the commodities compared with it, but that no commodity could be
found, which is not itself exposed to the same
causes of fluctuation as all other commodities.
My proposition is, that if the causes affecting
any one commodity continued unaltered, this
commodity would not be invariable in value,
unless the causes affecting all commodities
compared with it, continued unaltered. Mr.
Ricardo, on the contrary, maintains, that provided the causes affecting one commodity were
always the same, the commodity would be of
invariable value, in regard to commodities produced under the same circumstances, notwithstanding any changes in the causes affecting
them, provided those changes did not extend
to the proportions betwixt the fixed and circulating capital, the durability of the fixed capital, or the length of time required to bring the
commodity to market. What I assert is, that
if all commodities were produced under ex-

actly the same circumstances, as for instance, by labour alone, any commodity, which always required the same quantity of labour, could not be invariable in value, while every other commodity underwent alteration: he asserts, on the other hand, that such a commodity would be invariable, and, according to his doctrine hereafter to be examined, would form a perfect measure of other things.

Clear and definite ideas on the present subject are so essential to the political economist, that it will not be a vain labour to point out the mistakes of another eminent writer concerning it. Mr. Malthus has not avoided those of Mr. Ricardo. After defining value, in accordance with that writer, as expressing the power of commanding other objects in exchange; he proceeds to say, that this power "may obviously arise either from causes affecting the object itself, or the commodities against which it is exchanged*. In the one case, the value of

* In this passage there is a palpable inaccuracy in expression. Mr. Malthus has not even succeeded in bring-

the object itself may properly be said to be affected; in the other, only the value of the
commodities which it purchases; and if we
ing out his own meaning. He states two cases ; in one,
the power of purchasing, possessed by any object, is said
to arise from causes affecting the object itself; in the other,
its power of purchasing is said to arise from causes affecting the commodities against which it is exchanged. He
then proceeds to observe, that in the first case " the value
of the object itself may properly be said to be affected :"
i. c. " if the power of purchasing possessed by any
object arises from causes affecting the object itself, the
value of the object itself may properly be said to be affected." This must be allowed to be a very unmeaning
proposition. Mr. Malthus evidently intended to say,
not that the *power of purchasing* possessed by any object,
but that a *change* in its power of purchasing, might arise
either from causes affecting that object, or from causes affecting the commodities compared with it.

Many similar instances of negligence and inaccuracy of
expression disfigure the pages of Mr. Malthus's pamphlet,
the more unpardonable, not only because he is master,
when he chooses, of an excellent and perspicuous style,
but because such passages form serious impediments to
the progress of a science, which requires the utmost clear-
ness and precision of language, both for its improvement
and its diffusion.

could suppose any object always to remain of the same value, the comparison of other commodities with this one would clearly show which had risen, which had fallen, and which had remained the same. The value of any commodity estimated in a measure of this kind, might with propriety be called its absolute or natural value; while the value of a commodity estimated in others which were liable to variation, whether they were one or many, could only be considered as its nominal or relative value, that is, its value in relation to any particular commodity, or to commodities in general *."

We have here invariable, absolute, natural, nominal, and relative value; but, throughout the whole of the passage, the notion of value as something intrinsic or absolute is apparent. Departing at once from his own definition, he maintains, that the value of an object may be affected without affecting the value of the com-

* The Measure of Value - stated and illustrated, p. 1, et seq.

modities for which it is exchanged : that is,
that the power of A in commanding B in exchange may be altered, while the power of B
in commanding A remains as before. Mr.
Malthus has fallen into the same error, which
we have already noticed in Mr. Ricardo ; the
error of supposing, that if a commodity continued the same in the circumstances of its
production, it would retain the same value
amidst the fluctuations of other commodities.
The inconsistency of this with the definition of
value, has already been sufficiently exposed;
and as it is the basis of Mr. Malthus's notion
of absolute value, that notion necessarily falls to
the ground. The very term absolute value, implies the same sort of absurdity as absolute distance ; while the invariable value of one object,
amidst the fluctuations of all other things, is
as self-contradictory a notion as the invariable
resemblance of a picture, to the natural scenery
from which it was taken, amidst all the vi-
cissitudes of the seasons, the touches of time,
and the encroachments of art.

The same error runs through the whole of Mr. Malthus's pamphlet, entitled "The Measure of Value stated and illustrated;" and is involved in the position which it is the object of that pamphlet to establish. He maintains, after Adam Smith, that labour is always of the same value; that is, according to his own definition, always retains the same power of commanding other objects in exchange; and yet, in the same treatise, he speaks of the labourer earning a greater or smaller quantity of money or necessaries, and insists that it is not the value of the labour which varies, but the value of the money or the necessaries. As if produce or money could change in value relatively to labour, without labour changing in value relatively to produce or money. But we need not be surprised at any implied inconsistency in Mr. Malthus, when, after having set out with the definition which we have already quoted, that value is "the power of commanding other objects in exchange," or, in other words, "the power of purchasing," he subsequently makes the direct assertion, that "although money may increase in its power of purchasing, it does not necessarily increase in value*." If Mr. Malthus thus abandons his own definition, what other will he put in its place?

I have already shown, that the power of purchasing, or the power of commanding other objects in exchange, can be expressed only by quantity. In other words, the value of one commodity can be expressed only by the quantity of some other object for which it will exchange. When a hat is said to be twenty shillings in value, it is obvious that the value of the hat is expressed by the quantity of silver: when a yard of cloth is said to be worth two bushels of wheat, the value of the cloth is expressed by the quantity of wheat. It is impossible to designate, or express the value of a commodity, except by a quantity of some other commodity.

The power of purchasing, or the value of an object in relation to some other object, admits

* Page 62.

of degrees; it may be greater or less; which means, that the former object may command a greater or smaller quantity of the latter. In no other sense can the power of one commodity to purchase another be said to increase or decrease. As the value of an object A, can be expressed only by the quantity of some other object B, so an increase in the value of A, can be expressed only by an increase in the quantity of B.

Simple as these conclusions appear to oe, and directly flowing from the definition of value universally adopted, Mr. Ricardo has drawn contrary inferences. Although he agrees with Dr. Smith, in defining value to express the power of purchasing, and although, in the very first proposition in his book, he speaks of the value of a commodity as synonymous with the quantity of any other commodity, for which it will exchange *, yet in another chapter of his

* " The value of a commodity, or the quantity of any other commodity for which it will exchange, depends on the

work he says, " I cannot agree with M. Say in estimating the value of a commodity by the abundance of other commodities, for which it will exchange *." In accordance with the definition, this means that he cannot agree with M. Say in estimating the power of a commodity to purchase other commodities, by the quantity of the latter, which it will purchase. But if the power of a commodity to purchase be not measured by the quantity purchased, what other mode of estimation can be found? It is no great degree of boldness to challenge the whole body of economists to produce a different meaning of the word power, or a different measure of its degrees.

One of the most accomplished of Mr. Ricardo's disciples, the author of the Templars' Dialogues on Political Economy, whose writings

relative quantity of labour which is necessary for its production, and not on the greater or less compensation which is paid for that labour." See title of Section i, Chap. 1.

* Page 333, third edition.

can seldom be read without both pleasure and instruction, is still more explicit on this subject,
and more unmeasured in his language than
Mr. Ricardo himself. He asserts, in terms to
which nothing can lend additional positive-
ness, " that there is no necessary connection at
all, or of any kind, between the quantity commanded, and the value commanding * :" and
again, " I presume, that in your use, and in
every body's use of the word value, a high
value ought to purchase a high value, and that
it will be very absurd if it should not. But as
to purchasing a great quantity, that condition
is surely not included in any man's idea of
value †."

The plausibility of this passage will disappear on a little reflection. An article of high
value, A, will truly enough purchase another
article of equally high value, B, but these two
articles will not be high in relation to each
other : the term high, in this connection, must

* London Magazine for May 1824, page 552.
† Ibid. page 557.

be used to denote their value in relation to a
third commodity, or to commodities generally;
and the precise reason why A and B are said to
be high in relation to a third commodity, is,
that a small quantity of them commands in
exchange a large quantity of the latter.   Gold
is said to be fifteen times more valuable than
silver, because an ounce of gold, no matter
from what cause, will command fifteen ounces of
silver.   So far, therefore, from quantity being
excluded from any man's idea of value, it is essential to it, and to express value, except by
quantity, is impossible.   The mistake, both in
this writer and in Mr. Ricardo, evidently arises
from an inaccurate apprehension of the true nature of value.   Instead of regarding value as a
relation between two objects, they seem to consider it as a positive result produced by a definite quantity of labour.   If the quantity of labour necessary for the production of an object
is always the same, the value according to
them is always the same, however other objects
may have varied; so that, in fact, the circum-

stance of its being produced by a certain quantity of labour constitutes its value, independently of any other circumstances. Whatever variations there might be in the quantities of other things which this object commanded, it would be still of the same value, because produced by the same labour.

These authors appear to have had an unsteady apprehension of a sufficiently distinct proposition, and one, too, on which they have largely insisted, namely, that the values of commodities are in the same ratio as the quantities of labour bestowed upon them. Sometimes they have apparently construed this to mean, that the value of any one commodity is in proportion to the labour employed upon it. Because the values of A and B, according to their doctrine, are to each other as the quantities of producing labour, or, as it is sometimes expressed, are determined by the quantities of producing labour, they appear to have concluded, that the value of A alone, without reference to any thing else, is as the quantity of its pro-

ducing labour.   There is no meaning certainly
in this last proposition, but there is so much of
the appearance of it, that the most cautious in-
vestigator might be led astray by the semblance.

After these critical strictures, it is a pleasure to cite a passage from an author, whose
views as to the nature of value appear to me
to be sounder than those of any other writer.

" Even if a commodity," says he, " could
be found, which always required the same expenditure for its production, it would not therefore be of invariable exchangeable value, so as
to serve as a standard for measuring the value
of other things.   Exchangeable value is determined, not by the absolute, but by the relative
cost of production.   If the cost of producing
gold remained the same, while the cost of producing all other things should be doubled, then
would gold have a less power of purchasing all
other things than before; or, in other words,
its exchangeable value would fall one half;
and this diminution in its exchangeable value
would be precisely the same in effect, as if the

cost of all other things remained unaltered, while that of producing gold had been reduced one half. In the very term, exchangeable value, a relative and not an absolute quantity is implied. If gold should have a greater or a less power of purchasing all other things, then all other things would have a greater or less power of purchasing gold. It is impossible to increase the exchangeable value of one set of commodities, without at the same time diminishing the exchangeable power of the other set of commodities with which the first is compared *."

The following propositions may be stated as the results of the investigation in which we have been employed. Simple as they appear, we have seen that it is possible to overlook them.

1. Inasmuch as the term value denotes a relation between two objects, a commodity cannot be said to possess value, or to alter in value,

---

* An Essay on the Production of Wealth, by R. Torrens, Esq.

without an express or implied reference to some other commodity. Its value must be value in something, or in relation to something.

2. This relation between two objects cannot alter as to one, without altering as to the other. If A rises in relation to B, B cannot remain stationary, but must fall in relation to A.

3. The value of a commodity can be expressed only by a quantity of some other commodity.

4. A rise in the value of a commodity A, means, that an equal quantity of this commodity exchanges for a greater quantity than before of the commodity B, in relation to which it is said to rise.

5. A fall in the value of A, means, that an equal quantity of it exchanges for a smaller quantity of B.

In the examination of the present subject, as discussed by those writers on whose doctrines I have ventured to animadvert, I have been forcibly struck with the vagueness, the inconsistencies, and the errors, which have arisen

from speaking of value as a sort of general
and independent property; and I cannot too
strongly recommend the student of political
economy never to let the word value pass before him without putting the question, " value
in what?" or, " in relation to what?" The value
of a commodity must be its value in something,
and whenever the term is used with any definite meaning, that something may be assigned.
If it cannot be assigned, the reader may rest
assured that the author, whoever he be, is
writing without any determinate ideas. Whoever resolutely applies this rule in reading our
economical writers, will be surprised and pleased
at the light which it will pour over their pages.
The most difficult and obscure passages will
frequently brighten into perspicuity, and the
sum of their truth as well as of their error will
stand apparent. The brilliant paradox, the ingenious fallacy, the seemingly profound observation, will separate into two distinct parts,
one exhibiting the gaudy fragments of sophistry and delusion, the other the simple truth,

which they only served to hide with their cumbrous splendour.   We may apply to the ri-
gorous exaction of a uniform sense, from the
terms employed in discussions of this nature,
what an eloquent writer has said of the detection of a fallacy in a fundamental maxim.

" To discover error in axioms," says he, " or
in first principles grounded on facts, is like the
breaking of a charm.   The enchanted castle, the
steep rock, the burning lake disappear : and the
paths that lead to truth, which we imagined to
be so long, so embarrassed, and so difficult, show
as they are, short, open, and easy *."

* Of the True Use of Retirement and Study, by Lord
Bolingbroke.

CHAPTER II.

ON REAL AND NOMINAL VALUE.

A DISTINCTION of value into real and nominal, has been made by several of our most eminent economical writers. According to Adam Smith, the real value or price of a commodity is the labour which it will command, while the nominal value is the money for which it will exchange. As this definition of real value is evidently inapplicable to labour itself, he proceeds to say, that the real value or price of labour " may be said to consist in the quantity of the necessaries and conveniences of life which are given for it; its nominal price in the quantity of money*."

Mr. Malthus, in his Principles of Political Economy, has adopted similar, if not precisely the same distinctions. " The most proper de-

* Wealth of Nations, Book i, Chap. v.

finition," he says, " of real value in exchange, in contradistinction to nominal value in exchange, is the power of commanding the necessaries and conveniences of life, as distinguished from the power of commanding the precious metals *."

Mr. Ricardo also makes a distinction, in the case of labour, between real and nominal value. " Wages," he says, " are to be estimated by their real value, namely, by the quantity of labour and capital employed in producing them, and not by their nominal value, either in coats, hats, money, or corn†."

After the disquisition on the nature of value in the preceding chapter, the distinction of it in this way, into two kinds, must appear to be merely arbitrary, and incapable of being turned to any use. What information is conveyed, or

---

* Principles of Pol. Econ. p. 62.

† Principles of Pol. Econ. and Taxation, p. 50. He does not, however, confine his idea of real value to the case of labour only.— For a more particular examination of the use which he makes of this term, see the Notes and Illustrations at the end of the present Treatise, Note A.

what advance in argument is effected by telliug us, that value estimated in one way is real, but in another nominal? The value of any commodity denoting its relation in exchange to some other commodity, we may speak of it as money-value, corn-value, cloth-value, according to the commodity with which it is compared; and hence there are a thousand different kinds of value, as many kinds of value as there are commodities in existence, and all are equally real and equally nominal. We gain nothing in perspicuity or precision by the use of these latter terms, but, on the contrary, they entail upon us a heavy incumbrance of vagueness and ambiguity and unproductive discussion.

Of the latter we have a good exemplification in the Templars' Dialogues on Political Economy, dialogue the fourth, which contains much ingenious reasoning, founded altogether on this distinction. It would not probably have been written, however, had the author attended to the simple fact, that value must always imply value in something, and unless that something is indicated, the word conveys no information. Now as the terms *nominal* and *real* do not denote any thing in this way, they stand in the predicament just mentioned, they convey no precise information, and are liable to engender continual disputes, because their meaning is arbitrarily assumed.

In a subsequent chapter on the value of labour, I shall probably have an opportunity of examining some of the positions of this writer, founded on his doctrine of the real value of wages. At present it will be sufficient to confine ourselves to the value of commodities. Following Mr. Ricardo, he appears entirely to lose sight of the relative nature of value, and, as I have remarked in the preceding chapter, to consider it as something positive and absolute; so that if there were only two commodities in the world, and they should both from some circumstances or other come to be produced by double the usual quantity of labour, they would both rise in real value, although their relation to each other would be undisturbed. According to this doctrine, every

thing might at once become more valuable, by
requiring at once more labour for its production,
a position utterly at variance with the truth, that
value denotes the relation in which commodities stand to each other as articles of exchange.
Real value, in a word, is on this theory considered as being the independent result of labour; and consequently, if under any circumstances the quantity of labour is increased, the
real value is increased. Hence the paradox,
" that it is possible for A continually to increase in value — in *real* value observe — and
yet command a continually decreasing quantity
of B *:" and this although they were the only
commodities in existence. For it must not be
supposed that the author means, that A might increase in value in relation to a third commodity
C, while it commanded a decreasing quantity of
B — a proposition which is too self-evident to
be insisted on ; but he means that A might in-

* Templars' Dialogues, in London Magazine for May,
1824, p. 551.

crease in a kind of value called *real,* which has
no reference to any other commodity whatever *.

Apply to the position of this author the
rule recommended in the last chapter: inquire, when he speaks of value, value in what?
and all the possible truth on the subject appears
in its naked simplicity. The touch of this talis-
man will show, that the paradox above quoted,

---

* Unless it be to an imaginary commodity, to which, in
assertions of this kind, there seems to be a latent reference; a commodity namely, always produced by the same
labour. It is no matter, on this theory, whether such a
commodity exists or not. An object A is tried by this
ideal standard, and if it is found that it would have risen
in relation to it, had the standard existed, A is pronounced
to have risen in real value — so that any one in a jocular
mood might be tempted to define real value, "value estimated by a standard which has only an imaginary existence."
Nor is the reference to such a standard always a merely
tacit or latent one. Mr. Ricardo assigns as a reason for
calling an alteration in wages a fall, that it would appear
to be a fall if the value of labour were estimated in an hypothetical standard of this kind.

and which is asserted by its author to be "true in such a way and degree, as to oblige him who denies it to maintain an absurdity," is either a palpable contradiction in terms, or a mere truism scarcely worth a word of illustration, much less that display of logical dexterity which he has exhibited in its support. Since value must be value in something, or in relation to something, if there is any meaning at all in the proposition, " that it is possible for A continually to increase in value, and yet command a continually decreasing quantity of B," it must be either, (1) that A may increase in value in relation to B, and yet command a continually decreasing quantity of this very B; or (2) that A may continually increase in value in relation to other commodities, or what amounts to the same thing, to a third commodity C, while the said A commands a continually decreasing quantity of B. These are the only possible interpretations which can be given of the proposition, according to the received definition of value. Now in the first sense, the proposition is palpably absurd.

if tried by the principle laid down in our last chapter, " that a rise in the value of a commodity means, that an equal quantity of it exchanges for a greater quantity than before, of the commodity in relation to which it is said to rise." To maintain, therefore, that A increases in value to B, and at the same time that it commands a smaller quantity of B, is to affirm a rise and fall in A at the same moment.

In the second sense the proposition, as I have already remarked, is too self-evident to require any proof; and as the author of the Dialogues has expended so much labour and dialectical skill in explaining and supporting it, we might fairly infer that this is not the sense in which he meant it to be interpreted, even if he had not put the matter beyond dispute by his doctrine, so frequently and strongly expressed, " that there is no necessary connection at all, or of any kind, between the quantity commanded and the value commanding *."

The eminent writers on whose doctrines I

* Ibid., p. 552.

have hazarded the preceding observations, agree in defining value to be the power of an object to purchase or command other objects in exchange. Adhering to this definition, it is difficult to conceive what propriety they could have discerned in their use of the words real and nominal. A real power of purchasing implies, if it means any thing, that it is not a false or pretended power; while the counter phrase, a nominal power of purchasing, intimates that the power is only in name; that it is not what it professes to be. But the applicability of these epithets can have no dependence on the nature of the commodities in relation to which the power is possessed, nor on the causes affecting the production of the commodity in which the power resides. According to all proper usage, the epithets refer not to any thing in the power itself, but to the quality of the affirmation that the power exists, characterizing that affirmation as true or false.

CHAPTER III.

UNLESS we change the meaning of value in the case of labour from that which it bears when applied to any thing else, the value of labour must signify the power of commanding other things in exchange. The term in reference to labour, as in all other cases, denotes a relation, and the relation, in this instance, must be between labour and commodities. Labour, therefore, is high in value when it commands a large, and low when it commands a small quantity of commodities; and when labour is said to rise or fall in value, the expression implies, that a definite portion of it, a day's labonr for example, exchanges for a larger or a smaller quantity of commodities than before. This is obviously the only interpretation of which the terms rise and fall of labour admit, consistently with the definition of value.

Before proceeding to apply these positions to the current doctrines of the day, it will be necessary to call the reader's attention to a comparison of the terms "value of labour," and "wages," and to the way in which they are employed. The value of labour, as we have just seen, signifies the relation in which labour stands to commodities. The term wages has the same meaning — for we may say indifferently the wages of labour are three shillings a day, or the value of labour is three shillings a day; but it is often employed with greater laxity of signification.

Mr. Ricardo, for example, talks of "the labour and capital employed in producing wages," and of "the real value of wages *;" in which instances it is impossible to substitute

* " Wages are to be estimated by their real value, *viz.* by the quantity of labour and capital employed in producing them." Pol. Econ., p. 50.

the term value of labour instead of wages, as
might be done if the two expressions were
used as synonymous and equivalent. We could
not speak with propriety of " the labour and
capital employed in producing the value of
labour," or of " the real value of the value of
labour."

The term wages, when thus used, appears intended to denote the commodities or money
given to the labourer in exchange for his labour—not the value of his labour in money, but
the money itself. This is either an unwarrant-
able use of the term, or there is a double meaning in it as I think a little consideration will show,
although the distinction, which I shall attempt
to make, may seem on a first glance to be a distinction without a difference. It will be acknowledged, that the value of labour can be expressed only by the quantity of some commodity
given for a definite portion of it. Thus, if silver
is that commodity, the value of a day's labour is
expressed by the quantity of silver, or, what is
the same thing, the number of shillings which

the labourer receives. This quantity of silver
expresses the value of his labour, in the same
way that a certain quantity of silver expresses
the value of a yard of cloth. Now the quantity of silver by which the value of a yard of
cloth is expressed, we term the price of the
cloth, and, in a manner strictly analogous, the
quantity of silver by which the value of a day's
labour is expressed, we term the wages of labour. The price of cloth and the wages of labour
are so far exactly correspondent expressions.
But when I speak of the price of cloth as the
subject of causation or change, I do not intend
the silver itself. The price of the cloth may
be twenty shillings, but what causes the price
is not what causes that quantity of silver. To
consider the price as being or consisting in the
actual silver itself, is an error of the same kind
as to consider the length of a piece of timber
as consisting in the instrument which we employ to measure it. Were I to speak of the real
value of the price of cloth, or of the labour and
capital employed in producing the price of

cloth, I should be thought to make use of strange language. Could any meaning be attached to the latter expression, it would be the labour and capital employed in producing the cloth itself, and not in producing the silver in which I expressed the value of the cloth. The same remarks must equally apply to the use of the term wages, if it has only one meaning. If I speak of the labour and capital employed in producing wages, it is in this case equivalent to speaking of the labour and capital employed in producing labour itself, and not in producing the silver or any other commodity given for labour. Mr. Ricardo, however, by this phraseology, evidently means the labour and capital employed in the production of the money, or of the commodities in which the value of labour is expressed—a singular perversion of terms, arising probably from an unconscious identification of two distinct ideas; or, if it is not a perversion of terms, there are evidently two senses in which the same word is used.

Hence Mr. Ricardo, ingeniously enough,

avoids a difficulty, which, on a first view, threatens to encumber his doctrine, that value depends on the quantity of labour employed in production. If this principle is rigidly adhered to, it follows, that the value of labour depends on the quantity of labour employed in producing it—which is evidently absurd. By a dexterous turn, therefore, Mr. Ricardo makes the value of labour depend on the quantity of labour required to produce wages, or, to give him the benefit of his own language, he maintains, that the value of labour is *to be estimated* by the quantity of labour required to produce wages, by which he means, the quantity of labour required to produce the money or commodities given to the labourer. This is similar to saying, that the value of cloth is to be estimated, not by the quantity of labour bestowed on its production, but by the quantity of labour bestowed on the production of the silver, for which the cloth is exchanged.

From the preceding observations it appears,

that either the term wages has two meanings, or
it has been used with improper laxity.   In
order to avoid any ambiguity which might
arise from it, I shall in general employ in its
stead the expression, value of labour, by
which, in consonance with the usual definition
of value, I mean the power which a definite
portion of labour possesses, of commanding in
exchange any other commodity compared with it.

It has been already stated, that when labour
is said to rise or fall in value, the expression
implies, that a definite portion of it exchanges
for a larger or smaller quantity of some commodity or commodities than it did before. This
however is not the view taken by Mr. Ricardo
of the value of labour; for he enters into
various details to show, that although the labourer might receive more commodities in exchange for his labour, yet the value of his
labour, notwithstanding, might have fallen.

" It is not," says he, " by the absolute quantity of produce obtained by either class, that

we can correctly judge of the rate of profit,
rent, and wages, but by the quantity of labour
required to obtain that produce. By improvements in machinery and agriculture, the whole
produce may be doubled; but if wages, rent,
and profit be also doubled, these three will bear
the same proportions to one another as before,
and neither could be said to have relatively
varied. But if wages partook not of the whole
of this increase; if they, instead of being
doubled, were only increased one half; if rent,
instead of being doubled, were only increased
three-fourths, and the remaining increase went
to profit, it would, I apprehend, be correct for
me to say, that rent and wages had fallen while
profits had risen; for if we had an invariable
standard by which to measure the value of this
produce, we should find that a less value had
fallen to the class of labourers and landlords,
and a greater to the class of capitalists, than
had been given before. We might find, for
example, that though the absolute quantity of
commodities had been doubled, they were the

produce of precisely the former quantity of
labour. Of every hundred hats, coats, and
quarters of corn produced, if

The labourers had before 25
The landlords 25
And the capitalists 50
———
100

And if, after these commodities were double
the quantity, of every 100

The labourers had only 22
The landlords 22
And the capitalists 56
———
100

In that case I should say, that wages and rent
had fallen, and profits risen; though, in consequence of the abundance of commodities, the
quantity paid to the labourer and landlord
would have increased in the proportion of 25
to 44.   Wages are to be estimated by their
real value, *viz.* by the quantity of labour and

capital employed in producing them, and not by their nominal value, either in coats, hats, money, or corn. Under the circumstances I have just supposed, commodities would have fallen to half their former value, and if money had not varied, to half their former price also. If then in this medium, which had not varied in value, the wages of the labourer should be found to have fallen, it will not the less be a real fall, because they might furnish him with a greater quantity of cheap commodities than his former wages*."

In this passage may be noted several of those errors on which I have already animadverted in the preceding chapters. In one part he supposes the possibility of an invariable standard of value amidst universal fluctuation, a supposition which has been shown to involve contradictory conditions: in another part, he makes the unmeaning distinction of real and nominal value, and in another he asserts, that if *all* commodities were produced in double quantity

---

* Principles of Pol. Econ. and Taxation, p. 49, third edit.

by the same labour, they would fall to half their former value, the correctness of which will be hereafter examined in the chapter on the methods of estimating value.

The error, however, which it belongs to the purpose of the present chapter to point out, is a departure from his own definition of value. Instead of regarding labour as rising or falling according as it commands a greater or smaller quantity of the commodities exchanged for it, which is a direct corollary from the definition of value as the power of purchasing or commanding other objects in exchange, he represents it as rising or falling only when a larger or smaller *proportion* of the commodity produced goes to the labourer. This variation in the proportion of the product is undoubtedly one source of variation in the value of labour, but it is not the sole source. As value, when applied to labour, denotes its relation to other things, that value must vary, not only from causes which affect labour, but from causes which affect the commodities received in exchange for it. To take Mr. Ricardo's own case in the preceding extract. He says, that if by improvements in machinery and agriculture, the whole produce of a country were doubled, while the quantity of labour employed continued the same, and if before this increase of produce, of every hundred hats, coats, and quarters of corn, the labourer received 25, and after the increase only 22, then wages would have fallen, although the labourer actually received 44, where he before received only 25. But if by a fall of wages is meant a fall in the value of labour; if, further, by value we mean the power of commanding other things in exchange, and if the degrees of that power are in proportion to the quantity commanded, then it is evident, that so far from wages falling they would have risen, inasmuch as a definite portion of labour would command in exchange an increased quantity of hats, coats, and corn.

I have said, that an alteration in the proportion of the product assigned to the labourer is one cause of variation in the value of labour: for it is manifest, that if out of a fixed quantity of hats, coats, and corn, the labourer receives at one time a quarter, and at another time half, his labour at the latter period will be doubled in value in relation to these commodities. Mr. Ricardo's error, it deserves to be repeated, lies in considering this change in the proportion to be the only cause of change, or rather the only *case* of change in the value of labour*.

---

* Mr. Ricardo's inference is a legitimate deduction from his premises, if we concede certain postulates.   Grant him the kind of value called *real*, which has no relation to the quantity of commodities commanded, but solely to the quantity of producing labour, and it inevitably follows, that there could be no alteration in the *real* value of labour, but from an alteration in the proportion of the product which went to the labourer.   Neither, if money were always produced by a uniform quantity of labour, could there be any other alteration in the money-value of labour. But to say in this case, that although the labourer obtained a larger quantity of hats, coats, and corn, yet if he obtained less money, the value of his labour would have fallen, is altogether nugatory.   Money-value has no greater claim to the general term "*value,*" than any other kind of value; and the simple state of the case would be, that labour had risen in value in relation to hats, coats, and corn, and fallen in relation to money.   As to real value, the last chapter has shown that it is a nonentity.

His assertion in another place, that " the labourer is only paid a really high price for his labour, when his wages will purchase the produce of a great deal of labour*," is only another mode of stating the same doctrine, and amounts to this, that wages are high only when a great proportion of the article produced falls to the labourer. For wages at the same period being on a level in the different branches of industry, if a man's wages (to use Mr. Ricardo's language) will purchase the produce of a great deal of labour, they will purchase the produce of a great deal of any sort of labour, consequently the produce of a great deal of his own labour, that is, the proportion falling to him of the produce of his own labour will be great.

The author of the Templars' Dialogues, who pushes Mr. Ricardo's doctrines to their remotest consequences, and thus, if they are untrue, necessarily exposes their incorrectness by

* Principles of Pol. Econ. and Taxation, p. 322, 3d ed.

the paradoxes into which he falls, has not
failed to drive this doctrine of the value of labour to an extravagant result.   " Wages," says
he, " are at a high real value, when it requires
much labour to produce wages; and at a low
real value, when it requires little labour to
produce wages : and it is perfectly consistent
with the high real value—that the labourer
should be almost starving; and perfectly consistent with the low real value—that the labourer should be living in great ease and comfort *."

Well might the author's friend Philoebus
exclaim at this extraordinary passage, " this
may be true : but you must allow, that it
sounds extravagant."

Let us examine it by the test before given :
let us ask, value in what? If the labourer is
starving, in relation to what is his labour of
high value? In relation to corn? If so, he
would obtain a large quantity of corn in ex-

---

* London Magazine for May 1824, p. 557.

change for his labour, and could not starve. It will be replied, perhaps, that corn is high too, and therefore, although labour is high, the labourer obtains little corn. But if corn and labour are both affirmed to be high, the assertion must mean, that they are high in relation to other commodities, as it is an absurdity to say, that they are both at once high in relation to each other. If therefore the labourer ob tains little corn, labour must be low in relation to corn.

The same result will be obtained if the definition of value is substituted for the term. The author's proposition then would be, " it is perfectly consistent with a great power of commanding commodities in exchange for his labour, that the labourer should be almost starving, and perfectly consistent with a small power, that the labourer should be living in great ease and comfort." This is asserting power to be in an inverse ratio to the effects produced *.

* See Note B.

CHAPTER IV.

_____

In the last chapter I endeavoured to explain the true meaning of the value of labour, and to show, that a rise or fall of labour implies an increase or decrease in the quantity of the commodity given in exchange for it.

A rise or fall of profits is sometimes spoken of as analogous to a rise or fall of labour or of wages. But profits cannot be regarded as analogous to wages. Labour is an exchangeable thing, or one which commands other things in exchange; but the term profits denotes only a share or proportion of commodities, not an article which can be exchanged against other articles. When we ask whether wages have risen, we mean, whether a definite portion of labour exchanges for a greater quantity of other things than before; but when we ask whether profits have risen, we do *not* mean whether a definite portion of some article called profits will exchange for a greater quantity of other things than before, but whether the gain of the capitalist bears a higher ratio to the capital employed.

Mr. Ricardo appears to have considered wages, or the value of labour, and profits as equally shares or proportions of the commodity produced, and hence his doctrine, that as wages rise, or, in other words, the value of labour rises, profits must fall. " Whatever," he says, " increases wages, necessarily reduces profits;" and again, " nothing can affect profits but a rise in wages."

It has been shown, however, in the last chapter, that wages, or the value of labour, and profits may both rise together, because the value of labour does not entirely depend on the proportion of the whole produce, which is given to the labourers in exchange for their labour, but also on the productiveness of the labour; because, in fact, a rise of profits and a rise in labour are essentially distinct in their nature, the one signifying an increase of proportion, the other an increase in the quantity which a definite portion of labour will command.

The proposition, that when labour rises profits must fall, is true only when its rise is not owing to an increase in its productive powers. If labour rises while these productive powers remain the same, profits will inevitably fall. This may be easily proved from the principles already advanced; for if labour rises in value, whoever purchases labour must give a greater quantity of other things for it, and as the capitalist purchases labour, he must pay more for it. It will be said, perhaps, that he may raise the value of his goods, that is, he may require a greater quantity of other commodities than before, in exchange for his own. But the capitalist who produces these other commodities is in the same predicament, and they cannot both raise their goods. If A raises the value of his cloth, sells it at an advanced price, and purchases corn, or exchanges it directly for corn, the result is, that he gets more corn for the same quantity of cloth than he did before. If B the grower of corn does the same with his produce, he gets more cloth. But A cannot obtain from B more corn for the same quantity of cloth, at the same time that B obtains from A more cloth for the same quantity of corn. Consequently the value of goods cannot rise. Moreover, if all commodities rise, they must rise in relation to something, and as it is manifestly absurd that all commodities should at once rise in relation to each other, this something must be labour. But, by the supposition, labour itself rises in relation to all commodities; whence it is a contradiction to maintain, that a universal rise in the value of labour can increase the value of commodities.

It may be necessary to repeat the qualification with which the doctrine, that if labour rise in value profits must fall, is to be received. It is true only when the productive power

of labour continues the same, for if this productive power be augmented, that is, if the same
labour produce more commodities in the same
time, labour may rise in value without a fall, nay
even with a rise of profits.   This has been already shown in treating of the possibility of
labour rising, although the proportion of the produce assigned to the labourer were diminished.
In the case there stated it is supposed, that the
whole produce of a country becomes doubled,
while the quantity of labour remains the same;
and that of every 100 hats, coats, and quarters of corn, the labourer before the increase received 25, and after the increase 22, so that at
the latter period he would receive 44 for the
same quantity of labour which before obtained
25.   The capitalist for his share, before the increase, is supposed to receive 50 per cent., and
after the increase 56 per cent., making 112,
where he before obtained only 50.   In this
case, while the value of labour in relation to
hats, coats, and corn, is evidently increased,
that is, while a definite portion of labour ex-

changes for a larger quantity of those articles, the proportion assigned to the capitalist, or the rate of profits, is also augmented.

It may be asked, whether not only the proportion is raised, but the value of the same proportion? If the capitalist, for instance, receive 100 hats, coats, and quarters of corn at the latter period for every 50 at the former, would not the value of his profits have risen, although the proportion were left undisturbed?

A question whether the value of profits has risen, can have only one of three meanings: 1. Whether the proportion of the produce obtained by the capitalist has increased? 2. Whether the aggregate value of his share is greater, estimated in some of the commodities produced? 3. Whether the aggregate value has risen, estimated in labour?

1. The inquiry which I have supposed to be made, cannot be in the first sense, because one of the conditions is that the proportion remains the same.

2. If it be intended to ask whether he

value of the share has risen, estimated in any of the articles produced, the value of profits has undoubtedly risen.   Suppose, for instance, the value to be estimated in quarters of corn, and that at the first period the whole share of the capitalist was an aggregate of 1000 coats, hats, and quarters of corn*; and suppose further a quarter of corn to exchange for a coat or a hat, then his share estimated in corn would be worth 1000 quarters of corn; but after the produce was doubled, his share would be an aggregate of 2000 coats, hats, and quarters of corn, and would consequently be worth 2000 quarters of corn, or double its former value in corn.

3. If it is meant to inquire whether, when the product of labour was doubled, the profits of the capitalist would rise in their aggregate value estimated in labour, the reply is, evidently not. For as the labourer, by the supposition, obtains double the former quantity of commodities, double the quantity of commodities must be given for the same quantity of labour, and of

* See Chapter viii, on the Methods of Estimating Value.

course the share of the capitalist would command only the same labour as before. There could be a change in the value of profits estimated in labour only from an alteration in the proportions assigned to the capitalist and labourers. This is easily shown. Whatever the produce of the labour of six men might be, whether 100 or 200 or 300 quarters of corn, yet so long as the proportion of the capitalist was one fourth of the produce, that fourth part estimated in labour would be invariably the same. Were the produce 100 quarters, then, as 75 quarters would be given to 6 men, the 25 accruing to the capitalist would command the labour of 2 men: if the produce were 300 quarters, the 6 men would obtain 225 quarters, and the 75 falling to the capitalist would still command 2 men and no more. Thus a rise in the proportion which went to the capitalist would be the same as an increase of the value of profits estimated in labour, or, in other words, an increase in their power of commanding labour.

Should it be objected to the doctrine of profits and the value of labour rising at the same time, that as the commodity produced is the only source whence the capitalist and the labourer can obtain their remuneration, it necessarily follows that what one gains the other loses, the reply is obvious. So long as the product continues the same, this is undeniably true; but it is equally undeniable, that if the product be doubled the portion of both may be increased, although the proportion of one is lessened and that of the other augmented. Now it is an increase in the *portion* of the product assigned to the labourer which constitutes a rise in the value of his labour; but it is an increase in the *proportion* assigned to the capitalist which constitutes a rise in his profits; whence it clearly follows, that there is nothing inconsistent in the supposition of a simultaneous rise in both*.

* See Note C.

CHAPTER V.

ON COMPARING COMMODITIES AT DIF-
FERENT PERIODS.

PERHAPS no part of their investigations has perplexed political economists more than their attempts to compare the value of the same object at different periods of time.

It is a direct inference from the explanation of value in the preceding chapters, as denoting a relation between two commodities, a relation incapable of existing when there is only one commodity, that it cannot exist between a commodity at one period and the same commodity at another period. We cannot ascertain the relation of cloth at one time to cloth at another, as we can ascertain the relation of cloth to corn in the present day. All that we can do is to compare the relation in which cloth stood at each period to some other commodity. When we say, that an article in a former age was of a certain value, we mean, that it exchanged for a certain quantity of some other commodity. But this is an inapplicable expression in speaking of only one commodity at two different periods. We cannot say, that a pair of stockings in James the First's reign would exchange for six pair in our own day; and we therefore cannot say, that a pair in James the First's reign was equal in value to six pair now, without reference to some other article.

Value is a relation between contemporary commodities, because such only admit of being exchanged for each other; and if we compare the value of a commodity at one time with its value at another, it is only a comparison of the relation in which it stood at these different times to some other commodity. It is not a comparison of some intrinsic, independent quality at one period, with the same quality at another period; but a comparison of ratios, or a comparison of the relative quantities in which commodities exchanged for each other at two different epochs. If a commodity of in the year 100 was worth 2 B, and in 1800 was worth 4 B, we should say that A had doubled its value to B. But this, which is the only kind of comparison we can institute, would not give us any relation between A in 100 and A in 1800; it would be simply a comparison of the relation between A and B in each of those years.

It is impossible for a direct relation of value to exist between A in 100 and A in 1800, just as it is impossible for the relation of distance to exist between the sun at the former period and the sun at the latter. This perhaps will be still more apparent if we make use of the definition of value instead of the term. It will at once be seen how absurd it would be to talk of the power of A in the year 100, to command in exchange the same commodity in 1800.

It may, perhaps, be alleged, that I am here fighting with a mere shadow of my own creation; for that nobody ever imagined the possibility of comparing the value of any commodity at one period with its value at another, without reference to some other object, the bare notion of such a comparison being absurd, and scarcely susceptible of being stated in intelligible language; and further, that when the value of a commodity in one year is compared with its value in another, the very terms necessarily imply a reference to other articles, and are always so considered.

A slight inspection, however, of our principal writers will prove, that if I am fighting with a shadow, which I by no means deny, it is not one of my own creation. When Mr. Ricardo tells us, that a commodity always produced by the same labour is of invariable value, he implicitly maintains all I have been attempting to disprove. By the epithet invariable he clearly means, that its value at one time will be precisely the same as its value at another, not in relation to other commodities, for he supposes all other commodities to vary, but in relation to

itself.   He distinctly states, that if equal quantities of gold could always be obtained by
equal quantities of labour, the value of gold
" would be invariable, and it would be emi-
nently well calculated to measure the varying
value of *all other things*," whence it follows,
that this invariableness must be intended to be
affirmed of the value of gold compared with
itself, and not of any relation between gold
and some other commodity.

The same remarks apply to all attempts to
find out something of invariable value.   Adam
Smith and Mr. Malthus, in considering labour
alone as never varying in its own value, assert
by implication, that labour at one period may
be compared in value with labour at another
period, without reference to any other thing
whatever *.   I fully concede that such a notion

* For further instances see Wealth of Nations, Book i,
Chap. v, and Mr. Malthus's Pamphlet on the Measure of
Value, p. 24 and 25.   When we come to treat on the measurement of value, we shall find this notion at the bottom
of some important errors on that subject.

involves an absurdity, — that they might have talked with equal propriety of the possibility of comparing the distance of the sun in the year 100 with its distance in 1800, without reference to any other body in space — and that language can scarcely be found to express the idea in direct terms, without a palpable contradiction: but that such a notion has extensively prevailed no one will doubt, who attentively turns over the pages of the first writers on the subject.

The following passage from the Templars' Dialogues on Political Economy, is a conspicuous instance of the error in question.

" I wish to know," says he, " whether a day's labour at the time of the English Revolution bore the same value as a hundred years after, at the time of the French Revolution, and if not the same value, whether a higher or a lower. For this purpose, if I believe that there is any commodity which is immutable in value, I shall naturally compare a day's labour with that commodity at each period.   Some for instance have imagined, that corn is of invariable value, and supposing me to adopt so false a notion, I should merely have to inquire what quantity of corn a day's labour would exchange for at each period, and I should then have determined the relations of value between labour at the two periods *."

It scarcely needs pointing out, after the explanation I have given, that no relation of value could exist between labour at these two periods: the only point to be ascertained would be, whether the same or a different relation existed at both periods, between corn and labour, and this would be equally well ascertained, without supposing the condition of corn being immutable in value. This very supposition implies, either that the fact which it is wished to ascertain is already ascertained, or, that the value of corn at one period may be compared with the value of corn at another period, with no reference to any other commodity in the world.

* Dialogue v, London Magazine for May, p. 558.

Many errors appear to have arisen from this inattention to the real nature of a comparison of objects at different periods in regard to their value.

Much indistinctness has also proceeded from blending the comparison of contemporary commodities with that of the same commodity at different times, particularly when writers have been speaking of the comparative quantity, or the comparative value of the labour concerned in the production of commodities. It is not always clear to their readers, nor does it seem to have been clearer to themselves, whether they intended to compare the same commodity, as to the producing labour, at separate periods, or different commodities at the same period. There appears to me to be considerable confusion in this respect in Mr. Ricardo's first section on value; a confusion which is probably one of the latent causes of the obscurity felt by many to hang over that section, and which, if I mistake not, is perceptible in the very sentence which forms its title.

" The value of a commodity," says he, " or the quantity of any other commodity for which it will exchange, depends on the relative quantity of labour which is necessary for its production, and not on the greater or less compensation which is paid for that labour."

In the first part of this sentence he appears to be speaking of contemporary commodities, but in the latter clause he has changed his ground : it does not form a proper logical counterpart to the former : there is, I think, an implied although an unconscious reference to the same commodity at different periods. For if not, if he is speaking in the latter clause also of contemporary commodities, the amount of the proposition would be this :—

" The values of two contemporary commodities, A and B, are to each other as the quantities of labour necessary to their production, and they are *not* to each other as the *values* of the labour employed in their production." But if commodities are to each other as the quantities, they must also be to each other as the values of the producing labour; for the contrary would necessarily imply, that the two commodities A and B might be equal in value, although the value of the labour employed in one was greater or less than the value of the labour employed in the other; or that A and B might be unequal in value, if the labour employed in each was equal in value. But this difference in the value of two commodities, which were produced by labour of equal value, would be inconsistent with the acknowledged equality of profits, which Mr. Ricardo maintains in common with other writers *.

It is probable, therefore, that this was not Mr. Ricardo's meaning, but that he unconsciously confounded this proposition with another, and really intended to say, that the value of A at two different periods, No. 1 and 2, was

* In this chapter we are assuming, for the sake of argument, the truth of the doctrine, that commodities are to each other in value, as the quantities of labour respectively employed in their production. It will form a subject of examination hereafter.

not proportioned to the value of the labour necessary to its production at each period ; that
although, for example, the value of the labour
were doubled at the latter period, the value of
the commodity might not be affected. The
proposition expressed more simply is, that the
value of a commodity and the value of the labour employed in its production, do not bear
to each other a constant ratio ; or more simply
still, that labour may rise and fall in value without affecting the value of the commodity.

This is obviously a very different proposition
from the other, and depends in fact on the falsity of the other, or on the contrary proposition,
" that the values of two contemporary commodities *are* to each other as the values of the
labour employed in producing them." For as
value must be value in something, let us ask,
in relation to what object might the value of A
at period No. 2 be, as here asserted, the same
as its value at period No. 1, although the value
of the producing labour were doubled? In re-

lation to other commodities. And why? Because the rise in labour would be the same in all commodities; but if the values of commodities are to each other as the values of the labour employed in producing them, and if the labour employed in all commodities rose in equal proportion, there could not possibly be any disturbance of the relations existing between all commodities before the rise, and of course A would be of the same value at period No. 2 as at period No. 1.

The only alteration in this instance would be, an alteration in the relation of value between labour and commodities. It would be a simple case of a rise in labour, and (proceeding on the assumption that commodities are determined in value solely by the quantity of labour) the whole amount of the proposition is this, that the values of commodities in relation to each other are not disturbed by an alteration in their values in relation to labour; which is only a particular application of the more general proposition, that when one commodity or thing alters its value in relation to other commodities, the mutual relations of these other commodities, *cæteris paribus*, are not thereby affected *.

The reader will notice, that in supposing that while the value of the producing labour was doubled, the commodity remained the same, I have used the expression, " the value of the commodity *might not* be affected," for this reason, that whether it was or was not affected, would depend on the nature of the cause by which the value of the labour was doubled. In the proposition, the values of A and B are to each other as the values of their producing labour, the value of labour means aggregate value. Now the aggregate value of the labour necessary for the production of a commodity may be increased in two ways, either by an augmentation of the quantity of the labour at

* It may be necessary perhaps to state, that by the qualification *cæteris paribus*, it is meant to restrict the proposition to cases in which the altered commodity either does not enter at all into the composition of other commodities, or enters into them in the same proportion.

the same rate, or by a rise in the rate, that is in
the value of a definite portion of it, while the
quantity remains the same.   It is only in the
latter event (which is the one I have supposed
to take place) that the value of the commodity
would in general continue the same in relation
to other commodities, for the precise reason already assigned, that all commodities would be
affected in equal proportions.   It would be a
positive not a comparative rise in the value of
the producing labour of the commodity in question ; while on the other hand, should the increase in the value have arisen from an augmentation in the quantity of labour, such increase would be probably, although not necessarily comparative.

As the misconception on the part of Mr.
Ricardo here noticed is a fundamental one, I
make no apology for presenting the reader with
a further attempt to show it.   The confusion in the proposition will be more apparent
by a little alteration in the language.

" The value of a commodity A, or the quantity of any other commodity B, for which it will exchange, depends on the comparative quantities of labour necessary for the production of A and B." So far there is no obscurity, and the position can be construed only in one sense. When Mr. Ricardo, however, adds, " and not on the greater or less compensation which is paid for that labour," every one must be sensible of a confusion of ideas. In the former clause he is telling us on what circumstance the mutual value of A and B depends, or, in other words, what circumstance determines the quantities in which these two commodities are exchanged for each other; in the latter clause it was evidently his business, as it was his design, to tell us on what the mutual value of A and B did *not* depend; or, in other words, what circumstance did *not* determine the quantities in which these commodities are exchanged for each other. Now the only circumstance assigned is obviously " the compensation paid for the labour," and the proposition really asserted in this latter clause is, that the mutual value

of A and B does not depend on the compensation paid for the producing labour of A being
equal to, or greater, or less than the compensation paid for the producing labour of B : so that
this compensation might be equal in the two
cases, while the quantities in which A and B
were exchanged for each other were unequal.

As far, however, as any thing can be gathered
from the confusion of thought and language
in Mr. Ricardo's opening section, this is not
what he intended to assert. In the first clause
he was comparing A and B, and asserting the
cause which determined the relation between
them ; but dropping B by the way, in this latter
clause he is speaking of A alone. By quantity of labour in the first clause, he meant
quantity of labour necessary to produce A, compared with the quantity of labour necessary to
produce B ; but by compensation of labour in
the latter clause, he does not intend the compensation of labour in A compared to the compensation of labour in B, but the compensation
paid for the labour required to produce A at

one time, compared with the compensation paid for the producing labour of A at another time. Hence Mr. Ricardo's sentence is a completely false antithesis.

The author of the Templars' Dialogues on Political Economy seems to have followed Mr. Ricardo in confounding the two distinct propositions above pointed out. This appears the more extraordinary, since he has laid down the first proposition (which I have supposed Mr. Ricardo did not clearly perceive to be involved in the terms employed) in such bold and unmeasured language, as almost to preclude the possibility of its being mistaken either by himself or his readers for any other.

After telling us, that " Mr. Ricardo's doctrine is, that A and B are to each other in value as the quantity of labour is which produces A to the quantity which produces B," he says, " I assert in the most peremptory manner, that he who says, 'the value of A is to the value of B, as the quantity of labour producing A is to the quantity of labour producing B,' does of necessity deny by implication, that the relations of value between A and B are governed by the value of the labour which severally produces them." Again, " so far are the two *formulæ* from presenting merely two different expressions of the same law, that the very best way of expressing negatively Mr. Ricardo's law (*viz.* A is to B in value as the quantities of the producing labour) would be to say, A is *not* to B in value as the *values* of the producing labour*."

Let us examine the reasoning employed to support this extraordinary assertion. It is too long to be introduced here, but it amounts to this, that when the producing labour is increased in *quantity*, the commodity produced is increased in value; but when the producing labour is increased in *value*, the value of the commodity produced remains unaltered; and therefore the values of commodities are not to each other as the *values* of the producing la-

* London Magazine for April, p. 348.

bour.   For instance, if A and B were each produced by six days' labour, they would be equal
in value ; but if A should from some cause or
other require 12 days' labour, then the value of
A would be to the value of B as 12 to 6.   But
suppose that A in 1810 required six days' labour at 4s., making 24s., and in 1811, 6 days at
6s., making 36s., if the value of the commodity
was 40s. at the former period, it would still be
40s. at the latter.   And suppose that B in 1810
required 3 days' labour at 4s., making 12s., and
in 1811, 3 days' labour at 6s., making 18s., the
value of the commodity at each period would
be 20s.

Now this author's argument is, that because A
and B at these two periods do not vary in value
with the varying value of labour, therefore they
are not to each other in value as the values of
the producing labour. But it is evident that 40s.,
the value of A in 1810, is to 20s., the value of
B at the same period, as 24s., the value of the
producing labour in A, is to 12s., the value of

the labour in B; and again in 1811, 40*s*. is to 20*s*., the values of the commodities, as 36*s*. to 18*s*., the values of the labour.

The author appears to me to have vacillated unconsciously between two essentially distinct propositions. He has begun (not an uncommon case) by proposing one as the object of his attack, and ended by contending with the other.

This will be seen at a glance when they are placed together.

1. A and B are to each other in value as the values of the producing labour.

2. The value of A at one period is to the value of the producing labour, as the value of A at another period is to the value of the producing labour; or, to conform the expression of it to the preceding instance, the value of A in 1810, 40*s*., is to the value of the labour at that period, 24*s*., as the value of A in 1811, 40*s*., to the value of the producing labour in the same year, 36*s*., which is manifestly ab-

surd ; but I lie under a great mistake, if it is not really the proposition which X Y Z * has been attacking, while he supposed himself to be in logical combat with the first.

It is difficult to imagine how an error of this kind (if I am right in supposing it to be one) should have escaped a mind evidently well versed in the detection of ambiguities in argumentation.   It appears to have arisen, as in the case of Mr. Ricardo, from blending the comparison of contemporary commodities with that of the same commodity at different periods, which led them to the erroneous inference, that because the value of A at one period did not bear the same relation to the value of its producing labour as at another period, therefore the values of two contemporary commodities did not bear the same relation to *each other* as the values of the labour respectively bestowed on their production.

* X Y Z is the designation assumed by the Author of the Dialogues.

In this chapter I beg not to be understood as
contending, either that the values of commodities are to each other as the *quantities* of labour
necessary for their production, or that the
values of commodities are to each other as the
values of the labour: all that I intend to insist
upon is, that if the former is true, the latter
cannot be false; and I have endeavoured to explain the source of the misconception which
has regarded the two propositions as incompatible and contradictory*.   The fact is, that the
quantity of labour and the value of labour are in
the same case.   Any alteration in the comparative *quantities* of labour required to produce A
and B, would alter their value in relation to
each other; and an alteration in their mutual
value would equally follow from any change in
the comparative *values* of the producing labour,

---

* Of the two propositions, however, the latter is a much
nearer approximation to the truth, for reasons which will
be stated in a subsequent chapter on the causes of value.

while the comparative quantities of labour remained the same.

Again, an alteration in the positive quantities of the producing labour in A and B, which left the comparative quantities the same, would not affect the mutual value of these two commodities, any more than an alteration in the positive values of the producing labour, while the same ratio subsisted between those values as before.

CHAPTER VI.

ON MEASURES OF VALUE.

WE now come to the consideration of a subject which has made a conspicuous figure in
the writings of political economists, and than
which, none perhaps has been a greater source
of error and confusion; I mean the measurement of value.

Our first inquiry must therefore be directed to
the signification of the term. The analogies
suggested by the word measure seem to have
bewildered almost every author who has touched
on the subject. It has been taken for granted
that we measure value as we measure extension, or ascertain weight; and it has been consequently imagined, that to perform the opera-

tion we must possess an object of invariable value.

Let us examine, therefore, how far measuring value and measuring space are similar operations. In every case of measuring we merely ascertain ratios—the ratio which one thing bears to another. In measuring the length of an object we find what ratio it bears to the length of some other object, or in other words, how many times one is contained in the other. We measure the longitudinal extension of a piece of timber, for example, by a foot-rule; that is, we find how often the length of the latter is contained in the former, and this is effected by the actual application of the rule to the timber. It is a physical operation, by which we obtain the knowledge of a fact before unknown, the ratio of length subsisting between the object and the instrument we employ.

In measuring value, what resemblance to this operation can possibly be discovered? We may place two objects by the side of each other, or apply one to the other in any way we please,

but we shall never be able by such means to
discover the relation of value existing between
them.   We shall never extort from them a single fact with which we were before unacquainted.   What then is it possible to do in the
way of measuring value? What kind of measurement is intended, when the term is so frequently
employed? All that is practicable appears to
be simply this : if I know the value of A in relation to B, and the value of B in relation to C, I
can tell the value of A and C in relation to each
other, and consequently their comparative power
in purchasing all other commodities.   This is
an operation obviously bearing no resemblance
at all to the process of measuring length.   There
is no unknown fact discovered by a physical
operation: it is in truth a calculation from certain data, a mere question in arithmetic.   It is
not, let it be observed, what on a first glance
it may appear, like ascertaining the comparative length of two pieces of timber which cannot be brought into juxta-position, by means of
a foot rule or other instrument which we apply

first to one and then to the other: it is far from being so much as this: it is merely like calculating the ratio of length between the two pieces of timber, after we are informed how many feet are contained in each. For of each commodity A and C the value in relation to B must be given, or, in other words, their value must be expressed in a common denomination, before their mutual relation can be ascertained; just as in the case supposed the relation of each piece of timber to the foot-rule must be given, before their relation to each other can be deduced. The actual application of the foot rule is that part of the process which is alone entitled to the appellation of measuring, the rest being mere calculation, but to this there is nothing at all analogous in any possible attempt to ascertain value. The way in which the commodity B would be used, in the above instance, is in truth as a medium of comparison, not a measure, yet it is the only process which bears any analogy to measurement.

It appears, therefore, that all we can under-

stand by a measure of value, is some commodity which would serve as a medium to ascertain the relation subsisting between two other
commodities, that we had no means of bringing
into direct comparison. Thus, if I wished to
know the relation in exchange between corn
and cloth, and there happened to be no instance of direct barter of one of these commodities for the other, I could acquire the desired
information only by ascertaining their relations
to a third commodity. Supposing this commodity to be money, if a yard of cloth were worth
10s., and a bushel of corn 5s., I should learn
immediately that a yard of cloth was worth
two bushels of corn, and would have an equal
power of commanding all other things in exchange, silver in this instance being the commodity employed as a measure. This kind of
measure of value, which is merely a medium of
comparison, and obviously quite dissimilar to a
measure of length, is the only one which it is
possible to have; and although money is the
measure generally employed, and by far the

most convenient of all, yet any other commodity might answer the purpose.

Such a measure as this, however, has not
contented political economists; it is only, they
say, a measure of commodities at the same
time: they have wished for something to measure the value of commodities at different
periods.

Let us see what this amounts to: if it is
wished to measure or compare the value of corn
and cloth at one period with their value at another period, money will evidently answer the
purpose. We have only to inquire the prices
of corn and cloth at each period, and we shall
then be able to ascertain how they have varied
relatively to each other. If, in the year 1600,
cloth was 20s. a yard, and corn 10s. a bushel,
and in the year 1800, cloth was 10s. and corn
10s., then it would manifestly appear, that in
1600 a yard of cloth would command in exchange or be worth two bushels of corn, and in
1800 only one bushel. Thus by inquiring the
prices of the commodities we should ascertain

their variations in value with regard to each other, and money would be the measure of value or medium of comparison which we employed. This is evidently using money for a measure of value in the same manner as in the first case, the only difference being that we apply it to two periods, and make a subsequent comparison of the results obtained from each.

We have therefore not yet arrived at the sense in which the term is employed by economists, who are desirous of measuring the value of commodities at different periods. They do not wish to compare the mutual value of two commodities, or the relation subsisting between two commodities at one period, with the relation subsisting between them at another period, for this would be effected by a simple reference to their prices. They state their object to be, to find some standard commodity by which they might measure the value of the same object A, at two or more different periods, or, in other words, its fluctuations in value.

But in relation to what object is it wished to measure the value of A and its fluctuations? We cannot speak of value, as I have before shown, without meaning value in something, and as only A and the standard commodity which may be called B are here in question, the value of A must mean its value in B. It is wished therefore to measure the relation between A and B at two different periods by B, which if it has any signification must imply, that it is wished to ascertain the value of A and B relatively to each other at two different periods. These are historical facts, and when we have learned them as we learn other facts, we shall certainly know the fluctuations which the relation between A and B has undergone; but B is, in this procedure, by no means a measure of value, or a medium of comparison, any more than A. In a word, turn the matter as we please, we shall find that we can have no measure of value but in the sense already ex plained.

From this examination it appears, that a

measure of value can mean nothing but a commodity employed as a medium of comparison,
and that so far from its being impossible to
have any thing perfectly capable of performing
this function, we are in the daily use of one
possessing all the perfection which it is possible to conceive. In regard to measuring or comparing value, there is no operation which can
be intelligibly described or consistently imagined, but may be performed by the *media* of
which we are in possession.

It is astonishing, indeed, to find how slight
are the analogies with which economists have
contented themselves on this subject, and which
have served to preclude any close investigation
of processes essentially different, although confounded under the same appellation. One of
the most striking instances of this carelessness
of examination is the notion of its being necessary, that a commodity should possess invariable value, in order to form a perfect measure of value; a notion which has passed un-
questioned from one writer to another, and been

adopted without any suspicion of the false analogy and fundamental misconception on which it proceeds *. It is therefore essentially requisite, for a clear understanding of the present subject, to bring this opinion to the test of a close and minute examination.

The utter absurdity, however, of supposing, that a commodity to constitute a measure must be of invariable value, requires no deep research; it lies almost on the surface, and presents itself in numerous different aspects.

Invariable value must signify, as we have repeatedly shown, invariable in relation to some one or more commodities. Suppose A to be the commodity selected as a measure, and that it is invariable in value to B. I have here got an invariable value, but in what way am I to use it in regard to other things? When I have an invariable space, or an unvarying distance between two points, I can apply it mediately or immediately to all other spaces or distances within my reach, and ascertain their

* See Note D

respective ratios to it: but the invariable relation of value between A and B can tell me nothing of the mutual value of C and D; or, to
vary the language, the power which A has to
command B, can tell me nothing of that which
C has to command D.   I do not in any sense
measure the relation of value between two
commodities, by that existing between two
other commodities.   Invariable value, therefore, can be of no service.   The only meaning
to be attached to the phrase measuring value,
the only operation implied in it, is, as we have
seen, that comparison of the values of two objects which we are enabled to make by their separate relations to a third, or, in other words,
by having these values expressed in a common
term or denomination.   But the capability of
expressing the values of commodities has nothing to do with the constancy of their values,
either to each other or to the medium employed; neither has the capability of comparing these expressions of value any thing to
do with it.   Whether A is worth 4 B or 6 B,
and whether C is worth 8 B or 12 B, are cir-

cumstances which make no difference in the power of expressing the value of A and C in B, and certainly no difference in the power of comparing the value of A and C when expressed.

This supposition, of the necessity of invariable value in any commodity employed as a measure, proceeds, as I have already remarked, on a false analogy. Because a measure of space must be invariable in its length, a measure of value, it has been argued, must be invariable in its value *. To expose the fallacy of this inference, let us examine in the first place, what are the character and circumstances of that invariableness which is requisite for a measure of length. All that is required ap-

---

* "As a measure of quantity," says Adam Smith, " such as the natural foot, fathom, or handful, which is continually varying in its own quantity, can never be an accurate measure of the quantity of other things ; so a commodity, which is itself continually varying in its own value, can never be an accurate measure of the value of other commodities." Wealth of Nations, Book i, Chap. 5.

pears to be this, that when we measure the length of two objects by a third object, the length of the, latter, or the instrument employed, must remain the same until it have been applied to both the objects which are to be measured; or if it vary, it must vary in a known degree. Suppose it is wished to ascertain the relation of length between two trees lying apart from each other on the ground. The only requisite for doing this is a staff, or rod, or any other instrument which shall continue of the same length during the process of measuring. The process over, although the rod might be instantly altered in length, it would be as good a measure as before of the length of these or any other objects: for suppose the measurement to be repeated after this alteration in the instrument, the same relation of length between the two trees would be obtained. But if the rod varied in its length in an unknown degree, between applying it to the first tree and the second, whether this interval was a minute or an age, it is obvious that it could not serve as a measure of their relative length: there would in that case be no common medium of comparison. It is essential to the discovery of the mutual relation of two objects, which cannot be directly compared, that their respective relations to some third object should be known: but in this case, the ratio which the trees were found to bear would not be to the same object, and therefore nothing could be told as to the ratio of the trees to each other. It is thus indispensable, that the instrument employed as a measure should remain unaltered, or be altered in a known degree, during its successive applications to the objects measured, in order to give us their relations to one common object. By this means we obtain a common term or denomination, in which the lengths of the two trees are expressed. This is, in fact, all that is essential to the end in view: the measurement, that is, the actual application of the physical instrument to the object, is the means, and the unvarying length of the instrument, or its ascertainable variation during the process, is the necessary condition for obtaining that common expression of the length of the two objects, which will show their relation to each other. But it is obvious that this relation of length would be equally determined in whatever way the common expression was obtained.

Now in the case of value, we obtain this common expression without that physical operation here described. We learn the values of two commodities in relation to the third, not from the application of an instrument, first to one commodity and then to the other, but from intercourse with mankind, or from the inspection of documents in which they are registered. We equally obtain a common expression, but we obtain it by different means. But the invariableness in the length of a measure of space, as above described, is a circumstance belonging to the means employed to obtain a common expression of length; and as the means of obtaining a common expression of value are totally different, as in fact the common expres-

sion is necessarily implied in the supposition
of using any commodity as a medium of comparison, there is nothing in the latter case in
which invariableness of any kind, or in any
sense, can be required. In the one case there is
an instrument employed in a physical operation, and it is for the purpose of rendering this
instrument capable of performing its function,
that invariableness is indispensably necessary :
in the other case there is no instrument so employed, and therefore there is no invariableness
wanted : in the former case invariableness in
the instrument (under the modification which it
is needless to repeat) is essential to the attainment of the common term ; in the latter, the
common term being given, there is nothing in
which invariableness can have place, or of
which it can be predicated. If the length of
the rod varied in an unknown degree between
applying it to the two objects, we should have
two terms of unknown relation to each other,
and there could be no comparison of the objects to be measured ; and if the values of the

two commodities, which we were desirous of comparing, were expressed in different media, there would be the same impossibility. Hence, if in the case of value we were under the necessity of finding a counterpart to invariableness of length in the instrument employed to compare the dimensions of two objects, it would be, not invariableness of value in the commodity used as a medium to compare the value of two other commodities, but the condition that the value of these commodities should be given in relation to the same medium, or, in other words, expressed in a common denomination.

From all this it appears, that the analogy universally supposed to exist in this matter is altogether imaginary, and the phrase, invariable measure of value, proves to be absolutely destitute of a basis of meaning.

The doctrine which exacts invariableness in a measure of value, furnishes one corollary, which has been so frequently maintained and so generally adopted, that although its refutation is contained in the preceding observations, it appears to require a separate examination. It is argued, that money or any other commodity is a good measure of the value of commodities, only at the same time, because it is liable to vary; while to perform this function correctly, there should be a commodity the value of which did not vary from one age to another; as to measure the lengths of objects at different periods, there must be an object of invariable length *. Let us therefore endeavour to ascertain what this really amounts to. With regard to the measurement of space, the intervention of time occasions no alteration in the requisite conditions. The preceding remarks are as applicable to the measurement of the length of objects at different times as to the same time. The qualification necessary to constitute an instrument a good measure of space, is in each

* "At the same time and place, money is the exact measure of the real exchangeable value of all commodities. It is so, however, at the same time and place only." Wealth of Nations, Book i, Chap. 5.

case identical, namely, invariableness during its application to all the objects compared. Whether an hour or a century elapses between the successive applications of the instrument makes no difference. The essential requisite is the same in measuring objects in distant ages, or objects existing at the same time.

But in the process called measuring value, there is no application of any instrument, and therefore, as I have already shown, there is absolutely nothing to which the quality of invariableness can be attributed, or of which it can be affirmed. The requisite condition in the process is, that the commodities to be measured should be reduced to a common denomination, which may be done at all times with equal facility; or rather it is ready done to our hands, since it is the prices of commodities which are recorded, or their relations in value to money. If money, therefore, is a good medium of comparison at one time, it is at all times.

It may be objected, " Yes, good enough for commodities at each time, but not between commodities at different times."

This objection, however, proceeds on a fundamental mistake already exposed in a former chapter, namely, that the relation of value can exist between commodities at different periods, which is in the nature of the case impossible; and if no relation exists there can be no measurement of it. It is, in truth, only the value of commodities at the same time that can be measured; another point in which the supposed analogy between the measurement of space and of value completely fails. In the case of length, a direct comparison may be made between two objects, however separated by time, and their ratio to each other found. The length of an object now may be compared with the length of an object in former times, by means of an instrument actually handed down to us; by an uninterrupted transmission of the same object, or the same space through the medium of different objects, furnishing a com-

mon bond of connection between the measure-
ments of space in all ages.   But this circumstance can evidently have no existence in the
measurement of value, which is the ascertainment of a relation between contemporary commodities, and not between objects at different
periods.   The two cases would be analogous
if we supposed no physical measure of length
to be transmitted from one period to another, but
only a record of the lengths of different objects
expressed in a common denomination.   Under
these circumstances, all that we could do would
be to compare the relative dimensions of objects in our own days, with the relative dimensions of similar objects in past times, as recorded: but we should have no common medium of comparison between one age and another.   Now what in this case would be owing
to the want of a transmitted measure, arises in
the other case from the very nature of the relation with which we have to do.   The nature of that relation itself interposes as complete a disconnection between different ages, as

would result from the supposed want of a common instrument for measuring space.

It is obvious then, that if no relation of value can exist between objects in different ages, there can be no measurement of it, nor consequently can there be any measure or medium of comparison required.

The only thing to be done, with regard to different periods, is to compare the relation of value subsisting between any two commodities, A and B, at one period, with the relation subsisting between them at another; or, in other words, the quantity of A which purchased B at the former time, with the quantity of A which purchased B at the latter. This is evidently a simple comparison, in which neither A nor B perform the function of a measure, or medium, in any possible interpretation of the term. That office has in all likelihood been already discharged in ascertaining the relative quantities of A and B at each period; and if, as is probable, these quantities have been ascertained by means of the prices of the commodities, money has been the medium of comparison. But after these quantities have been ascertained, there can be no place whatever in the subsequent comparison for any medium, no conceivable function for it to perform.

Should it be urged, that when we compare the price of corn in one year with its price in another, we use money as a medium of comparison, in the same way as when we compare the prices of corn and cloth at the same point of time, the answer is not difficult.

In the latter case it is obvious, that the facts furnished to us are the relations of cloth and corn to money, or, the quantities of money for which definite portions of them are exchanged; and from these we infer another circumstance, namely, the relation of value between corn and cloth, and consequently their comparative power of purchasing all other commodities.

In the former case, on the other hand, the facts furnished to us are the prices of corn, or the relations between corn and money, at two different periods: but from these we deduce no other rela-

tion; we do not advance a step beyond the information given; there is no inference corresponding
to that which is drawn in the other case. We cannot deduce the relation of value, between corn at
the first and corn at the second period, because
no such relation exists, nor consequently can
we ascertain their comparative power over
other commodities. If we made the attempt,
it would be in fact endeavouring to infer the
quantities of corn which exchanged for each
other at two different points of time, a thing
obviously absurd. And further, money would
not be here discharging a particular function
any more than the other commodity. We
should have the value of corn in money, and
the value of money in corn, but one would be
no more a measure or medium of comparison
than the other.

These observations are enough to show, that
the only use of a measure of value, in the
sense of a medium of comparison, is between
commodities existing at the same time; and
consequently the proposition, that money is not

a good measure of the value of commodities at
different periods, is either false or amounts to
nothing.   If it means that money is not equally
a good measure of contemporary commodities
at any period, it is directly opposite to the
truth : if it means that it is not a good medium of comparison between commodities at
different periods, it asserts its incapability of
performing a function in a case where there is
no function for it to perform.

In applying the principles developed in the
preceding disquisition to the writings of Mr. Ricardo, we shall find that he has fallen into the
same errors as his predecessors and contempo-
raries, as well as into others peculiarly his own.
Misled by his radical misconception of the nature of value, and particularly by his notions
on the subject of real value, he has opened his
section " on an invariable measure," with the
following passage, the errors of which will be
sufficiently apparent to any one who has attended
to the foregoing part of the present chapter.

" When commodities," says Mr. Ricardo,

"varied in relative value, it would be desirable to have the means of ascertaining which of them fell, and which rose in real value, and this could be effected only by comparing them, one after another, with some invariable standard measure of value, which should itself be subject to none of the fluctuations to which other commodities are exposed. Of such a measure it is impossible to be possessed, because there is no commodity which is not itself exposed to the same variations as the things, the value of which is to be ascertained; that is, there is none which is not subject to require more or less labour for its production."

It has been already shown in the first chapter, not merely that such a commodity is physically impossible, as here conceded by Mr. Ricardo, but that the supposition of such a commodity, for such a purpose, involves contradictory conditions*. We could not in the nature

* Should Mr. Ricardo, or rather should any of his followers, shelter himself under the notion of real value, and thus escape the absurdity here charged upon him, it would only be taking refuge in another absurdity equally great.

of the case have any commodity of invariable value, by which to ascertain the fluctuations of all other things, unless all commodities were of invariable value, in which case there would be no fluctuations to ascertain.

We have also seen in the present chapter, that the demand for invariablenes of value in any commodity to be used as a measure, is founded altogether on a false analogy; that fluctuations in value are not ascertained by any measure, but by historical evidence; that a measure of value can signify nothing but a medium of comparison for contemporary commodities; and that we have as good a measure in this sense, not only as it is possible to have, but as it is possible to conceive.

Besides these errors, there is to be discovered in Mr. Ricardo's views, as to the uses of a measure of value, a singular confusion of thought, which I shall here endeavour to explain.

The specific error of Mr. Ricardo on the subject of invariable value consists, as before explained, in supposing, that if the causes of value affecting one commodity remained the same, the value of that commodity could not vary, overlooking the circumstance, that value denotes a relation between two objects, which must necessarily alter with an alteration in the causes affecting either of them. He incessantly identifies constancy in the quantity of producing labour with constancy of value. Hence he maintains, that if we could find any commodity invariable in the circumstances of its production, it would be in the first place invariable in value; and, secondly, it would indicate, or would enable us to ascertain, the variations in value of other commodities.

It is curious enough that he should never have clearly discerned what such a commodity would really serve to indicate: it would not, as he asserts, serve to indicate the variations in the value of commodities, but the variations in the circumstances of their production. It would enable us to ascertain, not any fluctuations in value, but in which commodity those fluctuations had originated. He has in truth

confounded two perfectly distinct ideas, namely, *measuring the value of commodities,* and
*ascertaining in which commodity, and in what
degree, the causes of value have varied.*

For suppose we had such a commodity as he
requires for a standard : suppose, for instance,
all commodities to be produced by labour
alone, and silver to be produced by an invariable quantity of labour. In this case silver
would be, according to Mr. Ricardo, a perfect
measure of value. But in what sense ? What
is the function performed ? Silver, even if invariable in its producing labour, will tell us
nothing of the value of other commodities.
Their relations in value to silver, or their prices,
must be ascertained in the usual way, and
when ascertained, we shall certainly know the
values of commodities in relation to each other :
but in all this there is no assistance derived
from the circumstance of the producing labour
of silver being a constant quantity.

But it is the fluctuations of commodities
which this invariable standard is to ascertain or

measure. Let us try to discover how far it would assist us here.

Suppose cloth in the year 1600 was worth 12s. a yard, and in 1800 only 6s. Here we have a fluctuation in the value of cloth, in relation to the standard commodity; in 1800 it was worth only half as much silver as it was in 1600. This, however, is not, let it be observed, a fluctuation ascertained by the circumstance of silver being produced by an invariable quantity of labour. Had silver varied in the circumstances of its production, our information as to the relation between cloth and silver would have been equally attainable, and equally complete. What then could be ascertained, in this case, from the metal being invariable in the quantity of its producing labour? What inference would this circumstance enable us to draw? No inference, obviously, as to the value of cloth and silver; for, on this point, the prices of the former tell us all that it is possible to know. The inference we should draw would be, that the cause of the change in the relation between cloth and silver had been in the former, and as labour is, by the supposition, the sole cause of value, we might more particularly infer, that the producing labour of cloth had been abridged to half its former quantity.

A commodity, therefore, under these conditions, produced by an invariable quantity of labour, would enable us to ascertain, not the fluctuations in value between two or more commodities (for these are facts to be gathered from appropriate evidence), but the fluctuations in the quantity of labour which produced them: and in truth, if we examine what is the particular advantage which Mr. Ricardo himself supposes we should be able to derive from the possession of such a commodity, we shall find it to be in reality that which is here described, the power of ascertaining, not the variations in value, but the variations in the producing labour of commodities. Speaking of the interchange of game and fish, in the earlier stages of society, he says,—

" If with the same quantity of labour, a less quantity of fish, or a greater quantity of game were obtained, the value of fish would rise in comparison with that of game. If, on the contrary, with the same quantity of labour a less quantity of game, or a greater quantity of fish was obtained, game would rise in comparison with fish.

" If there were any other commodity, which was invariable in its value, we should be able to ascertain, by comparing the value of fish and game with this commodity, how much of the variation was to be attributed to a cause which affected the value of fish, and how much to a cause which affected the value of game.

" Suppose money to be that commodity. If a salmon were worth £1, and a deer £2, one deer would be worth two salmon. But a deer might become of the value of three salmon, for more labour might be required to obtain the deer, or less to get the salmon; or both these causes might operate at the same time. If we had this invariable standard, we might easily as-

certain in what degree either of these causes
operated.   If salmon continued to sell for £1,
whilst deer rose to £3, we might conclude *that
more labour was required to obtain the deer.*   If
deer continued at the same price of £2, and
salmon sold for 13*s.* 4*d.* we might then be sure
that *less labour was required to obtain the salmon;*
and if deer rose to £2. 10*s.* and salmon fell to
16*s.* 8*d.* we should be convinced that *both causes
had operated* in producing the alteration of the
relative value of these commodities."

Here we have a very accurate description,
by Mr. Ricardo, of what a commodity produced by an invariable quantity of labour
(not a commodity of invariable value, as he
erroneously terms it) would enable us to ascertain, under the supposition that all things were
determined in value by quantity of labour.
He does not tell us that such a commodity
would enable us to ascertain the value of fish
or game, or their variation in value, but *this
variation being given,* that it would enable us
to infer how much of it was to be attributed to a

change in the labour required to obtain the salmon, and how much to a change in that required to obtain the deer.

In this and other passages it will be found, that although Mr. Ricardo is professedly speaking of a commodity produced by invariable labour, in the character of a measure of value, he is in reality, without being conscious of the difference, altogether occupied with the consideration of that commodity as capable of indicating variations in the producing labour of other commodities*. Instead of a measure of value,

* The same remark will apply to economists in general. Their real object in seeking for a measure of value (however little they may be aware of it) is to determine in which commodities any changes of value have originated, and not to ascertain the extent of these changes, which, as I have repeatedly stated, are matters of record and evidence, and a knowledge of which is in reality pre-supposed in any application of what they call a measure. It is not, therefore, a measure of value which they are in pursuit of, but a commodity which would indicate the sources of variation. Whether there is any one object which would do this better than another, would at all events be a rational, and might prove a useful inquiry.

such a commodity as he describes would be a
measure of labour, or a medium of ascertaining the varying quantities of labour which
commodities required to produce them. Before it could be employed in regard to any object, the value of that object, or its relation to
the standard commodity, must be given, and
then all that could be deduced from the datum
would be the quantity of labour bestowed on
its production.

But perhaps the most remarkable circumstance of all is, that for this latter purpose, that
invariableness in the quantity of labour, which
he has insisted upon as so essentially requisite,
would be of no peculiar service. On the supposition that labour was the sole determining
principle of value, a commodity produced by
an invariable quantity of labour would afford
us no assistance even as a measure of labour,
which could not be equally derived from a
commodity the producing labour of which
was variable, provided we were furnished with
the same data.

For in the above comparison of cloth in 1600 and cloth in 1800, mark all that is specifically ascertained.

If silver had been liable to variation in the quantity of its producing labour, we should still have been informed, from the same source that supplied the information in the other case, what was its relation to cloth, for this is equivalent to saying, that we should still have been informed of the prices of cloth at the two different periods specified. These are historical facts, and not deductions from the invariableness of the labour employed in the production of silver. Were this labour then a variable quantity, we should still learn, that a yard of cloth in 1600 was 12s. and in 1800 6s. ; but we should, it is alleged, be at a loss to discover, whether the change in the relation between silver and cloth had been owing to the former or the latter. This then is the sole circumstance by which the two cases are supposed to be distinguished, and in fact it amounts to this; we could tell that, in the former case, cloth in 1800 required only

half the labour necessary for its production in
1600, while in the latter case we could not tell
whether the quantity of producing labour in
the cloth had been reduced one half, or whether
that required for the production of money had
been doubled. In answer to this I say, that the
ratio between the quantities of labour necessary
for the production of cloth in 1800, and in
1600, might be equally ascertained, although
the quantity of labour employed in the production of silver had varied, provided that the data
in the two cases were equal.

The data in the first case are the prices of
cloth at each period, and the ratio subsisting
between the quantity of labour employed at
each period in the production of silver. The
circumstance of this ratio being that of equality
makes no difference.

Now suppose, in the second case, that we
are furnished with the prices of cloth at both
periods, and with the ratio subsisting between
the quantities of the labour necessary for the
production of silver, which ratio, by the sup-

position, not being that of equality, suppose
to be as 2 in 1600 to 1 in 1800, or, in other
words, suppose that silver in 1800 is produced
by half the labour required in 1600.

With these data it is obvious, that we could
deduce the ratio of labour employed in the
production of cloth at these periods, with as
much accuracy as we could under the conditions of the first case. If in 1600 the cloth
was 12*s.* per yard, and in 1800 only 6*s.*, the
producing labour of silver at the latter period
being only half of what it was at the former
period, then the producing labour of cloth
would have been reduced to a quarter of its
former quantity. For in 1600 a yard of cloth
being 12*s.* in value, the yard of cloth and the
12*s.* took equal quantities of labour to produce
them: but in 1800 the producing labour of 12*s.*
is by the supposition reduced one half, and
consequently the quantity of labour in 6*s.* must
be a quarter of the quantity which had been
necessary to produce 12*s.* in 1600. Now as 6*s.*
in 1800 exchange for a yard of cloth, the pro-

ducing labour of the yard of cloth must be
equal to the producing labour of the 6s.; that is,
a quarter of the quantity of labour employed to
produce a yard of cloth in 1600.

It may probably be alleged, however, as an
advantage peculiar to the first case, that the
quantity of producing labour being invariable,
we are saved from all that research into its comparative quantity at different periods which
would be necessary on the contrary supposition.
But it is to be recollected, that the circumstance
of a commodity having been always produced
by the same quantity of labour, is an historical
fact quite as difficult to ascertain as the variations of another commodity. We might, it is
true, be saved from all investigation of this
nature, if there existed a commodity, which,
from some obvious and insuperable necessity,
was always the product of the same labour; yet
even this advantage is not dependent on the invariableness of the labour; for if, what is
equally easy to suppose, and quite as likely to
happen, we had a commodity which necessarily

varied every year in a given proportion, we should be equally spared the pains of historical research. To have a commodity, whether produced by a variable or by an invariable quantity of labour, which saved us the trouble of inquiry, would doubtless be an advantage, but we might as well suppose fifty other arbitrary aids *.

In concluding this discussion, it may not be useless to advert more particularly to one of the objects, which economists have proposed to themselves in the attempt to discover an invariable measure or standard of value. It appears to have been to determine the efficiency of revenues, salaries, and wages of different classes of people at different periods, in what condition such revenues enabled them to live, or what power it enabled them to wield. This, it is supposed, would be accomplished, did we possess some object of immutable value.

" If we are told," says Mr. Malthus, " that the wages of day-labour in a particular coun-

* See Note E.

try are, at the present time, four pence a day ;
or, that the revenue of a particular sovereign,
700 or 800 years ago, was 400,000*l.* a year,
these statements of nominal value convey
no sort of information respecting the condition of the lower classes of people in the
one case, or the resources of the sovereign
in the other. Without further knowledge on
the subject, we should be quite at a loss to say,
whether the labourers in the country mentioned
were starving, or living in greater plenty;
whether the king in question might be considered as having a very inadequate revenue, or
whether the sum mentioned was so great as to
be incredible.

" It is quite obvious, that in cases of this
kind, and they are of constant recurrence, the
value of wages, incomes, or commodities, estimated in the precious metals, will be of little
use to us alone. What we want further is
some estimate of a kind which may be denominated real value in exchange, implying the
quantity of the necessaries and conveniences of
life, which those wages, incomes, or commodi-

dities will enable the possessor of them to command *."

Now to suppose that we can have any one object by which this information can be obtained, would imply a gross misconception of the nature of value. I have already repeatedly stated, that to know the value of an article at any period, is merely to know its relation in exchange to some other commodity. From this fact, which must be ascertained like other facts, no inference whatever can be drawn as to the value of any thing beyond the two commodities in question. From the relation of corn and money nothing can be inferred as to the relation of corn and labour, or of money and labour. If, proceeding a step farther, we learn from the proper records the relation also of labour and money, then we can deduce the relation of labour and corn; but we should not be able to make any inference to any other object. The only practicable inference on the subject

* Principles of Pol. Econ., p. 59.

of value, is the mutual relation of two commodities from their separate relations to a third.

It follows, that if we wish to ascertain the state of comfort or luxury in which any class of people lived at any assigned period, there is no possible method of effecting the object, but ascertaining from the proper documents the amount of their incomes, and then, particular by particular, the relation which these incomes bore to commodities. If the incomes are stated in corn, or silver, nothing can be inferred from the statement, as to their power over other things. Supposing the income to be a certain amount of money, then the inquirer must find records of the prices of those articles to which his curiosity is directed, and a simple calculation will teach him the power of the income to command them.

If he wishes, for example, to ascertain the condition of the labouring class at any given period, he must first find the rate of wages, or, in other words, the mutual relation of labour and money. This is one step in the investigation, but it will not of itself throw any light on the food, clothing, and comfort, which the labourers are able to procure; and he must therefore search in the proper registers for the prices of such commodities as constitute these necessaries and conveniences. He can ascertain nothing but what is shown by the historical documents which he consults. When he has found the price of labour, the price of corn, of cloth, of hats, of stockings, of fuel, of house-room, he will be able to tell how much of each of these commodities a week's or a year's labour could command: in other words, the condition of the labouring class of society in these respects will become manifest.

But these are all separate particulars, to be separately ascertained: one will not disclose another; each must be individually established by independent evidence. There can be no commodity, by a reference to which the power of a given income over any or all other commodities may be shown.

Conclusions such as these are so obvious, that they would scarcely require to be formally stated had they not been frequently overlooked. Even the author of the Templars' Dialogues, who observes, " that Mr. Malthus, in common with many others, attaches a most unreasonable importance to the discovery of a measure of value," seems to sanction the prevailing errors, when he goes on to remark, that such a measure " would at best end in answering a few questions of unprofitable curiosity*." Sufficient, it is hoped, has been said to show, that we are in possession of the only kind of measure which can be had or conceived, and that we must look for the gratification of our curiosity, not to any measure of value whatever, but to the records of former times, and a few simple calculations from the data which they furnish.

* London Magazine for May 1824, p. 560.

CHAPTER VII.

ON THE MEASURE OF VALUE PROPOSED
BY MR. MALTHUS.

AFTER the conclusions established in the preceding chapter, it would be a superfluous task to examine the various measures of value which may have been imagined or proposed by different economists. As that, nevertheless, which has been recently advocated by Mr. Malthus, and which was originally brought forward by Adam Smith, has attracted some attention, it may deserve a cursory notice.

This measure is labour, considered as an exchangeable commodity, or, in other words, the labour which commodities command: and proceeding on the false principle, that a measure of value must be itself immutable in value, Mr. Malthus maintains that the value of labour is invariable.

The discussions in which we have already been engaged, furnish a variety of methods in which the errors of this doctrine may be exposed.

It has been shown, for example, that the value of labour, like that of any other exchangeable article, is denoted by the quantity of some other commodity for which a definite portion of it will exchange, and must rise or fall as that quantity becomes greater or smaller, these phrases being in truth only different expressions of the same event. Hence, unless labour always exchanges for the same quantity of other things, its value cannot be invariable; and consequently, the very supposition of its being at one and the same time invariable, and capable of measuring the variations of other commodities, involves a direct contradiction.

It has also been shown, that to term any thing immutable in value, amidst the fluctuations of other things, implies that its value at one time may be compared with its value at

another time, without reference to any other
commodity; which is absurd, value denoting
a relation between two things at the same time:
and it has likewise been shown, that in no sense
could an object of invariable value, if attainable, be of any peculiar service in the capacity
of a measure.

These considerations are quite sufficient to
overturn the claims of the proposed measure,
as maintained by its advocate, but it may be
inquired, how far would it be useful in the sense
of a medium of comparison.   In order to satisfy this inquiry, let us suppose a simple case.
I wish to know, for instance, the mutual value
of corn and cloth in the year 1600 ; and in the
ordinary way I find, that corn was 6s. a bushel
and cloth 12s. a yard, and I thence perceive,
that a bushel of corn was worth half a yard of
cloth.   This appears to be the only information wanted ; but this is using money as the
medium of comparison ; and to apply Mr. Malthus's measure, we must find the value of corn
and cloth in relation to labour.   Of this, however, I probably shall find no record, and there-

fore the measure proposed cannot be used.   I
may find, it is true, the prices of labour, corn,
and cloth : I then may proceed to calculate the
value of a yard of cloth and a bushel of corn
in labour ; and their separate relations to labour
will show their relation to each other : but
this I have already learned from their prices or
separate relations to money.   Their value in
labour, therefore, is perfectly superfluous towards
ascertaining their mutual relation, consequently
labour in this case is perfectly useless as a measure of value.

The way in which Mr. Malthus attempts to
establish the invariable value of labour is remarkable enough, and his table, drawn up with
that view, is certainly one of the most curious
productions in the whole range of political
economy*.

In the first column he supposes certain
quantities of corn to be produced by ten men,

* As the subsequent remarks could scarcely be understood without a reference to this table, a copy of it is presented to the reader at the end of the present chapter.

according to the varying fertility of the soil.
In the second column he states the yearly corn
wages of each labourer, determined by the demand and supply. The first case supposes the
yearly wages of a labourer to be 12 quarters,
the last only 8 quarters ; in other words, the
value of labour in relation to corn is in the first
case 12 quarters, and in the last 8. Hence it
is obvious, that to prove the invariable value of
labour, he begins by supposing it to be variable;
singular premises, certainly, from which to deduce such a conclusion. And the process of
deduction is no less singular. Taking the first
case, he proceeds thus: If 1 man obtain 12
quarters per annum for wages, 10 men will obtain 120 quarters, and as the whole product of
these 10 men is 150 quarters, profits will be 25
per cent. Now as 150 quarters are the product
of 10 men, 120 quarters must be produced by 8
men, and the profits being equal to the labour of
2 men, the value of the whole 120 quarters is
10. But 10 what? Evidently 10 men's labour:
that is, in other words, the quantity of corn

given to 10 men for their labour, is equal in value to the labour of ten men, which is just equivalent to saying, that the number of shillings which any one gives for a yard of cloth, is equal in value to the yard of cloth for which the shillings are exchanged! In a word, Mr. Malthus sets out from the premises, that 120 quarters of corn are given as wages to 10 men, and, after journeying through two columns of figures, he arrives at the conclusion, that the said 120 quarters are worth the labour for which they are given. In the same manner he goes through all the other cases, and as whatever quantity of corn is given to 10 men as their wages must be equal in value to that for which it is exchanged, that is, to the labour of 10 men, he constantly succeeds in alighting at the point from which he set out. Having accomplished thus much, he appears to proceed as follows: "If I give a commodity, which is as valuable at one time as at another, for another commodity at each of these periods, that other commodity must be equally constant in value. Now the wages of

10 men having been proved to be as valuable at one time as at another, the value of the labour for which they are exchanged must be also constant." By wages he means the aggregate quantity of corn; and how has he shown these wages to be of invariable value? He has shown them to be invariable, estimated in labour: his argument consequently is, that because the wages of ten men are always of the same value, estimated in labour, therefore the labour for which they are exchanged must be of invariable value.

In the same way any article might be proved to be of invariable value; for instance, 10 yards of cloth. For whether we gave £5 or £10 for the 10 yards, the sum given would always be equal in value to the cloth for which it was paid, or, in other words, of invariable value in relation to cloth. But that which is given for a thing of invariable value, must itself be invariable, whence the 10 yards of cloth must be of invariable value.

It is scarcely necessary to expose the futility

of reasoning like this.   Instead of proving labour to be of immutable value, it proves the reverse.   An alteration in the mutual value of
two articles means, that the quantities in which
they are exchanged for each other are altered :
a definite quantity of one is exchanged for a
greater or smaller portion of the other than before.   Now the only commodities in question,
in Mr. Malthus's table, are corn and labour ;
and if, as he supposes, the labour of 10 men is
at one time rewarded with 120 quarters of corn,
and at another time with only 80 quarters, the
only condition required for an alteration of
value is fulfilled, and labour, instead of being
invariable, has fallen one-third.

The fallacy lies in virtually considering or
speaking of wages, as if they were a commodity ; while, as the term is used by Mr. Malthus, it really implies an aggregate quantity of
corn, in the same way as the term *sum* implies
an aggregate quantity of money; and it is just
the same kind of futility to call wages invariable
in value, because though variable in quantity

they command the same portion of labour, as to call the sum given for a hat, of invariable value, because, although sometimes more and sometimes less, it always purchases the hat. In speaking of the rise and fall in value of commodities, we have nothing to do with aggregate quantities which really vary in amount, and have no identity but in name; our business is with definite portions: and the precise reason why the labour in one case, and the hat in the other, are not of invariable value, is, that the quantities of corn and of money given for them have varied, although these quantities under every variation continue to be designated by the terms " wages," and " sum."

It is true enough, that if a commodity exchanges at one time for 10 men's labour, and at another time for the same, it has not altered in value to labour: both the commodity and the labour have been constant in value to each other; but as wages are not a commodity, as in Mr. Malthus's nomenclature they signify an aggregate quantity of corn, if this aggregate quantity, given for a definite portion of labour, is sometimes larger and sometimes smaller, the corn of which the aggregate is composed varies accordingly in value in relation to the labour for which it is given, and the labour varies in value in relation to the corn.

From these remarks the reader will perceive, that Mr. Malthus's " Table illustrating the invariable value of labour," absolutely proves nothing.   It exhibits merely the results of a few simple operations in arithmetic, as a slight inspection of the annexed copy will show.   Column 1 contains the quantities of corn produced, according to the varying fertility of the soil, by the yearly labour of 10 men, which quantities are assumed, and not deduced from other data. The second column exhibits the quantities of corn given yearly to each labourer, and these quantities are also assumed, not deduced. Column 3 contains the quantities of corn given yearly to 10 men, obtained by multiplying the quantities in column 2 by the number 10. Column 4 shows the rate of profit, or how much per cent. the quantities of corn in column 1 exceed the corresponding quantities in column 3 ; or, in other words, how much per cent. the quantities of corn produced by 10 men exceed the quantities given to 10 men for their labour. Column 5 exhibits the quantities of labour, or number of men required to produce the quantities of corn in the third column, obtained by a simple operation in the rule of three : if 10 men produce 150 quarters, how many will be required to produce 120 ?

Column 6 shows the profits estimated in labour, after the rate in the fourth column; or, what is the same thing, it shows the quantities of labour which the quantities of corn in column 3 will command, over and above what produced them.   Column 7 contains the quantities of labour commanded by the corn in column 3, and is nothing but a repetition of what was before told us in the third column : for we are there informed, that the quantities of corn enumerated, severally commanded the yearly labour of 10 men, and in this seventh column there

are fourteen distinct reiterations of the same
piece of information.   Column 8 is merely
another enumeration of results obtained by
simple operations in the rule of three.   It shows
the quantities of labour which 100 quarters of
corn would command, at the different rates according to which labour is rewarded in the
third column.

Column 9 is a similar enumeration of results,
obtained in the same manner, and exhibits the
quantity of labour which the products of the
labour of 10 men in column 1 would respectively
command, or the value of those aggregate quantities estimated in labour.

This cursory review evinces, that the formidable array of figures in the table yields not
a single new or important truth; and that the
seventh column, which was intended to afford
the grand result of this tabular argument, exhibits merely a constant repetition of one of the
assumptions on which the whole is built*.

---

* See Note F.

Mr. Malthus's Table illustrating the invariable Value of Labour and its Results.

1. Quarters of Corn produced by Ten Men, or varying Fertility of the Soil.	2. Yearly Corn Wages to each Labourer, determined by the Demand and Supply.	3. Advances in Corn Wages, or variable Produce commanding the Labour of Ten Men.	4. Rate of Profits under the foregoing Circumstances.	5. Quantity of Labour required to produce the Wages of Ten Men under the foregoing Circumstances.	6. Quantity of Profits on the Advances of Labour.	7. Invariable Value of the Wages of a given Number of Men.	8. Value of 100 Quarters of Corn, under the varying Circumstances supposed.	9. Value of the Product of the Labour of Ten Men, under the Circumstances supposed.
Qrs.	Qrs.	Qrs.	Per Cent.					
150	12	120	25	8	2	10	8.33	12.5
150	13	130	15.38	8.66	1.34	10	7.7	11.53
150	10	100	50	6.6	3.4	10	10	15
140	12	120	16.66	8.6	1.4	10	8.33	11.6
140	11	110	27.2	7.85	2.15	10	9.09	12.7
130	12	120	8.3	9.23	.77	10	8.3	10.8
130	10	100	30	7.7	2.3	10	10	13
120	11	110	9	9.17	.83	10	9.09	10.9
120	10	100	20	8.33	1.67	10	10	12
110	10	100	10	9.09	.91	10	10	11
110	9	90	22.2	8.18	1.82	10	11.1	12.2
100	9	90	11.1	9	1	10	11.1	11.1
100	8	80	25	8.88	2	10	12.5	12.5
90	8	80	12.5	8.88	1.12	10	12.5	11.25
		Quantity of Labour required to produce the corresponding quantity of Corn in the third column.		Quantity of Labour which the Corn in column 3 will command over and above what it cost.		Quantity of Labour commanded by the Corn in column 3, or Number of Men commanded.	Quantity of Labour commanded by 100 Quarters of Corn, under the circumstances supposed.	Quantity of Labour commanded by the Corn in column 1.

Explanations, as given in the present Chapter.

CHAPTER VIII.

ON METHODS OF ESTIMATING VALUE.

THE discussion respecting the measurement of value naturally leads to the consideration of the methods of estimating value. To measure and to estimate value are often considered as implying the same operation, and are used indiscriminately. The explanation, however, of the former, which I have given in a preceding chapter, establishes a useful distinction between them. By measuring value I mean finding the mutual relation of two commodities by their separate relations to a third. Estimating value is the same thing as expressing it *, except that

* See Note G.

the latter is more appositely used in regard to a single definite portion of a commodity, or at least in the simpler cases of valuation; while the former may be appropriated to cases of greater complexity, where we compute the value of a mass or number of commodities. When I say a yard of cloth is worth twenty shillings, or a pound, I express the value of the cloth in relation to silver. When I say that 1000 yards of cloth, 500 quarters of corn, and 20 tons of iron, are worth 3000 guineas, I estimate the value of these articles in gold. If it is necessary to establish a distinction between expressing and estimating value, it may therefore be stated to be, that the latter involves the idea of computation, which is not necessarily implied in the former. The distinction, however, is not essential, and the indiscriminate use of the terms can scarcely lead to error.

Mr. Ricardo frequently insists, that if by improvements in the methods of production the whole produce of a country were doubled, while the labour employed remained the same, this doubled produce would be only of the same

aggregate value as the former produce, while
each individual commodity would have fallen
fifty per cent. in value. It is obvious, however,
that the truth of this and similar positions entirely depends on the medium in which we estimate value.   Suppose, for the sake of simplification, that the country had no foreign commerce, and produced its own money : then if
all commodities (money of course included) were
produced in double quantity, the effect would
be, that while the value of the aggregate would
be doubled, the value of each individual commodity would remain as before.   For by the
value of an individual commodity we mean its
power of commanding other things in exchange.
If a pair of stockings were formerly worth a
shilling, it would still be worth a shilling.
Every commodity would in the same way continue to be exchanged in the same quantity
against every other commodity.   So far as to
the value of individual commodities.   With
regard to the aggregate, value being in strict
propriety a relation existing amongst the several
parts, it cannot be predicated of the whole, ex-

cept in reference to some of its parts. If the value of the whole means any thing, it can be only its value estimated or computed in some individual commodity; and in this sense, as the quantity of every thing would be doubled, the aggregate value would be doubled. If a pair of stockings continued to be worth a shilling, 2000 pair, which would now be produced for every thousand pair previously, would be worth 2000 shillings; and thus, with regard to every other commodity, we should have a double value in shillings, and the sum of all these values would be double.

Labour is the only thing in relation to which any commodity would not necessarily appear to be of the same value*, but here we are of course leaving labour out of consideration. On the sup-

---

* Commodities *might* appear of the same value even in relation to labour; that is to say, there would be no inconsistency or repugnance amongst the terms and ideas involved in the supposition, although the circumstance would be one not likely to happen: a point, indeed, in which it only resembles the other parts of this hypothetical case.

position that all commodities were doubled in quantity, this is the result, in whichever of the commodities or parts we choose to estimate the whole. But if any one commodity is supposed to be produced in the same quantity by the same labour as before, and the whole of the other commodities are estimated in this one, it will be true enough, that the whole produce continues of the same value, while the parts have fallen one half*. From this it is evident, that in all such cases the result depends on the commodity chosen as the medium of estimation. As by value we always imply value in something, a commodity may be said by one person to rise, and by another to fall, and with equal truth, if they speak with tacit reference to different commodities; but a general affirmation of this nature is worse than useless. The assertion of a rise or fall in any thing should be accompanied by a mention of the commo-

* Assuming that commodities are to each other in value as the quantities of labour concerned in their production.

dity in relation to which it has thus varied, or, at all events, the commodity should be clearly indicated by the tenour of the language employed. Otherwise, two disputants in Political Economy may share the fate of the two knights, who fell sacrifices to their obstinacy in maintaining, the one that a shield was of gold, the other that it was of silver, both being equally correct in their assertions, and their difference arising, as a thousand differences arise, from the simple circumstance of having looked at opposite sides of the same object.

The present subject may be further elucidated by citing a passage from Mr. Ricardo. " The labour of a million of men in manufactures," says he, " will always produce the same value, but will not always produce the same riches. By the invention of machinery, by improvements in skill, by a better division of labour, or by the discovery of new markets, where more advantageous exchanges may be made, a million of men may produce double or treble the amount of riches, of necessaries, conve-

niences, and amusements, in one state of society, that they could produce in another, but
they will not on that account add any thing to
value; for every thing rises or falls in value in
proportion to the facility or difficulty of producing it, or, in other words, in proportion to
the quantity of labour employed on its production*."

All this may be safely pronounced unmeaning
and nugatory†.   It conveys no information, nor
can we judge of its correctness or inaccuracy,
till we know what is the commodity, in relation
to which it is meant to assert, that the product
of the labour of this million of men will always
prove of the same value, or in other words,
until we are told what is the commodity employed as a medium of estimation.   If these
men produce treble the quantity of all articles
of exchange whatever, then the aggregate value
of the product of their labour will be treble,

* Principles of Pol. Econ., p. 320, 3d edit.

† See Note H.

estimated in any article we please. If any articles still require the same labour, and we estimate the rest in these, then the aggregate value
will remain the same.

In the sequel of the passage above cited,
Mr. Ricardo maintains, that when the labour of
a certain number of men, formerly capable of
producing 1000 pair of stockings, becomes by
inventions in machinery productive of 2000 pair,
the value of the general mass of commodities will be diminished, because the stockings
manufactured before the improvement must
fall to the level of the new goods. This again
depends on the mode of estimation. Estimated
in stockings, the aggregate value of the general mass of commodities would rise; estimated in any thing else it would fall: and although it may seem ludicrous to talk of estimating the value of all commodities in stockings,
the principle is still the same as if gold or
any other commodity happened to be the medium of valuation.

Hence it appears, that these propositions,

which carry so profound and paradoxical an air, really amount to nothing but this, that a commodity may rise or fall in relation to one commodity and not to another, and therefore that the estimation of commodities in different *media* will necessarily yield different results.

It may be here remarked, that Mr. Ricardo employs the term estimate in a manner altogether incorrect. In the preceding pages it has been shown, that we can express the value of a commodity only by the quantity of some other commodity, for which it will exchange. Now if to *estimate* has the same meaning as to *express* value, with the accessory idea of computation annexed, it follows that we can estimate value only in the same manner. Should we therefore at any time employ labour as the medium of estimation, it must be the labour for which a commodity will exchange. But Mr. Ricardo speaks of estimating commodities by the labour which is required to produce them. Nor is this to be regarded merely as a verbal inaccuracy, for it appears to have led him into that erroneous method of estimating the value of labour, which has been already pointed out. It may be said, at least, that a clear apprehension of the precise meaning of the term would have been incompatible with his doctrine on the real value of wages, if not with the fundamental error which runs through his speculations, and of which his doctrine on the subject of the real value of wages is but a ramification.

CHAPTER IX.

ON THE DISTINCTION BETWEEN VALUE AND RICHES.

In the last chapter the subject of the present one has been in some degree anticipated. It has been there shown what is the real amount of the assertion, that the riches of a society may be doubled or trebled without any thing being added to their value. The subject, however, is of so much importance, that it will be necessary to enter into a closer examination of it.

The distinction between riches and value is sufficiently obvious, riches signifying the commodities themselves (with one or more accessory ideas annexed), and value denoting the relation in exchange between any of these commodities.

Mr. Ricardo, nevertheless, has been singularly unfortunate in his attempt to discriminate them. His elaborate chapter, which contains it, appears to me to be a remarkable tissue of errors and uumeaning conclusions, arising from his fundamental misconception of the nature of value. Throughout the whole of this chapter, he speaks of value as the positive result of labour : whence it follows, that the same quantity of labour must always produce the same value, however much its productive powers may have increased. Riches, therefore, may be indefinitely multiplied, while no more labour is em ployed ; but the value of the riches, under this condition, remains invariably the same.

Such is the sum and substance of his argument. The error of stating the value to remain constant has been sufficiently considered. There is still, however, an ambiguity or obscurity in the meaning of the term riches, which requires to be cleared up. Mr. Ricardo has regarded it as synonymous, sometimes, with *commodities*, and at other times with *abundance of commodities.* It is evidently used in a collective sense ; it is a term expressive of aggregation, if not of plenty. The adjective rich is never applied but to denote the possession of abundance, or the means of commanding it, and it may be doubted whether the substantive riches is ever used without an implication of the same idea. If it were merely a general expression for commodities, without any accessory idea, it might be discarded from our speculations, and the latter word substituted in its stead. But such an experiment would not answer. We could not with any propriety change the title of Adam Smith's great work into " An Inquiry into the Nature and Causes of the Commodities of Nations." We should approximate more nearly to the meaning of the original, were we to translate it, " An Inquiry into the Nature and Causes of the greater or smaller abundance of Commodities possessed by Nations."

Whether the idea of abundance, however, is involved in the meaning of riches or not, the idea of aggregation or collection cannot be excluded. A single grain of wheat is not wealth, although it may be said to be an article of wealth. The idea of possession also seems essential to it. Riches are not simply commodities as things existing, but as things possessed. The most useful articles in an uninhabited country could not be termed wealth, because they would have no proprietor. The country, it is true, might be denominated rich in such articles, but only inasmuch as it would be the container or possessor of them. There would still be the same idea of possession involved in our language.

Whatever difficulty may be found in furnishing a good and complete definition of riches, there can be none in establishing the difference between the terms riches and value, as used in the science of Political Economy. Riches are the attribute of men, value is the attribute of commodities. A man or a community is rich; a pearl or a diamond is valuable. He possesses riches who is the owner of commodities which themselves possess value*; and, further, he is rich in proportion to the value of the objects possessed. Mr. Ricardo, indeed, denies that value is the measure of riches; but a slight consideration will show, that it is the only criterion by which we can determine whether one man or one community is richer than another. If the wealth of two men consisted in one single commodity, then, without entering into the question of exchange or value, we might determine that one was richer than the other, from mere excess of quantity. Even, however, in the simplest imaginable case of

---

* Colonel Torrens is of opinion, that value is not essential to the idea of riches: it may be questioned, however, whether it is not always implied, and whether the latter term would have been invented in a state of society in which there was no interchange of commodities. It is a point, at all events, of little importance; as, in those cases which come under the notice of the political economist, value in exchange is a constant adjunct of wealth. Vide Essay on the Production of Wealth, chap. i.

this kind, there would necessarily be a superiority of value, if such an idea came at all
into question, as well as of wealth. If the
sole commodity in possession of the two individuals were corn, of which one possessed 500
quarters and the other 1000, the latter would
not only be richer, but the proprietor of produce, the aggregate value of which was
greater.

In all but this very simplest case, it would
be impossible to decide with accuracy on the
superiority of two individuals in point of riches,
except by estimating their value in some
common medium. Suppose the individual
who possessed the 500 quarters of corn, was
worth also 500 yards of cloth, while the other,
who had 1000 quarters of corn, possessed only
100 yards of cloth ; in what imaginable method
could their riches be compared, and the superiority of one over the other be ascertained,
except by means of their value, computed in
some common medium of estimation, or reduced into one denomination ?

With regard to heterogeneous commodities, there are in fact only two conceivable *criteria* of riches: one, the utility of any possessions; the other, their value.   The first is in the highest degree unsteady and indeterminate, and altogether inapplicable.   Iron, as Mr. Ricardo remarks, may be more useful than gold, but the possession of a pound of the former metal would not constitute a man as rich as that of an equal weight of the latter.   Value, therefore, is the only criterion of riches which is left to us.

In determining, then, the question whether riches could be increased, without an increase of value, we must recur to the principles laid down in the last chapter.   The answer in each particular case will depend on the medium of estimation.   There is one additional remark, however, which may be here introduced.   In the chapter referred to, a case was supposed, in which all commodities were produced in double quantity by the same labour, with the exception of one solitary article, and it was admitted, that if the whole were estimated in this one commodity, the aggregate value would be unaltered. In this hypothetical case, nevertheless, it still remains to be determined how we are to estimate the value of the commodity chosen as the medium. In estimating the *whole* produce in this .medium, we necessarily include the latter, and compute it as *being worth itself.* But value is a relation between two objects, and had we in any case to express the value of the medium, we must have recourse to one of the other commodities, when its value would appear to be doubled. Hence, although according to the supposed estimate, the aggregate value of the other commodities would be the same, the value of the medium would be twice as great as before ; and thus it might be truly said, that let us adopt what medium of estimation we please, no increase of riches can take place without an increase of value.

CHAPTER X.

ON THE DIFFERENCE BETWEEN A MEASURE AND A CAUSE OF VALUE.

ANY one who takes the trouble of minutely examining the writings of the most celebrated political economists will be astonished, not only at the looseness of expression, but at the vagueness of design by which they are too frequently distinguished. It is often far from being manifest, what is the precise doctrine or proposition they are intending to support, or to overthrow; or rather, it is evident that they themselves have not succeeded in defining it clearly to their own understandings.

No department of political economy has suffered more from this indefiniteness of purpose, and ambiguity of language, than that which is occupied with investigating the measures and causes of value. It would seem, on a first view, that the ideas of measuring and causing value were sufficiently distinct to escape all danger of being confounded; yet it is remarkable, that both the ideas themselves, and the terms by which they are expressed, have been mixed and interchanged and substituted, with an apparently total unconsciousness of any difference existing between them.

The author of the Templars' Dialogues on Political Economy is the only writer who appears to me to have been fully aware of this confusion of two separate and distinct ideas*. He traces it partly to an ambiguity in the word determine. " The word determine," says he, " may be taken subjectively for what determines x in relation to our knowledge, or objectively, for what determines x in relation to itself.

---

* This was written before I had seen the second edition of Mr. Mill's Elements, in which the distinction is for the first time introduced. His language on this point, nevertheless, is not uniformly consistent, as will be shown in the next chapter.

Thus if I were to ask, ' What determined the length of the race course?' and the answer were, ' The convenience of the spectators, who could not have seen the horses at a greater distance;' or, ' The choice of the subscribers;' then it is plain, that by the word 'determined,' I was understood to mean ' determined objectively,' in relation to the existence of the object; in other words, what *caused* the race-course to be this length rather than another length: but if the answer were, ' An actual admeasurement,' it would then be plain, that by the word ' determined,' I had been understood to mean ' determined subjectively," *i. e.* in relation to our knowledge; what ascertained it*?"

The writer just quoted is wrong, however, in supposing Mr. Ricardo to be free from ambiguity in this point. A very cursory inspection of the Principles of Political Economy and Taxation will show, that he has fallen into the same confusion as other economists; and it is astonishing to find the author of the Dia-

* London Magazine, Dec. 1823, p. 588: article entitled " Measure of Value."

logues asserting, that Mr. Ricardo did not propose his principle of value (namely, the quantity of labour) as the measure of value. The fact is, that he sometimes speaks of it as the cause, and sometimes as the measure, in such a way as proves that he had not attained to any distinct conception of the difference between the two ideas.

Thus in the first section of his book he accuses Adam Smith of erecting the labour, which a commodity will command, into a standard measure, instead of the labour bestowed on its production, the latter of which he asserts to be, " under many circumstances, an invariable standard, indicating correctly the variations of other things*." Farther on he speaks of estimating food and necessaries " by the *quantity* of labour necssary for their production;" contrasting it with measuring them " by the quantity of labour for which they will *exchange*†."

In the second section, after speaking of la-

* Principles of Political Economy and Taxation, p. 5, 3d edition.

† Ibid, p. 7. The Italics are Mr. Ricardo's.

bour as being the foundation of all value, he adopts in a note the language of Adam Smith, which designates labour as the real measure of the exchangeable value of all commodities *.

In another chapter of his work he is still more explicit.

" A franc," says he, " is not a measure of value for any thing, but for a quantity of the same metal of which francs are made, unless francs and the thing to be measured can be referred to some other measure, which is common to both. This I think they can be, for they are both the result of labour ; and, therefore, labour is a common measure, by which their real as well as their relative value may be estimated †."

And to support this doctrine he cites a passage from M. Destutt de Tracy, the scope of which is to show that labour is the *cause* of value. Surely nothing can more decisively prove a confusion of ideas on this point than adducing a passage, which asserts labour to be

* Ibid., p. 13.   † Ibid., p. 333.

the cause of value, in confirmation of a proposition that it is the measure of value.

Mr. Malthus, who has himself fallen into the same confusion of ideas and terms, is sufficiently justified by these passages in attributing to Mr. Ricardo the act of bringing forward his principle as a measure. That Mr. Ricardo has more frequently spoken of it as a cause of value, only proves that he has deviated into inconsistencies. How the author of the Dialogues could be led to maintain, in the face of these passages, that " Mr. Ricardo never dreamed of offering it as a standard or measure of value," it is difficult to imagine.

It will possibly be urged by the admirers of Mr. Ricardo, in order to defend him from the charge of inconsistency or ambiguity of language, that if quantity of labour is truly the sole cause of value, then it must also be a correct measure or criterion of value ; and as one of these circumstances necessarily follows the other, it is indifferent in which capacity we speak of it.

It is certainly true, that, provided quantity of labour were the sole cause of value, we should always be able to deduce the value of two commodities from a knowledge of the quantities of labour which they respectively required to produce them; and in this sense, quantity of labour would be at once the cause and the measure of value. But even under these circumstances, an author would not be justified in an indiscriminate use of the terms; nor could he fall into such an error, had he a distinct apprehension of the difference between the two ideas.

It would by no means follow, however, from quantity of labour being the cause of value, that it would be of any service as a measure. On this point we may adopt the language of the author of the Dialogues: " If it had been proposed as a measure of value, we might justly demand that it should be ready and easy of application; but it is manifestly not so; for the quantity of labour employed in producing A, ' could not in many cases' (as Mr. Malthus

truly objects) ' be ascertained without considerable difficulty :' in most cases, indeed, it
could not be ascertained at all.   A measure of
value, however, which cannot be practically
applied, is worthless*."

It was probably some obscure and undefined
impression of this truth, which, when Mr. Ricardo deliberately set himself to treat on the
subject of a measure of value, influenced him
to speak, not of labour itself in that capacity,
but of a commodity produced by an invariable
quantity of labour.   If the quantity of producing labour really determines the value of
commodities, it seems on a first view useless to
require for a measure an object of which the
producing labour is invariable, when we **may**
have recourse to the labour itself.   But Mr. Ricardo probably perceived, that a knowledge of
the quantity of producing labour in objects
would be in most cases difficult of attainment,
and therefore betook himself to the considera-

---

* London Magazine for May, 1824, page 559.

tion of a commodity in which a definite portion of it was embodied *.

All that is really meant by a measure of value we have already seen, and what is implied by a cause of value will be examined in the following chapter. The object of the preceding brief discussion is not to consider the nature of either, but merely to show the essential distinction between the ideas which they involve.

* There was a further reason, namely, that the real object which he contemplated in a measure of value was to ascertain by it the changes which commodities might undergo in regard to the quantity of labour required to produce them. Now to use labour itself as a measure implies this object to be already accomplished. See Note I.

CHAPTER XI.

ON THE CAUSES OF VALUE.

IT may seem, that an inquiry into the causes of value should have had an earlier place in the present treatise; but it is in reality the natural method of proceeding to make ourselves acquainted with the nature of an effect, before we attempt to investigate its causes. Although, in point of time, a cause must precede its effect, yet in the order of our knowledge the case is commonly reversed, and we ascend from the phenomena before us to the active principles concerned in their production.

Our first object in this investigation must be to ascertain what is really meant by a cause of value, or what is its true nature, that we may have some criterion which will show us, on the

one hand, whether any circumstance assigned
as a cause can be correctly admitted to rank under this denomination, and, on the other hand,
whether any circumstance alleged to have no
influence can be justly excluded.

It was explained in the first chapter, that
value, although spoken of as a quality adhering to external objects, or as a relation between them, implies a feeling or state of mind,
which manifests itself in the determination of
the will.   This feeling or state of mind may be
the result of a variety of considerations connected with exchangeable commodities, and an
inquiry into the causes of value is, in reality, an
inquiry into those external circumstances, which
operate so steadily upon the minds of men, in
the interchange of the necessaries, comforts,
and conveniences of life, as to be subjects of
inference and calculation.   These circumstances may either act directly on the mind, as
considerations immediately influencing its views,
or they may operate indirectly, by only causing
certain uniform considerations to be presented

to it. In either case, if they are steady in their operation, they may be equally regarded as causes of value. We may often assign an effect to a cause, when perhaps we are unable to trace the exact series of changes occurring between them, or, in other words, the less prominent links in the chain of causes and effects by which they are separated in time, but connected in efficiency. In reference to the present subject, this may be easily illustrated. The equality in the cost of production of two articles, for example, is a cause of their exchanging for each other. This we know is the general effect of such circumstances; but it would be difficult to trace with precision the mode in which the effect was produced, and which indeed might vary on different occasions without disturbing the result. Suppose two persons, A and B, of whom the former has linen, which he wishes to exchange for woollen cloth, and the latter has woollen cloth, which he wishes to exchange for linen. The matter would be abundantly plain, if, besides knowing what his own article cost him, each had a knowledge of the producing cost of the article to be received in exchange. But it is likely enough that they do not possess this latter knowledge, and in this case the defect will be supplied by the competition of the producers, which is itself governed by the cost of production; and thus, although the two parties to the bargain may not be guided by a knowledge of what each article has cost to produce it, they are determined by considerations, of which the cost of production is the real origin. This is still more strikingly the case in other instances. A clergyman, who received his tithes in kind, and exchanged raw produce for cloth, might be ignorant of the cost of either, yet the terms of his bargain would be determined by the general cost of both. The cost would regulate the point at which the competition of the producers would fix each article, or their ordinary prices; and a knowledge of these prices would operate on his mind in the exchanges which he made.

Whatever circumstances, therefore, act with

assignable influence, whether mediately or immediately, on the mind in the interchange of commodities, may be considered as causes of value.

Although, in the subsequent remarks, I may sometimes have to bring into view the mental operations implied in all cases of interchange, yet, to avoid prolixity, instead of speaking of circumstances operating on the mind in regard to any commodity, I shall frequently speak of those circumstances as operating on the commodity itself. While this will save circumlocution, it will not, it is hoped, give rise to ambiguity, as such language will be employed with a tacit reference to the real nature of the occurrence which it is intended to designate.

I have already had occasion to remark, that since value is a relation between two objects, it requires no proof that it cannot arise from causes affecting only one of the objects, but from two causes, or two sets of causes respectively operating upon the objects between which the relation exists. If A is equal in value to B, this must be owing, not only to causes operating on A, but also to causes operating on B.   In investigating the sources of value, however, it will be necessary to treat of these causes separately; and it may not be useless to recollect, that although value must in every instance arise from the combination of two sets of causes, any alteration, any rise or fall of value, may proceed from only one. The value of A and B is the effect of causes acting on both, but a change in their mutual value may arise from causes acting on either: as the distance of two objects is to be referred to the circumstances which have fixed both of them in their particular situation, while an alteration of the distance between them might originate in circumstances acting on one alone.

What then are the causes which determine the value of commodities, and an alteration in which is followed by a change in their relations? Or, in other words, what are the causes which determine the quantities in which commodities are exchanged for each other?

In order to answer this question, it will be necessary to attempt some classification of exchangeable articles.

Commodities, or things possessing value, may be divided into three classes.

1. Commodities which are monopolized, or protected from competition by natural or adventitious circumstances.

2. Commodities, in the production of which some persons possess greater facilities than the rest of the community, and which therefore the competition of the latter cannot increase, except at a greater cost.

3. Commodities, in the production of which competition operates without restraint.

A cursory attention to these classes will at once show, that their respective causes of value cannot be the same. Let us therefore take them in detail, and examine the causes operating on each class.

1. Monopolies may be divided into two kinds; those in which there is only one interest con-

cerned, and those in which there are separate interests.

In the first case, "the competition," (as Mr. Ricardo justly remarks) " is wholly on one side — amongst the buyers. The monopoly price," he continues, " of one period, may be much lower or higher than the monopoly price of another, because the competition amongst the purchasers must depend on their wealth, and their tastes and caprices. Those peculiar wines which are produced in very limited quantity, and those works of art, which from their ex-cellence or rarity have acquired a fanciful value, will be exchanged for a very different quantity of the produce of ordinary labour, according as the society is rich or poor, as it possesses abun-dance or scarcity of such produce, or as it may be in a rude or polished state*."

The second kind of monopoly differs from

* Principles of Political Economy and Taxation, p. 290, third edition.

the first in the obvious circumstance, that there
may be a competition amongst the sellers as well
as amongst the buyers. Where there is only
one interest concerned in the monopoly, it may
be to the advantage of the party to withhold his
article from the market in times of dull demand,
or even to destroy a part of it to enhance the
value of the remainder; a policy which is said
to have been pursued by the Dutch in the spice
trade. But when a monopoly is in the hands
of different individuals, with separate interests,
such a line of policy is impracticable: for although it might be to the advantage of the whole
body if the quantity of the monopolized article were proportionately reduced to each
holder, yet as, by the supposition, there is no
combination of interest, every individual finds
it beneficial to dispose of all that he possesses.
To destroy any part of it, would be to injure
himself for the benefit of his brother monopolists. While on the one hand he is fenced in
by an exclusive privilege or possession from the
competition of the public, he is on the other

hand compelled by his own interest to bring to market the whole of his supply, and he is obliged by the same principle to produce the greatest supply in his power, so long as the average price pays him a higher profit than the ordinary employment of capital. It deserves to be remarked, that all commodities, which require any considerable period of time for their production, are liable to be occasionally forced into the class of articles owing their value to this second kind of monopoly, by a sudden alteration in the relative state of the demand and supply. Hence arises what is called by political economists market value. Should the relative demand for any of these commodities increase, as it could not, according to the supposition, be immediately answered by a correspondent supply, the possessors of the commodities would enjoy a temporary monopoly; for a while they would be protected from competition by the impossibility of producing a further quantity.

On the contrary, should the relative demand

decrease, the possessors of the commodities would be exposed to the necessity of bringing them to market at a reduced rate, especially if they were commodities of which the supply could be neither immediately stopped, nor adjusted to the new state of the demand. The holders, in this case, would be exposed to all the disadvantages incident to a monopoly in which there were separate interests. The competition amongst themselves would force the whole of their supply into the market.

Occurrences of this kind must not be considered as rare or unimportant. Mr. Tooke, in his recent valuable work " on the High and Low Prices of the Thirty Years, from 1793 to 1822," has most strikingly shown the frequency and extent of excesses and deficiences in the supply of corn, as well as the momentous effects which they occasion. These effects are all referable to the principle of a temporary monopoly. Foreign supplies being put out of the question, the holders of corn have obviously a monopoly of the article till

the ensuing harvest ; and as it is an article which
cannot be dispensed with, should the supply be
less than usually required, the price may rise
to an almost indefinite height. If, on the contrary, the supply should exceed the ordinary
demand, which from the nature of the commodity admits of little augmentation, the
holders suffer the disadvantages before described; the interest of each lies in the dis-
posal of as large a quantity as possible, and
the competition thus engendered infallibly
brings down the value. The larger quantity
may in this way become of less aggregate value
than the smaller quantity at the previous high
prices. Were the commodity in the hands of
an individual, or, what is the same thing, individuals combined by one interest, this is a
circumstance which could never occur.

Labour must be considered as falling under
this class of exchangeable commodities, and as
being determined in value by the same causes
which operate on articles monopolized in the
second method here described. If a man em-

ploy his capital in production, he must purchase labour, and the demand for labourers
will therefore be in proportion to the capital
destined for this purpose. But there are only
a certain number of labourers in existence ;
these cannot for the time be either purposely
increased or diminished, and they consequently
possess a monopoly of their peculiar commodity. The greater the demand, therefore, for
their labour, the higher it will rise, exactly as
other monopolized commodities in the same
circumstances. This monopoly, too, is attended with the disadvantages common to all
monopolies in the hands of conflicting interests.
Under all circumstances the labourers must live,
and must therefore sell their labour; and
should the demand for it decrease, as they
cannot purposely diminish or keep back their
numbers, competition will soon reduce the
value of their labour.

Besides the general monopoly which the labourers naturally possess, and which may be
advantageous or disadvantageous, according to

circumstances, there are divers subordinate monopolies, occasioning labour to be paid after different rates. In trades, which require application for a greater or smaller period before they are learned, the workmen are evidently protected from immediate competition; and should there be an increase in the demand for their work, their labour would rise in value, and remain enhanced till more artizans possessed of their peculiar skill had been formed.

It scarcely needs to be mentioned, in this place, that although labourers cannot be purposely augmented or reduced in number by the application of capital, or its diversion into different channels, like material commodities, yet they may be augmented or reduced in another way. The high value of labour, compared with commodities in general, enabling the labourers to live in abundance, marriages are encouraged, or at least more children are reared, and population is increased; so that, after the lapse of a certain interval, the same effect is produced as if men could be purposely created. On the other hand, a material fall in the value of labour operates to check population by the penury and hardship which it spreads among the labouring classes; and the supply of labour becomes eventually adjusted to the demand by disease and death.

2. The second class of commodities embraces articles of more importance (with the exception of labour) than that which we have just considered. When a commodity is of a kind which admits of being increased by industry and competition, but only at a greater cost, the possessor of the cheaper means of producing it has evidently a monopoly to a certain extent, and the value of the commodity will depend on the principles already explained, until it reach such a height as will afford the ordinary profit to those who produce it at a greater expense. The same causes will be in operation, but instead of the value of the article having no assignable boundary, it will be limited by the watchful competition, which is

ever ready to act upon it the moment it has exceeded a particular point.

Under this head we may class the important articles of corn, raw produce in general, metals, coals, and several others. As one commodity, however, will elucidate the rest, we may confine our observations to the first.

The value of that corn which is produced on lands paying rent, is not, it is acknowledged, in proportion either to the capital or to the labour actually expended in its production. It must be owing, therefore, to some other cause; and the only other cause is the state of the supply and demand, or the competition of the purchasers. This competition might raise the price to an indefinite height, if it were not for the existence of other lands, which although they could produce corn only at a greater cost, would be brought into cultivation as soon as the price had risen sufficiently high to pay the ordinary profits on the capital required. It is, therefore, the possibility of producing corn, or the actual production of it, at a greater cost, which forms the limit to its value. But although this is the limit beyond which its value cannot rise, it cannot be said to be the cause of its value. It is the cause of its being no higher, not the cause of its being so high. A perforation in the side of a vessel, at any distance from the bottom, would effectually prevent its being filled to a greater height with water, but it would be no cause of the water attaining that height. At the utmost it could be considered as only a joint cause of the result.

We accordingly find that the expression used by Mr. Ricardo on this subject is, not that the value of corn is *caused*, but that it is *regulated* by the cost of production on the least fertile lands. The owners of land of superior fertility enjoy a monopoly, which, however, does not enable them to raise their commodity in definitely, according to the varying wants and caprices of mankind, but which is bounded by the existence of inferior soils.

It is simply out of this monopoly-value that rent arises. Rent proceeds, in fact, from the extraordinary profit which is obtained by the possession of an instrument of production, protected up to a certain point from competition. If the owner of this instrument, instead of using it himself, lets it out to another, he receives from him this surplus of profit under the denomination of rent. In this view of the subject, the extraordinary profit might exist, although the land in cultivation were all of the same quality; nay, must exist before inferior land was cultivated; for it could be only in consequence of extraordinary gains obtained by the monopolizers of the best land, that capital and labour would be expended on soils of a subordinate order. Rent, therefore, might exist, while all the land under cultivation was of equal fertility. Perhaps it might not exist under these circumstances during any long period, but its existence at all would prove that it was the effect of monopoly, an extraordinary profit, and not the consequence of the cultivation of inferior soils.

The extraordinary profit out of which rent

arises, is analogous to the extraordinary remuneration which an artizan of more than common
dexterity obtains beyond the wages given to
workmen of ordinary skill. In so far as competition cannot reach them, the owner of the
rich soil and the possessor of the extraordinary
skill obtain a monopoly price. In the one case
this monopoly is bounded by the existence of
inferior soils, in the other of inferior degrees of
dexterity.

It has been made a question, whether rent
forms a component part of the price or value of
produce. " Rent," says Mr. Ricardo, " does
not and cannot enter in the least degree as a
component part of its price." The expression
is in reality figurative, and the only meaning
of the assertion, that rent is a component part
of price, must be, that it is one of the causes
of the value of produce. But we have just
seen that rent is a consequence of the extraordinary value of a monopolized commodity, and
it cannot therefore be one of the causes of its
value. Although not the cause of the value of

corn or other produce, rent must be an accurate
representation of the additional value consequent on the monopoly of the land on which
the corn is grown : therefore, if one part of the
price of corn, from any particular land, is considered as representing the share of the labourer, another the share of the capitalist, the
remainder, if any, will be representative of the
rent; and it is probably this consideration
which has led economists to speak of it as a
component part of price.   In whatever way the
expression is used, it is at the best vague and
indefinite, and ought to be banished from a
science, which owes half its difficulties to the
laxity and ambiguity of language.

3. The third class of commodities, those
which can be increased by industry, and on
which competition acts without restraint, are
the next to claim our consideration.

The value of these commodities owes nothing to monopoly ; what then are the causes
which determine the quantities in which they
are exchanged for each other?

There is, perhaps, at the bottom, little actual difference amongst economists as to these causes, but they do not agree either in their methods of explanation, or in the language they employ. It has been shown, that the immediate causes of value are the considerations which act on the minds of human beings, and that the circumstances, which form or furnish these considerations, must be the causes into which the economist has to inquire. Our present object, therefore, is to find those circumstances which act upon the mind with certainty and precision, in the interchange of commodities of the class under our notice.

A moment's reflection on the subject will suffice to discover, that the principal of these circumstances must be the cost of production. No man, who bestows his time and attention on the production of a commodity, will continue to produce it for the purpose of exchanging it against another commodity, which he knows costs less to the producer than his own: and, on the other hand, every producer will be willing

to sell as large a quantity of his commodity as
he can dispose of at the same price as his fel-
low producers.

It is not, indeed, disputed, that the main circumstance, which determines the quantities in
which articles of this class are exchanged, is
the cost of production; but our best economists
do not exactly agree on the meaning to be attached to this term; some contending that the
quantity of labour expended on the production of an article constitutes its cost; others,
that the capital employed upon it is entitled to
that appellation.   Let us look at the state of
the facts.   If a man exchanges an article which
he has produced by a day's labour, for another
article, also the produce of a day's labour, it is
plain that the cost of production is the labour
bestowed.   If another man expends £100 in
producing a quantity of cloth, that is, in the
purchase of materials as well as in the wages
of labour, and exchanges it for a quantity of
linen which has cost his neighbour £100, the
cost of production is the capital employed.

Cost of production may be, therefore, either a quantity of labour or a quantity of capital. What the labourer produces without capital, costs him his labour; what the capitalist produces costs him his capital.

Such appears to be the simplest view of the subject; but it is contended, that as the value of the capital itself has been caused by labour, it is more accurate to say, that cost of production consists in the quantity of labour. It must be recollected, however, that we are inquiring into the circumstances which determine men to give a certain quantity of one commodity for a certain quantity of another ; and what really acts upon the minds of two capitalists in exchanging their respective goods, is not the labour which in a thousand different ways has been expended upon the articles constituting the capital employed, but the amount of capital which they have parted with, in order to obtain the commodity produced. So that granting for the present that the value of capital may be resolved (to use the common language on this subject) into a previous quantity of labour, it would still be a correct statement of facts to say, that the cost of production consists in the quantity of capital expended : or to lay aside the term cost of production altogether, that the amount of capital expended is the cause which determines the value of the commodity produced.

It is impossible, under this view of the subject, to agree with the following passage in Mr. Mill's Elements of Political Economy.

" To say, indeed, that the value of commodities depends upon capital as the final standard, implies one of the most obvious of all absurdities. Capital is commodities. If the value of commodities, then, depends upon the value of capital, it depends upon the value of commodities ; the value of commodities depends upon itself. This is not to point out a standard of value. It is to make an attempt for that purpose clearly and completely abortive*."

---

* Elements of Political Economy, p. 94, 2d edition.

This passage, which seems to have a tacit reference to the speculations of Col. Torrens, appears to me to show the power of words over the clearest and strongest minds. By the potent magic of a term, the value of commodities is first made something single and individual; and then it follows of course, that an individual thing cannot depend upon itself as a cause. But this is not asserted by those who contend that capital causes or determines value. The value of commodities may not be capable of depending on itself, but the value of one commodity, which is one thing, may very easily depend on that of another, which is a different thing; and if it did not in point of fact, there would be no logical absurdity in asserting it. He who maintains that the mutual value of two commodities is chiefly determined by the comparative quantity of capital expended in their production, undoubtedly maintains that it is determined by the value of preceding commodities; and this is quite consistent with the value of those preceding commodities having been de-

termined by their comparative quantities of producing labour, or by any other cause. The
latter would be a step further back in the sequence of causes and effects. There can be
nothing absurd in assigning one thing as the
proximate cause of an effect, merely because it
is possible that another may be assigned as its
remote cause.

Mr. Mill's language, too, is unusually lax.
He confounds the standard with the cause of
value. The proposition, that the values of commodities are determined by the capitals expended in producing them, affirms a cause, but
certainly does not point out any standard of
value; nor would Mr. Mill's own doctrine furnish such an auxiliary. A standard, whatever
meaning it may have in this connection, must
at all events be something clearly defined and
easily accessible; and if Mr. Mill purposes to
set up the quantity of labour in a commodity
from first to last, through all its various meta-
morphoses, in that capacity, it will be one
seldom within his reach. In reality, however,

the preceding part of his section is occupied in
proving labour to be the cause of value; and it
is only at the conclusion that he deviates into
this laxity of expression*.

It appears, therefore, that if we do not aim at
undue generalization, but are content with a
simple statement of facts, the value of objects,
in the production of which competition operates
without restraint, may be correctly stated to
arise principally from the cost of production;
and that cost of production may be either labour or capital, or both. Whatever the mere
labourer produces costs him his labour: if a
man is a capitalist as well as a labourer, what

* In the second edition of his Elements, Mr. Mili himself,
in the section succeeding that containing the passage here
animadverted upon, has distinctly pointed out the difference
between what he calls " the regulator," and the measure of
value, and has mentioned two circumstances which, he
says, render it impossible that the former should be employed in the latter capacity. It is therefore surprising
that he should have retained a passage, which confounds
what he has subsequently taken express pains to distinguish.

he produces costs him both: if he is only a
capitalist, it costs him only capital.   In a civilized country instances of each kind may be
found, but the mass of commodities are determined in value by the capital expended upon
them.

The amount of capital is thus the chief, but
by no means the sole cause of value.   Other
circumstances which have a regular influence,
cannot with any propriety be excluded.   The
discredit, the danger, the disagreeableness of
any method of employing capital, all tend, as
well as pecuniary expenditure, to enhance the
value of the product.   The time, too, which
a commodity requires before it can be brought
to market, is another circumstance affecting value, and frequently to a considerable extent.
It would be an extraordinary phenomenon, indeed, if, in the interchange of commodities, the
minds of men should be influenced by one exclusive consideration: if, imbued as they are
with feelings of shame, and fear, and impatience, and others not necessary to enumerate,

these passions should leave no regular traces of their operation in the daily business of production and exchange.

I have hitherto been contending, that even if capital could be resolved into previous labour, it would still be a correct statement of facts to say, that the value of commodities is chiefly determined by the capital expended upon them. It is an interesting inquiry, however, how far this doctrine, which we have taken for granted, is true, and I shall therefore proceed to examine its claims to be received in that character.

It is manifest that if the unqualified doctrine, as laid down by some writers, were correct, the value of any commodity would be strictly representative of the quantity of labour expended on its production from first to last. " If," as Mr. Mill expresses it, " quantity of labour in the last resort, determines the proportion in which commodities exchange for one another * ; "

* Elements of Political Economy, p. 94, 2d edition.

or, as it is stated by the author of the Templars' Dialogues, " commodities are to each other in value as the quantities of labour employed in their production*;" or, as it is laid down by Mr. M'Culloch, " the exchangeable value, or relative worth of commodities, as compared with each other, depends exclusively on the quantities of labour necessarily required to produce them †;" then it follows, that any two commodities, which at any time exchange for each other (putting aside all fluctuations of market value), must have been produced by exactly the same quantity of labour. If a quarter of wheat is exchanged for a piece of linen, these two commodities must have required the same labour to bring them to the condition in which they are exchanged ‡.

---

* Dialogue 1, passim.

† A Discourse on the Science of Political Economy, p. 66.

‡ This is stated in the strongest conceivable terms by the second-mentioned writer. " No cause can possibly affect the value of any thing, *i. e.* its exchangeable relation to

Now this cannot be true if we can find any instances of the following nature :

1. Cases in which two commodities have been produced by an equal quantity of labour, and yet sell for different quantities of money.

2. Cases in which two commodities, once equal in value, have become unequal in value, without any change in the quantity of labour respectively employed in each*.

Cases of the first kind are exceedingly numerous. Every one at all acquainted with manufactures must know, that there are in the same, as well as in different occupations, various degrees of skill and rapidity of execution

---

other things, but an increase or diminution of the quantity of labour required for its production : and the prices of all things whatsoever represent the quantity of labour by which they are severally produced; and the value of A is to the value of B universally as the quantity of labour which produces A to the quantity of labour which produces B."— London Magazine, April 1824, p. 352.

* This last case is resolvable into the first, but the subject will be better illustrated by keeping them distinct.

amongst artizans, various kinds and gradations
of talent and acquirement, which enable some
of them to earn double the money obtained by
their less fortunate compeers in the same time.
There are also circumstances of insalubrity, or
disagreeableness, or danger, which affect the
pecuniary recompense. The value of the articles produced by these various classes of
workmen, and under these various circumstances, bears no proportion to the mere quantity of labour expended. It is no answer to
this to say, with Mr. Ricardo, that " the estimation in which different qualities of labour
are held, comes soon to be adjusted in the
market with sufficient precision for all practical
purposes ;" or with Mr. Mill, that " in estimating equal quantities of labour, an allow-
ance would, of course, be included for different
degrees of hardness and skill." Instances of
this kind entirely destroy the integrity of the
rule. Difference of skill is a circumstance
which practically affects value, as well as difference in quantity of labour, and therefore the

latter cannot, with any propriety, be said to be the sole cause of value.

What should we think of an assertion, that coats àre to each other in value as the quantities of cloth contained in them, or that their comparative value depends exclusively on the quantities of cloth required to make them? And if it were added, that due allowances must be made for the different qualities of the cloth, where would be the truth or the utility of the first mathematically strict position? The proposition would, in fact, be reduced to its negative, that coats are *not* to each other in value as the quantities of cloth contained in them.

In Mr. Ricardo's language on the subject of the different qualities of labour, there is some inconsistency and much indistinctness. The second section of his first chapter is headed, " Labour of different qualities differently rewarded. This no cause of variation in the relative value of commodities." By this it is to be presumed he means, not what the words really imply, that the different compensation

given to labour of different qualities does not
originally affect the value of commodities, but
that when the influence of this cause is once
adjusted, it subsequently occasions no variation
in value.   In the body of the section, however,
he softens this expression into " inconsiderable
variation."   " We may fairly conclude," says
he, " that whatever inequality there might originally have been in them, whatever the ingenuity, skill, or time necessary for the acquirement of one species of manual dexterity
more than another, it continues nearly the same
from one generation to another ; or at least that
the variation is very inconsiderable from year
to year, and therefore can have little effect for
short periods, on the relative value of commodities."

It is, however, a mere assumption, that " the
scale, when once formed, is liable to little variation ; " nor, if this could be established, would
it furnish any aid to the doctrine which we
have at present under consideration. If the differences of skill in different employments are so

little variable as here represented, it proves only that they are circumstances which permanently affect value, and that it must be altogether incorrect to designate *quantity* of labour the sole cause, when *quality* of labour is so steady in its effects. This cause of value is, in fact, on precisely the same footing as any other. A variation in it, small or great, would occasion a corresponding variation in the value of the article on which the labour was employed; and however inconsiderable its effects may be, they cannot be consistently either denied or overlooked. The whole of the section appears to have been dictated by a lurking impatience of any thing which seemed to break into the beautiful simplicity of the rule, that value is determined by quantity of labour. Else why not freely allow the exceptions wherever they occur, and qualify the expression of the general rule accordingly * ? "

* The only place in Mr. Ricardo's work, where I have been able to find the expression of the general rule pro-

But the most singular circumstance in this section is, that it unsettles all our notions respecting quantity of labour itself. The grand principle of Mr. Ricardo's work, which seemed as precise and definite as it could be, the doctrine that quantity of labour is the cause of value, which appeared to be fast anchored in the understanding, is unloosed from its moorings. We are here told of " the difficulty of comparing an hour's or a day's labour in one employment with the same duration of labour in another." The language of Adam Smith is quoted, to show " that it is often difficult to ascertain the proportion between two different quantities of labour. The time spent in two different sorts of work will not always determine this proportion."

If this be true, then quantity of labour has no determinate criterion, and Mr. Ricardo has

perly qualified, is the Index. He there says, " the quantity of labour requisite to obtain commodities the *principal* source of their exchangeable value."

proposed, not only as the cause but the measure of value, that which is itself unascertainable. There are only two possible methods of comparing one quantity of labour with another; one is to compare them by the time expended, the other by the result produced. The former is applicable to all kinds of ʃabour; the latter can be used only in comparing labour bestowed on similar articles. If therefore, in estimating two different sorts of work, the time spent will not determine the proportion between the quantities of labour, it must remain undetermined and undeterminable.

2. We are furnished with cases of the second kind (namely, those in which two commodities, once equal in value, have become unequal in value without any change in the quantity of labour respectively employed in aech) by Mr. Ricardo himself.

Take any two commodities of equal value, A and B, one produced by fixed capital and the other by labour, without the intervention of machinery; and suppose, that without any change

whatever in the fixed capital or the quantity
of labour, there should happen to be a rise in
the value of labour; according to Mr. Ricardo's
own showing, A and B would be instantly altered in their relation to each other ; that is,
they would become unequal in value. At the
former period being equal in value, they must,
according to the doctrine under consideration,
have been the products directly or indirectly of
equal quantities of labour; but if at the latter
period their values were taken as representative of the relative quantity of labour expended on each, the result obtained would be,
that they were the products of unequal quantities
of labour. The doctrine, therefore, that the
values of commodities are representative of the
respective quantities of labour required for
their production, which is a direct corollary
from the proposition that commodities are to
each other in value as is their producing labour
in quantity, cannot possibly be true.

This again, it may be said, is allowed by
Mr. Ricardo and his followers: but if they

allow it, why persist in calling quantity of labour the sole determining principle of value? Why attempt to give the science an air of simplicity which it does not possess?

To these cases we may add the effect of time on value. If a commodity take more time than another for its production, although no more capital and labour, its value will be greater. The influence of this cause is admitted by Mr. Ricardo, but Mr. Mill contends, that time can do nothing; "how then," he asks, " can it add to value?" "Time," he continues, "is a mere abstract term. It is a word, a sound. And it is the very same logical absurdity to talk of an abstract unit measuring value, and of time creating it*."

The alleged absurdity, however, will disappear, if we recur for a moment to the mental operation implied in every creation of value. The time necessary to produce a commodity,

* Elements of Pol. Econ. p. 99, 2d edition. The credit of this argument, however, is due to Mr. M'Culloch, whose authority is cited by Mr. Mill.

may, equally with the requisite quantity of labour, be a consideration which influences the
mind in the interchange of useful or agreeable
articles.   We generally prefer a present pleasure
or enjoyment to a distant one, not superior to it
in other respects.   We are willing, even at
some sacrifice of property, to possess ourselves
of what would otherwise require time to procure it, without waiting during the operation ;
as of what would require labour, without
personally bestowing the labour.   If any article were offered to us, not otherwise attainable,
except after the expiration of a year, we should
be willing to give something to enter upon present enjoyment.   On the part of the capitalist,
who produces and prepares these articles, the
time required for the purpose is evidently a
consideration which acts upon his mind.   If the
article is wine, he knows that the quality is improved by keeping; he is aware that the same
excellence cannot be imparted to any wine,
without the employment of capital for an equal
period ; and that people will be found to give

him the usual compensation rather than employ their own capitals in producing a similar result. Thus time is really a consideration which may influence both buyers and sellers; nor is it necessary here to enter into any metaphysical inquiry into its nature in order to prove its effects.

The author of the Elements of Political Economy has made a curious attempt to resolve the effects of time into expenditure of labour. " If," says he, " the wine which is put in the cellar is increased in value one tenth by being kept a year, one tenth more of labour may be correctly considered as having been expended upon it *."

Now if any one proposition can be affirmed without dispute, it is this, that a fact can be correctly considered as having taken place only when it really has taken place. In the instance adduced, no human being, by the terms of the supposition, has approached the wine, or spent upon it a moment or a single motion of his

* Elements, p. 97, 2d edition.

muscles. As therefore no labour has been
really exercised in any way relating to the wine,
a tenth more of labour cannot be correctly considered as having been expended upon it, unless that can be truly regarded as having oc-
curred which never happened.

Doctrines of this kind, which attempt to reduce all phenomena to a uniform expression,
ought to be rigidly scrutinized.   In the present
instance, the eminent writer just quoted appears to have been seduced by a preceding false
generalization, that, namely, which designates
capital as accumulated or hoarded labour. This
is at best an aukward mode of expression, which
can answer no good purpose.   When we accumulate we add one thing to another, and it is
essential to the process, that both should remain in existence.   But labour, consisting in
the mere exertion of muscular power, or in the
equally evanescent motions of the brain, continually perishes in detail, and therefore admits
of no accumulation.   It may be alleged, nevertheless, that when a series of days' labour

has been bestowed on any article, we may fairly say that there has been an accumulation of labour; one day's labour has been added to another day's labour till they have amounted to a given number, suppose, for example, a hundred. The only accumulation here, however, is not an actual but an arithmetical one, and admitting the accuracy of the expression in this sense, it amounts to this, that a hundred days' labour is an accumulation of labour, not that the article produced is accumulated labour. The article produced is the result of labour, not labour itself. To designate capital or commodities by the term accumulated labour is to call the effect an accumulation of the cause.

In a rhetorical declamation, in the compressed and vigorous eloquence of a great mind disclosing its own comprehensive views by a few master strokes of expression, such an identification of cause and effect is often a positive beauty. The " Knowledge is power" of Lord Bacon, is felicitous and forcible: but in philosophical discussion, phrases of this kind as grounds of reasoning, or as correct expressions of fact, mislead the mind intent on the pursuit of truth ; and I have no fear, that to those who are adequately aware of the importance of words in all moral and political researches, the objection, which I have urged to the language under consideration, will either appear frivolous or unfounded.

In this attempt to show that the value of capital cannot be traced entirely to the quantity of producing labour, I have taken into view those commodities only, the production of which is perfectly free to competition: and so far as we have proceeded, the strictures, which I have ventured to offer, apply rather to the manner in which the doctrine is asserted than to any thing actually maintained by its supporters. But the great defect of this theory is, its overlooking the important fact, that capital consists, not only of commodities of this class, but also of the commodities belonging to the other two classes of our enumeration. To assert, that the value of capital may be resolved into quantity of labour, is to lose sight both of the modifications generally admitted, and, what is of far greater moment, of causes which extend themselves in every direction through the mass of exchangeable products.

It must be recollected, that although we have arranged commodities under three divisions, yet they are all, not only promiscuously exchanged for each other, but blended in production. A commodity, therefore, may owe part of its value to monopoly, and part to those causes which determine the value of unmonopolized products. An article, for instance, may be manufactured amidst the freest competition out of a raw material, which a complete monopoly enables its producer to sell at six times the actual cost; and the quantity of the raw material necessary might be so proportioned to the quantity of labour required to work it up, that they would equally contribute to the value of the finished fabric. In this case it is obvious, that although the value of the article might be correctly said to be determined by the quantity of capital expended upon it by the manufacturer, yet no analysis could possibly resolve the value of the capital into quantity of labour. Nor must it be supposed that is this a case of rare occurrence. In scarcely any instance could the value of capital be traced to the quantity of labour as its only source, liable as every process of production is to the intrusion of articles deriving their value from other causes.

Hence for those economists, who object to the doctrine of the value of commodities being chiefly determined by the quantity of capital expended in their production, that it does not satisfy the whole of the inquiry, since they want to know what has determined the value of the capital, the answer is easy. The value of the capital was probably determined by the value of preceding capital, which was in its turn determined by preceding capital in the same manner. Does any one ask, what determined the value of the first of these capitals, trace them as far back as we will? I answer, perhaps monopoly, perhaps the quantity of labour, or perhaps the value of labour; or possibly some combination of these.

Let us take, for example, a piece of linen. The value of this has been proximately determined by the capital expended in its manufacture. The capital expended consisted, we will suppose, of food for the workmen and flax as the material. We have then to inquire what has caused the value of the food and the flax; and we might find it to be owing to the labour expended in raising it, or more probably to a monopoly possessed by the owners of land. In the former case it may be urged, the value of the capital is ultimately resolvable into the quantity of producing labour; and not the less so in the latter, since the value of the produce grown on superior soils is determined by the value of that grown on lands not coming under any description of monopoly, or in other words paying no rent. But it does not follow in the first case, that the value of the produce should have been determined by the mere quantity of labour: it may have been affected by the value of that labour, since the skill of those concerned in raising it may have been better paid than in other employments, or have done the work with half the usual number of hands, or there may be some peculiarity of hardship, arising from the nature of the employment itself. In the second case, if the value of produce from a superior soil is regulated by the quantity of labour necessary to raise the same kind on inferior soils, it is not determined by the labour actually employed in raising such produce, and therefore the value of the produce is not resolvable into quantity of labour.

Hence it appears, that the value of capital may possibly be traced to quantity of labour as its origin, but it is not necessarily traceable to it; and we therefore could not pronounce, that because A and B are equal in value, these two articles have been either directly or indirectly the products of equal quantities of labour, although no other circumstance existed to render such a conclusion erroneous. If two samples of corn of equal quality, but from different soils, were submitted to us, and we were told that their prices were equal, we could not pronounce with any certainty that they were the results of equal labour. One might have been produced by a fourth part of the labour required for the other, and yet they are of the same value. If gold and corn, or cloth and corn, were compared in the same way, there would be a similar impossibility of telling that portions of these commodities of equal value had been produced by equal quantities of labour.

We shall now be prepared to take a general survey of Mr. Ricardo's doctrine on the subject of the causes of value, and estimate it at its real worth. He commences by stating, that " commodities derive their exchangeable value from two sources: from their scarcity, and from the quantity of labour required to obtain them.' Articles of the first kind he regards as comparatively unimportant, and therefore professes to

restrict his inquiries to " such commodities only
as can be increased in quantity by the exertion
of human industry, and on the production of
which competition operates without restraint."
Instead, however, of confining himself to these
commodities, he enters into the consideration
of the value of labour, of corn, of gold, and
of other articles, in the production of which
competition certainly does not operate without
restraint ; but which he is obliged to bring under that head, from the imperfect classification
with which he sets out.   According to his own
division, the value of these things should be
determined by the quantity of labour necessary
to produce them: but of none of them can
this be asserted ; for the value of labour can in
no sense be said to be determined by the quantity of labour necessary to produce it: the
value of corn in general is determined, on
his own principles, by the quantity of labour
required to raise corn on the worst soils in
cultivation, and not by the quantity of its own
producing labour; and in the same way the

value of gold itself depends, not on the labour necessary to produce every individual portion of it, but on the labour necessary to extract it from the least fertile mines that are worked.

Mr. Ricardo did not, evidently, allow sufficient importance to that source of value which he calls scarcity; nor did he consistently bear in mind, that it was the very same principle which enabled the owner of land, or of mines, of more than common fertility, to raise the value of their articles beyond what would afford the customary profit. Instead of scarcity, or, in other words, monopoly, or protection from competition, being an unimportant source of value, and the commodities which owe their value to it forming a very small part of the mass of commodities daily exchanged in the market, we have seen that it is a most extensive source of value, and that the value of many of the most important articles of interchange must be referred to this as its origin.

With regard to the causes of the value of

these commodities, which are left in every way perfectly free to competition, the practical truth inculcated by Mr. Ricardo is this, that if the quantity of labour necessary for the production of a commodity is increased or decreased, it rises or falls in value in relation to other commodities, of which the quantity of producing labour is not altered. This, however, is a truth not dependent on the quantity of labour being the sole cause of value, but on its being one of the causes. The same is true of every other cause of value. Any effect is necessarily increased if we increase any of its causes.

Mr. Ricardo, indeed, explicitly allows the influence of other causes, such as time, differences in the proportion of fixed and circulating capital, and inequalities in the durability of capital, by which he admits the value of commodities is liable to be affected. Notwithstanding these modifications, however, his followers continue to lay down the position of quantity of labour being the sole cause of value in the most precise and positive terms; not that they deny the exceptions, but they appear to lose sight of their existence, and frequently fall into language incompatible with their admission; while they altogether overlook the source of value to be found in partial or incomplete monopolies, and the intermixture in production of commodities which are indebted for their value to different causes.

On a review of the subject it appears, that economists attempt too much. They wish to resolve all the causes of value into one, and thus reduce the science to a simplicity of which it will not admit. They overlook the variety of considerations operating on the mind in the interchange of commodities. These considerations are the causes of value, and the attempt to proportion the quantities in which commodities are exchanged for each other to the degree in which one of these considerations exists, must be vain and ineffectual. All in reality that can be accomplished on this subject is to ascertain the various causes of value; and when this is done, we may always infer, from an increase or diminution of any of them, an increase or diminution of the effect. If Mr. Ricardo, as his admirers allege, has really enriched the science of political economy with any new and important truths (a point which this is not the place to decide), we may safely pronounce that they are not inferences from the doctrine, that the quantity of labour employed in the production of commodities is the sole determining principle of their value. It may be affirmed, without any hazard of error, that there is not one of them, whatever they may be, which would not equally flow from the more accurate proposition, that it is the principal cause. A false simplification in matters of fact can be of no service, and can only tend to perplex the mind of the inquirer by those perversions of language, those distortions of expression, and those circuitous expedients of logical ingenuity, which it unavoidably engenders.

NOTES AND ILLUSTRATIONS.

NOTE A (*page* 38).

Mr. Ricardo introduces his notion of real value in a somewhat obscure and indirect manner.

He gives us no formal preliminary definition or explanation of the term, and had not perhaps, at the outset, defined it clearly in his own mind, although the idea seems to have mingled itself with all his speculations. In the opening of his book, the only kinds of value which he points out are value in use and value in exchange, as distinguished by Adam Smith; the latter of which is defined to be the power of purchasing. At the third page, nevertheless, we find another kind of value introduced, without comment or explanation, in an extract from the Wealth of Nations. " The *real price* of every thing, what every thing really costs to the man who wants to acquire it, is the toil and trouble of acquiring it. What every thing is *really worth* to the man who has acquired it, and who wants to dispose of it, or exchange it for something else, is the toil and trouble which it can save to himself, and which it can impose upon other people."

In adopting this passage, however, Mr. Ricardo makes
no use of the new kind of value introduced to his readers,
and we hear nothing more of real value, till he applies
the epithet to the value of wages, in the sense mentioned in the text.   See pages 11 and 12 of the Principles
of Pol. Econ. and Taxation, third edition.   At page 15
he introduces another kind of value, which he terms " absolute," in a sense which I have not been able to seize,
but this is only incidentally, and no consequences are deduced from it.   At page 41 he says, " when commodities
varied in relative value, it would be desirable to have the
means of ascertaining which of them fell and which rose
in *real value*." This appears to be the first passage in which
relative value and real value are fairly placed in contrast;
and we gather from it, that the value, which he calls *real*,
is not of a relative nature.   We subsequently come to the
passage quoted in the text, wherein he uses the phrase real
value as synonymous with the quantity of labour and capital employed in producing a commodity : whence it follows,
that the real value of an object has no relation to the quantity of any other object which it will command, but solely
to the cost of production, or rather it is the cost of production itself.   If the cost of production is always the
same, the real value is always the same.

It may perhaps be contended, that Mr. Ricardo had a
right to use the term real value in any sense he chose, and
that all which could be required of him was consistency in

its employment. Conceding this for the sake of argument, we may yet remark, that it is an apology inapplicable in the present case, because he had already given us his definition of value, and was therefore bound to adhere to it, by the very principle here supposed to be offered in extenuation.

If he had a right to use the term in any sense he pleased, he had no right to destroy the essence of his own definition by an epithet annexed to the term defined. His definition of the term, as the power of purchasing, makes it essentially relative to something to be purchased, and it is annihilating his own meaning to transmute value, by the force of an epithet, into something in which no relation of this kind is implied.

It may still possibly be urged, that Mr. Ricardo is not liable to the charge of having deviated from his definition of *value*, that he has strictly adhered to one meaning, and that the term *real* has not the neutralizing effect here assigned to it. If this were true, we might of course substitute the definition for the term, which would yield some curious results. The real value of an object in this case must be its real power of purchasing or commanding other objects in exchange; and we have already seen, that a power of commanding in exchange can be expressed only by a quantity of the commodity commanded. What then is the commodity in which *real value* can be expressed? Mr. Ricardo tells us, that the value of a thing in money, hats, coats, or corn, is only nominal value. In what commodity then shall we express real value? His answer must be, in none. This illustration is itself sufficient to show, that Mr. Ricardo's notion of real value is totally irreconcilable and incompatible with his previous definition of the only kind of value of which he professes to treat. The argument is short and conclusive : value, as the power of purchasing, can be expressed only by a quantity of the commodity to be purchased — real value cannot be so expressed — therefore value and real value are used in senses incompatible and contradictory.

In a foot-note to the text we have stated, that real value, as used by Mr. Ricardo, has no relation to any commodity unless it be to an imaginary one; namely, a commodity produced by an invariable quantity of labour. But it must be observed, that if we had such a commodity, it would still not enable Mr. Ricardo or any body else to furnish an expression of real value ; it would only enable him to express a *variation* in real value. For suppose gold to be such a commodity, and take any point of time, for example A. D. 1600 : suppose further, an object A to be worth at that period so much gold, so much corn, so much cloth : in this case, the value of A in gold would have no more claim to the title of real value (even on Mr. Ricardo's or any other person's theory) than its value in corn or cloth. But we next compare the value of A in gold, corn, and cloth, in the year 1800, and we find that it is worth only half as much gold, although worth as much corn as before, and worth more cloth.   Here then, according to Mr. Ricardo's doctrine, A has fallen to half its former real value, because worth only half as much gold, which by the supposition is invariable in real value.   But although we can tell how much A has fallen in real value, we are no nearer obtaining an expression of real value than we were before. Still the value of A in gold would be no more its real value, than the value of A in corn or cloth.   Hence it is plain, that real value, in Mr. Ricardo's sense, is not value in relation to any commodity whatever : consequently it does not mean power of purchasing, and Mr. Ricardo has used the word value, when coupled with the epithet real, in an acceptation which excludes the whole of his own definition.

The same remarks will apply to Mr. Malthus's notion of absolute value.   " If we could suppose," says he, " any object always to remain of the same value, the comparison of other commodities with this one would clearly show which had risen, which had fallen, and which had remained the same.   The value of any commodity, estimated in any measure of this kind, might with propriety be called its absolute or natural value," &c. &c.—*The Measure of Value stated and illustrated*, page 2.

To pass over the inconsistency already exposed, of supposing a commodity to remain of the same value, and to take it as implying constancy in the circumstances of its production, it is evident, that, at an assigned period, the value of any commodity ᴀ, in this invariable commodity which we may term x, would have no more right to ᴛᴜe appellation of real value than the value of ᴀ in any other commodity.   Assume another period, and the same remark would be applicable : if commodities had varied in the circumstances of their production, the change in their value to x would show such variation, which Mr. Malthus calls a variation in their absolute value, but still their value in x would not be absolute value, in Mr. Malthus's sense, any more than their value in B, C, or D.

It is to be remarked, that Mr. Ricardo is any thing but consistent in the use of the term under consideration, or of the doctrine which it implies.

In fact, the more I examine his writings, the more I am convinced that he had not formed any clear notions on the subject, that there was a radical confusion in his views regarding it.

It is only occasionally that he intimates to his readers that he is speaking of real value : in general he professes to be speaking of " exchangeable value," sometimes of " relative value," as contradistinguished from that which is " absolute" and " real."

It is, in truth, curious to note the different kinds of value of which he speaks in the course of his speculations. The following enumeration will show how far he is entitled to credit for the precision of his language and ideas on this subject.

Page

Value in use............   1

Value in exchange, or exchangeable
   value................................. 1, 4.

Real Ditto .... 11, 41, 50.

Absolute Ditto........................ 15.

Relative Ditto .... 15, 41.

Nominal Ditto........ .... 50.

Natural Ditto......................... 80, 85.

If the view of the subject unfolded in these pages is at all correct, all these epithets (except perhaps the last) may be at once swept away. Even the adjunct exchangeable is tautological, the term value implying in itself a relation in exchange, or the power of commanding in exchange, and consequently any epithet which merely expresses the same idea being perfectly superfluous. The word, too, is ill adapted to convey the meaning imposed upon it. It is easy to understand what an exchangeable commodity is; a commodity, namely, which is capable of being exchanged : and this is the proper meaning of the epithet; but what is meant by an exchangeable value is not so clear. The words import a value capable of being exchanged ; and although it is possible to speak of exchanging the value of A for the value of B without absolute absurdity, yet this is evidently not the sense in which the epithet is employed. All that is meant by it is value in exchange, and not value capable of being exchanged. The same epithet is sometimes coupled with the term relation, in which case the impropriety is still more glaring. It would be difficult for the greatest ingenuity to find out any way in which the relation between two commodities can be capable of being exchanged. If it were permitted to introduce a new term, perhaps the epithet *exchangive* might be useful to mark the particular kind of relation which we are now obliged to designate by the phrase " relation in exchange." The *exchangive* relation of a commodity would be less objectionable than the *exchangeable* relation; and if this term were adopted, it would supply a deficiency which most writers on political economy must have occasionally felt.

In the text, I have noticed the improper use of the terms real and nominal value, in our English economists only. The celebrated French writer, M. Say, commits precisely the same error.

" If different commodities," says he, " have fallen in different ratios, some more, others less, it is plain they must have varied in relative value to each other. That which has fallen, stockings for instance, has changed its value relatively to that which has not fallen, as butcher's meat; and such as have fallen in equal proportion, like stockings and sugar in our hypothesis, have varied in *real*, though not in *relative* value. — There is this difference between a real and a relative variation of price; that the former is a change of value, arising from an alteration of the charges of production; the latter, a change arising from an alteration of the ratio of value of one particular commodity to other commodities." — *Treatise on Pol. Econ. translated by C. R. Prinsep*, book ii, chap. 3.

NOTE B (*page* 61).

The source of such barren and paradoxical propositions as are noticed in the text, is to be found in the notion of real value; and that notion being conceded as a preliminary, these propositions logically follow from it. We must look for the original fallacy therefore in the notion itself, the intrinsic inconsistency of which has been already sufficiently exposed.

NOTE C (*page* 70).

To avoid misconception it may be necessary to state, that in this and the preceding chapter it has been intended simply to explain the nature of a rise in the value of labour and a rise in profits, not the causes on which they depend, or the way in which they actually take place. In maintaining that there is no inconsistency in supposing a simultaneous rise of labour and of profits, I profess not to enter into the question whether such a rise does ever or can ever take place, but contend solely, that in cases of improved productive power, the product might be so divided, that the rate of profits should be increased, while the value of labour was enhanced ; and that this would be necessarily the result, were the product divided in the way described in the hypothetical case adduced by Mr. Ricardo.

NOTE D (*page* 103).

The universality of the supposition, that a commodity must itself be invariable in order to serve as a measure of value, will appear from the following extracts.

" As a measure of quantity, such as the natural foot, fathom, or handful, which is continually varying in its own quantity, can never be an accurate measure of the quantity of other things ; so a commodity, which is itself continually varying in its own value, can never be an accurate measure of the value of other commodities. Equal quantities of labour at all times and places, may be said to be of equal value to the labourer. In his ordinary state of health, strength, and spirits, in the ordinary degree of his skill and dexterity, he must always lay down the same portion of his ease, his liberty, and his happiness. The price which he pays must always be the same, whatever may be the quantity of goods which he receives in return for it.

Of these, indeed, it may sometimes purchase a greater and sometimes a smaller quantity ; but it is their value which varies, not that of the labour which purchases them.

At all times and places, that is dear which it is difficult to come at, or which it costs much labour to acquire ; and that cheap which is to be had easily, or with very little la- bour. Labour alone, therefore, never varying in its own value, is alone the ultimate and real standard by which the value of all commodities can at all times and places be estimated and compared." — *Wealth of Nations, by Adam Smith,* book i, chap. 5.

" That money, therefore, which constantly preserves an equal value, which poises itself, as it were, in a just equilibrium between the fluctuating proportion of the value of things, is the only permanent and equal scale by which value can be measured." — *An Inquiry into the Principles of Pol. Econ., by Sir James Stuart,* book iii, chap. 1.

" Incapacities of the Metals to perform the Office of an invariable Measure of Value." — *Ibid.* Title to chap. iii, book 3.

" As nothing can be a real measure of magnitude and quantity, which is subject to variations in its own dimensions, so nothing can be a real measure of the value of other commodities, which is constantly varying in its own value." — *An Inquiry into the Nature and Origin of Public Wealth, by the Earl of Lauderdale,* page 25, second edit.

" Le principal caractère d'un *mesure* est d'être *invariable*. C'est en appliquant successivement une mesure invariable à des quantités variable, qu'on peut se former une idée de leur rapports ; mais quand on applique une mesure variable à des quantités qui le sont aussi, on n'apprend rien. Une poignée, une coudée, ne sont pas des mesures propre à comparer les dimensions, puisqu'elles varient dans chaque individu ; il en serait de même d'un numéraire dont la valeur varierait, soit dans le même temps dans différens endroits, soit dans le même endroit dans différens temps ; il ne pourrait guere servir à mesurer d'autres valeurs." — *Cours D'Economie Politique, par Henri Storch,* Première Partie, liv. v, chap. 2.

" Silver is more valuable, when it will purchase a large quantity of commodities, than when it will purchase a smaller quantity.   It cannot, therefore, serve as a measure, the first requisite of which is invariability." — *A Treatise on Pol. Econ., by J. B. Say, translated from the French, by C. R. Prinsep,* book i, chap. 21.

" When commodities varied in relative value, it would be desirable to have the means of ascertaining which of them fell and which rose in real value, and this could be effected only by comparing them, one after another, with some invariable standard measure of value, which should itself be subject to none of the fluctuations to which other commodities are exposed." — *Principles of Pol. Econ. and Taxation, by D. Ricardo, Esq.,* page 42, third edition.

" Labour, like all other commodities, varies, from its plenty or scarcity compared with the demand for it, and at different times, and in different countries, commands very different quantities of the first necessary of life ; and further, from the different degrees of skill, and of assistance from machinery with which labour is applied, the products of labour are not in proportion to the quantity exerted. Consequently, labour, in any sense in which the term can be applied, cannot be considered as an accurate and standard measure of real value in exchange." — *Principles of Pol. Econ., by Rev. T. R. Malthus,* page 125.

It is to be remarked, that in the preceding passage, Mr. Malthus rejects labour as an accurate measure of value, because it is *not* invariable. In his pamphlet on this subject he has altered his views, and maintains labour to be an accurate measure, because it *is* invariable. In both cases he proceeds equally on the doctrine, that invariableness of value is necessary in a measure of value.

" A standard, by a reference to which we may ascertain the fluctuations in the exchangeable power of other things, must itself possess an exchangeable value fixed and unalterable.

" Nothing can be an accurate measure of value, except that which itself possesses an invariable value." — *An Essay on the Production of Wealth, by R. Torrens, Esq.,* pages 56 and 59.

" There is no point so difficult to ascertain as a variation of value, because we have no fixed standard measure of value ; neither nature nor art furnish us with a commodity, whose value is incapable of change ; and such alone would afford us an accurate standard of value." — *Conversations on Pol. Econ., by Mrs. Marcet,* page 330.

" Money, that is, the precious metals in coin, serves practically as a measure of value, as is evident from what has immediately been said. A certain quantity of the precious metal is taken as a known value, and the value of other things is measured by that value; one commodity is twice, another thrice the value of such a portion of the metal, and so on.

" It is evident, however, that this can remain an accurate' measure of value only if it remains of the same value itself. If a commodity, which was twice the value of an ounce of silver, becomes three times its value; we can only know what change has taken place in the value of this commodity, if we know that our measure is unchanged."— *Elements of Pol. Econ., by James Mill, Esq.* second edit., page 108.

" A standard is that which stands still, while other things move, and by this means serves to indicate or measure the degree in which they have advanced or receded.*** And a standard of value must itself stand still, or be stationary in value." — *The Templars' Dialogues on Pol. Econ.*, London Magazine, May 1824, page 558.

" That great desideratum in political economy, an uniform measure of value." — *Observations on the Effects produced by the Expenditure of Government, by Wm. Blake, Esq.*

It will not be thought uninteresting to examine what notions on the subject of a measure of value were entertained by so clear a thinker as Locke. He considered, that the value of commodities is determined by " the proportion of their quantity to the vent;" that the vent of money being always "sufficient and more than enough,"—" its quantity alone is enough to regulate and determine its value, without considering any proportion between its quantity and vent, as in other commodities."   Hence he argues, that so long as the quantity of money in a country remains the same, its value is invariable, and it will serve to measure the varying value of other things.   In his own words —

" Money, whilst the same quantity of it is passing up and down the kingdom in trade, is really a standing measure of the falling and rising value of other things, in reference to one another : and the alteration of price is truly in them only.   But if you increase or lessen the quantity of money current in traffic, in any place, then the alteration of value is in the money : and if, at the same time, wheat keep its proportion of vent to quantity, money, to speak truly, alters its worth, and wheat does not, though it sell for a greater or less price than it did before.   For money, being looked upon as the standing measure of other commodities, men consider and speak of it still as if it were a standing measure, though, when it has varied its quantity, it is plain it is not."

In this passage may be remarked the same error, that I have pointed out in other economists, of supposing an alteration in value can take place in one commodity, while the commodity compared with it remains the same ; " money alters its worth and wheat does not."   Yet in the subsequent paragraph, the sound sense of this profound reasoner carried him to the truth, although into some apparent inconsistency; for he adds, " But the value or price of all commodities, amongst which money passing in trade is truly one, consisting in proportion, you alter this, as you do all other proportions, whether you increase one, or lessen the other." — *Considerations on the lowering of Interest and raising the Value of Money.*

It may be further remarked on the former of these passages, that, taking him on his own theory, the measure which he describes, like the measures of other economists, would not enable us to ascertain any variations of value, for these are necessarily exhibited in the prices of commodities, but would indicate in which commodities the changes originated. While money remained unaltered as to the causes of value operating upon it, which it would do on his principles as long as it remained the same in quantity, all variations in the prices of commodities must necessarily proceed from alterations in the proportion between the quantities of such commodities and their vent, and this is all that, under the circumstances supposed, Mr. Locke's standing measure would show.

On reviewing this subject from first to last, it appears to me, that nearly the whole of the vagueness, confusion, and perplexity in which it has been involved, may be traced to an unconscious vacillation between two distinct ideas. There are evidently two senses in which the term measuring value is employed, and it is the unconscious passing and repassing from one to the other, which has been the source of the mischief : one of these senses, and the only proper sense, is, ascertaining the mutual value of two commodities by their separate relations to a third ; the other is, ascertaining, when two commodities have varied in value, in which of them the variation has originated. The transition from one of these ideas to the other is, I think, perceptible in the doctrine examined in the text, that money is a good measure of value for commodities at the same time, but not for commodities at different times.   In the first part of this proposition, the term measure is used in the former sense, and it is meant to assert, that the value of commodities to each other is shown by their prices, or values in money.   In the latter part of the proposition, a transition is made to the second meaning, and it is intended to say, that the value of a commodity in money at different periods does not show whether there has been any alteration in the circumstances of its production ; whether any variation in its price has originated with it, or with the money in which its value is expressed.   If we do not suppose this transition to be made, but that one sense is rigidly adhered to, the proposition is liable to all the objections brought against it in the text.

It is probably the latter construction of the term measure, under which invariableness has been so generally supposed requisite.   But this, as is shown in the course of the present chapter, would not be invariableness of value, but invariableness of cost, or invariableness in the circumstances of production; and what would be measured by it would be that cost, or those circumstances, and not value.

NOTE E (*page* 133).

The reasoning in the text shows, that on the supposition that commoditities were to each other in value as the quantities of labour required to produce them, any commodity produced by labour alone, however variable the quantity of that labour, would enable us to ascertain all that Mr. Ricardo regards as to be derived exclusively from a commodity produced by an invariable quantity of labour; provided a register were kept of the varying quantities of the producing labour required.   In both cases, the prices of the standard (if we may so .call it) at different periods, would be equally necessary.   In the one case, the circumstance of invariableness in the labour expended would save the trouble of keeping such a register, and simplifv our calculations; but in the other case, the result would be attained, if not with equal ease, at least with equal certainty.

NOTE F (*page* 150).

The author of the Templars' Dialogues has also examined this table, but it appears to me that he has fallen into some singular misconceptions of Mr. Malthus's meaning. At least he has construed it differently from what it is represented in the text, and consequently either he or myself must be in error — possibly the latter. I can only say, that I have been at pains to understand and scrupulous not to misrepresent the scope of Mr. Malthus's argument. At the same time I must confess, that with all the patient attention which I have given to the speculations of the latter, there are many parts of "The Measure of Value stated and illustrated" which I am unable to comprehend.

NOTE G (*page* 15).

It is to be observed, that many writers consider measuring and expressing value as the same thing. This is directly maintained by M. Say, in the following passage.

" Quant à la mesure de la valeur de deux objets qui sont en présence, leur deux valeurs se mesurent l'une par l'autre. Si l'on a dix livres de blé pour une livre de café, le café vaut dix fois autant que le blé ; et chacune de ces choses est la mesure de l'autre. La monnaie n'a à cet égard aucun privilége. Trente sous sont la valeur d'une livre de café, et une livre de café marque la valeur des trentes sous aussi bien que les diverses choses que l'on peut acquérir avec cette monnaie." — *Note in M. Say's Edition* (page 124, vol. i) *of* " *Cours d'Economie Politique, par Henri Storch.*"

It is not correct, however, to regard these two operations as identical.   To measure implies, either directly or indirectly, the ascertainment of a ratio between two objects by the intervention of a third.   We say, it is true, that we have measured the length of a building, when we have found its ratio to a yard or a foot, but this is because the length of other objects in feet is known to us, and therefore, when we have the length of the building in feet, we have it in a common denomination : the ratio of the building to the foot, determines its place in the common scale ; or, in other words, determines its ratio to a variety of other objects.   We should scarcely consider the length of a building to be measured, if its ratio was determined only to a staff or rod, the length of which in relation to any other object could not itself be ascertained.

In the same way, when we say the value of a commodity A is measured when expressed in money, it is because we know already the relations in value between money and a variety of other commodities, and therefore the value of A in money instantly determines its relation to all these objects.   The idea of intermediation is still implied.   But although to express the value of a commodity in money may thus be considered as equivalent to measuring it, we could not with propriety apply the latter term to the expression of the value of a commodity in another commodity of no known or ascertainable relation to any thing else.

The following passage from one of Locke's able tracts on

raising the value of money, so accurately describes the only process which can be termed with propriety measuring value, that I cannot resist the temptation of inserting it here in confirmation of my own views.

" By this measure of commerce, *viz.* the quantity of silver, men measure the value of all other things. Thus to measure what the value of lead is to wheat, and of either of them to a certain sort of linen cloth, the quantity of silver that each is valued at, or sells for, needs only be known; for if a yard of cloth be sold for half an ounce of silver, a bushel of wheat for one ounce, and a hundred weight of lead for two ounces; any one presently sees and says, that a bushel of wheat is double the value of a yard of that cloth, and but half the value of an hundred weight of lead."— *Further Considerations concerning raising the Value of Money.*

NOTE H (*page* 158).

Many of the strictures which have been made on Mr. Ricardo's writings, in this and other chapters, would be in some degree obviated if two things were conceded, namely, if we assumed that he was constantly speaking of real value, and if we were to grant him the absurdity which we have shown this expression to imply; or, in other words, if we were to consider it as importing cost of production, without relation to the power of commanding in exchange. But then, although some inconsistencies would by this means be obviated or explained away, we should obtain in their place a number of others equally irreconcilable, and also a series of unmeaning and identical propositions.   For instance, the proposition that a million of men always produced the same value, but not the same riches, would be reduced to this, that what a million of men produced always cost the labour of a million of men : a = a.   The truth appears to be, that the idea of real value was seldom distinctly present to his mind, although there was almost constantly an obscure reference to it.

NOTE I (page 178).

In speaking sometimes of a commodity produced by an invariable quantity of labour as a measure, and sometimes of the labour itself in that character, Mr. Ricardo has in fact used the term in the two senses mentioned in note D, and passed from one to the other without being conscious of it.   When he says, that a commodity produced by an invariable quantity of labour would serve to measure the variations of other things, his meaning, as we have before shown, amounts to this, that such a commodity would serve to indicate the variations in the cost of production, or producing labour of other commodities.   But to employ the quantity of producing labour itself as a measure in this sense would be endeavouring to ascertain what is already presupposed.   When, therefore, he affirms labour itself to be a common measure of value, he makes a transition to the other sense of the phrase, and means, that when the quantities of labour respectively required to produce commodities are known, their values in relation to each other are thereby determined.

This distinction, constantly borne in mind, would, I am persuaded, throw great light upon the obscurity which clouds many discussions in political economy, and clearly show the source whence it has proceeded.

THE END.

REVIEW OF *A CRITICAL DISSERTATION*
[Sometimes Attributed To James Mill]
Westminster Review January 1826

Art. VIII. *A Critical Dissertation on the Nature, Measures, and Causes of Value ; chiefly in reference to the Writings of Mr. Ricardo and his followers.* By the Author of Essays on the Formation and Publication of Opinions, &c. &c. Hunter. London. 1826.

BEFORE we had seen this production, and when we had heard only of its size, we more than suspected what we have found. We knew that any one who understood the subject, would say all he had to say upon it, in twenty, instead of two hundred pages.

" A very long discussion," says an intelligent author, " is one of the most effectual veils of fallacy. Sophistry, like poison, is at once detected and nauseated, when presented to us in a concentrated form. But a fallacy, which, when stated barely, in a few sentences, would not deceive a child, may deceive half the world, if diluted in a quarto volume."*

Chap. I. *On the nature of Value.*—This chapter is logomachy, simply and purely. It makes profession, or rather ostentation and parade, of being a controversy with Mr. Ricardo. But it contains not an assertion to which, as far as *ideas* politico-economical are concerned, Mr. Ricardo would not have assented; it contains, not indeed, as far as such ideas are concerned, an assertion which is not implied in the propositions which Mr. Ricardo has put forth. It is a criticism on some of Mr. Ricardo's forms of expression, and the dissatisfied critic will presently find, that his own expressions stand in need of quite as much indulgence.

We are willing to admit, in behalf of this author, a matter of some importance, which he himself appears to be little aware of, that it is impossible to expound the doctrines of political economy in language altogether unexceptionable, without a new nomenclature ; or giving such a technical, and unusual meaning, to old terms, as would certainly occasion more obstruction to a learner, than using language as nearly as possible in its ordinary acceptation, when some degree of laxity is hardly to be avoided. This only becomes a vice requiring philosophical rebuke, when it introduces confusion of ideas ; that is, when a word of double meaning is so used, that the ideas belonging to one sense are suggested, when the truth of the proposition requires the ideas which are comprehended in the other. To make this clear by an example—the word " dog " signifies two things ; an animal, and a star. The words are never improperly

---

* See the Article Logic in the Encyclopædia Metropolitana.

applied, when the context shows in which of the senses it is that the word is employed. But if the context is such, that we are understood as speaking of the animal; as if we should say, " the dog has two ears and four feet ;" and then we should suddenly add, " the dog also shines," this would evidently be an abuse of the terms, and justly censurable.

Mr. Ricardo used the word " value " in two senses. He did so avowedly. It has always been remarked, as well by those who have adopted, as by those who have opposed, his doctrines. Mr. Ricardo conceived, erroneously we think, that it would be good to attempt the introduction of more precision into the language of political economy, by giving a technical meaning to the word " value." But he did not imagine, for that reason, that he could altogether dispense with the use of the word in its more ordinary acceptation ; nor could he have done so without such innovations of language as would have been very inconvenient to his readers, as well as himself.

It frequently happens, in fact, that when a new word, or a new acceptation of a word, is proposed, the best and sometimes the only expedient for procuring it admission is, to use it along with the more ordinary and lax expressions ; when, the value of it becoming more and more known, it gradually supersedes the less appropriate expressions.

Had the term " value " been the best that could have been chosen for the peculiar and technical sense in which Mr. Ricardo employed it, which we have always thought it was not, still it would, in our opinion, have been judicious to use the word in the sense of exchangeable value, in those passages where he could not avoid that use of it without further innovations in language. It would have been a sufficient reason for this, had there been no other, that too many innovations should not be attempted at once, unless where there happens to be, as in Chemistry, a pre-disposition to admit them. Had Mr. Ricardo ventured upon more, his book would have been still more embarrassing to the learner than it is. In introducing a new meaning of a term, without being able to dispense altogether with the old, it is incumbent upon writers to keep them distinct, and make their context always indicate clearly in which of the two meanings the word should be received. This, we think, Mr. Ricardo has done, with extraordinary vigilance and success.

Such being the case, to write a chapter, we should rather say a book, with a great expenditure of metaphysics, not very valuable, and not at all to the purpose, and many words in very comely phrase, not for the purpose of showing that Mr. Ricardo had confounded ideas that ought to be distinguished, that he had in any case drawn inferences from a word used in one sense which could only be drawn from it with correctness when applied in another, but simply to show that this distinguished author, having professedly made use of a particular word in a technical sense, found it necessary, on some occasions, to use it in its ordinary sense, where no mistake could possibly arise, was surely to employ ability to very little purpose.

The author delivers his opinion, in great variety of phrase, that the word "value" ought to be used in the sense of exchangeable value only. Be it so. Some of those whom he is pleased to designate by the title of followers of Mr. Ricardo, Mr. Mill, for example, have also thought, that, as a matter of convenience, it would be best to confine it to this acceptation, though they do not appear to recognize, with this author, a sort of divine right in the word, to be used in one sense more than another. It is a question of verbal convenience merely : and when it is taken as any thing higher, is both the consequence and cause of delusion.

The principal part of the chapter is employed in showing in what manner, if this sense is to be adopted, the word "value" ought, and ought not, to be used ; wherein the author displays intense persuasion of the importance of what he is about; wherein, however, all that is good is any thing in the world rather than new ; and all that is new, appears to us to be any thing in the world rather than good.

Value, in the sense of exchangeable value, he tells us, is a relative term. Well; there is surely nothing new in this. It follows from this, he says, that when any commodity changes in value, all commodities change in value. If one commodity falls, all other commodities rise, and rise in the same degree. Stockings, for example, fall in value, and a pair of them which would have exchanged for a pair of shoes, will only exchange for half a pair; the rise in the value of the shoes is as great as the fall in the value of the stockings. This is new, but this is not good. There is a great difference between the alteration in the value of the stockings, and the alteration in the value of the shoes. The stockings have fallen in value, as compared with every thing, but the shoes have risen in value only as compared with one. This is a distinction worth marking. In the alterations which take place in relative value, this divides commodities into two classes, which it is of great importance to have terms to distinguish. Mr. Ricardo adopted a method of distinguishing them. A great part of the vituperation which this author bestows upon Mr. Ricardo, is on account of his endeavour to mark this distinction. There appears to us, in what the critic says upon this subject, a complete oversight of the existence of the distinction, and of course of the importance of marking it.

Mr. Ricardo says, the ordinary and natural cause of an alteration in the value of a commodity, as compared with other commodities, is an alteration in its cost of production, meaning the last elements, whatever they are, into which cost of production can be resolved. Of the two classes of commodities which have just been mentioned, one is that of those in which, when values alter, a change in the cost of production has taken place; another, that of those in which a change in the cost of production has not taken place. " If," says Mr. Ricardo, " we had any commodity, to the production of which the same quantity of labour [meaning cost of production in its ultimate elements] was always required, this commodity would be a perfect test by which to distinguish one of those classes of commodities from the other, and also a perfect test to determine the degree in which the purchasing power of any commodity in the class wherein cost of production had been affected, was altered in respect to the other class, and in respect to any other commodity in its own class. To this commodity, answering thus extensively the purpose of a test, in all changes of value, Mr. Ricardo thought that the name of Standard of Value might not improperly be applied; and that it might be considered as invariable; not surely invariable in its own purchasing power; that is a meaning which no one can for a moment suppose was applied to it by Mr. Ricardo; but invariable in its accuracy as a test to mark the variations in the purchasing power of other commodities. Surely all this is very true; and all this is very clear and accurate developement. Yet there is no measure to the contempt which this author pours upon Mr. Ricardo for this part of his speculations. It will now be seen, by the dullest of our readers, that it is a contempt very ill deserved. And it is, we are sorry to say, a contempt which imports a very inadequate and shallow view of a subject which requires, after all, no very great depth of understanding to fathom it.

Who, that understands what he is about, would bestow contempt, or even censure, upon an author who used the word " exchange," for example, in a technical sense, such as that of the merchants, when they speak of " the par of exchange," " the rise and fall of the exchange," and so on; but who used it also in the ordinary sense, and spoke as other people do of value in exchange. So common is this practice, so familiar to all logicians, that Aldrich, in the Oxford Text Book of Logic, makes the famous distinction of words *primæ, et secundæ inten-tionis*, to correspond with it. " Nomen *primæ intentionis*," says he, " est vox in communi usu posita" [value in exchange]. " *Secundæ*, vox artis, quam ex communi sermone sumptam, philosophia recudit denuo et moderatur" [value in Mr. Ricardo's sense].

We shall now show our anonymous corrector, by his own example, that it is not so easy a matter, in the present state of our language, to avoid a degree of laxity in expounding the doctrines of political economy, as, from the contempt he expresses of those who have not always come up to his ideas of precision, he seems to suppose.

He makes vast use of the word " relation." But it is **very** evident to us, that he does not know what it means. Is he acquainted with Hobbes's profound remark, that there is nothing relative, but terms? With all his metaphysics, we will give him a month to explain what is meant by relation. He will find, if he likes, some excellent information in Hobbes's Logic, which may, perhaps, abate a little his admiration of Dr. Brown, who made use of the word " relative" as an occult cause, to explain whatever he did not understand.

This proposition—" A will exchange for B, merely states," says our author, " a relation in which they stand to each other." Again, " In the examination of the present subject, as discussed by those writers, on whose doctrines I have ventured to animadvert, I have been forcibly struck with the vagueness, the inconsistencies, and the errors, which have arisen from speaking of value as a sort of general and independent property."

When he calls it " a relative," instead of " an independent property," does he flatter himself that he has spoken with precision ?

This author's attempt reminds one of the mistake of Diderot, who wrote an eloquent and a much more plausible book than this, to show, what he too thought a great discovery, that Taste is a perception of relations ; aye, and Moral Sense the same thing. It was not difficult to see, that this was a solution in words merely ; not, however, more vain than that of the writers who resolve the principle of value into a relation ; and then imagine they have enlightened the world.

" The mistake both in this writer and in Mr. Ricardo, arises from an inaccurate apprehension of the true nature of value. Instead of regarding value as a relation between two objects, they seem to consider it as a positive result produced by a definite quantity of labour." This is a curious passage. Does the critic consider value, does he consider a relation, as not a positive result; as a thing that is not produced, and also annihilated? What does he say of the word effect? Is not that a term of relation? Is not effect a positive result? What inconsistency, too, in the man who says that cost of production is the *cause of value;* to quarrel with others who say it is a positive result produced by cost of production? This is not metaphysics; it is jargon. And when an author's skill in language enables him to write plausible jargon, it is only so much the worse.

The very title of the chapter is a misnomer; and shows that the author had not settled with himself what he was about; what in truth was his object in penning the pages. The proper title would have been, " On the meaning of the term value." When an author has said, that he means to employ the word value only in the sense of " purchasing power," any explanation of the nature of it would have been mere impertinence. Every body understands the nature of purchasing power, as well as the metaphysical author of the " Critical Dissertation." Accordingly he says not one word about the nature of purchasing power; the chapter is employed in stating the meaning he attaches to the term value, and giving specimens of what he thinks proper and improper applications of it.

He does not even know when he meets with laxity, and not laxity merely, but incongruity, of language, in others. He quotes with great eulogium, from Colonel Torrens, a passage in which that writer says, " Exchangeable value is determined not by the absolute, but by the relative cost of production." Now in the name of all that is risible, what is the distinction the author would have us put between absolute, and relative, in this expression? If he means, that a greater cost of production is attended with a greater value, a less with a less, has any other person ever said any thing else? Is the cost in the two cases less an absolute cost on that account? One bottle holds a quart and another a pint. Are the poor bottles, on that account, no longer absolute, but only relative bottles?

In the same short passage the colonel also says, " In the very term, exchangeable value, a relative, and not an absolute quantity, is implied." Surely, if any thing in the world be absolute, it is quantity. He might as well talk of a relative substance. Can there be within the compass of thought, two ideas more distinct than that of quantity, and that of relation?

And these are the men who are finding something to contemn in the language of Ricardo at every step! Metaphysical terms are edge tools, and should not be meddled with by those who are not used to the handling of them.

It is remarkable enough, that while these two writers are charging Mr. Ricardo with the highest degree of intellectual culpability, for using a term, avowedly, and guardedly, in two senses, they are confusing themselves most grossly by a double meaning of the same term, of which they are altogether ignorant.

Concerning the subject of relation the logicians have distinguished the following particulars : 1. *Relatio;* 2. *Subjectum;* 3. *Relatum;* 4. *Correlatum;* 5. *Fundamentum;* 6. *Terminus.* And of so much importance to the understanding of the *relatio* are the other particulars included in the enumeration, that the following is their rule for its definition:

Relatio definitur, subjecto, relato, correlato, fundamento, et termino.

When these things have separate names, the case is in general clear, and easily understood. In the case of value, it so happens, that the *relatio*, and the *fundamentum*, have not two names, but unfortunately one and the same name. By the authors who think they have done something great for political economy, when they have told us, that value is exchangeable value, and a relation, these two meanings are confounded in almost every page. We ask them, if value be the *relatio*, to tell us what is the *fundamentum*. Let them do so, and they will probably discover, that they have less ground, than they thought, of complaint against Ricardo and his followers.*

The anonymous dissertator sums up his first chapter, in the following manner:

' The following propositions may be stated as the results of the investigation in which we have been employed.

1. ' Inasmuch as the term value denotes a relation between two objects, a commodity cannot be said to possess value, or to alter in value without an express or implied reference to some other commodity. Its value must be value in something, or in relation to something.

---

* They would have performed a better service, than that of cavilling at Mr. Ricardo because he used the word value in a new sense, at the same time that he used it in the old, had they taught us how to dispense with a word which it is so very difficult to use with the requisite precision. It is great pity that the word exchange is so unmanageable a word ; otherwise it would have been highly convenient to have made from it a word to express value in exchange exclusively and definitely. Exchangeability would not do, because it has a passive signification. Exchangivity would have the proper signification ; but then it is an awkward word. It might, by dropping the *ex* be softened to changivity ; and would, if the public were reconciled to it, be exceedingly useful. We should then speak of the changivity of commodities instead of their value. We should call them changive, instead of valuable, and should talk of degrees of changivity, regulator of changivity, measure of changivity, and so on.

2. ' This relation between two objects cannot alter as to one, without altering as to the other. If A rises in relation to B, B cannot remain stationary, but must fall in relation to A.

3. ' The value of a commodity can be expressed only by a quantity of some other commodity.

4. ' A rise in the value of a commodity A, means that an equal quantity of this commodity exchanges for a greater quantity than before of the commodity B, in relation to which it is said to rise.

5. ' A fall in the value of A means, that an equal quantity of it exchanges for a smaller quantity.'

He says, " Simple as these results appear, we have seen that it is possible to overlook them." We affirm that nobody has ever overlooked them. They are mere identical propositions. When he has defined value to be exchangeable value, his " simple results" are merely repeating, that exchangeable value is exchangeable value five times over.

We will help him, however, to a simple result or two ; which will probably surprise him. In his meaning of the word value,

1. There is no one commodity more fixed in its value than any other.

2. Of the value of all the commodities possessed by any country, there never can be either increase or diminution.

3. The whole of the commodities of a country have no value at all.

It may amuse the author's leisure to go on adding to these results.

Chap. II. *On Real and Nominal Value.*—On this chapter we have not much to say. The author gives us his opinion, which is easily done, that this distinction is not useful. And then he finds fault with Mr. Ricardo and the Templar's Dialogues, because they predicate and predicate truly of value in their sense, what cannot be predicated of it truly in his sense. This is mere logomachy ; and these are the contents of the chapter.

Chap. III. *On the Value of Labour.*—Pretty nearly the same remarks will suffice on this, as on the former chapter. The only proper meaning of the term value of labour or value of wages, the author says, is value in exchange ; and having said this, he proceeds to accuse Mr. Ricardo and the Templar of deep errors, because they affirm of labour and wages what is true in their sense of the word value, but not true in his sense. They never meant it to be true in his sense.

Chap. IV. *On Profits.*—The object of this chapter is, to shew that Mr. Ricardo committed an error, when he stated that as wages rise, profits fall. This author begins by defining a rise or fall of wages, to be an increase or decrease in the quantity of the commodities given for labour. Now, in this meaning of the terms rise or fall of wages, neither Mr. Ricardo nor any body else ever maintained, that as wages rise or fall, profits fall or rise. Mr. Ricardo distinctly maintained the contrary. This author labours under a perpetual *ignoratio elenchi.*

CHAP. V. *On comparing Commodities at different Periods.* —The author is obscure in this chapter. The object still is, to accuse Mr. Ricardo of error, because he affirms of value in his own sense of it, what it would be absurd to affirm of it in the sense of the anonymous dissertator.

If there were any commodity which two hundred years ago was produced by seven days labour, and which had continued to be in demand and to be produced by the same quantity of labour to the present day, what does Mr. Ricardo say it would do? That it would remain invariable in its power of purchasing? that it would invariably command in exchange the same quantity of commodities? No such thing. Mr. Ricardo not only never advanced any such proposition; but it seems almost incredible that any body who has read his book should impute it to him.

What, then, is it that Mr. Ricardo really says? He says, that if this commodity exchanged for two pair of shoes two hundred years ago, and exchanges for four pair of shoes now, it shows that shoes are made at half the cost, at which they were made two hundred years ago; and he adds, that, according to his language, they are, therefore, one half cheaper than they were in those days.

In like manner, if this commodity two hundred years ago exchanged for 10 loaves of bread, and now exchanges only for five, this would show, according to Mr. Ricardo, that it requires twice as much cost to produce a loaf of bread now, as at that former period, and for this reason and this reason alone, he would call it twice as dear.

Is there any confusion in these ideas?

What, then, are we to say of an author who embarrasses himself by jumbling together two meanings, his own meaning and Mr. Ricardo's meaning of the same terms, and then imputes to Mr. Ricardo the confusion which reigns only in his own brains?

CHAP. VI. *On Measures of Value.*—The same thing is to be said of this author's chapters, one after another. The same *ignoratio elenchi;* the same fighting with a shadow. The author says here, that value is exchangeable value, and of exchangeable value there neither is nor can be any invariable measure. He imputes the absurdity of denying this proposition largely to all political economists preceding himself. In this, however, he indulges an idea of his own superiority, for which he is indebted solely to his own imagination. If invariableness in value means invariableness in power of purchasing, it supposes, of course, that no change takes place in any thing. When Mr. Ricardo says " standard measure of value," he means a commodity invariable in the labour which goes to its production. He does not mean invariable in its power of purchasing, quite the contrary. And we have already shown what is the use to which he would turn this commodity as a standard.

CHAP. VII. *On the Measure of Value proposed by Mr. Malthus.*—Mr. Malthus has said, that the reward of labour, that which is given for it, in other words, its wages, are always of the same value. On this our author makes his usual remark ; this, says he, is not true, in my sense of the word value; the wages of labour do not always command the same quantity of commodities ; therefore Mr. Malthus is absurd. When Mr. Malthus, however, takes as his standard what is given in exchange for labour, he takes it, not because it is invariable in its command of commodities, but because it is invariable in its command of labour. To this our author replies, as others had replied before him, that, to say a day's labour is always equal to what is given for it, is an identical proposition ; it is merely to say, that a day's wages is a day's wages ; from which it is evident that nothing can be inferred.

CHAP. VIII. *On Methods of estimating Value.*—In this the author returns to his supposition of a controversy with Mr. Ricardo. In illustration of his own peculiar meaning of the word value, Mr. Ricardo said that, if the productive power of the labour of a country were doubled, the amount of the commodities would be doubled ; but the value would be the same. In Mr. Ricardo's sense of the word this is strictly true ; and our nameless author abuses him because it is not true in a different acceptation of the term. You cannot speak, he says, of the alteration or non-alteration of a commodity in exchangeable value, without a reference to the commodities against which it is exchanged. True ; but in speaking of alteration of value in Mr. Ricardo's sense, you need a reference to nothing but the quantity of the labour which has been employed in production.

CHAP. IX. *On the Distinction between Value and Riches.*—The matter of this chapter is precisely the same as of the former. Assigning a new and technical meaning to the word value, it was necessary for Mr. Ricardo to mark, by some of the most striking instances, the distinction between that and the ordinary meaning.   According to the case supposed in the preceding chapter, of a doubled power of production in the labour of any country, without any increase of labour or of population ; as there would be double the quantity of commodities, there might be said to be double the riches that were in the country before, though, according to Mr. Ricardo's sense of the word value, there clearly would be the same value and nothing more.   In animadverting upon this, the author not only commits his usual *ignoratio elenchi ;* but shows that he does not understand the import even of his own term.   He affirms, speaking of the aggregate of a nation's commodities, that there can be no increase of riches without an increase of value ; not seeing that in the correct application of his meaning of the word value, the value of the aggregate of a nation's commodities is susceptible neither of increase nor diminution.

Chap. X. *On the Difference between a Measure and a Cause of Value.*—The author charges all writers but himself with the absurdity of confounding these two things.   None of the writers whom he names ever did.   His contempt of others and satisfaction with himself are, therefore, equally undeserved on this occasion.

Chap. XI. *On the Causes of Value.*—The principal object of this chapter is to maintain that cost of production, or the capital expended in production, cannot be resolved into any simpler elements.   Mr. Ricardo, Mr. Mc. Culloch, and Mr. Mill, think that it may, and we are fully satisfied that their analysis is sound.   This, however, is a controversy into which we do not mean to enter ; both because the disquisition would carry us to a greater length than we are inclined to go, and because it is more abstruse than the readers of a review are generally prepared to relish.   It is necessary, however, to show here, also, into what blunders of language the author has fallen in his zealous endeavours to fix charges of lax and inconsistent speaking upon others.

Exchangeable commodities may be divided into two sorts : those upon the value of which competition produces its full effect, and those upon which it does not produce its full effect. We shall confine our observations to the former, because they constitute the general rule.   The cases of exception falling under the latter head, our author thinks extend much further than is generally supposed. But that is a question of fact, not of principle; and, therefore, it does not concern our present purpose.

In answering the question, which forms the subject of this chapter, what are the *causes* of value, he assigns the principal place to cost of production, and talks at great length about " feelings or states of mind."

When a commodity is in demand, and has a class of purchasers, at a certain price, it may always be taken for granted, that they would give a little more for the commodity, if it could not be obtained at that price. What is the cause of this cheapness? Cost of production, of course. Cost of production instead of being the cause of value, is more properly the reverse; a cause of non-value, a cause of the non-existence of a higher degree of value, which, but for cost of production, the commodity would have attained.

Demand is the cause of value. There is no puzzle about that; about which, however, our language-master has puzzled himself through several pages. Cost of production, by preventing demand from raising value above its own level, limits and determines value; and, therefore may, with great correctness, be denominated the Regulator of Value. To call it the Cause, is a metaphysical blunder. As well might a tyro in physical science think to improve our knowledge by calling the pendulum the cause of motion in the hands of the clock. The pendulum performs a function to the motion of the hands of the clock, perfectly analogous to that which is performed by cost of production to the value of commodities.

A comment, in this chapter, on a passage in Mr. Mill's Elements, affords a specimen of that talent of the author which he rates so highly, his *talent at precision.*

He quotes the passage in the work of Mr. Mill as follows:

" To say, indeed, that the value of commodities depends upon capital as the final standard, implies one of the most obvious of all absurdities. Capital is commodities. If the value of commodities, then, depends upon the value of capital, it depends upon the value of commodities; the value of commodities depends upon itself. This is not to point out a standard of value. It is to make an attempt for that purpose clearly and completely abortive."

He then comments in the following words:—" This passage,
" which seems to have a tacit reference to the speculations of
" colonel Torrens, appears to me to show the power of words over
" the clearest and strongest minds.—By the potent magic of a
" term, the value of commodities is first made something single

" and individual; and then it follows of course, that an indi-
" vidual thing cannot depend upon itself as a cause. But this
" is not asserted by those who contend that capital causes or
" determines value. The value of commodities may not be
" capable of depending on itself, but the value of one com-
" modity, which is one thing, may very easily depend on that
" of another, which is a different thing; and if it did not in
" point of fact,—there would be no logical absurdity in asserting
" it. He who maintains that the mutual value of two com-
" modities is chiefly determined by the comparative quantity of
" capital expended in their production, undoubtedly maintains
" that it is determined by the value of preceding commodities;
" and this is quite consistent with the value of those preceding
" commodities having been determined by their comparative
" quantities of producing labour, or by any other cause. The
" latter would be a step further back in the sequence of causes
" and effects. There can be nothing absurd in assigning one
" thing as the proximate cause of an effect, merely because it
" is possible that another may be assigned as its remote cause.
" Mr. Mill's language, too, is unusually lax. He confounds
" the standard with the cause of value. The proposition, that
" the values of commodities are determined by the capitals
" expended in producing them, affirms a cause, but certainly
" does not point out any standard of value; nor would Mr.
" Mill's own doctrine furnish such an auxiliary. A standard,
" whatever meaning it may have in this connexion, must at
" all events be something clearly defined and easily accessible;
" and if Mr. Mill purposes to set up the quantity of labour in a
" commodity from first to last, through all its various meta-
" morphoses, in that capacity, it will be one seldom within
" his reach. In reality, however, the preceding part of his
" section, is occupied in proving labour to be the cause of value;
" and it is only at the conclusion that he deviates into this
" laxity of expression."

" The value of commodities is first made something single
and individual." The author appears to affirm, that Mr. Mill
here speaks of commodities individually, as if he said, that the
value of a particular commodity cannot depend upon the value
of that particular commodity. It is perfectly obvious that Mr.
Mill says no such thing. The passage occurs in that section
of Mr. Mill's book, which inquires " what it is that determines
the quantity in which commodities exchange for one another."
Mr. Mill traces it through it's several stages; first, demand
and supply; secondly, cost of production; so far our author
follows him. Mr. Mill goes on to a third stage, quantity of

labour, to which our author does not follow him. Now, when this author says that exchangeable value depends upon cost of production, does he make " the value of commodities something single and individual;" or does he not? For it is clear that Mr. Mill makes it depend upon labour in the same sense.

He evades the reasoning of Mr. Mill, which applies to commodities in general, by saying that the value of one commodity may depend upon that of another. Who has ever disputed that? Surely not Mr. Mill, who says, only a few paragraphs before that which the author has quoted—" Cost of production, then, regulates the value of commodities." But is it enough, in inquiring what it is that value depends upon, to say, that the value of one thing depends upon the value of a second, that upon the value of a third, and so on? If the inquiry related to sweetness, would not every one laugh at the pretended philosopher who should tell us, that " the sweetness of your tea depends upon the sweetness of the sugar you put into it, and that upon the sweetness of the sugar cane?" Is it not perfectly clear, that the question what sweetness depends upon, is not answered by a reference to a million of things that are sweet.

One number is the measure of another, and one is said to measure another exactly when it is the same. But when we talk of the cause of number, it would be absurd enough to say it is another number. Not more absurd than what we are told by the writers who, assigning the cause of value, tell us it is capital. A thing is of a certain value, when a certain value has been expended upon it. This is very true; but utterly useless when we come to inquire why the *expended* value was such and no more.

It would be just as proper to determine the value of the capital by the value of the produce, as the value of the produce by the value of the capital.

He is a poor metaphysician who does not see the pertinence, at least, of Mr. Mill's reasoning, and also its conclusiveness to the point in hand. It may be, or it may not be, that Mr. Mill has traced to its proper elements the regulator of value: but it is obvious that the man has not made a single step who accounts for the value of one thing, by only giving us a reference to the value of another; and that the man who thinks he has made a step by so doing, has the art, in great perfection, of imposing upon himself. Is not this, as Mr. Mill describes it, to explain value by itself; or, in other words, to tell us that value is value; a notable discovery—the upshot, however, of

this boastful volume; the sum and substance of its grand discoveries.

What should we think of a man who, pretending to be a
metaphysician, should expound the human will, by saying first,
that it is a relation, and next, that one will is produced by another! Does not every body assent to the truth of what is said
by Hobbes [*Humane Nature*, chap. xii. § 5.] "A man can no
more say he will will, than he will will will, and so make an
infinite repetition of the word *will*, which is absurd and insig-
nificant." Let us suppose the question to be—what is motion,
or space, or time? Would it be enough for the explanation of
motion, for example, to say, it is a relation, and to add that
one motion is produced by another; the motion of the billiard
ball by the motion of the mace, and that by the motion of the
hand, and so on; as our political economists of the exchange-
able-value school recommend to us with respect to value. A
passage relative to this very subject of motion, from an author
who hardly did justice to his own metaphysical powers, is
fraught with instruction to writers, who thus easily provide for
their own satisfaction.—"And now, perhaps, it may not be
amiss to inquire what physical motion is. Some philosophers
have found a short method here, by telling us 'tis a simple
idea, and therefore cannot be defined. Others, with more
reason, have called it hard to be defined, a circumstance not
unusual with other subjects equally obvious, there being nothing more different, both in accuracy and truth, than that
apprehension which is adequate to the purposes of the vulgar,
and that which ought to satisfy the investigation of a philosopher."—Harris *Philos. Arrangements*, chap. xvi.

It is curious enough, that the grand cause of the puzzle in
regard to value, and of the difficulties in expounding will,
motion, space, and time, should be the same : viz. the want of
distinct names for the *relatio*, and the *fundamentum relationis*.

" Mr. Mill's language, too, is unusually lax. He confounds
the standard with the cause of value."—This is worse than the
usual blundering of the author in his charges of laxity. In the
first place, in Mr. Mill's sense of the term *cause* of value,
namely *demand*, the author surely does not mean that Mr. Mill
confounds standard and cause. In the next place, it is very
evident from Mr. Mill's language, that by standard he means
regulator, and that by regulator he means cost of production,
which this author says is the cause of value. So that Mr.
Mill did no wrong in confounding, in this author's phrase, the
standard and cause, since he did no more than consider the
same thing as the same, or a certain thing the same as itself.

This specimen will shew, that an examination of this author's precision in detail, would yield some amusement; but we cannot afford to track him any further.

We have spoken of this book freely, and as we think it deserves; not only because it is " much ado about nothing," and, in every department of literature, that is a spirit which ought to be repressed; but because in Political Economy it is peculiarly noxious. While the knowledge of the science is still confined to a comparatively small number, it has two powerful classes of enemies, the interested, and the ignorant; who, we daily see, assume to themselves a merit in decrying it. One of the handles which best answers their purpose, is, the diversity of opinion which seems to prevail among those who pretend to the knowledge of the science. What better proof, cry its enemies, of the uncertainty of its conclusions, and of the folly of listening to its vain and fanatical admirers? This handle is made, and held out to them, by those writers, who, from lack of knowledge, or abundance of conceit, fancy they have made discoveries where there are none to be made, who confound diversities of expression with discordance of ideas, and magnify into importance objections, which are either trivial, or totally without foundation.   As, however, it sometimes happens, that a book may be said to be better than its author, in the present case we think it but just to say that the author is better, in our opinion a great deal better, than his book. We recognize sufficient marks, if not of a strong, of a cultivated, and even of a candid mind, though its candour is a little subject to injury from its self-complacence. His mistake has been, a mistake not unnatural to a juvenile author, such as we imagine this to be, of supposing he understood a difficult subject, when he should have performed a little longer the functions of a learner. We predict, that at a future time, we shall have a much more agreeable task to perform, that of bestowing upon him a large measure of well merited applause.

A LETTER TO A POLITICAL ECONOMIST

A

LETTER

TO

A POLITICAL ECONOMIST:

OCCASIONED BY

An article in the Westminster Review

ON

THE SUBJECT OF VALUE.

BY THE AUTHOR

OF

THE CRITICAL DISSERTATION ON VALUE

THEREIN REVIEWED.

Agedum pauca accipe contra. — HORACE.

LONDON:

PRINTED FOR R. HUNTER,

72, ST. PAUL'S CHURCHYARD.

1826.

ADVERTISEMENT.

THE article in the Westminser Review, which occasioned the following Letter, appeared in the ninth number of that journal, published about six months ago ; and the greater part of these remarks in reply to it were written immediately afterwards. Circumstances, which it is not needful to mention, have postponed the publication of them to the present time ; a delay, which the author does not regret, as it has afforded him the opportunity of giving the whole subject a deliberate re-examination.

Nov. 17, 1826.

A

LETTER

TO

A POLITICAL ECONOMIST,

&c. &c.

MY DEAR SIR;

I promised to lay before you a
few remarks on an article in the Westminster
Review, which takes for its text my Critical
Dissertation on the Nature, Measures, and
Causes of Value. You appeared to think, that
the credit of the Dissertation could not be ma-
terially affected by such a piece of criticism in
the opinion of any one, who had studied the
subject. On this point I am disposed to accord
with you. In the estimation of thinking men,
the merits of an argumentative work can seldom
be permanently either much enhanced or much

depressed by any thing extrinsic. The final result will be tolerably accurate, although some delay and disturbance may occur in the process: and surely a man of any proper ambition would despise a reputation, that could not stand the severest gale that ever blew against the fragile bark of a poor author. It would be a feeble gratification to preserve a precarious buoyancy, by the forbearance of hostility on the one hand, or the support of friendship on the other.

Entertaining these views, I write the present remarks, not so much in the expectation of modifying the ultimate decision, which will be pronounced on the Dissertation and the review of it by competent judges, as to bring the materials on which their opinion will be formed more clearly and prominently before them, and thus facilitate the result, which is sure to take place.

In proceeding to examine the statements and reasonings of this review, it is impossible to overlook the commencement. The spirit in which the critic enters on his task is an admirable preparation for the due performance of it. He had heard of the book, and of its size; and, without further data, instantly applying a ready measure of merit in common use with both dunce and philosopher, to wit, the extent of his own knowledge, which appears on this occasion to have most luxuriantly expanded itself to twenty pages, he finds the work guilty of at least one hundred and eighty pages (fractions neglected) too many, and condemns it at once to run the gauntlet of his ruffled feelings. Nor does he stop at the fact of this actual excess. The dimensions of the book dilate before his excited imagination, and he levels the heavy artillery of a quotation against it as if the really small volume lay before him in all the terrific amplitude of a quarto *.

* " Before we had seen this production, and when we had heard only of its size, we more than suspected what we have found. We knew that any one, who understood the subject, would say all he had to say upon it, in twenty, instead of two hundred pages. ' A very long discussion, says an intelligent author, ' is one of the most effectual veils of fallacy. Sophistry, like poison, is at once detected and nauseated, when presented to us in a concentrated form. But a fallacy, which, when stated barely, in a few sentences, would not deceive a child, may deceive half the

The temper manifested in the sequel is worthy of this spirited commencement. You were perhaps too severe in terming the article " a continuous snarl," although I will not pretend to deny a remote analogy between the criticism in question and that inelegant indication of disagreeable feeling. It is to be feared, that the critic, whoever he be, has had his passions irritated, or his complacency disturbed, by something inadvertently let fall in the course of the treatise, which he attempts to review : a circumstance, which I most sincerely lament.   In an argumentative work, who would not wish to avoid producing needless irritation, and be glad if errors could be rectified in such a way as would save the most sensitive vanity from a wound ?

It is only on the supposition of some cause of this kind, that we can account for the expedients to which the critic has had recourse.

world, if diluted in a quarto volume.' " — *Westminster Review*, p. 157.   The reviewer has here most triumphantly proved, that Mr. Ricardo himself is not to be ranked amongst those who have understood the subject, since his chapter on Value extends over fifty pages, and the other topics connected with it occupy above fifty more.

You must have been frequently amused by similar exemplifications of that artfulness, that dexterity, that cunning, which is manifested by some of the less dignified passions of our nature in the pursuit of their own gratification.   You must have smiled too at the contrast between the transparency of the artifices with which the passion seeks to cover itself from observation, and the full security in which it seems to be, that its proceedings are perfectly concealed.

In the present instance, the critic, scarcely conscious perhaps of the principle which ac-tuates him, appears to understand sufficiently well the art of avenging himself by the common expedients of plausible colouring and profuse assertion ; of using terms of personality and reproach in discussions abstruse enough surely to preserve them from the interference of spleen ; and of seeking extraneous topics by which he may, according to the direction of Hamilton in his Parliamentary Logic, " wound the opponent."

Thus the author of the Dissertation is politely nicknamed a " language-master ;" is charged with shallow views, with writing plau-

sible jargon, with mere logomachy, with a perpetual *ignoratio elenchi*, with a parade and
ostentation of controversy, with fighting against
a shadow. A confusion is said with much
elegance " to reign in his brains," and self-
satisfaction and complacency I presume in his
heart. As to young writers, it is extremely
mortifying to be told, that their productions
savour of their age, the author is affectedly
considered (in defiance I fear of the parish register) as juvenile. An earnestness in argument,
which is generally regarded as somewhat laudable, is characterised as an intense persuasion
of the importance of what he is about. Precision of language, or the attempt to attain it,
is sneered at in italics. Metaphysical being a
term, which has something of the same oppro-
brium attached to it as theoretical and visionary,
that epithet is liberally bestowed*. Free animadversions are exaggerated into abuse, and
perfect freedom from *awe*, either of Mr. Ri-

---

* " A man's conceptions," says Mr. Bentham, " must
be woefully indistinct, or his vocabulary deplorably scanty,
if, be the bad measure [or doctrine] what it may, he cannot contrive to give intimation of what, in his view, there

cardo's intellect or that of any of his followers,
is converted into measureless contempt. Other
charges are lavishly scattered : "blundering,"
"lack of knowledge and abundance of conceit,"
"much ado about nothing," and similar phrases,
render this critique a valuable magazine for
those, who do not disdain to handle the
common weapons of critical offence.

Such is the language and such are the expedients to which critics think proper to de-
scend. Whether they are indications of a
suitable spirit for the examination of an abstruse work; whether they exhibit any thing
of the moderation of a man of sense, or the
temper of a philosopher; whether they are
disgraceful to him who has employed them,
or to him against whom they are directed, every
one can decide for himself.

It is well remarked by Mr. Bentham, that
"nothing but laborious application and a clear
and comprehensive intellect can enable a man

is bad in it, without employing an epithet, the effect of
which is to hold out, as an object of contempt, the very
act of thinking, the operation of *thought* itself." — *The
Book of Fallacies, p.* 298.

on any given subject to employ successfully
relevant arguments drawn from the subject itself. To employ personalities, neither labour
nor intellect is required : in this sort of contest
the most idle and the most ignorant are quite
on a par with, if not superior to, the most in-
dustrious and the most highly-gifted individi-
duals. Nothing can be more convenient for
those who would speak without the trouble of
thinking; the same ideas are brought forward
over and over again, and all that is required is
to vary the turn of expression*."

There are as many artifices in criticism as
in political discussion, and many of Mr. Bentham's remarks in his Book of Fallacies might
be applied with slight modification to the art
of reviewing.

It would be rendering a service to the public, if any of that praiseworthy class of writers,
who have employed themselves in arranging
and familiarising the speculations of men of
more original minds, would adapt Mr. Bentham's exposition of political sophistry to the
practices of criticism. No one perhaps would

* Book of Fallacies, p. 141.

accomplish this task better than the author of those articles in the Encyclopedia Britannica, which have so clearly if not very eloquently explained the views of the greatest writer of the age on Legislation. We should then be able, on reading a review, to do what Mr. Bentham predicts we shall be enabled to accomplish at some future period on hearing a speech; namely, instantly to mark a fallacy or unfair artifice by its appropriate appellation; and as in the House of Commons " a voice shall be heard " (to adopt the language of Mr. Bentham) " followed if need be by voices in scores crying aloud, ' Stale ! Stale ! Fallacy of Authority ! Fallacy of Distrust * !' so in reading the Edinburgh, Quarterly, Monthly, or Westminster Review, there would instinctively rise to the lips the exclamation, Fallacy of Spleen ! Fallacy of Confusion ! Question-begging appellatives ! Hobgoblin argument ! Wasp-reply !

The expressions of irritation which I have noticed you will probably think are not the most reprehensible parts of the article in

* Book of Fallacies, p. 410.

question.   Every one will be disposed to overlook the transient effusions of splenetic feeling,
and to regard the subject of them with com-
passion, as suffering under a paroxysm which
naturally exhausts itself and leaves him as
harmless as before.   It is true "*nescit vox missa
reverti*;" but this only establishes a further claim on our pity, since it is an additional
misfortune when the irritation of the moment
has embodied itself in words, and thus become
the source of permanent humiliation.

It is not easy to exercise equal forbearance
in the case of palpable misrepresentation, although I shall be able to suggest an apology,
which even in this case may moderate the indignation of the upright and candid mind.
Amongst several instances of the nature alluded to, the following is not the least conspicuous : —

"Chap X.   *On the Difference between a
Measure and a Cause of Value.*   The author
charges all writers but himself with the absurdity of confounding these two things."

He, who is unacquainted with the candour
of criticism or the logic of system, could not

possibly imagine that so far from this being the case, the author of the Dissertation ascribes to a preceding writer (the author of the Templars' Dialogues) the merit of having clearly pointed out this distinction.

The assertion, therefore, that the author charges all writers but himself with confounding these two things seems to be a slight departure from the strictness of correct representation.

Another instance in which the reviewer trespasses beyond the limits usually observed by the accurate and discreet is the following. The author of the Dissertation says, in his first chapter, that the value of a commodity can be expressed only by a quantity of some other commodity, and that a rise or fall in its value means, that it exchanges for a greater or smaller quantity of that other commodity than it did before; to which he adds a remark, that "simple as these results appear we have seen that it is possible to overlook them."

In reply to this the reviewer, with all the suavity of manner which embellishes his writings, breaks out, "we affirm that nobody has ever overlooked them."

It is convenient to meet with an adversary who rejects the unworthy maxim which teaches discretion to be the better part of valour, and commits himself to the contest with uncalculating temerity. Could any one but a writer of this complexion hazard such an assertion as the above when the very chapter, one of the positions of which he so unhesitatingly contradicts, furnishes an instance in which the truth of the propositions in question is not only overlooked but in fact positively denied? If you will turn to that chapter you will find that the author of the Templars' Dialogues repeatedly affirms, that " there is no necessary connexion at all or of any kind between the quantity commanded and the value commanding." And again, "I presume that in your use, and in every body's use of the word value, a high value ought to purchase a high value, and that it will be very absurd if it should not. But as to purchasing a great quantity, *that* condition is surely not included in any man's idea of value."

It cannot be urged here, you will observe, that the writer considers himself as using value in a peculiar technical sense: he considers his assertions true in the common acceptation of the term, " in any man's idea of it." In the common acceptation of the term then he denies that the value of a commodity has any connexion with the quantity of any other commodity, and consequently he must deny my definitions of the terms rise and fall, which are asserted by the reviewer to be identical propositions, and which nobody he says ever overlooked.

The same laudable figure of speech, the same divergence from the strict line of correct representation occurs in a subsequent passage. " The author says here" (writes the reviewer in reference to the sixth chapter), " that value is exchangeable value, and of exchangeable value there neither is nor can be any invariable measure. He imputes the absurdity of denying this proposition largely to all political economists preceding himself. In this, however, he indulges an idea of his own superiority, for which he is indebted solely to his own imagination. " Never was there a more beautiful exemplification of the candour of controversy than the charge here brought against me.

What is the fact? Far from imputing to all economists the absurdity of denying that there neither is nor can be any invariable measure, I do not in this chapter impute it to a single one. I make no imputation of the sort. On the contrary, in a preceding chapter, I had already said, " Mr. Ricardo so far agrees with the view here taken, as to maintain the impossibility of finding any commodity of invariable value ; " and in the sixth Chapter itself I quote from his Principles of Political Economy the very passage in which this impossibility is asserted.

The impossibility of a measure of invariable value has been likewise maintained by the Earl of Lauderdale, Col. Torrens, and others : and although the contrary has been held by Adam Smith and Mr. Malthus, the merest novice in political economy could not possibly run into the mistake of imputing the latter opinion to all economists. It is an error into which even a reviewer in all the rashness of his irritability could hardly precipitate himself. What in the chapter referred to I have really imputed to political economists is a proposition of a very different character. I have not said that they deny the impossibility of an invariable measure, but that they maintain, almost without exception, invariableness to be necessary to constitute a measure of value, while I contend that invariableness has nothing to do with it. There must be something exceedingly peculiar in the moral or intellectual structure of a mind capable of confounding two propositions between which there is not a single point of resemblance. What renders the matter more remarkable is, that this false representation is made the ground both of a preliminary charge of *ignoratio elenchi* against the author of the Dissertation, and of a concluding sarcasm against his conceit.

These misrepresentations, you will observe, are in direct opposition to the real facts of each case : others present themselves in the form of exaggerations, and although from this circumstance they may wear some colour of truth, they are actually quite as successful in diverging from accuracy as the rest. Of these the charge of abusing Mr. Ricardo I shall briefly notice, not having any vehement inclination to be regarded as one of a class in which the reviewer's self control seems insufficient to preserve him from being ranked, and to which he seems anxious to reduce every body else; probably on the principle that actuated the fox in the fable, who, having suffered a mutilation not of the most reputable kind, endeavoured to involve his fellows in the same ignominious misfortune. No one who has any tolerable share of self respect would wish to be classed among those who cannot discuss an important subject with temper, nor enter into controversy without descending to language, the disgrace of which recoils on him who utters it. When therefore the reviewer represents the author of the Dissertation as " abusing" Mr. Ricardo, as " bestowing vituperation" upon him, as " charging him with the highest degree of intellectual culpability, " as " pouring upon him contempt to which there is no measure," I am not inclined to let such a representation pass without exposing its real character. All that is necessary for this purpose is a simple statement of facts. The unsuspicious reader will be surprised to learn, that the strongest expressions unfavourable to

Mr. Ricardo in the Dissertation are the following : "there was an original perplexity and confusion in some fundamental ideas from which he
was never able to extricate himself;" and, in
another passage, " his elaborate chapter on this
subject" (value and riches) " appears to me to
be a remarkable tissue of errors and unmeaning
conclusions arising from his fundamental misconception of the nature of value." Other similar expressions might be cited, but these are I
believe the most forcible of any to the dis-
paragement of Mr. Ricardo to be found in the
volume ; and as they neither contain any term
of wanton censure, nor are mere unsupported
assertions, but are followed by explanations of
the grounds on which they are made, they will
be generally regarded as keeping within the
limits of fair criticism. From all this the reader
will probably conclude in opposition to the
critic, that if there is no measure to the contempt
which the author of the Dissertation bestows
on Mr. Ricardo, it is for the most excellent reason that there is no contempt bestowed at all.
He will be further confirmed in this conclusion when he learns, that as there was no

hesitation in that work to pronounce an unfavourable judgment when necessary, so there
was no reluctance to express a favourable
opinion when the opportunity presented itself.
Thus in one place Mr. Ricardo is termed an
eminent writer, in another a man of strong faculties, in a third the possessor of remarkable
logical powers.   It is not every one, it appears,
who is able to comprehend that impartiality,
which can distinguish faults and expose errors
(faults and errors inseparable from the progressive nature of human knowledge), while
it entertains and expresses a sincere respect for
the mind from which they have emanated,
along with successful processes of reasoning
and discoveries of truth.

The foregoing are a few instances of the misrepresentations scattered through the review,
and for which it seems at first sight difficult to
account on any principle adequate to repress
the contempt or indignation of the reader.
They admit, nevertheless, of several explanations tending to soften the moral turpitude of
the offence.   Some of them may be imputed to
a courageous neglect on the part of the reviewer

to possess himself of what is considered, by humbler individuals, a requisite qualification in all critical enterprises. He seems to have magnanimously disregarded the convenience and security arising to a critic from a competent acquaintance with the work which he makes the subject of his animadversions. While this high-minded omission will account for several of his trespasses, his other deviations from rigid accuracy of statement may take refuge in an explanation which as soon as it is suggested to any one acquainted with a certain school of Political Economy will convert his indignation into a much lighter and pleasanter emotion.

He will recognize in them the achievements of that dexterous logic which he has already learnt to admire, and which holds pretty nearly the same relation to the true art of reasoning that the skill of the juggler, or the miraculous magic of the harlequin, bears to the useful arts of life. Under this dialectical power of transmutation, plurality is converted into unity, effects into causes, nothing into something, propositions into their opposites: one particular cause becomes the *sole* regu-

lating principle of value amidst the admitted
operation of other causes; a commodity is
reconverted into the toil which produced it*;
additional labour, in defiance of bars and
bungs, pertinaciously settles upon a cask of
wine which has been scrupulously preserved
from the touch of human hands in the security
of a well locked cellar†; and as the climax of
this sleight of intellect, an author's declara-
tions empty themselves of their identity and
become the opposite of what they are!

This art of transmutation seems to assume
in many cases the features of imagination, and
things are gravely put forth as true which teem
with all the characteristics, except the graces,
of fiction. An instance of this kind presents
itself almost at the beginning of the review,
and as it involves the main point of the con-

---

* "Capital is commodities." "Capital is allowed to
be correctly described under the title of hoarded labour."
— *Mill.*

† " If the wine which is put in the cellar is increased
in value one-tenth by being kept a year, one-tenth more
of labour may be correctly considered as having been expended upon it." — *Mill.*

troversy I shall task your patience by quoting the entire passage : —

" We are willing to admit, in behalf of this author, a matter of some importance, which he himself appears to be little aware of, that it is impossible to expound the doctrines of political economy in language altogether unexceptionable, without a new nomenclature ; or giving such a technical, and unusual meaning to old terms, as would certainly occasion more obstruction to a learner, than using language as nearly as possible in its ordinary acceptation, when some degree of laxity is hardly to be avoided. This only becomes a vice requiring philosophical rebuke, when it introduces confusion of ideas ; that is, when a word of double meaning is so used, that the ideas belonging to one sense are suggested, when the truth of the proposition requires the ideas which are comprehended in the other. To make this clear by an example:—the word ' dog' signifies two things ; an animal, and a star. The words are never improperly applied, when the context shows in which of the senses it is that the word is employed. But if the context is such, that we are under-

stood as speaking of the animal; as if we
should say, 'the dog has two ears and four
feet;' and then we should suddenly add,
the dog also shines,' this would evidently be
an abuse of the terms, and justly censurable.

"Mr. Ricardo used the word 'value' in two
senses. He did so *avowedly*. *It has always
been remarked, as well by those who have
adopted, as by those who have opposed, his doctrines.* Mr. Ricardo conceived, erroneously
we think, *that it would be good to attempt
the introduction of more precision into the
language of political economy, by giving a
technical meaning to the word 'value.'* But
he did not imagine, for that reason, that he
could altogether dispense with the use of the
word in its more ordinary acceptation; nor
could he have done so without such innovations of language as would have been very inconvenient to his readers, as well as himself.

"It frequently happens in fact, that when
a new word, or a new acceptation of a word,
is proposed, *the best and sometimes the only
expedient for procuring it admission is, to use
it along with the more ordinary and lax expressions; when the value of it becoming more*

and more known, it gradually supersedes the less appropriate expressions.

" Had the term ' value' been the best that could have been chosen for the peculiar and technical sense in which Mr. Ricardo employed it, which we have always thought it was not, still it would, in our opinion, have been judicious to use the word in the sense of exchangeable value, in those passages where he could not avoid that use of it without further innovations in language. It would have been a sufficient reason for this, had there been no other, that too many innovations should not be attempted at once, unless where there happens to be, as in Chemistry, a predisposition to admit them. Had Mr. Ricardo ventured upon more, his book would have been still more embarrassing to the learner than it is. In introducing a new meaning of a term, without being able to dispense altogether with the old, it is incumbent upon writers to keep them distinct, and make their context always indicate clearly in which of the two meanings the word should be received. *This, we think, Mr. Ricardo has done, with extraordinary vigilance and success.*"

In the midst of the dry discussions of Political

Economy, a touch of the imagination is like an oasis in the desert. I have seldom met with a purer fancy-piece than the whole of this representation. Poetry and Science occasionally appear to change characters. A modern minstrel tells us, that

"Song is but the eloquence of truth ;"

and here we have strong evidence that philosophy sometimes degenerates into the colouring of fiction.

Could Mr. Ricardo revisit the scene of his labours, he would be astonished at this representation of his meaning and intentions ; and while he would not fail to admire the speciousness of the defence set up in his behalf, he would most certainly feel no disposition to incur the dubious credit which it would entail upon him.

In fact nothing is more easy, when an author has used a word in two senses without being conscious of it, than for any one to make out a plausible case to save his reputation. Begin by asserting without proof (for that would encumber you) that he had the two meanings distinctly in view, notwithstanding the circumstance that only one appears in his definition, and that he was in fact wonderfully successful in making them visible. Cite no instance yourself; but if any objections are brought against any of his conclusions on the ground of the original definition, boldly assert that, in the passage referred to, he used the term in the second meaning and never dreamed of employing it in the first. And if any instance is brought in which the second meaning will not apply, immediately revert to the other. By this intellectual *see-saw* you will gain a double advantage, for it will appear not only that your client has had a perspicacious discernment of the subject, but that his opponents have been employing themselves in drawing conclusions against his doctrines in which he himself would perfectly coincide. The objections are good if the term is taken in one sense, but neither he nor any one else ever dreamed of taking it in that sense, and therefore the objections are pure logomachy, fighting with shadows, conclusions which no one ever disputed, instances of mere ostentation and parade of controversy.

But the reviewer is not even content with

all this, but enters into a defence of the practice of using the same word in two senses. Laying Heaven and Earth under contribution for an illustration, he shows how very innocent it may be by the instance of the word dog, which he tells us signifies both an animal and a star, and yet the term is never improperly applied, nor are the ideas ever blended. He is perfectly right: stars and quadrupeds have passed under the same name without being confounded, without any one gravely maintaining "stellam latrare quia stella quædam Canis dicitur." Nay he might have pushed the matter further, for not only have stars been called dogs but many heterogeneous things have been called stars, and yet no obscurity or confusion seems to have ensued. These luminaries of Heaven are (to borrow the language of a noble poet)

" A beauty and a mystery, and create
In us such love and reverence from afar
That fortune, fame, power, life, have named themselves
　　a star."

A most triumphant proof of the harmlessness of calling two things by the same name.

I would beseech the critic, however, to recollect the way in which all confusion has been
obviated, and to consider seriously whether in
the case of the term " dog," as applied to a
four footed animal and a star, the impossibility
of confounding the two things has not arisen
from one being an opaque and the other a
luminous body, and both of determinate figures;
and whether the same practice could possibly
be equally harmless in the case of the term
" value," when the two ideas for which it stands
in the minds of certain economists are both of
them evidently destitute of native light and
definite outline ?

I would beg him further to consider whether a more appropriate illustration of the
subject would not be attained by dismissing
the star altogether, descending from the clouds,
and substituting the hypothesis that he (the
reviewer) kept two dogs, both of which from
one of those whims incident to great minds,
he called by the same name : and, in this case,
whether when he summoned one dog to his
side, the wrong animal, owing to this parsimony
of appellation, might not make his appearance,

or whether both might not come running to him at once, quarrelling perhaps for precedence, and urging discordant claims to his notice, while his hand, stretched out to bestow the usual caress, remained suspended in all the fixed irresolution of the ass between the two bundles of hay, or perchance oscillated irregularly from one to the other, or what would be still worse, received an unforeseen wound from the mordacious eagerness of the rival claimants.

Seriously, it would be quite as much as could be demanded, if the exposition of Mr. Ricardo's views above cited were met by simply pronouncing it altogether the progeny of the reviewer's imagination ; but I shall attempt to exhibit its true character at full length.

It represents Mr. Ricardo, you will observe, as deliberately and purposely using the word value in two senses, one a lax and ordinary, the other a peculiar and technical sense, and this with the express design of introducing precision into the language of political economy : further, that he always successfully indicated by the context in which of the senses he wished the term to be understood; and that his double employment of it has always been remarked by his supporters as well as opponents.

In contradiction to these assertions, and to the tenor of the whole passage, I shall endeavour to show,

1. That the use of the word value in two meanings by Mr. Ricardo has not been always remarked both by his supporters and opponents.

2. That Mr. Ricardo did not avowedly use the word in a double sense, but on the contrary professedly used it in one sense only.

3. That Mr. Ricardo did not keep the two meanings distinct and make the context clearly indicate in which of the two meanings the word should be received, and this for the simplë reason that he was unconscious of employing it in more than one.

4. That Mr. Ricardo did not consider himself as employing the word value in any

new, peculiar, and technical sense, and therefore could never entertain the ingenious design here imputed to him of giving more precision to the language of political economy by the profound expedient of using the same term sometimes in one sense and sometimes in another.

5. That Mr. Ricardo's employment of the term value in what the reviewer styles a new, peculiar, and technical sense, or in other words Mr. Ricardo's unconscious departure from his own definition, had not even the merit of originality, as a similar unconscious departure from the received definition of the term is to be observed in the economists who preceded him.

It is fortunate that in the statements of the reviewer on this subject there is the valuable quality of explicitness. There can be no mistake as to what he means, no misconception of the position which he has taken. On consulting the review, nevertheless, you will perceive one lamentable deficiency — a de-

ficiency which I greatly deplore : there are
unfortunately no instances adduced in support
of the representations there given of Mr. Ricardo's views and meaning. All rests on the
assertions of the critic : he seems to labour
under some indomitable shyness of proof.
Surely, if Mr. Ricardo avowedly used the word
in two senses, it would be easy to cite his
avowal : if he successfully made the context
clearly indicate the meaning, it would be easy
to take his first chapter and show how invariably this was the case.

Such a procedure was the more necessary
as, in the Dissertation under review, a particular citation is given of Mr. Ricardo's definition, and an attempt is made to show, by
quotations from his work, that the second meaning of the term was unconsciously introduced ;
that Mr. Ricardo was not fully aware of it ;
that he lapsed from his own definition without
an adequate apprehension of what he was
about.

To any one who replies to such an analysis
and examination by mere assertion, no courtesy
can deem an answer necessary ; but the task

is, in the present case, so easy that there is no
inducement to decline it.

1. First, let us examine the assertion, that the
   employment of the word in two senses by
   Mr. Ricardo has always been remarked
   by both his supporters and opponents.

Two of Mr. Ricardo's principal followers,
who have expounded his doctrines in elementary works, are Mr. Mill and Mr. M'Culloch.
On a careful perusal of the first and second
edition of the Elements of the former, and of
the article Political Economy written by the
latter for the Encyclopedia Britannica, I can
find no intimation whatever in either of these
works, that the term value was employed in
two senses by Mr. Ricardo. It might naturally be expected that if so important a word
had been employed in such a manner by the
most celebrated economist of the day, thus
necessarily giving a colouring to his doctrines
and his language, two elementary works, pro-
fessing to explain the most recent doctrines of
the science, would apprise us of the circumstance, were it merely to warn the student
against any ambiguity to which it might lead.

Not only however is there no intimation given that Mr. Ricardo used the word in two distinct acceptations, but not the slightest expression is dropped throughout the whole of these treatises from which it could be inferred that the writers were aware of the term being liable to such a double use.

This circumstance would be more remarkable in the case of Mr. M°Culloch, if the assertion of the critic were true, because he has bestowed considerable pains at the outset of his treatise to guard his readers against the confusion arising from another double employment of the term value, namely in the sense of value in use as well as of value in exchange ; an ambiguity first pointed out by the author of the Wealth of Nations.

" To confound these different sorts of value," says Mr. M°Culloch, " would evidently lead to the most erroneous conclusions. And hence, to avoid all chance of error from mistaking the sense of so important a word as *value*, we shall never use it except to signify exchangeable worth, or value in exchange*."

* Encyclop. Britt. Sup. Vol. vi, p. 217.

Now if Mr. McCulloch had been aware of a third sense of the word, if he had " remarked" that Mr. Ricardo used it in a peculiar technical sense, distinct from value in exchange, it would have been extraordinary indeed not to take the opportunity of apprising his readers of it when he was professedly engaged in clearing the term from ambiguity.

There is also presumptive proof that Mr. Mill had not " remarked" the use of the term in two senses by Mr. Ricardo. In his sections, which treat professedly of exchangeable value, that is, power of purchasing, he gives us no intimation of the existence of any other sort of value; and yet he affirms that a commodity can " remain an accurate measure of value only if it remain of the same value itself." Here, according to the reviewer, Mr. Mill must have passed from the sense of exchangeable value to the " peculiar technical" meaning; for he (the reviewer) tells us, that when Mr. Ricardo asserts that a measure must be invariable in value, " he does not mean invariable in its power of purchasing, quite the contrary," and it may be presumed that his followers are entitled to the benefit of the same remark when they maintain the necessity of invariableness.

But if Mr. Mill has used the word in Mr. Ricardo's peculiar and technical sense, without any intimation to his readers, and in a section, too, where he is professedly treating of exchangeable value, there is only one inference to be drawn; namely, that he did not remark the use of the word in two senses either by Mr. Ricardo, or what is still more extraordinary by himself.

In the third edition of Mill's Elements, and in the second and amended edition of the article Political Economy, published in a separate form by Mr. McCulloch, there are indeed explanations introduced for the first time intimating that the term value is used in two senses, one having reference to the power of purchasing, the other to the quantity of producing labour. Both these editions, however, appeared after the authors had seen the Critical Dissertation on Value, to which indeed one of the writers (Mr. McCulloch) has had the candour to refer; the inference therefore is, that these explanations were introduced in consequence of the remarks in that work, and it is scarcely possible to imagine that these writers were previously at all aware of any double meaning of the term in the writings of Mr. Ricardo.

But there is a still stronger and more direct refutation of the reviewer's assertion, that the employment of the word by Mr. Ricardo in two senses was always remarked by those who adopted his doctrines.

The author of the Templars' Dialogues, who as an expounder of Mr. Ricardo's views on this subject takes his place in the first rank, and against whose exposition many of my strictures were directed, far from agreeing with the Westminster critic, affirms that " Mr. Ricardo sternly insists on the true sense of the word value, and (what is still more unusual to most men) insists on using it but in *one* sense *."

The next authority, which I have to produce, is if possible still more to the purpose. You will be startled when I name the Westminster

---

* London Magazine, p. 344.

Review itself. Yet so it is. In an express defence of Mr. Ricardo against the Quarterly Review there is the following passage, which I did not see till my own treatise had been committed to the press : otherwise I might have been tempted to support my opinions by so *indisputable* an authority.

"Value is a relative term : if it is not this, it is nothing : if any one talks about *absolute value, or any other kind of value than exchangeable value we know not what he means**."

It appears, then, that in the year 1825 the Westminster Reviewers could not understand any one who talked about any kind of value but exchangeable value.

In the year 1826, however, they discover, not only that there is another kind of value distinct from exchangeable value, but that they had always remarked it ! And, far from not being able to understand any one who talks about it, they regard Mr. Ricardo as having talked about it with great perspicuity.

Is this—can it be—an instance of the new rhetorical figure called *see-saw*, on which the

* Westminster Review, Vol. iii, p. 224.

Westminster Reviewers delight to expatiate when they detect it in the writings of others? The see-saw of private passions is quite as worthy of admiration as that of political interests.

What then is the unavoidable conclusion from all these citations? If we find expositions of Mr. Ricardo's doctrines omitting all notice of any double use of the term; if we find another exposition of his doctrines possitively asserting that he sternly insisted on using the term in one sense and one sense only; and if we see the Westminster Reviewers themselves unreservedly declaring that they know not what any one means who talks of any kind of value but exchangeable value, have we not conclusive proof that Mr. Ricardo's followers were entirely ignorant of his having employed the word in two senses?

Would it be possible for professed disciples of Mr. Ricardo to write in this way if the assertion of the reviewers were true, that the use of the word in two senses by that writer had always been remarked both by his supporters and opponents?

2. Let us proceed, in the second place, to examine the assertion, that Mr. Ricardo himself avowedly used the word in two senses, and was of course perfectly aware of both.

If an author purposely uses an important word in two senses, particularly a word which designates the subject of his reasonings, we should naturally expect to find such an intention manifested at the time he professes to define the said word. It would be a very extraordinary sort of procedure, if when engaged in the preliminary business of definition, he should not only suppress all intimation of his design to make a double use of the term, but lead us to suppose that there was only one sense in which he purposed to employ it. This would at all events be a strange way of *avowedly* using the word in two meanings. But this course of proceeding might be alleged against Mr. Ricardo, if the assertion of the reviewers were correct. He begins by adopting the language of Adam Smith, which ascribes indeed two meanings to the word value, namely value in use and value in exchange : but in consonance with the practice of other writers on Political Economy and the design of the science, the consideration of the former is dropped, and consequently the only remaining kind of value is the latter*. In this preliminary adjustment of the meaning of the term, there is not the slightest hint of a third meaning : we have no intimation given us that we have still two kinds of value left on hand : and as this was the proper place to avow his intention of using the word in two senses, we may presume that he had no intention of the sort.

Further, it sometimes happens that an author's view of his subject may be gathered from the titles of his chapters or divisions. It is generally conceived that he places them there to inform his readers what he is writing about. In the present instance Mr. Ricardo, not con-

---

* It is to this distinction that the reviewer's quotation from the Oxford Rudiments of Logic is applicable. Value in the sense of value in exchange is a technical term of precise meaning " vox artis, ex communi sermone sumpta," while in the sense of utility or importance it is " vox in communi usu posita."

tent with giving us in the body of his first
section a definition of the sense in which he
employs the word value, has actually explained
his acceptation of it in the title; "the value of
a commodity, or the quantity of any other commodity for which it will exchange." There
can be no doubt, therefore, that the author in
this section considered himself as treating of
value in exchange alone; and that if he used
the word in any other sense, it was not only
unconsciously and without design, but in direct
contradiction of his own declaration at the
outset. If we track him in the other parts of
his book we shall in vain look for any avowal
of using the word in two senses. But on this
point to say more would be useless. If there is
any avowal of the kind, the proof of it is simple.
His followers have only to cite it.

3. But if Mr. Ricardo did not make any
avowal of using the word in two senses,
it might still be true that he was conscious
of so using it, and that he always indicated by the context in which sense he
wished it to be received. Not avowing

his design of using it in two senses might be merely an informality (a strange one it is true) at the commencement, subsequently remedied by extraordinary vigilance and success in distinguishing in each instance the acceptation in which it was employed.

Let us do what the reviewer himself ought to have done before he hazarded this eulogium on Mr. Ricardo's extraordinary success in the use of the term; let us try how far it is borne out by the fact; let us put to the test some of the positions in which the term is employed.

" Adam Smith," says he, " who so accurately defined the original source of exchangeable value, and who was bound in consistency to maintain, that all things became more or less valuable in proportion as more or less labour was bestowed on their production, has himself erected another standard measure of value, and speaks of things being more or less valuable in proportion as they will exchange for more or less of this standard measure. Sometimes he speaks of corn, at other times of labour as a standard measure; not the quantity of

labour bestowed on the production of any object, but the quantity which it can command
in the market."

This passage, it must be recollected, occurs
in the first section, which sets out with the definition of value as the power of purchasing,
and which bears the title before quoted. It is
evident too on the face of it, that Mr. Ricardo
had in his view value in exchange or purchasing power. Let us try to carry this sense
all through the sentence. It will then read
as follows : —

"Adam Smith, who so accurately defined
the original source of purchasing power, and
who was bound in consistency to maintain that
all things became possessed of more or less of
this purchasing power in proportion as more
or less labour was bestowed on their production, has himself erected another standard
measure of purchasing power, and speaks of
things being more or less powerful in purchasing in proportion as they will exchange for
more or less of this standard measure. Sometimes he speaks of corn, at other times of labour
as a standard measure ; not the quantity of

labour bestowed on the production of any object, but the quantity which it can command in
the market."

Now this is evidently what Mr. Ricardo did
not intend to say. He could not intentionally,
and with a distinct conception of what he was
about, find fault with Adam Smith or any one
else for maintaining that a thing, A, became
more powerful in purchasing because it would
exchange for more corn. Nor could there be
any inconsistency between this proposition and
the other, if the other was intended to assert
that A became possessed of more purchasing
power in relation to B, as more comparative
labour was bestowed upon it. One proposition would have reference to the effect, or rather
it would be a mere definition of the phrase
" becoming more powerful in purchasing," and
the other to the cause of that effect, but there
would be no inconsistency between them. As
Mr. Ricardo, nevertheless, supposes they are
quite inconsistent with each other, he must
have unconsciously changed the meaning of
the term, and the attentive reader will perceive
that he did in fact, labour under such a confu-

sion of ideas. Although he begins the passage
with speaking of exchangeable value and has
just defined it as the power of purchasing, yet
he suddenly passes to another meaning and
tells us that a commodity, A, becomes more
valuable (in a sense which has no reference to
purchasing power but to cost of production)
as more labour is bestowed upon it, and does
not of necessity become more valuable (in
the same sense), because it exchanges for more
corn. Hence, he argues, that those are wrong
who contend that because A exchanges for
more corn it has become of greater value :
that is, he infers from a sense of the term,
which he has himself unconsciously substituted, the erroneousness of a proposition which
is perfectly true in that sense of the term with
which he commences.

In fact there are only three possible suppositions on the subject. Either Mr. Ricardo,
in this passage, used the term solely in the
sense of purchasing power, or he used it solely
in that sense of the term which we are told
has reference to cost of production, or he used
it in both senses. If he used it solely in the

first sense, his argument is self-evidently erroneous. He could not use it solely in the second sense, because he begins the passage by
speaking of exchangeable value. The only
remaining supposition is that he used it in
both senses. But if he used it in both senses,
it must have been unconsciously, for he imputes
inconsistency to those who maintain two propositions which are perfectly compatible in the
sense of the term with which he sets out because they are incompatible in the sense which
he himself has substituted.

Let us try further a passage in the same
section, in which Mr. Ricardo engages in a
controversy with Adam Smith and Mr. Malthus, as to the occasions on which it is proper
to say that any thing rises or falls in value.
According to the definition in which these
three writers coincide, and to the explanation
prefixed by Mr. Ricardo announcing the subject of the section, there could not possibly be
any doubt in the mind of any one, who had
a clear view of the subject, as to what should
be called a rise and what a fall of any commodity whatever. A rise in A would be an

increase in its power of purchasing some other commodity B : a fall in B, a decrease in its power of purchasing A.

When therefore Adam Smith and Mr. Malthus contend, that if labour and corn exchange for less gold, it is the gold which has risen in value while the labour and corn have not risen but remained stationary, the right answer would be, " if you mean stationary to each other you are correct, but if you mean stationary in value to gold you are incorrect; because according to your own definition of value as the power of purchasing, if labour and corn purchase less gold they have become of less value or have fallen in relation to gold."

But this is not the answer given by Mr. Ricardo : he contends, that if the cause of corn exchanging for less gold is a diminution in the labour necessary to produce corn, he is bound to call the variation of corn and labour a fall in their value, and not a rise in the value of the things with which they are compared : *i. e.* (following his own definition) he is bound to call the variation of corn and labour a decrease of their purchasing power, and not an

increase of the purchasing power of the things
with which they are compared, as if one could
take place without the other. Here is evidently another unconscious transition from his
adopted acceptation of the word value. He
no longer means by it the power of purchasing,
although the title prefixed declares that to be
the subject of the section.

The whole chapter on the distinction between value and riches is a decisive proof of
the confusion of Mr. Ricardo's ideas on this
subject. If we suppose him to use the term
value in the sense of cost of production, or in
a sense referable to the quantity of producing
labour, the whole chapter is a series of truisms,
or a truism constantly repeated, that what the
labour of a given number of men produces,
always costs their labour to produce it. If
we suppose him on the other hand to use the
term in the sense annexed to it by his own definition, his remarks would be almost altogether
incorrect. He says, for instance, that the labour of a million of men in manufactures always produces the same value. If he intends
by this "purchasing power," the assertion is

evidently incorrect, for the labour of a million
of men may produce an aggregate of commodities, varying very much in their power of
commanding other articles in exchange.   If
he intends to assert, that the labour of a million
of men will always produce a mass of commodities which, however varying in quantity, will
have cost the same quantity of labour, he is
undoubtedly correct; but whether it was worth
while formally to enunciate such a proposition,
to insist upon it at length, to repeat and to
illustrate it, is another question.

Most of Mr. Ricardo's other positions in the
same chapter coincide with this in proving,
that instead of knowingly using the word value
in two senses, and making the context clearly
indicate in each case the acceptation in which
it should be received, he was labouring under
an ambiguity of which he was totally unconscious.

That he really considered himself as using
it in the ordinary sense annexed to it by political economists, and in that sense alone, is
shown by the circumstance of his finding fault
with M. Say, who speaks of it as denoting the

power of commanding in exchange, for what he considers as an improper use of it.

Now, although it might be conceded to Mr. Ricardo that he should use the term in any sense he liked, provided he did it consistently, he could have no plea for attacking the language of others, who used it in the ordinary sense of purchasing power. The very circumstance, of his animadverting on others for employing the term as he thought improperly, proves, that he himself considered it as only legitimately possessing one meaning. Why should he find fault with M. Say for saying "the value of incomes is then increased, if they can procure, it does not signify by what means, a greater quantity of products": a position perfectly correct if the term value is construed in the sense of purchasing power; in other words, perfectly correct according to Mr. Ricardo's own definition? Surely had he possessed that clear and distinct perception of the subject which has been attributed to him, that perfect consciousness of two senses in the term value, he would not have failed to make the remark, that the proposition was correct in one acceptation of the word and not in the other. Far from doing this, however, far from pointing out a distinction of this kind, he evidently conceives that there is no other distinction to be made than the common one between value in use and value in exchange; and it is accordingly with confounding these two meanings that he charges the French economist.

So far then from its being true, that Mr. Ricardo makes the context clearly indicate in which of the two meanings the word should be received, it appears that he confounds them in the same sentence, in a section where he professes to employ the word in only one meaning : further, that he lays down propositions, the enunciation of which can be accounted for only by supposing a confusion of the two meanings, since if we construe them in one sense they are incorrect, if we take them in the other they are nugatory : and, lastly, that he animadverts on the language of others in a way which implies that he considered only one legitimate meaning to exist.

These illustrations you will probably regard as sufficiently conclusive, as to the reviewer's accu racy and knowledge of the subject on which he professes to treat. In the Dissertation itself, I have already shown, how Mr. Ricardo was led into the errors, which he has committed on this point; but it may not be unacceptable to the reader, if I here present the explanation again in different words and at greater length.

We have seen, that while Mr. Ricardo professedly used the term value in one sense only he insensibly lapsed into a different sense'; and the way in which he did this it is not difficult to trace: it was in attempting to explain the cause or regulating principle of value, or, in other words, the circumstance which determines in what quantities commodities are exchanged for each other. Having adopted the principle, that the value of commodities depends on the comparative quantities of labour required to produce them ; that is, that an article A exchanges for 2 B, or is double the value of B, because one of the former requires as much labour to produce it as two of the latter, he inadvertently concluded, that if A always required the same labour it would always remain of the same value. Had he constantly taken along

with him, or borne in mind, his definition
of value as the power of purchasing, this is a
conclusion to which he could never have come;
for the proposition, that A would always have
the same purchasing power if produced by an
invariable quantity of labour, would have immediately carried his mind to the consideration of some commodity in relation to which
this purchasing power was to exist. But the
term value, from the vagueness of its common
use, does not necessarily or even ordinarily carry
the mind to the consideration of any correlative; and hence Mr. Ricardo, in common with
Adam Smith and other writers, appears to have
lost sight of a correlative being necessarily implied by the definition with which they set out.

The right conclusion from his doctrine, which
affirms labour to be the sole regulating principle of value, is, that two commodities would
always be of the same value in relation to each
other, so long as they required the same labour
to produce them; but Mr. Ricardo, losing sight
of relativeness in the term value, concluded
that one commodity, without reference to any
other, would always be of the same value, if

produced by the same labour : and hence that a thing would increase or decrease in this property of value, not in relation to other commodities, but considered in itself, in proportion as it required more or less labour for its production.

Now here we have clearly, first, an unconscious transition from the original meaning, a substitution of one sense for another, in consequence of not keeping the definition properly in view, but suffering a different and laxer sense to displace it ; and, secondly, we have an inference deduced from this substituted meaning which does not follow from the original one.

The passage in Mr. Ricardo's book where this transition is made, the turning point, if I may so call it, is in the very first section. Having quoted a few sentences from Adam Smith, which explain that in rude ages the quantities in which commodities were exchanged would be determined by the quantities of labour necessary to acquire them, he proceeds, " If the quantity of labour realized in commodities regulate their exchangeable value, every increase of the quantity of labour must augment the value of that commodity on which it is exercised, as every diminution must lower it." Now here Mr. Ricardo begins with using value in the sense of exchangeable value, or purchasing power, and as he uses it in that sense in the premises, he is bound to do it in the conclusion : and the conclusion is true enough, if he means that every increase of the quantity of labour must augment the value of that commodity on which it is exercised in relation to other commodities, which continued to require only the same labour as before. This, however, although perfectly consonant with his doctrines, will not be found to have been Mr. Ricardo's peculiar meaning. In this proposition he did not extend his view beyond the one commodity : the word value did not carry him over, as the phrase power of purchasing would have done, to the consideration of some other. An attentive reader will perceive his meaning to have been, that every increase of labour would augment the value of the commodity on which it was exercised, without reference to any other commodity. This proposition is the hook, from which all his other propositions inconsistent with his

own definition depend. This one false step
made, he very logically falls into the ob-
scurities and paradoxes which have excited the
admiration of his disciples, and the astonishment of every body else.

4. I proceed, in the next place, to show, that
   Mr. Ricardo did not consider himself as
   employing the word value in any new,
   peculiar, and technical sense, and therefore
   could not entertain the ingenious design
   imputed to him in the Review, of giving
   more precision to the language of Political
   Economy by the profound expedient of
   using the term sometimes in one sense
   and sometimes in another.

In the first section he says, " If I have to
hire a labourer for a week, and instead of ten
shillings I pay him eight, no variation having
taken place in the value of money, the labourer can probably obtain more food and necessaries with his eight shillings than he before
obtained for ten ; but this is owing, not to a
rise in the real value of his wages, as stated by
Adam Smith, and more recently by Mr. Malthus, but to a fall in the value of the things on

which his wages are expended, things perfectly distinct: and yet, for calling this a fall in the real value of wages, I am told that I adopt *new* and *unusual* language, not reconcileable with the true principles of the science. To me it appears that the *unusual*, and indeed *inconsistent*, language is that used by my opponents."

Now the whole of this passage would be erroneous, if the term value were to be taken in the usual sense of purchasing power; it must, therefore, on the reviewer's hypothesis, be taken in the new, peculiar, and technical sense, which Mr. Ricardo is represented as designing to introduce; and yet we find Mr. Ricardo himself disclaiming the imputation of novelty, and persisting that there is nothing unusual in his employment of terms.

Nay, so unconscious was Mr. Ricardo of treating of any kind of value but exchangeable value, that we find him in one place combining the two epithets by which he is supposed to distinguish one from the other, and speaking of *real value in exchange**.

* Principles of Pol. Econ. p. 506, Third Edition.

It is also maintained by his followers — by some of them at least — that there was nothing novel in Mr. Ricardo's use of the term value, except the consistency with which he employed it. The author of the Templars' Dialogues, after eulogizing him for his strict adherence to one meaning, denies that there was any thing new in his mode of using it; and in answer to Mr. Malthus's complaint, of the obscurity arising from Mr. Ricardo's unusual application of common terms, maintains, that "there is nothing at all unusual in his application of any term whatever, but only in the steadiness with which he keeps to the same application of it*."

5. Having disposed of the four first propositions which I undertook to substantiate, I hasten to the last, and shall endeavour to show, that Mr. Ricardo's departure from the received definition of the term had not even the merit of originality, since a similar deviation is to be observed in prior writers ; so that, if to save his credit it is maintained that he purposely used the

* London Mag. April 1824, p. 345.

word in two meanings, the same plea must be extended to the economists who preceded him; a circumstance quite fatal to the assertion of the reviewer, as to Mr. Ricardo's design of introducing more precision into the language of the science.

When Adam Smith, after having defined value to be purchasing power, goes on to say, that labour never varies in its own value, he evidently deviates from that definition, and passes into a sense of the term in which no power of purchasing is implied. Labour, he says, sometimes purchases a greater, sometimes a smaller quantity of goods, but it is their value which varies, not that of the labour which purchases them; a conclusion not true in the sense of purchasing power, and therefore, if true at all, it must be so in some other sense.

Almost all economists agree in telling us, that a measure of value must be invariable in value, which, according to their own definition, means, that a measure of purchasing power must be invariable in its own purchasing power, or, in other words, must always command the same quantity of all other commodities in exchange : they further tell us, that the use of such a measure is to ascertain variations in value, that is (pursuing their own definition) in the purchasing power of other commodities. But, if the measure is invariable in its purchasing power over other commodities, those other commodities must necessarily be invariable too ; consequently there can be no fluctuations to ascertain ; consequently an invariable measure can be of no use for the purpose to which they destine it. In saying, therefore, that a measure of value must be invariable in order to ascertain what commodities have varied, they must have substituted some meaning not included in their definition ; and they have undoubtedly by so doing forestalled the claims to originality in using the word value in two meanings now put forth in behalf of Mr. Ricardo. Or, if these two meanings are not precisely those of the latter author, the economists in question are entitled to the praise of having got the start of him in this singularly adroit expedient for introducing precision into the language of the science.

This expedient is itself a thing so extraordinary, that, now we have got through the five positions which I have endeavoured to establish, it really deserves a share of attention. I had always, I own, been accustomed to consider it as an imperative rule never to use a term in two senses, in any scientific or philosophical discussion. I had always thought with Locke, that the least that can be expected is, "that in all discourses, wherein one man pretends to instruct or convince another, he should use the same word constantly in the same sense: if this were done (which nobody can refuse without great disingenuity) many of the books extant might be spared; many of the controversies in dispute would be at an end; several of those great volumes, swoln with ambiguous words, now used in one sense and by and by in another, would shrink into a very narrow compass; and many of the philosophers' (to mention no other) as well as poets' works, might be contained in a nutshell *."

In another place the same eminent philosopher observes, "A great abuse of words is inconstancy in the use of them. It is hard to

* Locke's Essay, Book iv, Chap xi.

find a discourse written of any subject, especially of controversy, wherein one shall not observe, if he read with attention, the same words (and those commonly the most material in the discourse, and upon which the argument turns) used sometimes for one collection of simple ideas, and sometimes for another; which is a perfect abuse of language. Words being intended for signs of my ideas, to make them known to others, not by any natural signification but by voluntary imposition, it is plain cheat and abuse, when I make them stand sometimes for one thing and sometimes for another; the wilful doing whereof can be imputed to nothing but great folly or greater dishonesty*."

Regarding these views as universally entertained by philosophers, the plan of the reviewer took me by surprise; nor, after all the pains I have taken to comprehend the design, can I distinctly perceive how the employment of a word in two senses is to bring about its employment in only one of those senses, and thus introduce greater precision of language. I am

* Ibid. Book iv, Chap. x.

perplexed to discover in what manner the continued use of a word in its old and lax acceptation can lead to its disuse in that sense, or at all contribute to the reception of a new and stricter meaning. The critic theorises as if old meanings of words could be treated like old servants, who, having grown supine in their offices, are only retained to teach their successors the mysteries of the service on which they have entered. To one of my humble capacity it appears, that the old meaning, instead of lending any assistance to the new, would take every opportunity of thwarting its movements. In fine I am irresistibly led to think, that the simplest way of establishing the strict employment of a word in one sense is to use it in no other. My hesitation at differing on such a point from the authority of the reviewer is a little relieved by knowing that I am supported in my opinion by some distinguished philosophers. Mr. Dugald Stewart, in whose works there are some admirable remarks on the subject of language as an instrument of thought and communication, thus describes the plan which he has pursued in trying to intro-

duce some degree of precision into his peculiar department of study.

" I have frequently had occasion," says he,
" in the course of the foregoing disquisitions,
to regret the obscurity in which this department of philosophy is involved, by the vagueness and ambiguity of words ; and I have
mentioned, at the same time, my unwilling-
ness to attempt verbal innovations, wherever I
could possibly avoid them, without essential
injury to my argument. The rule, which I
have adopted in my own practice, is to give
to every faculty and operation of the mind its
own appropriate name, following, in the selection of this name, the *prevalent* use of our
best writers ; and endeavouring afterwards, as
far as I have been able, to employ each word
exclusively in that acceptation in which it
has been hitherto used *most generally*. In
the judgments which I have formed on points
of this sort, it is more than probable, that I
may sometimes have been mistaken ; but the
mistake is of little consequence, if I myself
have invariably annexed the same meaning to
the same phrase ; an accuracy which I am

not so presumptuous as to imagine that I have uniformly attained, but which I am conscious of having, at least, uniformly attempted*."

Such is the simple plan which naturally suggests itself in cases of this nature. The ingenious theory of verbal double-dealing propounded by the critic, seems to have originated in that fruitful source of crude speculation, a half-mastery of the subject in hand, sufficient to afford casual glimpses, but not complete and steady views. The inventor of it, whoever he was, had probably heard, that the best method to be pursued of introducing precision into the language of science is the careful use of a word in one uniform sense, a procedure which if it were adopted by the best authors would gradually supersede the more lax employment of the term by writers in general. In the subtle theory before us, however, this method has undergone a slight metamorphosis : two meanings are to couch themselves under the same term in the same treatise, and like two curs turned into one kennel, they are to snarl and

* Elements of the Philosophy of the Human Mind, vol. ii, p. 3, Second Edition.

wrangle till the inharmonious contest has terminated in the expulsion of the prior occupant.

While on this part of the subject, I may own that I admit the force of the reviewer's appeal against the word value being considered as having a divine right to be used in one sense more than another ; or, perhaps more properly, against one meaning being considered as having a divine right to the term in which I have endeavoured to re-instal it, and I beg expressly to declare, in order to allay any republican horror which I may have inadvertently excited on this head, that I intended to set up no claim of the kind. My views were entirely limited to rights acquired by election, and I simply meant to contend, that economists having by free choice elevated one meaning to the sovereignty, should not exhibit the discreditable spectacle of divided allegiance.

If I have been at all successful in establishing the preceding five positions, almost all the assertions of the critic respecting Mr. Ricardo's doctrines fall to the ground ; for most of them, without the shadow of argument or evidence, proceed on the false assumption that Mr. Ricardo purposely employed the word value in two meanings, and clearly indicated, in each instance, the acceptation in which he wished it to be received. The following passages of the Review, for example, scarcely need another word to overturn them : " If there were any commodity, which two hundred years ago was produced by seven days' labour, and which had continued to be in demand and to be produced by the same quantity of labour to the present day, what does Mr. Ricardo say it would do? That it would remain invariable in its power of purchasing? That it would invariably command in exchange the same quantity of commodities? No such thing. Mr. Ricardo not only never advanced any such proposition, but it seems almost incredible, that any body who has read his book, should impute it to him." * * * *

" When Mr. Ricardo says ' standard measure of value,' he means a commodity invariable in the labour which goes to its production. He does not mean invariable in its power of purchasing, quite the contrary."

To all this it is a sufficient answer, that
Mr. Ricardo, in his first section, defines value
to be the power of purchasing; in the same
section, a few pages further on, without any
intimation to his readers of a change in the
meaning of the term, he tells us, that a commodity which always required the same labour
to produce it would be invariable in value.
According to his own definition, therefore, the
phrase implies invariable in purchasing power.
That he would have denied this to be his
meaning, if any one had asked him whether he
intended it, is probable enough; since it is a
very common case for a writer, by losing sight
of his original definition, and passing to another acceptation of an important term, to be
led to conclusions which he would instantly
disown, if the definition were recalled to his
mind. To say in defence of such a one, that
in a subsequent part of his work he did not
intend the term to be received in the sense
which he began by ascribing to it, is only an
acknowledgment of the confusion of his ideas,
and presents itself to the mind as rather a ludicrous attempt at justification. There is no

better test of such a confusion than his shrinking from propositions, which seemed plausible enough while invested in the vagueness of ambiguous language, as soon as their absurdity has been made apparent by the substitution of the definition for the term.

In the passage last quoted the reviewer says, that by an invariable standard of value Mr. Ricardo meant " a commodity invariable in the labour which goes to its production : " in another part of the review he tells us, that by an invariable standard Mr. Ricardo meant a commodity " invariable in its accuracy as a test to mark the variations in the purchasing power of other commodities." According to the first description here given of Mr. Ricardo's meaning, he becomes chargeable with a number of identical propositions. His position, that if a commodity could be found, which always required the same labour to produce it, it would be of invariable value, sinks into the nugatory assertion, that if it required the same labour it would require the same labour.

By the second description here quoted of Mr. Ricardo's meaning, the reviewer's complete mastery of the subject is rendered still more conspicuous.   In what sense a commodity, such as Mr. Ricardo describes as necessary to constitute an invariable standard, can be said to be " invariable in its accuracy as a test to mark the variations in the purchasing power of other commodities," it is not for me to divine.   Nothing can show these variations but the actual facts of the market: the recorded prices of articles show us, as far as they extend, the relations of these articles to money and to each other ; but this has no sort of dependence on the invariableness of the quantity of labour required to produce the money.   In the Dissertation it has been already explained what such a commodity as Mr. Ricardo describes would do.   It would enable us to tell the variations in the quantity of labour required to produce commodities ; and even its power of accurately doing this would depend on the condition, that commodities were to each other in value as the quantities of labour required to produce them.

While examining such passages as those on which our attention has just been employed, one is tempted to exclaim, in the language of the Westminster Review itself on another ocasion, " Can there be a spectacle more repugnant to that candour and sincerity, which are so essential a part of morality, than a continued attempt to varnish over inconsistencies, and to reconcile in appearance doctrines which are really irreconcileable * ?"

You will not imagine that I am going to notice all the remarks of the critic. It is sufficient to have exhibited the extent and accuracy of his acquaintance with the writings of the economist whom he professes to defend. There are still remaining, nevertheless, a few of his observations, on which I shall take the liberty of detaining your attention for quite as long a time as their merits require.

The charge of logomachy you will notice is often repeated. The discussions in the Dissertation are frequently represented as disputes about words. Independently of showing, as I have already done, that they are discussions about ideas, it would be easy to reply to this accusation in the language of a hundred eminent writers. I might quote the words of the Westminster Review itself : —

* Vol. i, p. 527.

" With respect to the controversy being a mere dispute about words, we reply in the lan- language of Condillac, ' that we think only through the medium of words; that the art of reasoning is nothing more than a language well arranged ; that however certain the facts of any science may be, we can only communi- cate false or imperfect ideas of them to others, while we want words by which they may be properly expressed ; and that the sciences in general have improved, not only because philo- sophers have applied themselves with more attention than formerly to observe nature, but because they have communicated to their lan- guage that precision and accuracy which they have employed in their observations. By cor- recting their language they have reasoned better."—Vol. iii, p. 522 *.

I might also quote the authority of a writer

* In quoting this passage I would not be understood as coinciding in every expression. Against some of Con- dillac's first positions, judicious objections have been urged by several writers.—*See Dugald Stewart's Elements*, vol. ii, chap. ii, sec. 2 ; and *Elemens d'Idéologie, par M. Destutt de Tracy,* troisième partie, chap. ix.

who must be allowed to have paid some attention to points of this nature; "The sentence,
'It is a fruitless verbal debate,' is an assertion
of the same complexion with the contemptuous
sneers at verbal criticism by the contem-
poraries of Bentley. In questions of philosophy or divinity, that have occupied the
learned, and been the subjects of many suc-
cesive controversies, for one instance of mere
logomachy, I could bring ten instances of
logodaedaly, or verbal legerdemain, which
have perilously confirmed prejudices, and with-
stood the advancement of truth, in consequence
of the neglect of *verbal debate*, i. e. strict
discussion of terms*." But perhaps it will be
better to let the critic receive the merited
reprimand from the hands of a brother Ri-
cardian. The following passage might have
been written expressly for the purpose:

"For once Phaedrus" (says one of the inter-
locutors in the Templars' Dialogues to another)
"I am not sorry to hear you using a phrase
which is in general hateful to my ears. 'A
mere dispute about words' is a phrase which

* Aids to Reflection, by S. T. Coleridge, page 119.

we hear daily: and why? Is it a case of such daily occurrence to hear men disputing about mere verbal differences? So far from it, I can truly say that I never happened to witness such a dispute in my life — either in books or in conversation: and indeed, considering the small number of absolute synonymes which any language contains, it is scarcely possible that a dispute on words should arise, which would not also be a dispute about ideas (*i. e.* about realities). Why then is the phrase in every man's mouth, when the actual occurrence must be so very uncommon? The reason is this, Phaedrus: such a plea is a '*sophisma pigri intellectus*,' which seeks to escape from the effort of mind necessary for the comprehending and solving of any difficulty under the colourable pretext, that it is a question about shadows and not about substances, and one therefore which it is creditable to a man's good sense to decline: a pleasant sophism this, which at the same time flatters a man's indolence and his vanity! For once, however, I repeat, that I am not sorry to hear such a phrase in your mouth, Phaedrus: I have heard it from you before; and I will frankly tell you, that you ought to be ashamed of such a plea, which is becoming to a slothful intellect, but very unbecoming to yours. On this account it gives me pleasure that you have at length urged it in a case where you will be obliged to abandon it. If that should happen, remember what I have said : and resolve never more to shrink effeminately from the toil of an intellectual discussion, under any pretence that it is a verbal dispute*."

So much for accusations of logomachy. Another charge (that of dealing in bad metaphysics) I am not particularly anxious to repel, especially as it is made by one who is evidently an adept in the science, of which even the most obstinate scepticism would be satisfied by any of the ensuing specimens. At the conclusion of the first chapter of the Dissertation on Value, I have stated the following propositions amongst others, as the results of the reasonings in that chapter :—

"The value of a commodity can be expressed only by a quantity of some other commodity."

* London Magazine, April 1824, page 349.

"A rise in the value of a commodity A, means that an equal quantity of this commodity exchanges for a greater quantity than before of the commodity B, in relation to which it is said to rise."

These propositions the reviewer asserts to be mere identical propositions. "The value of a commodity can be expressed only by a quantity of some other commodity," an identical proposition! It is hardly necessary to prove the ingenuity of this assertion, which transcends the achievements of the continental mathematicians, who contended, that all the operations of arithmetic and algebra were constant repetitions of the formula $a = a$. On the ingenious system of the critic, all propositions, which could not be denied, would be reduced under this class. For instance, the assertion that the eighth article of the ninth number of the Westminster Review is a masterpiece of candid, elegant, courteous, and upright criticism, being quite beyond dispute, would be a mere identical proposition, a nugatory sentence, an idle assertion, for the utterance of which even a schoolboy ought to be whipped.

The same ingenuity relieves us at once from the labour of becoming acquainted with a number of elaborate works heretofore thought essential, and this, in the present superabundance of books, would be a happy deliverance from part of an intolerable pressure. If an explanation of what a rise in the value of a commodity *means*, comes under the class of identical propositions, we may at once disburthen ourselves of those weighty incumbrances on our shelves, lexicons and vocabularies. On this sweeping principle, Dr. Johnson's two folios are a string of nugatory propositions wanting the copula, and even Crabbe's technological quartos a continual repetition that a thing is what it is. What a cheap victory over the difficulties of a language! To learn a word, parrot-like, is every thing; all explanation is nugatory ; and to define what a word means is merely asserting that the same is the same.

To some authors this doctrine would be of inestimable value. To define their terms, which is often inconvenient, would be a superfluous elaboration of identical propositions. Freed from this troublesome necessity, they might astonish their readers with all the magic of paradox, without any fear of having their own definition hurled amidst the gay creation, putting the whole to flight as instantaneously as the short exclamation of Tam O'Shanter routed the merry party of midnight witches.

The same profound acquaintance with metaphysics doubtless prompted its possessor to tax the author of the Dissertation with having committed " a metaphysical blunder" in calling cost of production a *cause* of value. " Cost of production," says the critic, " instead of being the cause of value, is more properly the reverse ; a cause of non-value :" whence it follows, according to common logic, that as an increase of the cause must be attended with an increase of the effect, you have only to keep adding to the cost of production, in order to reduce a commodity to the extreme of worthlessness.

Not venturing to repel an attack so skilfully supported, I feel happy in being able to shelter myself under the authority of one, who, it requires no sagacity to conjecture, has hitherto maintained a high place in the reviewer's estimation, but who, unluckily for his future standing there, may be shown to have pronounced a prophetic sentence of absurdity on the passage just quoted, long before it had been conceived. It is scarcely necessary to premise, that the author (Mr. Mill) whom I am about to cite is engaged in resolving cost of production into labour. Speaking with this view of a hypothetical commodity, made purely by capital, he affirms, " it would be absurd to say that labour has nothing to do *in creating the value* of such a commodity, since, demonstratively, it is labour which *gives to it the whole of its value;* and if it could be got *without labour it would have no value at all**.*"

Now the Westminster critic will hardly deny, that his little theory on the causation of worthlessness is here pre-stigmatized as an absurdity, unless that which creates value, which gives to a commodity the whole of its value, and without which it would have no value at all, is not in his opinion entitled to the appellation of a cause of value. But this he will not commit himself by asserting; for as his acquaintance with logicians has extended to Aldrich, it has possibly

* Mill's Elements, page 98, 2d edition.

reached another writer skilled in the art, and
he may opportunely chance to recollect the
perspicuous definition of the facetious Dean of
St. Patrick's,

> " That without which a thing is not
> Is *causa sine quâ non*."

Having mentioned Mr. Mill in connection with
this part of the subject, I might seize the
occasion for replying to the critic s laboured
defence of that author, on whose behalf he
seems peculiarly sensitive, against a few slight
animadversions which I hazarded on a passage
of his elementary book on political economy ;
but as they are quoted at length in the Review,
I leave them without inquietude to appear by
the side of the counter-criticism, unencumbered
with further comment, especially as I am not
sure that I comprehend every part of the reply.
It is scarcely worth while deviating into the
single observation, that he does not in one
instance at least prove an advo ate on whom
his client will have much reason to congratulate
himself; for in repelling an imputation against
Mr. Mill, of confounding the standard with th·
cause of value, he owns, that Mr. Mill, by

standard, means regulator of value, that is, uses one expression for the other, and this, which is in fact the substance of the charge, he gravely alleges as a refutation of it.

The author of the Elements of Political Economy is not likely to be overpowered with gratitude to such a defender, especially as in his third edition he has discarded the expression commented on, and therefore may be presumed to have considered it as justly liable to objection. Should he feel annoyed at the indiscretion of his advocate, he will not be singular. We are all, like himself, occasionally embarrassed by the injudicious assistance of people whose zeal outruns their judgment, and who involve their friends in no very enviable predicaments, not from any propensity to malice or mischief, but from a wrong-headed alacrity of kindness, which no frequency of miscarriage can repress.

The whole of the reviewer's speculations on the subject of relation form another conspicuous proof of his metaphysical acuteness. On this topic he is so profound that I do not profess to be able to fathom his meaning; so powerful, that I do not pretend to cope

with his strength. There is one point, however, on which I must beg to set him right,
and it will then perhaps be apparent, not
much to the credit of his generalship, that
he has assembled his principal forces for an
attack where they could be of no service, when
prudence required them to be distributed
amongst the many posts of his own which he
has left defenceless. The point to which I
allude is the charge brought against the author
of the Dissertation and others, of " resolving the
principle of value into a relation, and then
imagining they have enlightened the world."

This is equally candid and sagacious.
Whatever may be the propriety of my use of
the word relation, as applicable to value, one
thing must be obvious to any one who has
read the work with attention; namely, that
none of the reasonings at all depend on this
word, so that it might be extirpated from the
book without impairing its conclusions, which
would all follow from the received definition
of the term value as the power of purchasing,
quite as strictly as from the designation of
value as a relation. To call it a relation is to
use the common language of metaphysicians

and logicians on the subject. The property, which we call value, belongs to that class called relative properties, relative mor' s, or relations.

To all the strictures and speculations with which the reviewer has unhappily perplexed himself on the subject of relation, this is a sufficient answer. There are one or two of his assertions, nevertheless, which may afford you amusement if not instruction. He maintains,

1. That there is nothing relative but terms; or at least he calls Hobbes's remark to this effect " profound," and therefore it may be presumed that he considers it to be true.
2. That quantity and substance cannot be relative.
3. That quart and pint bottles are absolute bottles.
4. That Dr. Brown made use of the word relative as an occult cause to explain whatever he did not understand.

In what sense Hobbes's remark is true I should be sincerely indebted to the reviewer or any one else to explain. It seems pretty much on a level, in point of correctness and intelligibility, with another remark of the same philosopher, that truth consists in words and not in things*, which induced Leibnitz to say that he appeared to him an ultra-nominalist, " plus quam nominalis." If by the proposition, that there is nothing relative but terms, it is meant to assert, that there are no relations existing between things, but only between words, the slightest consideration is sufficient to show its groundlessness. I may quote the words of a writer, who, according to the Westminster critic, " hardly did justice to his own metaphysical powers," and whom I cite on the present occasion on that account, rather than from any admiration on my own part of the manner in which he treats the subject.

" When beings," says he, " are produced, we must not imagine them to exist, like pebbles upon the shore, dispersed and scattered, without *dependence* or mutual *sympathy*. 'Twould be difficult out of *such* to compose a universe or *perfect whole*, because every perfect whole

* See his Logic. chap. iii.

has a respect to its parts, as well as the parts a respect both to such whole and to each other. Hence the rise of that *genus* called *relation*, a genus which *runs thro' all things, holding all of them together*, inasmuch as there is no member of the universe either so great or so minute, that it can be called *independent*, and *detached* from the rest*."

2. The second proposition, "that quantity and substance cannot be relative," seems to be only an assertion in two particular instances of the general proposition quoted from Hobbes, and I should certainly feel under a load of obligation to any one who would explain its meaning. The way in which the reviewer introduces this doctrine and the use he makes of it are worth attention. After quoting a passage from Col. Torrens, in which that able writer affirms, that, " in the very term exchangeable value, a relative, and not an absolute, quantity is implied," the critic sagely remarks, " Surely, if any thing in the world be absolute, it is quantity. He might as well talk

* Philosophical Arrangements, page 213.

of a relative substance. Can there be within the compass of thought two ideas more dis tinct than that of quantity and that of relation?" Such is the doctrine. What it means, or how it is intended to bear on Col. Torrens's remark, I am at a loss to conjecture. The ideas of quantity and relation are certainly quite distinct; but the inference which is suggested, that quantity cannot therefore be relative, is not more correct than it would be to conclude that figure cannot be coloured, because the ideas of figure and colour are essentially different. Every one is thoroughly aware that "quantity" (to borrow the words of Reid) "admits of a much greater variety of relations than any other subject of human reasoning*."

And now for the critic's application of the doctrine. He employs it to make good a charge of laxity, or rather incongruity of expression against Col. Torrens and the author of the Dissertation, the latter as accessary after the fact. The use of the phrase "relative quantity" not only provokes the laughter of the reviewer, but appears in his eyes to disqualify

* Essay on Quantity, read before the Royal Society.

any one for criticising the great economist of the
age. " These are the men," he exclaims, " who
are finding something to contemn in the language of Ricardo at every step." It is a pity,
that in passing this severe condemnation on
others for the employment of the simple expression " relative quantity," his knowledge of
Mr. Ricardo's writings should not have been
sufficient to tell him that he was condemning
Mr. Ricardo himself, in whose pages the same
phrase is frequently to be met with. Thus in
page 13, third edition, he speaks of " the *relative quantity* of labour as almost exclusively
determining the relative value of commodities,"
unconscious of the embryo ridicule which was
lurking in the mind of one of his disciples, and
which was at a future day to burst forth at such
a juxtaposition of terms. In fact, this sentence of
Mr. Ricardo's corresponds almost exactly with
another proposition from Col. Torrens's Essay
on the production of Wealth, over which the
reviewer makes a resolute effort to be merry;
namely, " Exchangeable value is determined,
not by the absolute but by the relative cost of
production." " Now, in the name of all that

is risible (asks the critic, with unrivalled intensity of humour), what is the distinction the author would have us put between absolute and relative in this expression?" He will certainly be at no loss to answer this question himself, when he has fully mastered the meaning of Mr. Ricardo's position, that " the relative values of commodities are governed by the relative quantities of labour bestowed on their production :" in which it will require no great discernment to perceive, that all which he ridicules in the position of Col. Torrens is either expressed or implied.

3. The position which I have cited, respecting quart and pint bottles, is intended as a humorous illustration of his comment on Colonel Torrens. " One bottle," says the critic, " holds a quart, and another a pint. Are the poor bottles on that account no longer absolute, but only relative bottles ?"

The defence of these *poor* vessels, as absolute entities, is full of pathos as well as humour; and I, for my own part, perfectly coincide with the opinion, that they are to all intents and purposes such as he contends them to be. I should be sorry to think for a moment that the bottles in my cellar had not an absolute existence, especially as some of them contain a liquid on which I have bestowed a good deal of that truly *economical* labour, which although never exerted except hypothetically, succeeds in producing an actual result*. Mr. Harris, nevertheless, with his "metaphysical powers", would have probably discovered, that even amongst bottles the existence of relations is not impossible.

4. The fourth assertion above quoted, " that Dr. Brown made use of the word relative as an occult cause to explain whatever he did not understand," will not detain us long. What is meant by making use of a word as an occult cause would require an effort to comprehend it, greater than the result could possibly be worth. One thing, however, is clear ; such a sentence could not have been written by any one who had not predetermined that a know-

---

* " If the wine which is put in the cellar is increased in value one-tenth by being kept a year, one-tenth more of labour may be correctly considered as having been expended upon it."—*Mill.*

ledge of the book on which he was passing
sentence might be dispensed with.

The four propositions above noticed form
altogether a happy exemplification of a remark
thrown out by the reviewer, the elegance of
which cannot certainly enter into competition
with its truth, that "metaphysical terms are
edge tools, and should not be meddled with by
those who are not used to the handling of them."
It is not always that the critic condescends, as
he has done in this instance, to furnish us with
any proof or elucidation of his own assertions.
In the whole of this reputable series of critical
animadversions, indeed, he has warily lavished
his strength on the expression instead of the
proof, reversing Lord Chesterfield's maxim, *sua-
viter in modo, fortiter in re.* The major part of
them are admirable illustrations of the cheap rate
to which the improvements in the machinery of
modern reviewing have succeeded in reducing
its products. It seems that it is not cottons,
or woollens, or stockings alone, which have been
lowered in value by modern inventions, but the

art of reviewing has proceeded *pari passu*, and turns out its commodities with such an economization of labour as to bring their *real* value almost to an evanescent quantity.

It has been usually thought heretofore, that argument should be met by argument; that a sophism should be exposed by some proof of its character; that a simple contradiction of a doctrine was not sufficient to overthrow it; that a charge of error should be supported by some instance where it was committed. But this is a tedious process : the power-loom of criticism produces its results with one hundredth part of the toil.

Thus if any one shows by detailed proofs, that former writers have overlooked certain distinctions or inferences, the whole answer is, "we affirm, that nobody has overlooked them." If a chapter is written to explain what the author supposes has been heretofore misconceived, the entire refutation is despatched in four words, "this is mere logomachy." In the same ready way Colonel Torrens and the author of the Dissertation are charged "with confusing themselves most grossly by a double meaning of the same term, of which they are altogether ignorant ;" an accusation heavy enough, to be sure, but not on that account the less likely to fall to the ground, being left without a single instance to support it. With equal ease the reviewer taxes the author of the Dissertation with ignorance of the meaning of his own term, in saying that there can be no increase of riches without an increase of value ; but leaves the allegation to maintain itself, neglectful of the consideration, that a charge requires assistance to uphold it in proportion to its native weakness.

This is indeed " the cheap defence" of doctrines, "the unbought grace" of controversy. It is so ready a method, that had I not a strong suspicion that what excites a feeling very different from admiration in the reader, cannot be accompanied by very elevated emotions in the writer, I might be tempted to make use of it in the course of my reply. In defending one's-self against the same artifice, there would be some justification for such a step. Assertions after the model above exhibited would of course be of trivial value, but it would be enough if they were equivalent to those which they were intended to meet in the market.

And now, my dear Sir, you will be capable of deciding, whether it is the author or the reviewer that has shown lack of knowledge and abundance of conceit: you will be able to pronounce on whom the charge of *ignoratio elenchi* is to be fixed; who has been guilty of the mistake of supposing he understood a difficult subject, when he should have performed a little longer the functions of a learner; who has been blundering and fighting with shadows; whose brains have been the territory of confusion; and who has fallen into the rash errors, although he has perfectly succeeded in escaping all the redeeming qualities of juvenility.

What a noble exemplification does the style of criticism which we have been examining afford of the lofty aim of the Westminster Review! How well it is calculated to contribute to the greatest happiness of the greatest number! How admirably does it stand the test of utility! Who does not see how much it

would diminish the happiness of mankind, if
critics did not come to the examination of
a work prepossessed against it on account of
its size; if they took the trouble to make themselves passably well acquainted with its subject;
if they examined its pretensions with candour;
if they suppressed every feeling of irritation;
if they replied to arguments by proofs and not
assertions; if they made no attempt to varnish
over inconsistencies; if they were anxious not
to misconceive and scrupulous not to misrepresent! Imagination is at a loss to set bounds
to the mischief which might arise to the human
race from critical coolness, candour, and equity.

In concluding his task, the critic, sensi-
tively alive to the interests of science, gives us
some insight into the motives which have
.actuated him in his strictures. The beginning
of my letter has done him some injustice on
this head. I attributed much of the less creditable matter of the article to some irritation of
feeling. It appears from the close, however,
that the whole has originated in a chivalrous
design of repressing "much ado about nothing,"
a spirit, we are told, peculiarly noxious in

Political Economy. The self-devotion of such an enterprise cannot be too highly estimated, since the result has proved the magnitude of the risk to reputation, to magnanimity, to complacency of feeling, and to placidity of temper. He might, nevertheless, have directed his weapons against a more formidable enemy. The spirit from which Political Economy has to fear the most is of a different character. The science has suffered and still suffers infinitely more from that arrogance, which looks upon certain names and doctrines as sacred from attack, that intolerance which would repress every symptom of free examination, that confidence which rejects with scorn any suspicion of the possibility of error, that pertinacity which clings to opinions once expressed, because the credit of individuals appears to be involved in maintaining them.

It is a spirit of this kind which opposes the most formidable obstacle to the progress of Political Economy, as well as discredits it in general estimation. Fortunately, however, even such an obstacle is comparatively powerless, and this, in common with other kinds of knowledge, will advance in its career in spite of the faults and the follies, the "blunders" and the "boasting" of Critical Dissertations or Westminster Reviews. A few years will probably consign them both to that oblivion which generally awaits works employed in clearing away, or in struggling to retain, the mere rubbish of a science; or if they should be recollected at all, the future economist will probably smile, that questions, then appearing so abundantly plain, should have occasioned any loss of temper, or any sacrifice of correctness, candour, and good sense to momentary irritation.

In the mean time I shall have the satisfaction of reflecting, that the work which has provoked the spleen of the reviewer has contributed in some degree, if by nothing else than compelling a closer examination of points before neglected, to relieve the science from that load of perplexity which lay on its very threshold; and that the subject of value can never again be placed in that state of obscurity and confusion, which deterred many from intellectual application to a department of knowledge of such vital importance to society.

It is but justice to take care before I conclude not to leave the impression, that the Review is a uniform effusion of splenetic feeling. It has laid me under obligations by one of those acts of kindness, which, although unfortunate in their issue, demand all the gratitude due to good intentions. As after a day of gloom and tempest the sun sometimes breaks out from the western clouds, and lights up the landscape with one of his most brilliant smiles; so the Westminster reviewer, at the close of his task, emerges for a moment from the sullenness in which he had enwrapped himself, and emits the radiance of his approbation. Not only does he generously acknowledge some faint symptoms of candour and cultivation of understanding in the work before him, but with the magnanimous condescension of a mind not prone to undervalue the importance of its own award, he holds out to the author the prospect of a large share of future applause. What a spirit-stirring summons to the field! What a splendid object of ambition!

"Visions of glory! spare my aching sight."

I would put it to the reviewer, however, whether he has not been rather indiscreet in the
abruptness of this communication ; whether he
should not have opened the prospect with a
more delicate regard to the overpowering effect
of sudden bursts of brilliant hopes on a mind
which he had just led through long and gloomy
passages of monotonous criticism, where the
darkness of the censure was not relieved by the
luminousness of the doctrine ?

" I could have borne my woes ; that stranger Joy
  Wounds while it smiles.   The long-imprisoned wretch,
  Emerging from the night of his damp cell,
  Shrinks from the sun's bright beams, and that which flings
  Gladness o'er all, to him is agony."

Grateful as I must feel for kind intentions,
however injudiciously manifested, I am only
apprehensive that my ambition will not be
strong enough for the occasion, and that it will
be satisfied with humbler laurels and less in-
toxicating applause.   It will content itself, I
fear, with directing its wishes to competent
and well-informed judges, and with looking for
nothing but that fair, candid, and dispassionate

estimate, both of faults and of merits, which must be the only desire of any writer who has entered on his task with correct and sober views; and which, although critics cannot withhold it without detriment to their own reputation, he may think himself more than commonly fortunate if he happen to meet with. There is much truth in the following observations of an eminent writer, and I have been frequently reminded of them in the course of the present Letter.

" What you have acquired by patient thought and cautious discrimination, demands a portion of the same effort in those who are to receive it from you. But applause and pre-ference are things of barter ; and if you trade in them, experience will soon teach you, that there are easier and less unsuitable ways to win golden judgments, than by at once taxing the patience and humiliating the self-opinion of your judges. To obtain your end, your words must be as indefinite as their thoughts : and how vague and general these are, even on objects of sense, the few, who at a mature age have seriously set about the discipline of their faculties, and have honestly *taken stock*, best know, by recollection of their own state*."

With this quotation, I must conclude the present Letter. There are other passages in the Review to which I could easily reply, but I have already bestowed as much attention upon it as the occasion requires, and must content myself with having urged all that is material to the defence of the work, which has been so temperately and candidly assailed.

The importance of these discussions about value I do not, I trust, overrate. It is of a factitious nature, arising, like that of many other controversies, in morals, metaphysics, and politics, from the errors which have been engendered by the efforts of the human mind to grasp the truth. He, however, must know little of the history of science, who is not aware of the magnitude to which such errors have sometimes expanded themselves, the obstacles which they have thus presented to the progress of knowledge, and the extensive good which has been effected by their removal. When this is accomplished, the means will

* Aids to Reflection, by S. T. Coleridge, p 186

often seem disproportioned to the end ; the exposure of a mistake will appear unnecessarily prolix ; and the consideration, that voluminous error sometimes requires still more voluminous refutation, will be forgotten by those who bring to the subject understandings familiar with the brief and simple truth, but which, without such a refutation, could never have approached it.

In the particular case before us, I cannot convey my own sentiments of the controversy better, than by repeating an expression in a preceding page : I consider it as an attempt on the one side to remove, and on the other to retain, a mass of mere scientific rubbish, which has been frequently turned over and thrown into new forms, but seldom without sending dust into the eyes of those who ventured on the experiment.

I am,

My dear Sir,

Yours very truly,

* * * *.

August 30, 1826.

OBSERVATIONS ON CERTAIN VERBAL DISPUTES

OBSERVATIONS

ON

CERTAIN VERBAL DISPUTES

IN

𝕻olitical 𝕰conomy,

PARTICULARLY

RELATING TO VALUE, AND TO DEMAND AND SUPPLY.

" What *do* they signify," said my Uncle Toby ?
" Nothing at all," quoth Yorick.

Tristram Shandy.

LONDON:

PRINTED FOR R. HUNTER,

SUCCESSOR TO MR. JOHNSON,

Nº 72, ST. PAUL'S CHURCHYARD.

1821.

OBSERVATIONS

ON

CERTAIN VERBAL DISPUTES,

&c. &c.

———◆———

THE difficulty of those sciences, which consist principally in what is called moral or metaphysical reasoning, is always owing, in a much greater degree than people are aware of, to inattention and inaccuracy in the use of *words*. Political economy has its share. Questions are thus debated, which need never have been raised at all; while those questions, which the nature of things does really present, are rendered more difficult of solution. The votaries of the science are checked and disheartened by the differences of opinion which they meet with, even among the most distinguished writers; and, on the other hand, those who dislike or despise such inquiries altogether, the lazy, the "*practical*," or the interested enemies of speculation, gather strength from this disunion, and make the uncertainty of the science a strong argument against it:

Ἦ κεν γηθήσαι Πρίαμος, Πριάμοιό τε παῖδες,
Εἰ σφῶϊν τάδε πάντα πυθοίατο μαρναμενοῖϊν.

They find, that these inquiries, " instead of a fruitful womb for the use and benefit of man's life" (to use the words of Bacon), end " in monstrous altercations and barking questions."—" So as it is not possible but this quality of knowledge must fall under popular contempt; the people being apt to contemn truth upon occasion of controversies and altercations, and to think *they* are all out of the way, which never meet."

There is no necessity, I should think, to *prove*, in England, in 1820, that political economy is an useful science; as Mr. Malthus does, page 12 of his Principles of Political Economy. It is not *arguments*, that people principally stand in need of, to allure them to the study; they want to be relieved from the repulsiveness arising from perpetual uncertainty and dispute. It is just the same in metaphysics; many people feel a disgust at metaphysics which they would not feel, if they did not consider it a pursuit, where little was to be obtained but a knowledge of the disputes of men. You will not remove this disgust by *arguing* in favour of the science; they will very likely admit it to be useful, if you will find it, and show it them; but " where are its conclusions?" they say, " where is this science? We can find nothing but the opinions of A, B, C, &c., all differing from each other."

The disgust with which such interminable controversies are regarded is peculiarly great, when the question at issue is not even pretended to be of any practical importance, and appears to end merely in words. This is especially the case, I think, with some of the discussions about the term *value*, and about the nature of *riches*. When we are told (as we are by M. Say, " Lettre V, à M. Malthus") that these are questions which " seem to interest most specially those who cultivate political economy *as a science*, and without any view to its applications*," we are tempted to ask, who are those? " Science" is here rather singularly put in opposition to any useful or practically interesting object of pursuit. Questions, to which the above expression of M. Say applies, appear ill to deserve the name of " propositions *principales*," which he gives them in the next page. Some of them hardly amount to propositions at all, being merely definitions. If, indeed, they are useful and necessary definitions, it is, as he observes, desirable that people should *agree* on them ; because, though to have a correct notion of them may advance us but little in knowledge, wrong or vague ideas about them may injure us a great deal. But if they really belong to the class he had before described, that is, are principally interesting to those, who do not care for the " application" of the science, I suspect they will often be found to be mere disputes for the sake of disputing, definitions for the sake of definitions of words, that we might very well do without altogether. If a writer thinks technical terms have been misused or confounded by others, he is too apt to remedy it by introducing new terms or new definitions of his own†. He seldom thinks of trying to " remove th' occasion of the ill‡,"—to do without technical terms altogether on the particular subject where they have been misused, and have led to error or difficulty. Yet it would be merely putting down four or five plain words here and there, instead of one that is not plain. M. Say calls this a " périphrase pénible;"

---

* " Semblent intéresser plus spécialement ceux qui cultivent l'économie politique comme science, et sans aucune vue d'application."

† See that part of Mr. Malthus's Principles of Political Economy which relates to Demand.

‡ Spenser.

but the trouble does not much signify, if it is useful. Especially as a confusion in the use of a term is much more easily introduced than cured. It is difficult to forget the old meaning, or use, to which we had been once accustomed: and then, between the two, we find our understandings, perhaps, in a worse puzzle than before. The particular instance of periphrasis, which M. Say is here speaking of, *viz.* that which the French are obliged to use instead of our terms " demand" and " supply," would, if it were always adopted by ourselves, prevent much error now incurred* in using those two words, and save more ink in the end, and a great deal of endless perplexity, and fruitless, unsatisfactory controversy. — " Brevis esse laboro, obscurus fio."

I confess it appears to me, that writers in general, especially those who are laying down any thing like a system, are too fond of giving us a number of new definitions, and introducing a technical language. Half-learned, conceited, readers are pleased with this. They can by this means soon pick up enough to be unintelligible, and puzzle other people, and then they seem profound. They think, to have got the nomenclature, the *learned slang*, by heart, is to have learned a great deal. It is the way children are often taught; but it is when they are taught by those whose information is but little above their own, and whose understandings, perhaps, are a little below. " What is cosmography ?" " What is an isthmus ?" " What are the antipodes ?" " What is orthography ?" and what not.

> " Confine the thought, to exercise the breath,
> " And keep them in the pale of words till death."

* See hereafter.

A proposition has very often a new striking appearance in the eyes of some readers, and a paradoxical or startling air in the eyes of others, from its being expressed through the means of technical terms; when, if turned into plain English, it either dwindles into a humble truism, or turns out to be wholly false, or even contradictory.

M. Say, in particular, seems to attribute an over importance to *terms*. He has an appendix to his work, to which he gives the title of an "epitome," but which is, in substance, a glossary. If it were really an epitome, it would not have been in the form of an alphabetical list of words to be explained. He himself is obliged, in order to make it serve as an epitome, to give an index raisonné to it, that we may get it into a more convenient order. The merit of a work of reasoning is surely in no respect in proportion to the number of definitions it gives us, or the number of new terms it obliges us to get by heart. Even its novelty and originality do not, in the slightest degree, arise from these sources. On the contrary, it will, cæteris paribus, be better, if it tells us what it has to tell without using one single word that we were not familiarly acquainted with, in the same sense, before. It will be shorter, and its doctrines more easily learned. Our bias ought always to be against technical terms, rather than in favour of them. The *only* use of them, in sciences such as this, is where the periphrasis would be so long as to occasion confusion in sentences where it was used. To set out with a number of terms and formal definitions, gives, it is thought, an air of resemblance to mathematical accuracy. But the accuracy of mathematics does not consist in having many technical terms, which require definitions, but in having no term that *has not*, where it *is* necessary, a clear definition, and that definition constantly borne in mind. New terms are more necessary there, as the subject is out of the common way. In mathematics, too, the language is so clear, and the limits of ideas so distinctly marked, that a word once defined hardly ever afterwards wanders from its definition. In such subjects as we are now speaking of, on the contrary, this happens perpetually; and not least, I am afraid, to those who are most full of definitions; therefore the more we can introduce, in practice, the definition itself instead of the term defined, the better. New terms where they are not wanted, or old terms, which, as commonly used, have no very clear unambiguous meaning, or old terms which are new defined so as not to coincide with their common use, or whose meaning has been the subject of difference of opinion, are better avoided wherever it is possible to do so.

The way in which the term "value" introduces itself into speculations on political economy is, I believe,

1. We sometimes say, that the object of these speculations, the *end* of which they are in search, is "public wealth," or "the wealth of nations," or "riches;" and that this consists in the "*value*" of the things we possess, and not in their bulk or quantity.

2. The *price* of commodities, of labour, and of land, is a constant subject of our consideration. Now the price of a thing means, in common language, the money which is given for it. Things are said to rise or fall as they exchange for more or less *money*. But every body agrees, that if we wish to reason accurately on these subjects, we must look a little further than this. It is admitted, that money itself may be said to rise or fall; and that, therefore, a conformity or a difference of price estimated (as is usual) in money, may sometimes be only an apparent (or,

as Dr. Smith calls it, *nominal*) conformity or difference of price. The question, then, is, when we *call* this a nominal price, what is the other sort of price, the real price, the existence of which we thus recognize and refer to? And since money is not the measure, criterion, or definition of it, what is? It is obviously only when we are considering the money price of a thing in *different* times or countries, that this difference between nominal and real price makes its appearance. This is stated by Smith, b. i, ch. v, p. 49, edit. 1806. It is desirable to bear this in mind. For "money price," or "nominal price," the term "price," by itself, is by some writers adopted; and then "value" supplies the place of "real price." By A. Smith, "value," when restricted to the sense of "exchangeable value," is considered as synonymous with "real price." The question, then, is repeated, When we say that the quantity of money which will purchase a particular thing, is only the nominal or apparent price of it, or is a sign of its nominal or apparent value only, and that, consequently, it has besides a real price, or a real value (call it which you please), what is it we thus refer to? What do we mean? Now the case in which the money price of a thing is said not to be its real price, or its real value, or the sign of its real value, is when, though the rate at which the thing exchanges with money is *different* (in some other place or time), the rate at which it exchanges with certain *other things* is the *same* (or vice versâ). Then the question is, *what* are those other things with which, when in such cases it exchanges at the *same* rate, we say its real price or value is the same. Various answers are given to this. Some say, labour; some say, all things taken together, or the average of them; and perhaps add, that as this last is a criterion difficult to ascertain and apply, some one or more individual things must be resorted to, and used as a *sample*, or *specimen*, of the rest; such as corn, the labour which *produced* the thing in question, the labour it will *command*, &c. I am not now deciding between the merits of these answers: but whatever answer we give, we must recollect, that we are inquiring what the import of the word *is*, not what it *ought* to be. Nothing can be more inconvenient than to introduce, in any degree, an arbitrary definition of our own, while we are professedly only explaining a term already admitted. It may, indeed, happen that the term has not, when used as it commonly is, *any* precise or determinate meaning attached to it (for this is the case with a great many words, as Locke and Bacon long ago complained); but then that would only show that we had better discard it altogether; in which case we must take the trouble, whenever we are speaking of the price, or value of a thing, to specify distinctly *against what* other thing or things the exchange, which we thereby mean to allude to, is supposed by us to take place: as is recommended by Mr. Ricardo (page 484, second edition).

There is an obvious difficulty in supposing that *labour* is what we mentally allude to, when we talk of value or of real price, as opposed to nominal price; for we often want to speak of the value or price of labour itself. Where by labour, as the real price of a thing, we mean the labour which *produced* the thing, there is another difficulty besides; for we often want to speak of the value or price of *land*; but land is not produced by labour. This definition, then, will only apply to commodities; and therefore it supposes, that value means, when applied to commodities, something different from what it does when applied to la-

bour or land. I have all along used the word " thing,"
instead of " commodity," in order to include labour, land,
and any thing else, if any such there be, that can be said
to have a value, or bear a price. Some writers have, with
the same view, called labour a commodity (see, for instance, Mr. Malthus's Principles of Political Economy) ;
but this is giving an arbitrary definition ; for we do *not*
mean to include labour, ordinarily, when we use the word
" commodity:" and many things previously asserted of commodities, and truly asserted, will *appear* not to be true
by this new definition. So M. Say calls labour a *product*,
vol. ii, 227, &c. But we generally mean by product,
product of labour.

There is, too, a difficulty, when we set up the *whole
mass of things* as the measure; and I have alluded to it
above, by using the word " *average.*" I mean this :—
Suppose the money price of the thing we are speaking of
to remain fixed, and that its price, measured in *some*
things besides money, has remained fixed too; while its
price, measured in *other* things, has altered—which things
are we to go by ? The majority, probably. But it is not
always easy to be ascertained which is the majority ; and
this is what principally leads me to think, that the word
value, or price of a thing, when used thus absolutely, that
is, without specifying against what you are supposing the
particular thing in question to be exchanged, has not any
very accurate or definite meaning; except in the case
where we can say that a change of the money price of a
thing is only nominal, because the same change has been
undergone by *all* things without exception, and therefore
is to be called a change in the price of money. Mr.
Ricardo tells us indeed, in page 13 (second edition), that
" the inquiry to which he wishes to draw the reader's at-

tention relates to the effect of the variations in the *relative* value of commodities, *and not* in their *absolute* value;" as if he there considered that there *is* such a thing as exchangeable value which is not relative.

He says, in page 40, " no commodities rise in exchangeable value merely because wages rise," &c. But he thinks some *fall*. Then the two sets of commodities exchange with one another at a different rate from what they did before. Then the value of one set in exchange for the other *rises*, just as that of the other in exchange for the first *falls*.

In page 43, he says, if the whole produce is increased, but a less *proportion* of the new mass goes to rent than before, though a greater absolute quantity, " it would, I apprehend, *be correct* for me to say, that rent had *fallen,* while profits had *risen."* Surely it would be most " correct" to state plainly the exact truth ; without searching for a short way of expressing it, which requires something to be *understood* by the reader. " For," he adds, " if we had an invariable measure of the value, we should find," &c. That is, an invariable measure of the exchangeable value of the whole produce. I want to know what exchangeable value, when applied to the *whole* produce, *means ?*

I will refer to another word, which I think is something in the same predicament. All value is relative, as M. Say observes; and as we should more easily bear in mind, if the word " exchangeable," or " in exchange," which in this sense it always *implies,* were always uttered and expressed. Now all *motion* is also relative; for by motion we merely mean, an alteration in the distance or interval between two things. But we have been accustomed, to save time, to use the word " motion," *absolutely.* When the distance between a ship and the whole mass of the country from which it set out, is altered, we say, absolutely, that the ship moves; and if we were asked whether the country moves too, should generally answer, no, it is at rest. That is, because the ship is small compared to the country. Yet this same country, perhaps, at the same time, alters its distance with regard to the heavenly bodies, and is itself said, when considered in that point of view, to *move ;* the heavenly bodies being now said to remain at rest: but we still *mean* only that the *distance between* these bodies and our earth, or that particular part of it, is *altered;* and that they are more, and larger, than it. Yet from this way of speaking, from this habit of saying, for shortness, that the ship, or the earth *moved,* absolutely, in order to express that a *relative* motion or change of distance took place between them and some other things, philosophers long maintained that motion was inherent, and that if there were but one thing in the universe it yet might move; that the earth (for instance) might be said to move, absolutely, though the heavenly bodies were annihilated; and if they were reminded that motion was relative, they would then assert, that the earth in such case would move relatively to the *parts of space ;* that is (by the very definition of space), relatively to *nothing at all**. " There is nothing" (as Mr. Malthus observes, in the Essay on Population), " which has given occasion to such a host of errors, as the confusion between relative and positive."

As far as relates to commodities only (but this, I have already observed, is an incomplete view of the question),

* See the Scholium to the Definitions in Newton's Principia, book i; and Berkeley, De Motu.

the difficulty above mentioned is sometimes thought to be removed by pointing out a *cause* of the rise of exchangeable value; and then, where a change in the relative exchangeable value of two commodities, that is, of the rate at which they exchanged with one another, has taken place, that commodity on which this *cause* has operated, would be said, absolutely, to be risen in value, while that, as to which the cause had remained stationary, would be said to have remained at the same value. For instance, take the cause to be, the increase of the quantity of labour, which produces the commodity. This is what Mr. Ricardo has done. Then he says of a commodity, which still requires the same quantity of unassisted labour to produce or raise it, that it is still of the same value, amidst any changes that may have arisen as to all, or many, other commodities*. But this cannot be admitted. Whether you assign this or that *cause* for a thing, cannot alter the question, " *What is* the thing you are assigning the cause for?" " The increase of the labour which produces commodities makes them rise in value." Be it so; provided we recollect, that the *meaning* of this is only, " makes the rate at which they exchange for certain other commodities different from what it was before." The

---

* " I am supposing money to be always of the same value, *in other words, to be* always the produce of the same quantity of unassisted labour." Ricardo, page 41, second edition. It is only the expression, " of the same value" that I am objecting to, as producing confusion; it would have been sufficient to have said, that money would then serve for a *criterion* or measure of relative value, *viz.* that the relative values of things would *be as* the relative quantities of money they would then exchange for. So, page 343, " That commodity alone is *invariable,* which at all times requires the same sacrifice of toil and labour to produce it."

other commodities may just as well be said to have *fallen*. All you *mean* is, a change in the *relation* between them; and the *cause* ought to be stated in a relative form too, as well as the fact which it is the cause of. A hat, for instance, it should be said, rises in value in exchange for a coat, not " because the labour required to produce a hat is *increased*," but " because that labour bears a larger *proportion* to the labour required to produce a coat, and the latter a less *proportion* to the former." If the absolute quantity of labour, which produces the greater part of commodities, or all except one, is increased, would you say that the value of that one is unaltered ? In what sense ? since it will exchange for less of every commodity besides. If, indeed, it is meant to be asserted that the *meaning* of increase or diminution of value, is increase or diminution in the quantity of labour that produced the commodity spoken of, the conclusions I have just been objecting to might be true enough. But to say, as Mr. Ricardo does, that the comparative quantities of labour that produce two commodities are the cause of the rate at which those two commodities will exchange with each other, *i. e.* of the exchangeable value of each, understood in relation to the other,—is very different from saying, that the exchangeable value of either *means* the quantity of labour which produced it, understood without any reference to the other, or to the existence of any other. If Mr. Ricardo *understands* by the value of a thing (as M. Say does, in part, by " real price") its value *in exchange for* the quantity of labour which produced it, his inquiries about the reasons for exchanging a deer for two salmon, &c. &c. are superfluous ; for we need not inquire whether *that* is or is not the *cause* of a thing, which we have already determined to be the very *essence* and *definition* of it.

" When we speak of high or low value," &c., says Mr.
Ricardo, p. 484, " we should always mention some
medium in which we are estimating them, or no idea can
be attached to the proposition," &c. I ask nothing more,
than that this rule be always borne in mind. I take it, it
is not *only* true in the case of different countries. But
this *medium* is the answer to the question, " value—in
exchange for *what* ?" and is not always what is meant by
the term *standard,* or *measure,* of exchangeable value;
a fact which Mr. Ricardo in some places forgets. Thus;
" corn is risen in value :" apply the above rule, and ask,
" in exchange for what ?" suppose the answer to be,
" hats;" then hats are the *medium* in which we are estimating it. Afterwards we want to know (what is a perfectly different point), *why* has the value of corn in exchange for hats risen ? Mr. Ricardo would answer, because the proportion between the quantities of labour,
which each costs, has altered. The quantities of labour,
which each costs, come then to be called, in one sense,
the *standard,* or *measure,* of the exchangeable value of
the two articles. But that does not prove that when you
said, " corn was risen in value in exchange for hats," you
meant that corn required more labour to produce it, still
less that you meant that it was risen in value *in exchange
for the labour* of producing it; according to what M. Say
calls the " exchange of production." Mr. Ricardo, in
some places, departs from that which appears to be the
great merit of his reasoning on this subject; namely, that
he had confined himself to the consideration of the rate
at which two commodities exchange with one another, to
" relative value," as he says, p. 13; and therefore denied
that any thing is a component part of price, which enters
in an equal proportion into the price of *every thing.*

In Mr. Malthus's book on Political Economy, p. 97, it is observed, that rent should be considered as a component part of price, because it enters into the price of almost all commodities. If it did, and in equal proportions, that would be exactly why it should *not* be considered as a component part of price, if by that is meant a cause of the rate at which commodities exchange with one another. Whatever claims it may have to be considered as affecting price, must be just owing to its *not* entering into the price of all things, or not by any means in an equal degree. So of profits. But if " component part of price" means only, that part of the price of almost every thing is, in fact, distributed to the landlord and capitalist, of course all agree as to that. Smith himself considers rent, on the whole, as depending on price, rather than price on rent.

The doctrine of Mr. Ricardo is not open to the observations made upon it in p. 86 of Mr. Malthus's book, except where he departs from his original point in the manner above noticed. Mr. Malthus says, it is obviously false where " applied in a *positive* sense," that is, where we say of a given commodity, considered without reference to others, or where we say of all commodities, that its value, or their value, positively, or absolutely, is increased, by their being produced by more labour. But the beauty of Mr. Ricardo's reasonings, for the most part, is, that he does *not* speak of it " in a positive sense;" but merely asserts, that the *relative* quantities of labour determine the *relative* values, *i. e.* the rate at which the two commodities will exchange with each other. " Gladios potuit contemnere, si sic omnia dixisset."

That Mr. Ricardo has departed from his original use of the term value, and has made of it something absolute, instead of relative, is still more evident in his chapter, entitled "Value and Riches, their distinctive Properties." The question there discussed, has been discussed also by others, and is purely verbal and useless; though people are fond of supposing that they are engaged in a difficult investigation into the nature of things, when they are only disagreeing about the meaning of words.

It may be thus stated :—" Raise the quantity of labour required to produce article A. Its value is raised. Do the same to B. *Its* value is raised. So on to C, &c., till you have thus raised the quantity of labour required to produce *all* articles. Is not then the value of *all* raised, and are not therefore, supposing the *quantity* to remain as before, the owners of all, the country, the world, richer ?"—No. The rise of value of article A, only *meant* value *estimated* in articles B, C, &c. *i. e.* value *in exchange for* articles B, C, &c. They, taken together, fall just as much with reference to A, or, *estimated in* A. The reaction (if I may use the metaphor) is equal to the action. So when B rises in its turn, that again lowers the value of A (and of all others except B) *estimated in* B, and so on. The value of the whole, then, has not risen at all.

" Value, then," Mr. Ricardo observes, p. 340, " essentially differs from riches." One would think, it could hardly have been supposed they were the same. Value is a property of things, riches of men. Value, in this sense, necessarily implies exchange, riches do not.

Mr. Ricardo derives the above inference from the position in Smith, that " a man is rich or poor according to the degree in which he can afford to enjoy the necessaries, conveniences, and amusements of human life." I would here observe, that I believe the terms rich and poor, as commonly used, imply a comparison of one man with another. A man, who has only those necessaries, &c., which nature gives to every body, is not said to be rich in a small degree, but not to be rich *at all;* as a man, who has no more honesty than the generality of people, is not praised for his goodness. His first step to riches must be to have something *more* than that which *every man* has. But this by the way.

Smith deduces his notion of *value* from this proposition of his, concerning *riches,* as I will presently show.

Taking it for the present that the above is a correct account of the meaning of " riches," it is clear, that where you are speaking of the riches of " *a man,*" i. e. of one single person's property, of a portion of property small compared to the general mass, the exchangeable value of what this man possesses, *i. e.* the number of certain other things, or the degree of purchaseable gratification, which it will procure him in exchange, may be of more consequence to the question of his *riches,* than the actual enjoyment he could derive from it while in his possession. But the more you multiply the number of your " men" in this case, the larger and more various you conceive the whole property to be, on the riches of whose owners you are pronouncing, the less will this be true. The more important will it be, what enjoyments their property will actually afford them in use or consumption; and the less important will it be, what enjoyments it would afford if parted with for other things. The exchangeable value of the property becomes less and less an important ingredient in the owner's *riches.* At last it becomes no ingredient at *all,* viz. when you come to consider, collectively, the owners of *all* the property that is in the world. But at the same point, where riches become thus entirely independent of exchangeable value, exchangeable value itself, as applied to the property we are speaking of, taken together, ceases to mean any thing; for there are no more things left (by the supposition) to exchange these with. You are speaking of *all*. Mr. Ricardo, however, talks of the " value of the general mass of commodities" being " diminished," (p. 341.) Value in exchange for *what?*

If the labour necessary to make hats is lessened, the owner of one thousand hats will, according to Mr. Ricardo, own less *value* than before. And does he not own less *riches?* " But that," it may be said, " is only because he can get fewer of *other* commodities for them, if he were to part with them." Certainly; and that is the reason why they are of less *value* too. It is the *meaning* of their being of less value.

Perhaps it may be said, " that the general mass of all commodities, though not actually exchangeable, *might* become exchangeable; supposing more things to exist, the owners of the present whole *mass of commodities would* then be the owners of more value." The moment you have supposed that, it will follow that they would be the owners of more *riches* too, if the new discovered commodities can be exchanged for those now possessed; and if they cannot, they will not affect the *value* of those now possessed. Riches, it is very true, do not depend *wholly* on the consideration of what the owner could get in exchange for what he possesses, for he may keep it himself, and enjoy it; but neither do they ever wholly *exclude* that consideration, where he can exchange them at all.

In p. 341, Mr. Ricardo says, that if equal labour comes to produce a greater quantity of some commodity than it did, the value of the new quantity produced by it will be equal to that of the former quantity; but yet that the whole value of the general mass of commodities will be diminished, because there will be a *stock on hand* of the newly cheapened article, which, he observes, will *come down* in price. But that *means*, that it will exchange for fewer of other articles; then other articles will exchange for more of *it*: what has this to do with the value of the general mass?

He then observes on the different measures of value adopted by different writers, and inquires, " why should any commodity, or *all commodities together*, be the standard, when such a standard is itself subject to fluctuations of value?" " All commodities together" are taken as a standard of value in exchange, because they are the *meaning* of value in exchange. We *mean*, if we mean any thing, by " a greater value in exchange" (when we do not add, " in exchange for corn," or for some particular thing) the exchanging for a greater number of other commodities in general (see Malthus, p. 131.)

" All commodities" cannot be subject to fluctuations of value, because they are not subject to *value*; value is inapplicable to them; they may fluctuate in value among themselves, compared to each other, but the whole mass cannot. " But how can any thing measure value that has not value itself?" Very easily; if you will only consider the *meaning* of value. When you ask that question, you are sedulously shutting up your mind to the meaning of the word you are using; and, because the term *measure* is used, are thinking of *length*, or *quantity*, or some such thing.

" That commodity," Mr. Ricardo adds, " is alone invariable, which at all times requires the same sacrifice of toil and labour to produce it." By "invariable," is meant always of the same value in exchange. I ask then, in exchange for what other things? Not for " all commodities together," else *they* might have been the standard as well; whereas he says they cannot, because subject to ' fluctuations in value." In exchange for labour? But labour is liable to fluctuations of value too. If the proposition is meant for a *new definition* of " invariable," then it can throw no light on the defects of former systems; they must be tried by what their *own meaning* was.

Mr. Ricardo thinks that the value of the necessaries, conveniences, and enjoyments of human life would be raised by diminishing their number ; " because by scarcity the value of commodities is raised." But this is not true of the *whole mass* even of *one* commodity, always. For instance; scarcity, owing to increased difficulty of production, would make *a pair* of stockings more valuable; but not, perhaps, the *whole mass* of stockings. Spoken of all commodities, it appears to have no meaning; because the " value" of *all* commodities has nothing left in which it can be estimated.

" It is true," he says, " that the man in possession of a scarce commodity is richer, &c., but as the general stock, &c., is diminished in quantity by all that any individual takes from it, other men's shares must necessarily be reduced in proportion as this favoured individual is able to appropriate a greater quantity to himself." This is to show that people will be less *rich*. But is it not equally true, that the " other men's shares" will be " reduced in *value?*" They can command less of this particular article, which has become scarce; and that is not made up for, by their commanding more of any other. In the next page, where he puts *water* as this article, he says, " they are poorer;" I add, and their property is of less *value;* it will not exchange for so much of the " necessaries, &c., of life," including water, as before.

Mr. Ricardo adds, " it may be said, then, of two countries possessing precisely the same quantity of all the necessaries and comforts of life, that they are equally rich, but the *value* of their riches would depend on the comparative facility or difficulty with which they were produced." I should say, that this last would only be true if they could exchange some of their riches for something from another country. If they could not, to talk of the value, *that is, the exchangeable value* of their riches, appears to be unmeaning. If they could, in order to which we must now suppose that they do *not* possess *all* the necessaries and comforts of life, I do not know that the country, whose riches had been produced with the greatest difficulty, would be that which would command the greatest quantity, of foreign " necessaries and comforts of life." But whether it was or not, that country of the two, at all events, would find the *value* of its riches the greatest, which could command, for a given portion of them, the greatest quantity of foreign " necessaries," &c.; and that would also (though not in the same proportion) be the *richest;* for riches do not, according to the definition of Adam Smith, which Mr. Ricardo set out with, depend on the degree in which we *possess,* merely, but in which we " *can command,*" that is, by exchange as well as possession, the " necessaries, &c., of life." See Malthus on Political Economy, p. 338.

We have, in p. 328 of Mr. Ricardo's book, a case put, of a country being no longer able to import so much, as it did before, of foreign commodities; and then he adds, " although the total value of the productions of the country will probably be but little altered, since the same capital will be employed, yet they will not be equally abundant and cheap," &c. What, but puzzle, is obtained by introducing " the total value" here in this manner? Total value, in exchange—for foreign commodities? But in this sense it *is* altered; because he says the country cannot get so much foreign commodities in exchange as before; and if it is not meant with respect to foreign commodities, what meaning has it?

But the case supposed by Mr. Malthus, p. 340, requires attention. If all the roads, &c., were suddenly broken up, " there would," says he, " be a great fall of exchangeable value of the whole mass of articles." That which would happen would be, not that each article would exchange (when it came to exchange) for a different portion than before of other articles, but that many of them would not exchange at all; and therefore would not answer to the owners the purpose for which they were made. For the most part of a vast stock of an article made to sell, may, if it loses its value in exchange, leave absolutely no value in use to the maker of it. In no sense of value is it true, that a certain article has a certain rate of value, whatever may be the quantity, or wherever it may be.

Exchangeable value becomes, in Mr. Malthus's opinion, p. 337, essential to wealth, because man cannot get the necessaries, &c., of life, without his own exertions, to which the great stimulus is " the desire to possess what can only be had by some labour or *sacrifice*." The real reason obviously is the advantage to be derived from *division* of labour; else we might all work hard, and yet never exchange.

Mr. Ricardo has pointed out much confusion and inconsistency in the use of the term " valeur," by M. Say.

It is singular that instances of this inconsistency should, notwithstanding, still be retained by this writer ; but inconsistency is rather valuable to any writer, who is fond of giving to his observations a paradoxical air. "Lorsqu'un homme," says he, vol. i, p. 5, "vend à un autre un produit quelconque, il lui vend l'utilité qui est dans ce produit : l'acheteur ne l'achète qu'à cause de son utilité, de l'usage qu'il en peut faire. Si par une cause quelconque" (he is alluding to *monopolies*) " l'acheteur est obligé de le payer au delà de ce que vaut pour lui cette *utilité*, il paie une *valeur* qui *n'existe pas*, et qui par conséquent, ne lui est pas livrèe." Now really this means nothing at all. A buyer never can be obliged to pay for a thing " more than the utility of the thing is worth to him ;" if by that is meant, to forego entirely, in order to get it, some other thing whose utility to him is greater ; if he can no otherwise get it than so, he *will not* pay for it at all : and if that is not the meaning, I really do not know what is. " If by any cause the buyer is obliged to pay, beyond" (it should have been) " what he would pay but for that cause," and then all the wonderment and air of paradox ceases. Or " obliged to pay for this article, if he purchases it, something which would have procured some other article, that, if he had not been already in possession of it, would have been of more utility than the article in question." But what then ? this is true of many articles. When I have got as much bread as I want to eat, I forego the acquisition of more, in order to obtain things of far less consequence. M. Say, himself, elsewhere, does not pretend, that the value of things is in proportion to their utility ; nay, he does not pretend that, even here ; for he says, " la valeur échangeable, ou le prix, n'est une indication de l'utilité que les hommes reconnoissent dans une chose, *qu'autant que* le marché qu'ils font ensemble n'est soumis à aucune influence étrangère à cette même utilité." Why then talk of a man " paying for a *value* which does not exist," when he pays more than in proportion to the *utility ?*

M. Say, in p. 163, of his " Lettres," says, that riches are composed of value, because the value of each thing I possess (as a horse, &c.), depends on the quantity of *other* things I can get in exchange for it, "*quand* j'ai besoin d'échanger un cheval, &c. contre du froment," &c. But he omits the other case, viz. *when* I do *not* want to exchange, but to consume; and yet to this last case the former case must always *tend,* for exchange is only in order to consume. When I have *got* the corn he speaks of, how am I to measure my riches then ? It seems that the end is to be considered of less importance than the means. He then supposes Mr. Ricardo to put it to him, that he cannot deny that " on ne soit plus riche lors qu'on *a plus* de choses agréables et nécessaires à *consommer, quelle que soit d'ailleurs* leur *valeur ;*" which means, of course, " even though their *value* should be *less.*" To the astonishment, I should think, of his reader, he answers, " J'en *conviens en effet!*" To reconcile this contradiction, he resorts to another contradiction : " n'est-ce pas avoir plus de choses à consommer, que d'avoir la puissance d'en acquérir en plus grande quantité ?" " Posséder plus de *richesses, c'est avoir* dans ses mains le *pouvoir d'acheter* une plus grande quantité de choses utiles," &c. He just before agreed, that one was richest when one had the most of agreeable and necessary things *to consume :* now he says, to *part with.*

In his Traité d'Econ. Polit. ii, 26 (edit. 4), he says himself, " C'est, comme on voit, la quantité des produits *et non leur valeur* qui fait le revenu de la nation vu en masse :" the very proposition he condemns in Mr. Ricardo. Surely, the shortest way would be to discard the term if we cannot agree about it, and submit to the necessity of speaking plain, and at full length.

According to Mr. Ricardo, Smith is unjustly represented by M. Say as having considered *labour* as a measure of *riches* as well as of value. But I believe it will be found, that Smith has not in fact kept sufficiently clear of what is here imputed to him; for he comes to the consideration of value, and of labour as its measure, as flowing from his definition of riches already cited.

The expression quoted from M. Say, at the end of this chapter of Mr. Ricardo (and there is a similar one, vol ii, p. 501), "that a man is infinitely rich without valuables, if he can for nothing obtain all the objects he desires," is merely an example of the practice of using a word in a sense which it does not bear, and by that means dressing up a striking and paradoxical sentence. We do *not* call a man rich who is without valuables. Nor *should* we, in the case he has supposed, of a state in which every thing should be supplied without labour, by nature, for the reason I have already mentioned; viz. that "rich" imports something not possessed by *every man*. And if we did, it would, as observed by Mr. Ricardo, be at variance with M. Say himself, who makes riches to be synonymous with value. Vol. i, p. 1, 2, &c.; and Lettres à M. Malthus, p. 163. There is a great deal in M. Say's work that is very sensible, and very clearly explained. But whenever he concerns himself with inventing or systematically defining *terms*, he seems to feel himself out of his element.

" Des richesses *naturelles*," M. Say says, vol. i, p. 5,

" n'ont point de valeur échangeable." Valeur échangeable, according to him, is the only sort of value ; so much
so, that he thinks Smith need not have mentioned value in
use, even for the purpose of rejecting it. Then, surely,
here again, it appears that riches and value are not always
synonymous.

M. Say, as well as Mr. Malthus, appears to me to be much
too apt to treat mere definitions as if they were axioms. The
former often calls an explanation of a word " un prin-
cipe *," and is therefore naturally led to think that a definition, though professedly of a common word, may have
other merits than that of correctness. For instance, the
opinion of M. *Louis Say*, which he refers to, as contrary
to his own, may be wrong; but certainly it is not because
M. Louis Say's interpretation of " utility" *would make it*
" une quantité arbitraire." The question is, what *is* the
meaning in common acceptation; what *do* we understand
by it? I have the same objection to the sort of praise he
bestows on Smith; *viz.* that by his definition of value in
exchange he *elevated* political economy into the rank of a
science, *gave it* accuracy, *made it* to be employed about
appreciable things, and delivered it " de la domaine des
reveries ;"

Immotamque coli dedit, et contemnere ventos.

So Mr. Malthus, in the beginning of his work on Political
Economy, talks of the question "what is wealth," as *fundamental*. Surely it is only a verbal question. "It may
lead to great practical changes." So may any dispute
about words, if you choose to *suppose* it to be a dispute

* Vol. ii, p. 4; and Lettre v, à M. Malthus, init.

about things. If two persons lay it down that "robbery should be punished with death," and *then* begin to discuss what "robbery" means (as, whether picking pockets or house-breaking), doubtless, this is now a discussion of great practical importance. But that is only because they chose to begin at the wrong end; chose to establish, at first, a supposed maxim, which they had not settled the meaning of, and which was therefore no maxim at all, only so much empty noise. Whether robbery should be punished with death, ought to have been left to *depend* on the meaning to be *previously* affixed to the term "robbery." The *substantial* question which they differed about (we will suppose, for instance, whether house-breaking and picking pockets ought both to be punished with death, or only the former) would then have remained unaffected by the *verbal* discussion as to the meaning of the word "robbery." So, if you first agree that "wealth" (or value, or what not) is the object of our inquiries and pursuit in political economy, it becomes a *practical* question to inquire afterwards what wealth or value mean. But that is owing to your having agreed to the truth of a proposition before you had settled its meaning. A proceeding very common, certainly, but wholly irrational. It would be better, of the two, to limit our inquiries and object by a new definition of *political economy*, an artificial and technical word, than by a new definition of *wealth*.

This never happens in mathematics. We do not there adopt a proposition from another writer, or from common use, without being quite sure that we understand it, nor without having gone to the bottom of it, and, as it were, proved it for ourselves. In order to make any science approach to the accuracy of mathematical conclusion, one would think that it might be desirable to imitate, as far as it *is* possible, the process adopted in mathematical reasoning; instead of folding our hands, and lamenting that the "nature of the subject" has excluded the possibility of attaining to the certainty which belongs to the "stricter sciences*."

"The comparative merits of Smith's system and that of the French Economists, depend," in Mr. Malthus's opinion, p. 26, "mainly on their different definitions" of wealth, &c. I should say, that if the Economists assume that wealth is the main object to be pursued, or in any way assume as true any proposition about it which is commonly maintained by those who use it in its ordinary sense, and at the same time define it themselves in a different way from the ordinary sense, and lay down propositions of their own in which they use it in their own peculiar sense, all this mixture, to be sure, will probably produce error; or if they say that wealth is commonly understood in one sense, when in fact it is commonly understood in another, that too must be an error, of course. But the avoiding and pointing out these errors cannot surely be the main merit of Smith's system, unless it is merely of a *redargutive* and negative kind. A bad definition certainly may be a very great positive *evil*.

> Ut in fabricâ, si prava'st regula prima,
> Normaque si fallax rectis regionibus exit,
> Et libella aliquâ si ex parti claudicat hilum,
> Omnia mendosè fieri atque obstipa necessum'st,—

but a true definition is no great positive *advance*, or addition to knowledge.

* This relates to the two or three first pages of Mr. Malthus's book on Political Econom

Mr. Malthus prefers material products to immaterial, as criterions for the definition of wealth, because alone capable of "definite valuation." But we want to know what the word *means*, I apprehend, not what it would be convenient for our present purpose that it *should* mean. Besides, the fact is not true; immaterial products may often be measured, in respect of *value*, which is what we are considering; and material products sometimes cannot. So M. Say excludes such a thing as water, because not appreciable: yet it is sometimes bought, sold, and rented. His definition would prove, that *land* has no value, for he says ("Lettres," p. 157), that things that cannot be increased or consumed are not valuable. In his "Lettres à M. Malthus," p. 157, after excluding from the title of riches such things as a glass of water, friendship, reputation, he adds, "Quelles sont donc les richesses *du ressort de cette science?* Celles qui sont susceptible de création et de destruction, de plus et de moins; et *ce plus, ce moins,* qu'est-ce encore une fois? de la *valeur.*" Are then water, and friendship, and reputation, not susceptible of more and less? He says the same, p. 163, "Qu'est-ce en effet que la valeur, que cette qualité susceptible d'appréciation, susceptible de plus et de moins," &c. I cannot conceive how the being susceptible of more and less is the same thing with being susceptible of appreciation. Appreciation means a capability of being *measured ;* or, of being *valued.* M. Say must here mean the former, or it is a mere identical proposition. I can conceive it may be said, as it was by Aristotle, that to be susceptible of more and less, in *one* sense, is what *prevents* appreciation. One thing is not *more four ounces weight* than another, it is either four ounces weight or not. But one thing *is* more *white, smooth,* &c., than another; hence quantity is accurately appreciable, and quality not.

To confine wealth to material things is what M. Say much disapproves. " Et nos talens (he exclaims) pour quoi les prenez-vous donc? Je connois des artistes habiles qui n'ont d'autre revenu que celui qu'ils *tirent de* leur talens, *et* qui sont *dans l'opulence.* Selon vous" (he says to Malthus) " ils ne seraient pas plus riches qu'un bar-bouilleur d'échoppes." No; you are talking of people who have got riches, *in addition to* their talents; they *derive these* from their talents; then the talents *are not* the riches. They *might* have had the talents, and not derived any riches from them. " *Et* qui sont dans l'opu-lence." " Je *connois des* artistes," &c. That is *admitting* that *merely* to be " un artiste habile" is not to be rich, that *all* such are not rich. If mere talent is riches, one might serve him as Diogenes served Plato, send a starving poet, or painter, into his lecture-room, in rags, and cry, " Voilà le riche de M. Say !" Such persons are *not called* rich.

Smith, he says, would not allow immaterial products to have value, " a méconnu des valeurs échangeables très réelles," &c. (Lettres, p. 41.) But Smith treats of the *value* of menial service, &c. Vol. ii, p. 84, 85 (edit. 1806).

One is astonished to find M. Say, after all, saying (Lettres, p. 167), that whatever has exchangeable value, makes *part* (only) of our riches, and that " elles" (our riches) " se composent *essentiellement* des *fonds pro-ductifs* que nous possédons : des terres ou des capitaux ou des facultés personnelles." I do not know what " essen-tiellement" means. M. Say considers production " comme un échange dans lequel on donne les services productifs de *son* travail, de sa terre, et de ses capitaux, pour obtenir des produits." It should be, the services productifs, not of *one's own* labour, &c., but of the labour, &c., one employs or hires. For the *owner* of the labour does not exchange his labour for its product, nor does the owner of the land, his land; but for their wages and rent. However, there is then, it seems, one sort of exchange which takes place between one product and another, and another sort of exchange which takes place between services productifs and products. Though, therefore, where products cost more, and are more valuable, *their* owners are richer, yet the light in which people are to be considered for this purpose is, it seems, as the owners of *services productifs*, which he calls nos *premiers revenus* (but they should be our *only* revenues, in order to make out his proposition), and *then* they are richest in the *contrary* state of things; viz. " when in the exchange, called production, the *services productifs* obtain a greater quantity of useful things." Is he speaking of what they *have actually* obtained or produced? If so, it is merely saying that people are richer because they have a greater *quantity* of products, which it would have been much better to have said directly. And if he is speaking of the quantity which their services productifs *are capable* of producing, I can only say, that we do *not* mean that, when we talk of riches. We call that "*means,*" or "power, of acquiring riches;" but we do not call it riches, except perhaps as to land, till the addition is actually produced. And even as to land, fertility may not, when we are considering a *whole country,* be a cause of riches. See the chapter in Malthus on that subject.

In another place (Livre ii, chap. iii, to page 35, fourth

edition), he says the revenue is greatest, when the *value* of the " services productifs" is greatest, and when that of products, consequently, is least. As the use of *land* is one of the services productifs, the above maxim is liable, without some further limitation, to be misinterpreted into an authority for the position, that the exchangeable value of the use of land, *i. e.* the quantity of products which the owner obtains in return for the use of it, that is, rent, is an addition to general wealth; which is the opinion of the Economistes. But M. Say's meaning of course is, that the revenue is greatest, when the value of all the sorts of *services productifs* taken together is greatest; and he would say probably, that high rent, or the high value of the *service productif* of land, is at the expense of some or both of the other *services productifs* (labour and capital) which are so much the worse paid.

But suppose we have learned to produce some article with less of the services productifs than before; are we, as he thinks, richer? If we employ as much of the services productifs as before, I grant we are; *because* we *have more produce.* If we choose (he says in page 36, of vol. ii, that we never do, but at least, I may put the case) to take advantage of this our saving, so as to cease to work so much, or use so much *services productifs,* as before, and thereby no more of the article is produced than before, we are *not* richer. In that case, we have gained either nothing, or at most only leisure and rest; and these are gains to which the term *riches* is *not* applied. And, on the other hand, if we *have* produced more, though it were *not* by any saving, but only by working harder, or employing more services productifs, we *are* said to be richer. The introducing of the *middle term, value,* seems then to have answered no end, in helping us to estimate general wealth, but only to have been a more roundabout, or less correct, way of saying what might have been said without it. M. Say was *once* so fond of this word *value*, that he *defined* the value of one thing to be the *value of other things* which it would exchange for! (Vol. ii, page 4, note.)

In vol. ii, page 26 (note), the comparative riches of two nations are stated still more *widely ;* as depending on " une appréciation morale du bien-être de l'un et de l'autre." For one cannot, he says, compare *values* that are not in the same place. But no two things are exactly in the same place; it is merely a question of *degree,* whether we are comparing two towns or two nations.

The above discussions are introduced by M. Say, in his " Lettres," to explain how it happens that " a million of persons may produce two or three times as much riches without producing more value" (page 168) "quoique la richesse soit de la valeur." He seems to admit these propositions to be *true,* and professes only to explain them. Can any explanation make them not *contradictory ?* But " telle est la *doctrine bien liée,*" he exclaims, " sans laquelle," &c. Lettres à M. Malthus, page dernière. In his Discours Préliminaire, page liv, he introduces two difficult problems, " *questions épineuses ;*" 1. " Un impôt ou tout autre fléau, en faisant renchérir les denrées, augmente-t-il la somme des richesses" (why should any body ask this question unless he thinks the *denrées* are undiminished in *quantity* as well as raised in price?) 2. " Les frais de production composant le revenu des producteurs, comment les revenus ne sont-ils pas altérés par une diminution dans les frais de production ?" A question which cannot be *answered,* because it is simply a statement of a contradiction. Not a paradox, but a falsehood on the face of it. Either part of it may be *denied,* if you please; but then, why was the question asked? What pretensions has such a question to be called a *problem,* or ranked among those, the resolving of which " constitue le science de l'Economie Politique." The way to answer such questions, where they have any pretensions to meaning, is to beg the proposer to put his meaning into precise terms; then the question will cease to seem " épineuse," or to require any answer.

Smith (Mr. Malthus says, page 30) is blamed on various grounds for defining *productive labour* as he does. Perhaps he might have been more properly blamed for defining it at all, or rather for using a term at all which he need not have used, and which he meant to use in a different sense from that which had been annexed to it by the only persons who had used it before.

I do not much admire Mr. Malthus's own definition. I object to calling three classes (distinguished from each other not by degree but by strict definition) " productive," " more productive," and " less productive." The simple distinction between the two first and the last of Mr. Malthus's classes is, that *they* produce something tangible, and capable of accumulation, and the last does not. The simple distinction between the first and the two last is, that it relates to land, and they do not. Why not denote them accordingly? Why say any thing about *productiveness* at all? " This mode," says Mr. Malthus, " would determine, in the very definition, the pre-eminence of agricultural labour," &c. That is my objection to it. A definition has no business to *determine* questions of pre-eminence. Nor does the *definition* determine it; it is the *name* that is arbitrarily made to determine it. The different degrees and the different modes in which these three sorts of labour (if they can* be accurately distinguished from one another in the way Mr. Malthus proposes) contribute to wealth, may be an interesting inquiry; but we do not want the *names* to help us in it; they hinder it by the prejudice which they create, and for creating which Mr. Malthus likes them. The term " unproductive," as used by Smith, is, generally, aimed at stock-holders, sinecure placemen, buffoons, opera singers, or menial servants. But, surely, whatever may be the per-nicious effects of a too great encouragement of these species of animals, they might have been enlarged upon in plain English, without its being necessary to invent or keep up an inaccurate and loose *term*.

Mr. Malthus thinks it absurd to call menial service productive, or to say that a *product* can be *immaterial*. And his *correspondent*, M. Say, observes in reply (page 35), with ridiculous " pomp and circumstance" of capi-tals and notes of admiration, that *all* products are imma-terial; as of course they are in one sense, because we do not increase the *quantity of matter*, but only work it up into a more desirable or useful form : but really we knew this before, and M. Say, of course, did not suppose that Mr. Malthus meant to deny that, or meant any thing at all about it, or used the word in that sense. This wonderful discovery, of all products being immaterial, only serves, then, to show, that *its author* made a foolish dis-tinction when he divided products into *material and im-material*, when he talked, a few pages before, of indigo

---

* See the Edinburgh Review on Lord Lauderdale's Inquiry con-cerning Public Wealth (1804). It is there observed, that upon the principle which sets aside the soldier, judge, &c., as unproductive labourers, a hedger might as well be called so ; because he only protects the corn which another rears.

being a *material product.* There is a whole chapter on *immaterial products* in his work : and yet he now tells us, with an air of triumph, that there is no such distinction, that one product is immaterial as well as another.

M. Say dislikes the maxim, " Quand tout est cher, rien n'est cher." Dearness, according to him, is high value, and a product is dear when it costs much. But when this is the case with *all* products, dearness or exchangeable value does not (in his opinion) vanish, as one would have expected; because, though we can now no longer contemplate the exchange between one *product* and another, we can that between products and the *labour,* &c., which produced them. Then products are now to be called valuable, or *dear* (which he says is the same), not (according to the definition in the epitome, article Valeur) because of the " quantity of things which you can obtain in exchange *for them,*" which things have themselves also a value*; but because of the quantity of things (*viz.* labour and other productive services), *in exchange for which* you did obtain *them* (the products); which things have *not* themselves a value, because, in order to have value, things must, he says, be " modified" and " laboured," or worked up, which is not the case with labour or land.

M. Say is fond of speaking of certain words in common use as having a particular meaning *in political economy,* which they have not elsewhere†. I cannot see the convenience of this; of announcing, for instance, that‡, in political economy, " la chose la plus

* Vol i, page 2.
† See his Lettres à M. Malthus, pages 156, 157, 160, 168.
‡ Vol. ii, page 506.

inutile" is to be spoken of as possessing utility. It seems merely meant to make us stare. The common idea of utility certainly is, that which contributes to something else: and not that which in itself satisfies some inclination, or affords any gratification. To make his idea of utility seem to agree with the common one, M. Say is obliged, vol. i, page 4, to use *besoins* in a new sense. He says (page 165 of the Lettres), " la limitation de l'idée de l'utilité est d'être egale à une autre utilité quelconque, que les autres hommes consentent de donner," &c. The limitation of an idea is the same as a definition, I presume (though it is an expression which would not be the worse for a little *limitation* itself); but the definition of utility cannot be, to be equal to another utility. M. Say is pleased with this, because he finds in it an " equation." This seems to be an application of the formal or verbal part of mathematical reasoning, where it does not apply. We had better seek to use the *substantial* part of mathematical reasoning where it *does* apply. The French philosophers (if I may venture to say so of our superiors in mathematical science) seem to make their mathematics impede rather than assist them in the prosecution of those speculations which are not mathematical. I cannot consider this a *necessary* consequence of mathematical habits, though we have the opinion of Gibbon that it is. (On the other hand, in his Discours Préliminaire to his Economie Politique, xxviii, M. Say disclaims the interference of mathematics, and tells us, value is *not* " susceptible d'aucune appréciation rigoureuse.") What M. Say means by utility being equal to another utility, &c., is simply that we must keep in mind the *average*, or *general* value set by mankind on a thing, and not the peculiar value set on it by some one

individual. But the way to express this is by the excellent term " valeur reconnue," which he elsewhere uses,
and not by " valeur échangeable," or " utilité," which he
introduces here.

Smith, he says, discards value in use, and treats of value
in exchange only; and so, says M. Say, we all do, " par la
raison *qu'il n'y a pas* d'autre valeur en économie politique."
If you choose to say political economy does not *treat* of
any other sort of value, well and good: but the limited
nature of political economy cannot alter the meanings
in fact affixed to words. And why is there no other?
i. e. why is value in use discarded? Because, he says,
" celle-là seule (value in exchange) est sujette a des lois
fixes," &c. Now value in exchange, according to M. Say,
depends in part on value in use, or what he calls utility.
How then can it be exclusively subject to fixed laws,
when it depends on that which is without fixed laws?
In making this observation he probably supposes, what is
not true, that value in use means, in Smith, only the
value set on things by particular individuals, as opposed
to valeur *reconnue*.

He is of opinion, that Smith has very improperly used
the term value in use (Lettres, &c., p. 159). Smith does
not profess to *invent* the term; therefore, whether it is an
inconvenient one or not is nothing to the purpose. I
suspect, that M. Say's criticism is in part owing to the
difference of language; *valeur en usage* may be unmeaning and bad French, and yet *value in use* may be good
English. I own, I think, however, that " value in use" is
not applied by Smith quite conformably to its actual acceptation. Such a term is wanted, partly to denote the opposite
to " valeur *reconnue*" of M. Say. For this, as to the
word *value*, at least, it answers well enough. We do in

fact speak of setting a high *value* on a keepsake, a picture of a friend, &c. &c., clearly independent both of *valeur reconnue,* and of market value in exchange. But then the word " use" appears inapplicable.

It is wanted, again, to express the opposite to *exchangeable* value; to denote that quality which water has, more than diamonds; to denote what Mr. Ricardo considers as the constituent of riches, and M. Say terms utility. " *Use*" here applies well enough, though only to a certain extent; but I do not think we speak of *value,* in this sense. *Desirableness* would perhaps answer the purpose better.

Mr. Malthus doubts, page 51, whether we are in the habit of using value in the sense of value in use, as Smith has done. But then he ought not to have spoken, in p. 48, of the " value and importance" of many sorts of unproductive labourers, some of whom he observes " possess a value," &c., which he obviously understands to be, not their price, but their indirect effect on the happiness of mankind. He even adds, " to estimate the *value* of Newton's discoveries," &c., " by the price at which their works have sold, would be but a poor measure of the degree in which they have elevated," &c., distinguishing value from price, or exchangeable value, in these cases. The expression, " the value of Newton's discoveries" is certainly English; so we call a man, sometimes, a very *valuable* man; though the last is rather colloquial. But both mean *useful.* Perhaps, therefore, I am wrong in supposing, that value is not sometimes used for utility or desirableness.

With respect to *valeur reconnue,* we must observe, that there is a line, here, rather difficult to draw. An

article may have exchangeable value, though there may
be but *one* man in the world to whom it is sufficiently
desirable to induce him to pay for the trouble or difficulty
of procuring it; if it is not in that man's possession.
When it gets into his possession, its exchangeable value
will be lessened, and may quite disappear; because there
being then no person (by the supposition) who is much
in want of it, it will command no quantity, or a much
less quantity, of other things. Is it very difficult to conceive a thing very valuable in one man's hands, and not
at all valuable the next moment in another's? If it is,
the puzzle arises only from your thinking of value as
some quality *inherent* in the *particular thing*, considered
by itself. Translate value into *what it means*, viz. that
this particular thing will exchange for so much of other
things, and there is no difficulty at all.

" The second main cause," says Mr. Malthus, " favourable to an increase of exchangeable value, is internal and
external commerce. Every exchange which takes place
in a country effects a distribution of its produce better
adapted to the wants of the society. It is, with
regard to both parties concerned, an exchange of
what is wanted less for what is wanted more, and
must, therefore, raise the value of both the products."
This last conclusion does not follow, as to value *in exchange*. Each party is more *comfortable*, but that is
not exchangeable value. If, indeed, two commodities,
by a mutual exchange of which their respective owners
would derive a great increase of gratification, are at a distance from one another, he who *conveys* each from the
one place to the other, will confer on it an increase of
exchangeable value, as M. Say very clearly states it:

and this is what Mr. Malthus has in view when he uses
the above proposition, which, in the general form, as he
gives it, is false.

Smith's reason for fixing on labour, p. 39, vol. i, as the
" real measure of exchangeable value," is clearly a bad
one. " The necessaries, conveniences, and amusements of
human life," are first introduced, as the criterion or definition of riches. " Every man is rich or poor, according
to the degree in which he can afford to enjoy the necessaries, conveniences, and amusements of human life."
Then, because " the far greater part" of these are got by
other people's labour, and " but a very small part" by
one's own, " the quantity of other people's labour which
one can command or afford to purchase," is substituted
for " the necessaries, &c., of life," as the test of riches.
(" But after the division of labour has once thoroughly
taken place, it is but a very small part of these with which
a man's own labour can supply him. The far greater part
of them he must derive from the labour of other people,
and he must be rich or poor according to the quantity of
that labour which he can command, or which he can
afford to purchase.") This conclusion would have followed
more naturally, first, if instead of " a *very small* part," he
could have said " *no* part;" secondly, if the only alternative modes of getting the " necessaries, &c., of life," were
other people's labour and our own. But without reckoning those necessaries, &c., which have not value in exchange, and which cost no labour, as water, we must
apply to other sources as well as those, even for such
" necessaries," &c., as have value in exchange. We must
go to the owner of appropriated land, and to the owner of
capital, and ask their help; in short, we do not, when we
want the necessaries of life, procure them by hiring other

people to labour for us. Thirdly, if " the quantity of other people's labour," &c., be the measure or test of exchangeable value, only because it is a criterion of the " necessaries, &c., of life," which he says are the *same thing as riches,* we must measure value, not merely by the " quantity" of labour, but by its productiveness, *i. e.* by the quantity of these same " necessaries, &c.," which a given quantity of the labour will produce. " The quantity of labour we can command," &c., in short, professes to be a measure of value, only inasmuch as it accurately represents (or is an accurate measure or criterion of) the quantity of the " necessaries, &c., of life" we can command. If, then, the same quantity of labour produces at different times different quantities of the " necessaries, &c., of life" (which it does in fact, and very different quantities of *different* articles, even at the *same* time), it is (for this reason alone, even if there were no other) a bad criterion of the amount of those " necessaries," &c.

When we are taught to look only at the labour, and to take *labour* simply as the criterion, we shall be led to think, that a thing may be more valuable if it commands more labour, though that labour commands a less quantity of the necessaries, &c., of life.

Smith having got thus far, sums up in these words : " The value of any commodity, therefore, to the person who possesses it, and who means not to use or consume it himself, but to exchange it for other commodities, is equal to the quantity of labour which it enables him to purchase or command." Now here we are told to confine ourselves to the case of a man who does *not* mean to use or consume his property himself. How can this answer to the *more general* case supposed in the definition of riches from which it was deduced ? " Labour, therefore, is the

real measure of the exchangeable value of commodities."
" *Labour*," in general, is foisted in here instead of " the
quantity of labour which a commodity enables its owner
to purchase or command." We are next told, " the real
price of every thing" (which appears from p. 39 to be the
same thing as the real measure of exchangeable value),
" what every thing really costs to the man who wishes to
acquire it, is the toil and trouble of acquiring it. What
every thing is really worth to the man who has acquired it,
and who wants to dispose of it, or exchange it for something else, is the toil and trouble which it can save to
himself, and which it can impose upon other people.
Labour was the first price, the original purchase money
that was paid for all things. It was not by gold or by
silver, but by labour, that all the wealth of the world was
originally purchased ; and its value to those who possess
it, and who want to exchange it for some new productions,
is precisely equal to the quantity of labour which it will
enable them to purchase or command *." " In that early
and rude state of society, which precedes both the accumulation of stock and the appropriation of land, the proportion between the quantities of labour necessary for
acquiring different objects seems to be the only circumstance which can afford any rule for exchanging them for
one another. If among a nation of hunters, for example,
it usually cost twice the labour to kill a beaver which it
does to kill a deer, one beaver should *naturally* exchange
for, or be worth two deer. It is *natural*, that what is
usually the produce of two days', or two hours' labour,
should be worth double of what is usually the produce of
one day's or one hour's labour†." To prove this last fact,

---

* Smith, chap. v, p. 39, 40.   † Chap. vi, p. 63, edit. 1806.

it is not at all necessary, surely, to say that labour *was price,* purchase money, &c.; or that " what every thing is really worth," &c.; and it might have been better to have said more by way of proving it, than that it was " *natural.*" This seems meant to explain more fully the doctrine already laid down; coupled with what follows, it is meant to lead to the doctrine, that *labour, generally,* i. e. what the thing *cost, or* what it will purchase (being, according to Smith, the same, as I understand him), is the measure of value : and to enable him to use the word *labour,* by itself, and unexplained, as the measure of value ; by which unconfined, general use of the word *labour,* he saves much trouble to himself, and produces much confusion to his readers. However, the way he now treats it is widely different from the way he first treated it at the beginning of chapter v. There, the quantity of necessaries, &c., was value, and the power of commanding labour was the measure of it, because most part of the necessaries, &c., are derived from the labour of other people. The value of labour being wholly owing to the necessaries, &c., it would procure. Here, the value of commodities, on the contrary, is owing to the labour they cost, or command ; and labour is considered the measure, because we may learn in what degree a man values a thing, when in the act of getting or parting with it, by seeing how much trouble it took him to acquire, or how much it saves him when acquired, which may be two very different things. It is arguing in a circle, I suspect.

Mr. Ricardo, p. 4, 5, considers Smith as having *first* laid down the labour things *cost* as the measure, and then the labour they will *command ;* whereas Smith does just the reverse ; Mr. Ricardo not having quoted the beginning of the chapter (down to " commodities"), nor adverted to the words "which it can impose upon other people," which he does quote. In fact, Smith, on the whole, mixes the two completely together. Now the " toil and trouble of *acquiring* it" is an expression admirably adapted for confusion. The trouble of acquiring a given portion of fuel, for instance, is to one person the trouble of picking up sticks, or cutting faggots; to another, that quantity of labour which will earn so much wages as will buy the quantity of fuel from those who sell it. "The toil and trouble," *i. e.* "that quantity of toil and trouble," &c. What does *quantity* of toil, &c., mean? When are two quantities of toil, &c., equal? When are they related to each other in a certain *proportion?* Smith tells us himself (p. 41, of vol. i, sentence 2, &c.), *he does not know!*

" It is often difficult to ascertain the proportion between two different quantities of labour." So, then, properties, which, according to himself, constitute part of the meaning of " more labour," properties which must be valued and measured, before we can tell *what* the "quantity of labour" (our criterion) is, are very difficult to value and measure, and are never, in fact, valued or measured at all; matters being settled (as far as relates to those properties) "not by any accurate measure, but by the higgling and bargaining of the market," &c. This seems to be rather like "making crooked the ruler you are proposing to measure with," as Aristotle says, ὅμοιον εἰ ᾧ μέλλει τις χρῆσθαι κανονι, τοῦτον ποιήσαι σρεβλον. Nay, Smith says (beginning of this paragraph), that this difficulty of "ascertaining the proportions between two different quantities of labour" is one reason (he puts it the first reason) why labour *is not* the measure commonly used. If the reason had been only that it could not be so conveniently got at, applied, or carried about; that things are more frequently exchanged for other things than for labour; that labour is too "abstract" a thing, and not "palpable" enough for common use; all these would have been reasons, why labour is not the *practical* measure of value, and yet might be consistent with the supposition, that labour (if it *could* be practically applied as a measure) would be a better one than that which is commonly used. (We cannot practically measure every thing by the standard in the Exchequer, but that standard is the real criterion of measure, and more accurately so than the various pots, bushels, &c., used about the country.) But when one of the reasons why labour is not used as a measure, and other things are, is because its quantity is not always so ascertainable as that of other things, and is to be ascertained by *the help of* those other things; this seems an objection, not merely of a practical nature, but applying to the root of its pretensions to be considered a measure even in theory. "Labour" (says Smith, ibid.) "is an abstract notion, which, though it can be made sufficiently *intelligible*, is not altogether so natural and obvious." I think it has *not* been "made sufficiently intelligible." I think he has shown just before why it *cannot* be made *sufficiently* intelligible, to serve as a measure. "Labour was the first price:" be it so : we want to know, not for *what sort* of price all things were *first* bought; but we want to know whether *now*, their value when bought can be measured by equal quantities of that or any other single thing. The using the conjunction "and" does not *prove* that one of these questions involves the other. However, "and" what? "And its value" (*i. e.* the value of all the wealth of the world) "*to those who possess it, and who want* to exchange it for some new productions, is precisely equal to the quantity of *labour*" (of productions one would have thought) "which it can enable them to purchase or command." This is *prop.* 1 again. Nothing here of the labour it *cost to acquire it.*

"Equal quantities of labour, at all times and places, may be said to be of equal value to the labourer" (Smith, i, p. 43). Surely this is not true. That it is not, seems to me so plain, that I can hardly tell where to go for instances by preference. In one country a man values his ease more, in proportion to the comforts labour would procure him, than in another. The Englishman will often observe in many foreign countries, "why don't these people just take the trouble to do so and so, instead of submitting to an inconvenience they could so easily avoid." The disposition to be "content," as they call it, is well pointed out, in a tale of Miss Edgeworth's, as the bane of the Irish poor: that is, setting less value on comforts and conveniences, and more on ease, than people do here. There is the same difference among those who live in easy circumstances. One man chooses to lead an indolent, *Will Wimble* sort of life, and leaves off no better than he began, but with the satisfaction of never having given up his *ease* and *liberty ;* while another, in order to gain the luxuries and the consequence of wealth, slaves at a profession or laborious business, til! he has, in the opinion of many people, undergone greater annoyances than he can ever earn pleasures. Is their own ease of equal value to these two men? And what is true of two individuals, may it not be, and is it not, true of two different countries, or two different periods?

On this consideration depends, in a very great degree, the question, "what will the real reward, price, or value of *labour,* at a given place and time, be?" A question which Smith's definition of value tends to keep out of sight; because it mixes together the question of the quantity of things which a given portion of labour will *produce*, and that of the quantity which it will *earn*.

Mr. Malthus seems to consider, that the measure of the comparative value of two things at different places or times is, the quantities of things in general which the two things will respectively exchange for; but he considers the most convenient *sample*, or *sign*, or *test* of this to be, the respective quantities of labour which the things in question would command; he does not mean to say, that this will be more than an *approximation* to a complete and accurate test. See p. 54, 60 (line 7), 61. In p. 61, at the bottom, he speaks of "the necessaries and conveniences of life, *including labour*." Is this quite accurate? He had excluded labour from being part of *wealth*, because not *material*. He cannot, then, adopt Smith's definition of wealth, else nothing could be part of the necessaries, &c., of life which was not part of wealth. He arrives at this test by steps, which appear rather singular. "In looking for any one object as a measure of exchangeable value, our attention would naturally be directed to that which was most extensively the subject of exchange." Why? What has that to do with the question, "what is a test likely to give the same results, as to the value of a thing, as the whole mass of things in general (the real measure of value) would give, if it could be resorted to?" And besides, if this circumstance recommends labour as a test, it must recommend money *à fortiori*, money being still more extensively the subject of exchange than labour; yet the whole of this inquiry, as I before observed, is founded on the supposition, that money will *not* do, as a measure of value.

His next reason is, " because this test can alone express

the degree in which they (commodities) are suited to the wants and tastes of society; the important effects of facility of production, &c. &c." If it is an accurate, or the most accurate test, surely that is a sufficient commendation, is what he professed to be in search of; and if it is not an accurate test, are we to say it is, in order to *express* certain "*effects*" however "important?" Besides, one would think the " facility of production" would be more readily "expressed" by directly including it in the question of value (as Mr. Ricardo does); yet this is what he *rejects*, and substitutes what has nothing to do with facility of production.

So of the third reason, which is, that the accumulation of capital, &c., depends entirely on its power of setting men to work. What is this to the purpose? We are wanting to know, whether if the quantities of *labour* which a hat and a jacket, for instance, will command, are equal, so will be the quantities of *things in general* which a hat and a jacket will respectively command.

He then comes nearer to the point, but only by degrees. " In the *same* place, and at the *same* time, the different quantities of day-labour, which different commodities can command, will be exactly in proportion to their relative values in exchange," and vice versâ. *If* this is true of labour, it is just as true of any thing else. Of money, for instance, as he himself points out. This is exactly what we are *not* in search of. We do *not* want, as I have already observed, a measure of real price at the *same* time and place. *Money* does very well as a measure at the same time and place; or we can exchange the two commodities, whose comparative values we want to know, directly against one another. But it seems *not* to be true of labour. Labour is not a measure even at the same time and place. Take a portion of corn, such as is at the same time and place said to be of equal value with a given diamond; will the corn and the diamond, paid in specie, command equal portions of labour? It may be said, 1. No; but the diamond will buy *money*, which will command an equal portion of labour. I answer, then the test is of no use, for it cannot be applied without being *rectified* by the application of the other test, which it professed to supersede. We can only infer, that the corn and the diamond will command equal quantities of labour, *because* they are of equal value, in money. But we were told to infer, that two things were of equal value, because they would command equal quantities of labour. 2. It may be said, the labourer may sell the diamond again. No. Corn and the diamond may exchange for each other, or be of the same value, in the *market;* but not in the hands of the *labourer.* He can eat the one; he does not know how to dispose of the other; if he does dispose of it, it will be at a loss; therefore he will give less labour for it.

"It is evident that no commodity can be a good measure of real value in exchange in different places, and at different periods, which is not at the same time a good measure of nominal value in these places, and at these distant periods." I do not pretend to understand this sentence, but "it is evident" that "*measure*" must be used in two different senses in it; otherwise, as real value is something *opposite* to nominal, the sentence could not be true. Nominal value means value in money. Of course, nothing but money can be a perfectly good measure of nominal value. The above sentence, then, understood literally, would show, that money is the only good measure of real value!

With respect to the ascertaining, by the application of a measure, whether two things, or equal portions of the same thing (silver for instance), are of equal values in different times and places; we must recollect, that we do not thereby mean, whether the two portions would exchange with one another, for by the supposition they are so situated that they *cannot* exchange; but whether the one would exchange, in its time and place, for the same quantity of other things, as the other would exchange for in *its* time and place. Taking, for instance, Mr. Ricardo's measure of value, the labour that produced each, I say we must not inquire whether the two cost equal portions of labour, but whether the quantity of labour, which the first cost, was in the same proportion to the quantities which other things cost in that time and place, as the quantity which the second cost was to the quantities which other things cost in *its* time and place.

Mr. Malthus very justly observes, that a medium of two measures is better than one; as Adam Smith had observed before. He proposes corn and labour. " Where corn compared with labour is dear, labour compared with corn must be cheap," p. 128. That is, if *a* is bigger than *b*, *b* is less than *a*. This might be said of any two things in the world, just as well as of corn and labour, and cannot be a reason for selecting *them*. What we want is two things, of which when one errs on one side, the other will probably err on the other side. *Their* medium may be nearly right. Mr. Malthus indeed adds, " at the period when corn commands the smallest quantity of the neces-saries, &c., of life, labour will command the greatest," and vice versâ; but this is a very different proposition from the former, though it comes in as if it were a corollary from it. But how is it *proved ?* It seems to me to be erroneous. The principal difference between two times or places, as to price, is the different rates at which necessaries exchange with superfluities, or the produce of land with manufactures. Now where manufactures command less *corn*, do they not usually command less *labour* too? Mr. Malthus, p. 300, observes that they do.

By saying that the produce of a country is of greater value because it commands more labour, Mr. Malthus (as he informs us in p. 451) sometimes means only, that it will *pay labour higher ;* though the number of labourers or degree of their exertions be not increased. So that giving more produce for a given quantity of labour, or getting more labour for a given quantity of produce, are one and the same thing in his " view;" instead of being, as one would have supposed, just the contrary !

This arises out of his confusing together, by the help of words, two things which are perfectly different. The rate at which commodities exchange for labour (that is, the quantity of labour which a given portion of each commodity will exchange for), and the quantity of labour which the *whole mass* of commodities will command, when increased in its quantity, or in the degree of enjoyment it will confer. Now it is quite obvious, that the whole mass of commodities may, in such case, command more labour than it did; and yet if it does not command so much more labour as is in proportion to its own increase, a given portion of each commodity will exchange for less labour now than before.

I do not undertake here to discuss the question, what is the *cause* of the relative value of commodities, *i. e.* of the rate at which two commodities will exchange with one another. If that cause can be ascertained, and if it is a simple cause, it may serve, of course, also as a *measure* of value, in some cases. If, for instance, it could be shown, that the cause was simply " the total quantity of labour necessary to manufacture the commodities, and bring them to market" (Ricardo, p. 17), then if we wanted to know if a given sum of money would have commanded, A. D. 1400, as much as it does now, we might simply inquire whether the labour of producing it was the same then, in proportion to that of producing other things, as now. If the inquiry were easily answered, it might be a convenient way of getting at the conclusion, as to whether the value of the money in exchange for other things were the same, at the two periods, or not. But if the inquiry were difficult, that is, if it were difficult to know, what *were* the quantities of labour that had been then respectively necessary to manufacture the particular commodities in question, it would only be a more roundabout way of coming to the conclusion ; and so it would be, if the cause were not so simple as that I have just mentioned, but were mixed up, and modified with others.

It does not, therefore, necessarily follow, that to point out the cause of relative value is to afford us any additional facility in measuring it, or ascertaining what it *is*, when different times and countries are to be compared. " The *relative* value of two things," by the way, is open to two meanings; the rate at which two things exchange or would exchange with *each other*, or the comparative portions of *a third* for which each exchanges or would exchange.

Mr. Ricardo's doctrine (which I will assume, for the present, to be completely correct) would be more readily received, if in the general statements or enunciations of it, its whole import had been included. For instance, it is not meant to be asserted by him, that two particular lots

of two different articles, as a hat and a pair of shoes, exchange with one another when *those two particular lots*
were produced by equal quantities of labour.   By " commodity," we must here understand " *description of commodity*," not a *particular individual* hat, pair of shoes,
&c.   The whole labour which produces all the hats in
England is to be considered, to this purpose, as divided
among all the hats.   This seems to me not to have been
expressed at first, and in the general statements of his doctrine, where such occur, so clearly as might have been
wished.   In the place above referred to, for instance, the
value is said on one side of the page to depend on " *the
total* quantity of labour necessary," &c. ; while on the
other, in enumerating the divisions and classes of this total
quantity, Mr. Ricardo says, " *a portion* of the labour of
the ship-builder, of the engineer, &c., in making machines,"
&c.   Yet the " total labour" that produced each single
pair of stockings, if it is of a single pair we are speaking,
includes the *whole* labour of the engineer; not " a portion ;" for one machine makes many pairs, and none of
those pairs could have done without any part of the machine ; and if, on the contrary, we are speaking of the
whole mass of stockings produced, then still less can the
expression in the following page, " a portion of the labour,"
apply ; for the *whole* labour of the engineer must of course
reckon into the exchangeable value of the *whole* mass.
Besides, on reading the words " a portion," &c., we are
tempted to ask, " what portion ?" and to complain that we
are told nothing accurate or useful, till we know what
definite portion is meant.

So of rent. Mr. Ricardo does not mean to say that *every
bushel* of corn exchanges at a rate dictated by the labour
it has cost; for this is true, in his opinion, only of certain

particular bushels, comparatively very few in number *viz.* those which are raised on the portion of land whose cultivation adds nothing to rent, or those which may be considered as produced by the portion of capital whose employment adds nothing to rent. Surely, then, his general proposition as to the cause of value ought to have been so worded, where it occurs, as to admit this case. " The exchangeable value of all commodities" (he says, in p. 56) " is always regulated, not by the less quantity of labour that will suffice for their production, under circumstances highly favourable, and exclusively enjoyed by those who have peculiar facilities of production, but by the greater quantity of labour necessarily bestowed on their production by those who have no such facilities." All this, then, ought to be included and incorporated in the general proposition, in which he so often states the cause of the exchangeable value of commodities to be in proportion to the greater or less quantity of labour employed in their production. It is not by any means self-evident, nor, therefore, implied as a part of that general proposition, if not expressed. We might have thought the " quantity of labour" meant the *average* quantity of labour, instead of the greatest quantity of labour employed by the least favoured producers, as we are now told to understand. It does not at first strike us, that the *large majority* of producers of an article can be the persons answering to the description of those having " *peculiar* facilities."

Where he puts the case of money being always of the same value, he adds, " or, in other words, to be always produced by the same quantity of *unassisted* labour ;" but elsewhere he says, " that commodity is alone invariable which at all times requires the same sacrifice of *toil and labour* to produce it;" without saying " un-

assisted." So, p. 41, we have " their real value, *viz.* the
quantity of labour *and capital* employed in producing
them." It is precisely on account of these and such like
instances of too general a mode of expression, that his doctrine of value has not been more readily received. But
it must be owned, too, that it is indebted to them for
much of its air of *originality.*

Many controversies arise from different persons
entering on the consideration of a subject in different
directions, as I may say. Suppose two causes must
concur in order to produce a particular effect. You
shall often have an apparent controversy, which of
those two ought to be called the *primary* cause.
M. Say considers himself and Mr. Ricardo at variance,
because he himself calls *utilité* the " premier fondement
des valeurs," and price as depending first on that, and
secondly on " frais de production;" while Mr. Ricardo
" fonde la valeur sur les frais de production;" that is, *if*
the article has *utilité* enough to admit of its being purchased at all (See vol. i, p. 9, fourth edition, and vol. ii,
p. 507, article Valeur). But these two opinions are just
the same, however the words may differ. Mr. Ricardo
does not think labour bestowed upon a thing will alone
give it value in exchange, unless it has sufficient "utilité"
to make it be purchased; but he thinks, that if it be
not desirable enough to induce people to exchange other
commodities for it at the rate which is pointed out by the
labour which its production cost, it will not, in the long
run, be produced at all. M. Say thinks the same. Both
must agree, that either without *utilité,* or without any
difficulty of production, it would never be exchanged at
all. Each is a *sine quá non.* There are opportunities
enough, surely, for people to dispute, without its being

necessary for them to do so, when they are really, at bottom, of the same opinion : though I believe there are few cases in which people dispute more eagerly, and more unceasingly.

A similar dispute exists about rent. Mr. Malthus contends, that it is owing " first, *and mainly*," to a certain property in land. But he knows that without the concurrence of *other* causes it would not exist. What does " first and mainly" mean then? We do indeed sometimes say, where two conditions are required in order that a thing should exist, of which one is much more easily fulfilled than the other, that the latter is the *main* point. But this is merely in a *practical* sense ; *viz.* that *our endeavours* must principally be directed to that, as being the least easy to attain.

Value, or valeur in French, is not only used absolutely instead of relatively as a quality of things, but is even used by some writers abstracted from any thing, and spoken of in the same terms as you would speak of a commodity, and a measurable commody, " Possessing a value," " transferring a portion of value," " the sum, or totality of values" (valeurs), &c. I do not know what this means. The definition of the value of a thing, in M. Say's epitome, is, the quantity of other things it will exchange for. Then, what does value, *not* saying value *of a thing*, mean? " The quantity of things which— will exchange for." Where is the meaning of this ? Again, what does " la somme des valeurs" mean ? " The quantity of other things which the whole quantity of things will exchange for ?" Here, too, I can go no farther than to say with Fluellen, " I do *partly* understand your meaning." Or, " The quantity of other things which each thing will in turn exchange for ?" Is not this merely the

same as " the sum, or totality, of *things*," " the quantity
of things," or, " of valuable things?" We need not
have had then so puzzling an abstract word as *valeur*
introduced on the occasion, and then used as if it was
not an abstract word. This use of *valeur*, or value, is
taken, I suspect, from the sort of language we use with
regard to bills of exchange, &c., " *value received*,"
" drawn, accepted, &c., *for value*." Here, the *value*
meant is, perhaps, a certain quantity of goods or money.
But to suppose, therefore, that the word value means goods
or money, absolutely, is like the Clown in Shakspeare,
supposing, that remuneration meant three farthings.
Value, here, is only *short for*, " goods or money of
equal value with the sum named in the bill," &c., and
denotes a *relation* (of equality), not a particular thing.
While we stick to nominal price, so much *money*, or so
much money's worth, may, perhaps, be said to be denoted
by the term value, without reference to any other commodity or thing: but when we talk of *real* price, one
commodity, whose value we may be talking of at one
time, becomes, in its turn, a constituent part of the value
of another: value, therefore, abstracted and distinct from
commodities, and from all notion of comparison, does not
seem to apply.

From this mode of using it arise those difficulties
which M. Say labours (in vol. ii, p. 80 and 228) to
remove, *viz.* " Si avec cette *valeur* acquise (100 écus)
on achète par exemple, des livres, comment se fait-il que
cette valeur-revenu, transformèe en livres, et qui se con-
sommera sous *cette forme,* serve pourtant de composer
le revenu de l'imprimeur, &c. &c.; revenu qu'ils con-
sommeront de leur côté?" (p. 80) And he is obliged to
tell us (p. 228), that it *does not* follow, that because two

values exchange for each other, they are one and the same *value*.

Of course, I mean here, by the "quantity" of things, not mere bulk or weight, but power of contributing to the various wishes of man. I mention this, to obviate the remark of Mr. Malthus (p. 339), who says, "but neither does it (wealth) increase in proportion to the mere quantity of what comes under the denomination of wealth, because the various articles, of which the quantity is composed, may not be so proportioned to the wants and powers of the society," &c. It may be said, wealth, so far as it depends on this, is difficult to be estimated. I cannot help that; the populousness of Africa, for instance, certainly consists in the number of people in it, however hard it may be to tell what that number is. I am not to say, it depends on the number of square miles, in order to get something more easy to be estimated. Besides, how does *your* definition assist us in estimating it? How does the use of value in exchange, as a criterion, help us to estimate the wealth of the owners of all commodities taken together? You may say, it is in proportion as they cost more labour. Another may just as easily say, in proportion as they cost *less;* as M. Say does.

Mr. Malthus, in pages 265, 266, talks in the same way, as I have already noticed, of the increased *value* of the general produce, meaning what I should call increased quantity; and he talks of it as a cause of the increase of wages. If he means value in exchange for labour (which is the criterion of value he elsewhere sets up), the proposition is merely identical, and therefore useless. If he does not mean in exchange for labour, in exchange for what else does he mean it?

The disputes concerning *demand and supply* are entirely owing to the use of words in different senses by different persons; to the disputants looking, like the knights in the story, at different sides of the shield. " The opinion," says Mr. Ricardo, " that the price of commodities depends solely on the proportion of supply to demand, or demand to supply" (meaning by " solely," independently of the cost of production), " has become almost an axiom in political economy, and has been the source of much error in that science." This "opinion" is not that of Adam Smith, at least. He calls that price of commodities, which depends on their cost of production, their natural price ; and if at any time the quantity of a commodity supplied, or brought to market, is greater or less than the quantity effectually demanded (that is, wanted by those, who are willing and able to pay this, which he has called the natural price), the price, which under these accidental circumstances is given, is, in his opinion, but temporary, and is sooner or later, by an alteration of the rate of supply, reduced to the natural price ; unless there are some insurmountable obstacles, either natural or artificial, standing in the way of such alteration of the rate of supply. This appears to be, precisely, the opinion which Mr. Ricardo himself entertains. It follows, that where the quantity of wages, capital, and land, required to produce an article, are become different from what they were, that which Smith calls the natural price of it is also different, and that price, which was previously its natural price, becomes, with reference to this alteration, its market price ; because, though neither the supply, nor the quantity wanted, may have been changed, that supply is not, *now*, exactly enough for those persons, who are able and willing to pay *what is now* the cost of production, but is either greater or less than that ; so that

the proportion between the supply, and what is with
reference to the new cost of production the effectual
demand, is different from what it was. An alteration in
the rate of supply will then take place, if there is no obstacle in the way of it, and at last bring the commodity
to its new natural price. It may, then, seem good to some
persons to *say*, that, as the commodity gets to its natural
price by an alteration in its supply, the natural price is
as much owing to one proportion between the demand
and supply, as the market price is to another; and, consequently, that the natural price, just as much as the market
price, depends on the *proportion* that demand and
supply bear to each other. (" The great principle
of demand and supply is called into action to determine
what Adam Smith calls natural prices, as well as market
prices." Malthus p. 75.) This *proportion*, however, if
we still *mean* by " demand" and " natural price," what
we meant just now, when referring to Adam Smith, must
always be a proportion of equality; for it is only when
the supply is equal to the effectual demand, that is, to
that demand which will neither more nor less than pay
the natural price; that the natural price is in fact paid;
consequently, there may be two very different natural prices,
at different times, for the same commodity, and yet the proportion, which the supply bears to the demand, be in both
cases the same, namely, the proportion of equality. That
demand, which was before effectual, is now become more
or less than effectual, for bringing to market, at the altered
cost of production, the same quantity as was formerly
brought to market; this has occasioned an altered rate of
supply, and the demand has become at last neither more
nor less than what is effectual for bringing to market, at
the present cost of production, the quantity actually

brought there. To say, therefore, as M. Say does (quoted by Mr. Ricardo, p. 494, second edition), that the value of every commodity rises always in a direct ratio to the quantity demanded, and in an inverse ratio to the quantity supplied, is absurd, if by demanded he means, as he expressly says (vol. ii, p. 10, fourth edition), effectually demanded, because the quantity effectually demanded must always, ultimately, where the rate of supply *can* be altered, be the *same* quantity as the quantity supplied, whether the natural price (of Smith) is greater or less; *i. e.* whether the effectual demand be at the time a greater or a less demand.

The use of these words, by M. Say, is evidently undefined and inaccurate. The price, he tells us (vol. ii, p. 15) regulates both the quantity of a thing supplied, and the quantity demanded: if it were not for price, every thing might be demanded in an unlimited quantity, and supplied in an unlimited quantity: price, then, *restrains both*. It should follow, that the higher the price is, the *less* ought both the quantity demanded and the quantity supplied to be. But by his *formula* in the next page we find, that the higher the price is the greater is the quantity demanded. It is clear, that he has here used " demanded" in two different senses, while he appeared to be using it but in one. It would be better not to talk about *formulas* and *direct ratios*, then, as if we had attained to the accuracy of mathematics.

It is certain, that in talking of demand people often mean mere desire, or liking for a thing; without annexing to it the idea denoted by the term *effectual,* as used by Smith. Even when considered in this sense, demand probably means the demand of such only as have *something* to give; which will include all persons, who have property of their own, or who have the power of working. In this sense of demand, supply would never be *equal* to demand, but when all such people had all they wanted; that is, when there would be no price at all. Mr. Ricardo (p. 78) says, " no commodity continues for any length of time to be supplied in such quantities as the wants and wishes of mankind require, and therefore there is none which is not subject to accidental and temporary variations of price." Is any commodity so supplied even for a *short* time? If it is, is not the effect to *destroy* price, not to make it steady? It is true, we may *conceive* a particular article *capable* of being supplied, by moderate *exertion*, in as large a quantity as the wants and wishes of mankind would require, and yet, of course, it would bear a price. Yet the whole of that exertion would probably not be made, if at the same time there were *other* articles, of which people could *not* get so much as they wished, without diverting, to the production of them, part of the exertion I have just mentioned. And there must be such other articles; for to suppose the wishes of men *completely* satisfied as to *all* articles is absurd.

Unless, however, we take into the account the increase of numbers, it is not quite true, that " *every* or *each* useful or agreeable thing (Say, ii, 10 and 16), would be demanded indefinitely," &c. " Who is there," M. Say asks, " that would not be disposed to receive *ce qui peut* contribuer à son utilité on à son agrément?" *Something* which would contribute to his use, certainly, he would be glad to receive; but that might not be *more* of *the particular things* he had got already. There are some useful and agreeable things, of which, yet, a man would not take beyond a certain quantity, even if you would give it him. He may, sometimes, indeed, if it is a perishable article, *buy* more than that quantity, if there happens to be a great fall in its price, which is expected not to last; by way of laying it in.

Mr. Malthus, like M. Say, understands by demand, the will combined with the power to purchase (p. 64). He does not, like M. Say, deliver his doctrine on this subject in the form of strict *proportion*, but more cautiously says, " that the relative values of commodities in money, or their prices, are determined by the relative demand for them, compared with the supply of them :" which does not necessarily import more, than that an increase of demand will always increase price, cæteris paribus ; and a lowering of demand lessen price ; and so, *vice versa*, of supply : but not that the increased demand, &c., will increase in price in the same *proportion* as it has itself increased. The proposition itself, therefore, is as indefinite as the words introduced into it are vague.

Mr. Malthus sets this in *opposition* to cost of production, in many cases, as a measure of permanent price ; at least, as far as I can understand from the language he makes use of (p. 73), and the instances he gives. Mr. Ricardo, on the other hand, directly asserts (p. 492), that " it is the cost of production which must ultimately regulate the price of commodities, *and not*, as has been often said, the proportion between the supply and demand."

The expression, " an increase in the number or *wants* of purchasers" (Malthus, p. 67), means, of course, *desire or wish*, not general indigence, which the word sometimes means, but which would diminish the price of a particular article, of which they were the purchasers, rather than raise it.

He (p. 67) supposes an article suddenly wanted by two thousand persons, instead of one thousand, who demanded

and consumed it before; and unless (says he) the intensity of demand of some of these, or their wills and
powers, should increase, no rise of price could take place.
The increase of the intensity of demand must mean (for
Mr. Malthus's definition is not exact enough to help us)
the existence of a disposition to give more for the quantity
actually taken, or to buy more at the same rate. But each
of the two thousand may be willing to buy *half* as much
as each of the one thousand bought, at an increased rate;
though none would be willing to buy *as* much as each of
the one thousand bought, at the former rate: would you
call that an increased intensity of demand? Half the
quantity we use of any article is generally *more* than half
as intrinsically desirable, as the whole. Then the price of
the whole *would* rise, in the case Mr. Malthus puts. The
case, as disposed of by him, teaches us that price does *not*
depend on the proportion between intensity of demand and
supply. For he is supposing, that there would not be any
increased intensity of demand; and yet if there is an
equally intense demand felt by twice as many people, there
will be an increased supply, and yet the price will not fall!
Indeed, having defined intensity of demand to be the degree of will and power to purchase it, one would have
thought equal will and power possessed by twice as many
people was an increase of that intensity. Mr. Malthus
here puts *cases*, which I believe we may safely abstain in
practice from troubling ourselves with; namely, of equal
tastes, wishes, &c., on the part of many human beings.

When he comes to talk of a " fall of price," p. 69, that
it " would in the same manner be occasioned by an increased abundance of supply, either actual *or contingent*,"
it is clear that his proposition about demand and supply is
original *merely* by his having dressed up an idea under the

disguise of a word that did not belong to it before. This
" contingent" supply is not what we before meant by supply; and *is* what we mean by " cost of production."
There might, in his opinion, be at two different times the
same supply, and yet a different price, and yet this difference of price be owing to the supply; *because he means*
contingent supply. These new definitions are really a
mere trap for disputations. He says indeed, just after, that
the *demand* has become less: then the fall was *not* owing
to change in the supply, but in the demand. Here it is
clear we are again got into a new *nomenclature*. " It
cannot be said that the demand is the same." It is me-
lancholy that we should be writing books to consider what
" may be said," or not. Why *need* we " say" either one
way or the other? Why can we not do entirely without
these concise, unintelligible forms of expression, " summi
materiam mali ?" In Smith's sense of demand, one would
think it was *increased* rather than fallen off: there is, for
the present, *more* than an effectual demand for the article
at its *new* natural price. Besides, the fall of demand here
is a *consequence* of what Mr. Malthus calls an increase of
supply. But could that be the meaning of demand, when we
were told that price depended on the proportion between
it and supply? If the degree of demand can itself be altered by the degree of supply, what information is given
us by saying, that something depends on the balance of
forces* (as it were) between the two? If a varies in-
versely as b, to say that c varies as $\frac{a}{b}$ is needless. That
part at least of the increase of demand, in his sense of it,
which depends on diminished supply, may be laid out of
the question; supply alone will do.

* Say.

In p. 70, that which raises prices on the part of *demand* is stated to be " such a change in the relation between supply and demand, as *renders necessary* the expression of a greater intensity of demand," &c. The " change" in question means merely a change of the cost of production: and therefore we may here, too, observe, that if diminished contingent supply *causes* greater intensity of demand, the price ought, according to Mr. Malthus's maxim, to be raised both ways. If the cost of production be doubled, for instance, that implies, as I understand him, a reduction of the supply, *i. e.* contingent supply, to half what it was: that alone, then, would double the price, upon his principles. Then, it is also a cause of a greater intensity of *demand.* Then, the price, on this account, must have another lift; so that it will be more than double. But of course Mr. Malthus does not suppose this.

" And, in the same manner, it is *not merely* extent of *actual supply,* nor the extent of the actual supply compared with the actual demand, *that lowers prices;* but *such* a change in the relation of the *supply* compared with the demand *as renders a fall of price necessary,* in order to take off a temporary abundance, or to prevent a constant excess of supply contingent upon a diminution in the *cost of production,* without a proportionate diminution in the price of the produce." This seems to me to mean, that the fall of price is owing after all to a fall in the cost of production. The first part of it, taken alone, would look like saying, that *that sort* of change in the supply, which lowers prices, is, such a change as lowers prices !

Mr. Malthus observes, very properly, that the sense in which Mr. Ricardo uses demand, p. 493, where he says, that more cannot well be said to be demanded, if no more comes to market, is quite contrary to the sense in which he himself and every body else understand it. It is making demand and supply the same thing.

Mr. Malthus says, p. 73, " in all the transactions of bargain and sale there is evidently a principle in constant operation, which can determine, and does actually determine, the prices of commodities, quite independently of any considerations of cost, or of the quantity of labour and capital employed upon their production. And this is found to operate, not only permanently upon that class of commodities, which may be considered as monopolies, but temporarily and immediately upon all commodities, and strikingly and pre-eminently so upon all sorts of raw produce." This is really rather singular ; for Mr. Ricardo, against whom it is directed, only asserts that the price of commodities depends on cost of production, where the price in question is *not* the " temporary and immediate" price, and where the commodities in question are *not* monopolies. So Mr. Malthus adds, that the price of raw produce differs widely in different years, owing to the seasons, though the cost may have been the same; an observation, which is not in the slightest degree at variance with Mr. Ricardo's rule, and which has been made by Adam Smith, vol. i, p. 78 (edit. 1806). The actual price of corn is never *exactly* the natural price, but *tending* to it. The case he puts, of farmers exempted *during a year* from any cost in producing corn, &c., is not at all in point, therefore; even if it were any way instructive to suppose any thing so unlike all human affairs as that in such case " no change should be made in the quantity brought to market."

The observations he makes in p. 75 I have already noticed. Adam Smith himself is the person who points out that an alteration in the supply is what brings down the market to the natural price. But what brought it up ? What made the old natural price become a market price ? An alteration in the cost of production. Demand and supply, *understood as Smith understands them*, are at a level now, as they were at the former natural price, and must always be in every *permanent* state of things, except where there are obstacles to increased production, or to the withdrawing of some particular sort of capital, or land, or labour to another use. Such an obstacle may exist by the *will* of the suppliers, as in the case of a bank restricting its issues; in which case they act, so far, as government, not as traders; or by miracle, as in the other case put by Mr. Malthus, of farmers able for ten years to raise corn, &c., without cost, and yet not raising any more than the present periodical rate of supply. So in the case of curates, which he next cites from Adam Smith; the *capital* which produces them (fellowships, &c., at colleges) is by law *irremoveable*, is devoted to that purpose only : it is what we may call the *converse* of a monopoly. In the cases of bounties, and of labour paid out of poor-rates, the price *is* in proportion to the cost of production. The cost of production *to the producer* is lessened by the act of the state.

Mr. Malthus proceeds to consider the rate of wages, profits, and rent, in *general*. But it is the *relative* prices of commodities he was considering, and that does not include any consideration of the rate of wages, profits, &c. It is sufficient to say, as Smith does, that those prices will settle at that proportion which gives *equal* rates of wages, &c., whatever those rates may be. I must, however, observe, that the high wages given to clever workmen are *not* on account only of their " rarity" (Malthus, p. 79).

If *all* were clever, the wages of all would, cæteris paribus, be higher. The master pays such an one more, because he makes more by him. Besides, in some cases a thing acquires part of its desirableness *by being* rare; in which case its rarity doubly raises its value in exchange, once because it is more difficult to get, and once more because it is more prized and desired. Men set more value, as Smith observes (though Mr. Malthus, p. 245, blames him for it), on a species of labour which requires an *uncommon* degree of dexterity and ingenuity.

Mr. Malthus, p. 83, thinks Smith's term " natural price," and definition of it, are bad. He calls the *same thing* " necessary price," and defines it " the price necessary in *the actual circumstances* of the society, to bring the commodity *regularly* to the market." This, he says, is a shorter description of what Smith means: Smith having, according to him, used much " circumlocution." That sort of *circumlocution* is the great merit of Smith's style ; which makes it delightful and satisfactory, above all styles, to any reader whose first desire is to understand and learn. It is " linked *reason* long drawn out." It is the serene and steady dignity of a philosophic mind, patiently and securely feeling its way; brooding with complacency on its own clear and well-pondered conceptions. If Mr. Malthus means by " actual circumstances," in *his* definition, actual rate of rent, profits, and wages, it is much *better* to say so : there is no conceivable merit in leaving it unexplained. We have time enough to attend to the additional words. We have not time enough to attend to the disputes and puzzles which arise from this zeal for " shortness."

Mr. Ricardo (p. 521, second edit.) well observes, that Mr. Malthus had twice used, in his Essay on Rent, " real price;" nay, had *defined* it, in the very manner which in another place he condemns. He did so because it suited what was his purpose at the time, *viz.* to denote the particular distinction which is the subject of that Essay; and the other term of which he calls High Price. But this sort of inattention is exactly what occasions rather more than half the difficulties in Political Economy.

The " natural price" of Smith implying the existence of a certain actual rate of rent, profits, and wages in general; the price or hire of land, capital, and labour in general cannot have any natural price in the sense Smith uses that term; nor any effectual demand, for this means a demand that suffices to pay the natural price. Particular portions of each, at particular times, may be said to have a natural or market price, meaning a price the same as the ordinary rate, or different from it. Indeed, the natural and market price of commodities are made up of these natural and market prices of labour, &c., in this sense. But the general price or rate is said to depend merely on demand and supply. Demand must here mean simply *wish*, or *desire*, with the limitation I above mentioned, *viz.* that it be felt by those who have *something* to give for the thing demanded. To say, then, that the price or hire of these three " productive services," as M. Say calls them, depends on the proportion between the supply of them and the demand, means on the degree in which the supply is *less* than the demand. *Equal* they cannot be, it seems to me, while any price is given. The *degree* of demand may indeed be estimated (if we choose to understand the term so) by increased *ability* to buy, possessed by the demanders of a thing, as well as by increased *desire*. But it is more simple to consider *that* as increased supply of the other thing, which is the other party to the exchange;

that is, of the thing with which the purchase is to be made. Then in the exchange between labour and capital (for instance), or the bargain they drive together as to the shares in which they are to divide the product, the event will depend on the wish the labourer has for capital to give him employment, and the amount of capital that is seeking some investment; on the desire of the owners of this capital to find an investment, and the amount of labour which is offered to be exerted. We may, by new definitions, apply " natural and market price" to land, labour, or capital; but it does not seem desirable to do so, nor is it done (except in the sense I just mentioned, *viz.* of particular sorts of each, which is *not* a new definition) as to any of them but labour.

With respect to labour, however, Mr. Ricardo pronounces, p. 85, that " it has, like all other things which are purchased and sold, and which may be increased or diminished in quantity, its natural and its market price. The natural price of labour is that price which is necessary to enable the labourers, one with another, to subsist, and to perpetuate their race without either increase or diminution." In the chapter " On Natural and Market Price," he seemed to consider the latter (as to commodities whose rate of supply can be increased and diminished) as applying to temporary and accidental variations of price only. But as to *labour*, it may apply to *permanent* states of price, which is what he would call *natural* price, if speaking of other things. For the price of labour may be, as he himself observes, p. 88, for centuries, such as enables labourers to *increase* (Malthus, 247). Because an increased supply of labour is an increased supply of that which is to purchase labour. If we say, then, with Mr. Ricardo, that labour is at every moment *tending* to

what he calls its natural price, we must only recollect, that
the increase made in its supply, in order to *tend* to that,
is itself one cause of the counteracting power, which prevents the *tendency* from being effectual. Whereas, when
we are talking (with Smith) of two *commodities*, the increased supply of one, which is exchanging at an exorbitant
rate with another, does not promote, in the least, the increased supply of that other, but on the contrary is in part
probably effected by the withdrawing of capital, &c., from
the production of that other : except where the former of
the two commodities is the *material* of the other.

In the next place, that particular price, which leaves the
amount of labour periodically supplied, or the number of
labourers in existence always the same, is different at
different times and places; as Mr. Ricardo himself observes, after Smith. One of these is no more an accidental price than another; and though this depends on
the tastes and habits of the labourers, " *essentially* depends," according to Mr. Ricardo (p. 91), yet those tastes
depend on *it*, too. That which people have been used to,
they come to expect (Malthus, 248); and the different
comparative prices of food and luxuries alter these " *tastes*"
very greatly. I do not see the advantage, then, of applying the term " natural price" to labour, since its meaning
must be altered a little, to fit. Or else the definition of
natural price of labour should at least be, as that of commodities is, " that price which it bears when not disturbed
by any temporary or accidental cause." I cannot see how
the line can be drawn between the natural and market
price here. In speaking of the price of a particular commodity the distinction is clear, because we refer to the
quantity of land, capital, and labour necessary to produce
it, and inquire whether its price is or is not such as to

pay the same profits as are made by producing other
things. No such consideration can enter into the question
as to the price of labour *in general*. The use of the term
has, as applied to labour, a certain resemblance to its use
when applied to the price of particular commodities, but
it is not the same; it therefore produces, I think, the same
sort of confusion and inconvenience as is produced by
metaphorical language. We are always forgetting how
far the resemblance holds, and where it fails; and we gain
nothing! Why could we not, when we mean to talk of
the price which will at any time keep the numbers of labourers stationary, say so in plain terms.

" In different stages of society, the accumulation of
capital, or of the means of employing labour, is more or
less rapid, and must in all cases depend on the productive
powers of labour. The productive powers of labour are
generally greatest where there is an abundance of fertile
land." If, in the first sentence, the productive powers of
labour mean the smallness of that aliquot part of any produce that goes to those whose manual labour produced it,
the sentence is nearly identical, because the remaining
aliquot part is the fund whence capital can, if the *owner
pleases*, be accumulated. But then this does not generally happen where there is most fertile land. It does in
North America, but that is an artificial state of things.
It does not in Mexico. It does not in New Holland.
The productive powers of labour are, indeed, in *another*
sense, greatest where there is much fertile land, *viz.* the
power of man, if he chooses it, to raise much *raw produce*
in proportion to the whole labour he performs. It is, indeed, a gift of nature, that men can raise more food than
the lowest quantity that they could maintain and keep up
the existing population on; but " surplus produce" (the

term used by Mr. Ricardo, page 93), generally means the excess of the whole price of a thing above that part of it which goes to the labourers who made it; a point, which is settled by human arrangement, and not fixed by nature.

The natural price, understood as it is by Mr. Ricardo, has nothing to do with cost of production, that is, with the lowest subsistence, that will keep life and soul together, at the existing rate of numbers; except as a limit. And if " cost of production" means the wages, that the labourer will take, without increasing or lessening numbers, it is a *metaphor*.

The only accurate and tangible *fact*, that is conveyed by the terms " natural and market price of labour," as used by Mr. Ricardo, is, that when wages are so low that they do not admit of the physical *possibility* of the existing population remaining alive, let them work ever so hard, the numbers will diminish; and, on the principle laid down by Smith, wages will rise, till they be again sufficient to admit of what will then be the existing population remaining alive.

If what Mr. Ricardo calls the cost of production of labour were extinguished, and labourers could get, without the slightest difficulty or trouble, enough to maintain their existing numbers, that would diminish and not increase their disposition to work; you would take away almost the whole of what is now the counteracting force to their indolence; and, of course, if you wanted to employ them (in raising necessaries you would not, but in other things) a higher inducement rather than a lower would become necessary. If you call labour a commodity, it is not like a commodity which is first produced in order to exchange, and then brought to market where

it must exchange with other commodities according to
the respective quantities of each which there may be in
the market at the time; labour is *created* at the moment
it is brought to market; nay, it is brought to market
before it is created, and if the inducement that offers is
not satisfactory, it will not be created at all. Mr. Ricardo
cannot be supposed to mean by saying, " and not on the
proportion between demand and supply," that the principle, by which supply, when it can be increased or diminished, is proportioned to demand, has *nothing* to do
with price; because it would have been unnecessary to
have limited his proposition to the case where supply can
be increased or diminished, if that was an immaterial
point. But he denies, for instance, that where the
supply can be increased, increased demand will, necessarily, permanently raise price: he says, that effectual
demand may match supply exactly at two periods, and
yet the prices be very different at the two periods: Mr.
Malthus says this too. Mr. Malthus goes no farther
than to say, that the principle by which supply is proportioned to demand has an influence on price. On what
fact, then, do they differ among themselves, or either of
them from Smith? I am, really, unable to conceive,
how it can enlarge the bounds of our knowledge, when
a certain matter of fact has been once already stated in
a complete and clear manner, to discuss, whether it ought
to be anew expressed in the one, or in the other, of two
laconic propositions, *neither* of which can express it or
convey it to the mind *at all*, unless the studied scantiness
of their phrase is eked out by something, which is to be
supplied by the imaginations of those, who are to use
them, but which is on no account to be uttered in words.
Mr. Malthus appears to understand, by his short phrase,

" *the principle* of demand and supply" something different from what I should, as a reader of Smith only, have understood it to mean : I should have said, it meant that principle, which tends to bring the respective prices of things into such a state as will equalize, as nearly as is possible, the profits, &c., obtained in the production of each. But that principle does not then determine, what that state is. That principle is, as Smith lucidly explains, the flowing of capital, &c., where it can flow, from less profitable to more profitable lines. Which *are* the most profitable must be settled from causes extrinsic to the principle. You can new-christen the principle, so as to include those causes, if you please. But do not then suppose you have made a *discovery*, or done any thing more than the most ignorant person might have done : nothing is more easy than to introduce confusion of terms into any subject,

———ἀλλ' ἐπὶ χώρας αὖϑις ἔσσαι δυσπαλὲς δὴ γίνεται,

it takes a deal of trouble to set it straight on its legs again.

" Where disadvantages or difficulties of any kind (Malthus, p. 245) accompany particular employments, it is obvious, that they must be paid comparatively high; because, if the additional remuneration were not sufficient to balance such disadvantages, the supply of labour in these departments would be deficient. The deficiency so occasioned, whenever it occurs, will naturally raise the price of labour, and the advance of price, after some little oscillation, will rest at the point where it is just sufficient to effect the supply required." What does this mean ? If it means, that there will be, at the new, and high price, that supply which was required at the low price, it is not true. Some of those who required a supply must have been *thrown out* at every step of the advance. If it means, that all those who *effectually* require, or have an *effectual* demand for a supply, when it is at the advanced price, will be supplied, it means nothing but an identical proposition; for effectual demand *means* a demand for such a supply as can be " effected."

Mr. Malthus thinks the definition given by Mr. Ricardo of natural price of labour absurd : *therefore* he new defines it to be " that price, which, in the actual circumstances of the society, is necessary to occasion an average supply of labourers, sufficient to meet the average demand." One would think the great business of life was to use terms which cannot be understood without an explanation, and yet which people cannot agree in explaining. What possible occasion have we for this term " natural" or " necessary price of labour," at all? In order to set up an *analogy*, which is in fact a confusion, between the price of labour in general and the respective prices of some commodities in particular. " Average." Of different employments at the same time? One would think so from the term " actual," which goes before. Then the average price of labour would always be natural. But it is opposed (as we find from the definition of market price just after) to *temporary*. (*Average* and *temporary* price would have been better terms then). However, it must then mean, average of a certain number of months, or years. *How many?*

When we talk of the market (or monopoly) price of certain products of land, such as certain vineyards, mentioned by Smith, we may recollect that the land in question is an article of a different *kind* from common land, and, therefore, it is no wonder it should bear a different

rent. So have the lands in Taunton Dean, and those in Bagshot Heath, different prices from each other. "If" (you say) "the vineyards were to become larger, this monopoly rent would cease, the rent would not be so high." Nor would the rent of England, if it were to become twice as big.

We cannot say there is more than an effectual demand for any sort of article, so as to induce a rise of price, unless there is, over and above all those who could and would buy up the whole stock of it, at what Smith calls the natural price, at least one person (or else a number *disposed* to club and subscribe) who possesses (or who together possess) funds sufficient to buy, at the natural price, the smallest lot into which the stock of the article can be divided; such as, *one* coach, one pair of stockings, one hat, &c.; and who is or are willing so to employ those funds. The circumstance, that one person possesses less than this, or that there are thousands of people who possess each less than this, if they cannot or will not *club*, does not add at all to the effectual demand, in the sense Smith gives to demand. It is obvious, that there is a great difference, in this respect, between different sorts of articles: as for instance, between coaches, or race horses, and corn. If the additional demander or demanders is able and willing to buy but a grain of corn per month, at the natural price, it adds to the effectual demand for corn so as to raise the price, though a bushel per month might have been the smallest quantity any one person demanded before. We often get into confusion by not specifying whether we mean by "the article," the whole mass of it, or a given lot or portion of it.

When the demand for an article exceeds, in the sense I have just explained, that which is, with reference to the present rate of supply, the effectual demand; and when, consequently, the price has risen, either additions can be made to the rate of supply at the same rate of cost of production as before; in which case they will be made till the article is brought to exchange at the same rate as before with other articles (whether the general rate of profits or wages will have altered or not during this process is not material) : or, 2dly, *no* possible additions can be made to the former rate of supply: and then the price, which has risen, will not be brought down again, but continue to afford, as Smith says, a greater rent, or profits, or wages (or all three), to the particular land, capital, or labour, employed in producing the article, than the ordinary rent, &c.: or, 3dly, the additions which can be made will require proportionally *more* land, or capital, or labour, or all three, than were required for the periodical production of the amount previously supplied. Then the addition will not be made till the demand is strong enough, 1st, to pay this increased price for the addition; 2dly, to pay the same increased price upon the old amount of supply. For the person who has produced the additional quantity will be no more able to get a high price for it, than those who produced the former quantity; and, therefore, as he certainly will get a high price for it (or else he will not go on producing it, since that, to him, is a mere natural or remunerating price), they will too. There will then be surplus profits in this trade: it being an intermediate case between the first and second, will partake of both. The surplus profits will be either in the hands of some particular producers only (as above supposed); or, if the *additional* produce cannot be *distinguished* from the rest, will be a surplus shared by all; or will be partly one and partly the other. People will give something to belong to a trade in which such surplus profit can be made : just as they pay a premium to belong to the Bank, and such like limited companies, if thriving; which are like trades of the *second* class. What they so give, is rent.

If, in the third case, the demand, though it rises above the effectual demand, never rises so much above as to make even the first step of addition worth while ; that will of course exactly resemble the second case. And there must always be an interval, in the progress of demand, during which this will be the state of things. Besides which, that which brings down market price is, the temptation to lay out more capital which it holds out, either to the former producers *or others.* Now in farming, *others* cannot so well come in as they can in many other lines ; the existing farmers exclude the capital of the rest of the world, during the currency of their leases : therefore the supply will not so soon be extended, in consequence of demand increasing, as in other lines. Both these causes, then, keep the price of raw produce (while demand is on the increase) *high,* i. e. of the nature of a monopoly, more than would be the case with regard to a manufacture. It is obvious, that in this third case an addition to the demand, say of one-tenth beyond the effectual demand, will add considerably less than one-tenth to the supply.

In the process of reducing the price of an article from a market price to a natural price, by an increase of supply, we must recollect, that an addition, say of one-tenth, to the supply, may bring down the price by much more than one-tenth ; or, in other words, the prices of the two periods will not be in a proportion indicated by the quantities of supply at the two periods. The knowledge on the part of the holders or producers of the quantity previously produced, that an increased supply can be afforded to new competitors to such an extent as would oblige them to come down in their price, will induce them to do so without waiting till the whole of such increased supply shall actually have taken place; if they see that it has commenced, and is likely to take place, the same cause which induces this new competitor to undersell them, and which makes him able to afford to do so, will equally induce them to undersell him, and they will probably be still better able to afford to do so. It is a common observation, how great a fall is suddenly effected in the price of corn, in a scarcity, by a very trifling importation. It is this consideration which made it necessary for Mr. Malthus, who maintains that price depends on the proportion of supply to demand, to explain supply to mean *contingent* supply, and not merely actual supply. But when he has explained it in this manner, his contingent supply means (when supply is free) exactly the same as cost of production; and there does not appear to be any difference remaining between his opinion and that of Mr. Ricardo. He says, indeed, that cost of production never affects price except by affecting either actual, or what he calls contingent supply; but that is only saying what is not at all denied by Mr. Ricardo, nor, I should imagine, by any other person: and contingent supply, as a criterion, is absolutely useless, and conveys no information, till we know what the cost of production is.

The observation I have made above, will, I believe, apply to the instances put by Mr. Ricardo, in his chapter on this subject.

The *conclusion* Mr. Buchanan draws, as cited by Mr. Ricardo, p. 493, " that a tax on the wages of labour would not raise wages, *because* it would not alter the proportion of the demand of labourers to the supply," appears by no means to follow. If the price of labour did not in such case rise, the supply would certainly ultimately diminish; and upon that event happening, or on the immediate prospect of its happening, wages would rise. At the same time, people would work harder, which would increase the proportion which the remuneration would bear to the *number of people working*, though not to the *quantity of work done*. Now natural price of labour, in Mr. Ricardo's sense, applies to the *former ;* it is the cost of maintaining *labourers*, and is in proportion, cæteris paribus, to the number of *them*, and not of the portions of work they do, or of the hours they labour. If a man chooses to work harder, there is no such thing as the *cost of production* of that addition.

Mr. Ricardo says (same page), if money falls in value, a commodity rises, and yet no increase has taken place in the demand for it. But of course, when it is said that the price of some one article depends on its demand and supply, we mean its price measured in something that has not altered in value, or else we include in its *demand,* that is, *effectual* demand, the question whether people have more or less of the other thing to give for it. Now to say that the value of money is fallen, is to say that people have more money to give for the commodity in question; the effectual demand for that commodity may therefore be said to be increased: or it may be said (which comes to the same thing), that though neither the demand nor supply of the commodity is increased, the proportion of the supply of *money* to the demand for *it* is increased, and therefore more money exchanges for less of the commodity.

" Conversion of revenue into capital" is another of these *verbal* sources of controversy. One man means by it, that the capitalist lays out part of the profits he has made by his capital, in making additions to his capital, instead of spending it for his private use, as he might else have done: another man means by it, that a person lays out as capital something which he never got as profits, or any capital of his own, but received as rent, wages, salary, &c. One, therefore, says, that capital can no otherwise be increased but by converting revenue into capital; while the other stoutly denies it. It would be quite absurd to expect them to lay aside this ambiguous *phrase*, and speak plain; bècause, then, they must submit to *agree*.

THE foregoing Tract will, perhaps, be rejected with contempt, as a mere discussion about words. It is so; it professes to be so. It has for its object to *prevent* some discussions about words, which *do not* profess to be so, but pass themselves off for discussions about *things*, instead of what they really are.

Books are something like commodities. M. Say tells us, that if there is a glut of commodities, the way to cure it is to produce more. Bacon, in like manner, says, that the too great number of books must be remedied by writing more. The success of both these rules must, of course, entirely depend upon what is the description and quality of the *particular article* that is *produced* in obedience to them. Whether the *preceding pages* are at all calculated to answer the purpose (for that a *glut exists* in the market of *Political Economy*, is pretty clear), or, on the contrary, only to aggravate the evil, must be left to the decision of the candid *consumer*.

T H E   E N D.

AN INQUIRY INTO THOSE PRINCIPLES
RESPECTING THE NATURE OF DEMAND

AN

INQUIRY

INTO THOSE

PRINCIPLES ADVOCATED BY MR. MALTHUS,

RELATIVE TO

THE NATURE OF DEMAND

AND

THE NECESSITY OF CONSUMPTION.

AN

INQUIRY

INTO

THOSE PRINCIPLES,

RESPECTING

THE NATURE OF DEMAND

AND

THE NECESSITY OF CONSUMPTION,

lately advocated by

MR. MALTHUS,

FROM

WHICH IT IS CONCLUDED, THAT TAXATION AND THE MAINTENANCE OF
UNPRODUCTIVE CONSUMERS CAN BE CONDUCIVE

TO

THE PROGRESS OF WEALTH.

LONDON:

PRINTED FOR R. HUNTER,

SUCCESSOR TO MR. JOHNSON,

N° 72, ST. PAUL'S CHURCHYARD.

1821.

I N Q U I R Y,

&c. &c.

——◆——

IF each man should form a wish for something, which he thought would tend to his own advantage, though each might be quite right in his choice, as related to himself, the way to promote the good of all, probably, would not be to grant all these wishes, because it would very likely turn out, that they were not all compatible with one another. In some cases it is very easy to see, that such wishes would not be compatible; as, if every man were to wish for a share of land larger than the whole land would afford if divided among them; but in some cases it is rather difficult to see it, and that difficulty is sometimes still further increased by prejudices, and by certain established modes of expression, which puzzle instead of assisting. This is the case with regard to some questions, which are raised about the necessity of *consumption,* in order to furnish a *demand* for the various articles of trade taken together. Many persons talk on this subject in a way, which might apply very well to their own particular business, and to its interests as compared to others, but which does not, and cannot, apply to the interests of all the different branches of business taken together, or to those of the public. They may now derive considerable support from the name of Malthus; and more support perhaps (owing to the unfortunate vagueness of statement, reasoning, and conclusion, in the late work of that celebrated writer) than he really intended to afford them. That part of his work to which I allude is in the form of an Inquiry into the immediate Causes of the Progress of Wealth. I propose to consider it, and the subject of which it so professes to treat.

We want to know, then, by what causes mankind, or the inhabitants of a particular country, are led to increase their wealth ; that is, to produce every year a greater quantity of the " necessaries, comforts, and conveniences of life" (to use a phrase which I know is somewhat vague) than they did the year before.

In this statement of the question there would be no particular object in using the word " year" rather than any other period of a given length ; and we might say, that wealth was the *periodical* produce of land and labour, as well as that it was the " *annual,*" which is Smith's word. A regular continual increase is the object, measured at any equal intervals you please. Were it not that the time for receiving the returns from land is, by the laws of nature, in most instances once a year : a year, or some multiple of a year, therefore, must be the period ; or else a rate of increase, as to produce from land, might often seem retrograde, or irregular, when it was in fact increasing with the greatest degree of regularity which the laws of nature could possibly admit of.

There are some other important objects, which the question as above stated does not include. For instance : it is to be wished, first, that the increase of wealth should be itself at a given rate, or else at an increasing, and regularly increasing, rate ; that is, that the additional produce, obtained at the end of this year, should bear the same proportion to the whole produce of last, as the addition obtained last year bore to the whole produce of the year before ; or else should bear a greater proportion ; and if a greater proportion, that this increase of the *proportion* should also go on steadily, and free from reverse or fluctuation.

The relative importance of these objects, or the question which of them ought, where we are obliged to choose, to be sacrificed to another, differs under different circumstances. It may be desirable, sometimes, to abstain from a present increase, if it is likely to produce a start that we cannot keep up to, and which therefore, especially through the medium of the principle of population, may in the end, taking a period of ten or twenty years, do more harm than good . and yet, on the other hand, it would clearly be absurd to abstain from opportunities of increasing our wealth for scores of years to come, merely because at the end of many centuries we should be obliged to draw in, or merely because we could not expect to go on increasing wealth at the same rate *for ever*, but must look forward to arriving at an absolute stand still, at some period indefinitely remote.

In the next place, it is a great object, that every such increase of wealth as I have been speaking of should not be less in proportion than the increase of numbers during the same period. For, in this case, though the world, or the nation, may be said, if you please, to have more wealth than it had before, yet it would consist of individuals, each of whom, one with another, would have less. It is farther to be wished, that the distribution of the increase of necessaries, &c., produced, among the same or increased numbers, should not be such as that any persons should have less than a certain quantity, or should suffer more than a certain degree of privations ; or at least it is to be wished, that the number of such persons should form a diminishing, or not increasing proportion of the whole ; and the *degree* of their privations be also diminishing. These objects, like those just mentioned, may sometimes be considered as *over and above* the main object stated at first, and sometimes be considered as interfering with, or at least qualifying it, so as that we may be obliged to choose between the two. Thus, though the sudden invention and rapidly extended use of some machine may at once add greatly to the wealth of the people, taken one with another, we may in some cases deprecate it on account of the injury it occasions at the time to certain individuals, which we may think may be so great as to more than counterbalance the good; and yet if the injury had been less, or the benefit greater, we might have thought otherwise. This is a case of actual diminution of the wealth of some; but in a case of *increase*, we could scarcely ever think, that an opportunity of increasing the wealth of *every* man should be foregone, merely because it was likely to increase it in such proportions as to leave the relative inequality between different conditions greater than before. It is an object, too, that more human beings should exist, rather than fewer; and it is hardly possible to state exactly how far this object must be sacrificed to, or preferred to, one or more of the others, nor with what limitations. It is not so necessary, perhaps, to point this out as a distinct object, because it forms part of individual well-being. If you wish, that where people are at ease and comfortable more should come into the world to partake those advantages, you may in almost all cases be sure, on the whole, that *those people* wish it themselves full as much; and it rests with them (Note I).

It is also to be wished, that the increase of wealth should be obtained so as to admit of labour,

or the more irksome kinds of it, being saved on
the whole. This is a question of degree
(Note II).

I have not said any thing about the excess of
production above consumption, as an object, which
may seem strange to those who have been used to
consider it as the very essence of wealth. But if
we produce ten times as much, and *consume* it, we
seem to be ten times as well off: it was the great
end for which the production took place : I do not
care whether it is *called* wealth or not. The
excess of production above consumption is important only as a *means* of obtaining, through
the help of capital, greater consumption. There
may indeed be an excess of production above consumption in another sense, *viz.* by the increased
use of *durable* articles, not used as capital : for
though in practice we generally mean by consumption the arrival of an article into the hands of
those who want it for their own use and not as
capital, yet we sometimes mean its final destruction by those persons, or by time. The production
of durable articles has been eulogized by Smith
(vol. ii, 107, 108, edit. 1806), and, to a certain
degree, with reason; but for the most part I should
be inclined to say, that the buyer is the best judge,
and that if he derives more satisfaction from what
is gone in a moment than what lasts ten years,
you cannot, in general, pretend to tell him he is
mistaken (Note III).

There will, indeed, where production and consumption are comparatively great, naturally be, at any given moment, a comparatively great surplus in the intermediate state, in the market, on its way from having been produced to the hands of the consumer; unless indeed the quickness with which things are sold off should have increased so as to counteract what would else have been the consequence of the increased production.

Neither have I mentioned the "increase of the exchangeable *value* of the whole produce," which forms so constant a topic with Mr. Malthus. It is because I am not so fortunate as to understand what it means, if intended as a description of some *object*, or *end*.

Much of our trouble would be saved, in discussions about the way of promoting *wealth*, if we were to keep clearly in mind, when using that word, which and how many of the various objects just enumerated we had particularly in view.

As I am considering a *given* portion of territory, and therefore no increase to wealth from obtaining more land, it is clear, that to increase the wealth each year, there must be either more work done each year than the former, equally productive of human means of enjoyment, or else the same or a less quantity of work, but so managed as to produce, on the whole, more of the means of human enjoyment; or both combined; taking into the account the altered productiveness (if any) of the natural agents or materials, in proportion to the labour employed on them: and it seems to me, that one or both these ends are sure to be obtained by an increased disposition in rich men to save their property, and employ it as capital, or to undertake the labour of superintending the employment of capital, or both ; and obtained not merely at the expense of a future diminution of production to the same extent by reaction, but so as to have made a real addition in the long run, beyond what would have otherwise existed. That every such addition of capital, or of labour of management, adds to the wealth and betters the condition of the world or of the country, at the *time*, seems quite plain. An addition of capital, by adding to the whole inducement to labour, makes the quantity of labour performed be greater than it otherwise would have been; and an addition to the labour of management is itself an addition to the quantity of useful labour performed, its use being in making more effective the labour of those who work with their hands. Now, in neither case is there any reason why the *whole* benefit thus conferred should be given away ; in all cases where you confer a benefit on mankind, embodied in the production of a commodity, you may get something in return, so that both you and they will be better on the whole. The question is, how much you will get; whether as much in proportion to your capital, &c., as was got before, or less; and whether, if you get less, that will not lead to the withdrawing of capital, so that in the end no good will have been gained by the addition made ?

Adam Smith thought (book i, chap. ix), that accumulation or increase of stock in general lowered the rate of profits in general, on the same principle which makes the increase of stock in any particular trade lower the profits of that trade. But such increase of stock in a particular trade *means* an increase more *in proportion* than stock is at the same time increased in other trades : it is relative.

In such case the profits fall, certainly. If the capital employed in cutlery is increased as 100 : 101, and can only produce an increase of cutlery in the same proportion, the degree in which it will increase the command which its producers have over things in general, no increased production of *them* having by the supposition taken place, will be in a less proportion ; and this, and not the increase of the quantity of cutlery, constitutes the employers' profits, or the increase of their wealth. But if the like addition of one per cent. had been making at the same time to the capitals of all other trades, &c. (which is a very likely case, if those additions came out of profits) and with the like result as to produce, this conclusion would not follow : for the rate at which each article would exchange with the rest would remain unaltered, and therefore a given portion of each would give the same command as before over the rest. Suppose the addition to be made to some at one time, and to the rest at another time, it will come to the same in the end, but with temporary and partial variations one way

and the other. For instance: in the case I first
put as to cutlery, the cutler found the rate of his
profits less (and probably this fall was not felt by
the added portion of capital only, but distributed
through the whole trade) ; but all other trades
found their command of cutlery increased, and
their profits, so far as they were measured in cutlery, somewhat higher : and when they in return
added to their capital and produce, their produce
fell again, compared to cutlery ; the rate of their
profits estimated in cutlery was less, and the profits
of the cutler, estimated in *their* produce, recovered
in a great degree their former fall. It is a mistake
therefore to infer, as Smith appears to have done,
that, because an addition of capital confined to one
particular trade would lower the rate of profits in
it, the like addition of capital in all would, for the
same reason, and in the *same manner*, lower the
rate of profits in general.

Smith was led to form the opinion I have just
mentioned, partly by wishing to account for a fact,
which he thought he perceived in history. He
thought, that profits in general had in fact fallen
very greatly in the course of the last two or three
centuries in the same countries, while capital had
increased ; and that they are lowest in the same
periods in those countries where there is most
capital, as in Holland, for instance, compared to
India. But, however true this may be to a certain
extent, it appears extremely probable, that he much
overrated the degree, and *that*, owing to the na-

ture of the criterion, which he made use of to estimate it. This was the market rate of interest (book i, chap. ix; and see vol. ii, page 9, ed. 1806). " To judge of what the average profit may have been formerly, or in remote periods of time, with any degree of precision," he thinks, " must be altogether impossible;" but that, " some notion may be formed of them from the interest of money. Wherever a great deal can be made by the use of money, a great deal will commonly be given for the use of it," and vice versâ. Now admitting this last observation to be perfectly true, and certainly it is so far true, that nobody will borrow *capital* at an average rate higher than the average rate of profits he can make by laying it out, the market rate of interest does not denote what is actually *given* for the use of money (Note IV). Part of the rate of interest, which each lender charges and contracts for, is always in the nature of insurance, on account of the uncertainty of being repaid at all ; and would not be charged or contracted for if the repayment were certain. Now this part is not in fact received, or actually *given*, at all, on the whole. It always represents the average danger of loss, which is the value of the risk. The receipt of it by some people merely balances the whole amount of the losses sustained by others. The whole rate of interest actually received on the whole mass of money lent is only the residue. In bottomry this appears plain enough : the marine interest is allowed by law to amount to any height:

we see two coexisting rates of interest, five, perhaps, and thirty. Every body sees here (what
Blackstone observes), that the excess of marine
over other interest must be mere risk, and that the
real returns of money are not greater there than
elsewhere ; for capital would flow to that mode of
investment, and reduce the rate to an equality. In
comparing different places or times, this last proof
not being applicable, the fact does not strike us so
forcibly.

This uncertainty of repayment is partly in the
want of power, and partly in the want of will.
We think now, in civilized countries, but little,
comparatively, of the latter, because the law assists
the creditor. But the law was a mere farce for
the Jew in the time of King John, against a king
or great baron. His creditor would draw his teeth,
or throw him behind the fire. He had to insure
the morality as well as solvency of his debtor. One
wonders that the rate of interest, under such circumstances, did not become something *infinite*.
M. Say goes so far as to infer, from these considerations, that we may deduct so much as eighty-two
out of eighty-six, a rate of interest, he says (vol. ii,
p. 131, fourth edit.), given in 1360, in order to get
at the real return for the money lent. The defect
of laws diminishes the *power* of the debtor too,
where he is not a powerful person, such as I just
alluded to ; owing to the insecurity of property : I
mean here, not his power to pay this or that *sum*
rather than another, but his power to pay whatever

it be that he has *contracted for*, be it more or less,
which of course must depend on the *certainty* with
which he can calculate his prospects. The returns
of his trade or employment may be as uncertain,
fluctuating, and unequal, as the gains of the person
who lends to him ; and it is because they are so
uncertain, rather than because they are ordinarily
high, that the interest charged by the lender is
great. In the observation of M. Say (which
Mr. Ricardo has remarked upon in page 374 of his
book) he forgets this; and the remark he makes
(vol. ii, p. 152), "que les profits du capital sont
d'autant plus grands que l'entreprise est plus ha-
sardeuse," is not quite correct. They are greater
when there are any received at all. Prices are
charged so as to allow for the risk : but the whole
return to the whole capitals employed, taking in
what fail, need not be greater than in other trades.
We see large gains made ; but must inquire, as the
philosopher did, "Where are they painted that
were drowned?" Now in flourishing trading
countries, as Holland, the amount of interest
charged, as for risk, is less; because if the risk
were not there small, they *never could have* become
so flourishing in trade, or laid out so large capitals.

The error of Smith, in thinking that general extension of capital lowered general profits, because
extension of capital in a particular line lowers the
profits in that line, was pointed out I believe by
M. Say; and he, on the contrary, advances, that
production always opens a market for production ;

that " chaque produit créé est un débouché ouvert," and that "chaque produit détruit ou consommé est un débouché fermé." Now the term débouché or " market" is all comparative. Nobody denied, that a new product will always, or almost always, find *a market:* the question is, at what price? Whether a profitable market? Whether its production and sale will bring in what were before the usual average profits of stock, or less? The term, un débouché, does not decide this (Note V). The difficulty being, whether it will answer to a man to produce some commodity : you tell him the production will open a market. But not for the thing produced.

If M. Say means, by opening a market or vent (*débouché*), opening a means of profitable traffic, it is not true that the creation of *any* product (*chaque produit créé*) will have that effect, it depends entirely upon what particular article you produce : for where a glut of any particular article exists, the production of more of that, must often be merely mischievous : it is the production of other articles, such as are fit to exchange with it, that is wanted.

The maxim of M. Say is expressed in a short form, and, as a natural consequence, puzzles more than it instructs. He means, that in the production of many things, each furnishes a market for the other. Each, therefore, taken singly, stands in need of a market for itself, just as much as it furnishes one for another commodity produced, or to be produced. He does not mean that it opens more

débouchés than it fills. He does not mean that the
production of an additional article increases by so
much the whole quantum of demand for articles in
general. He only means that it does not, as vul-
garly supposed, diminish it.

M. Say applies his maxim to the glut of English
manufactures in Italy, Brazil, &c. (Lettres, p. 15.)
What is wanted, says he, to put an end to this is,
that there should be some articles produced in those
countries to exchange with the English ones. This
is not a very *practical* way of stating it, because he
himself observes that they *could not* produce any
such articles. " There is a glut of English goods in
Italy, *because* there is not enough produced in
Italy." But *fewer* goods have not been produced
in Italy than formerly. It would be simpler to
say, the English should not have produced (which
was possible), than to say, as he does, that the
Italians and Brazilians *should.*

Where he puts a case (Lettres, p. 7), of a man
having taken a rich cargo, two hundred years ago,
to Philadelphia, of course it would have been better
that it should never have been produced, that the
capital which produced it should have been consumed, than that it should have been taken there
then.

It might be said (though not by M. Say), that
every exchange must be an advantage to both parties, or else they would not make it ; but that only
shews that the producer is at least better off when
he has exchanged his stock on hand than while it

is on hand; which every body knows. But that is saying little, since if it is to continue on hand, it is absolutely of *no* advantage to him whatever, beyond the very small portion he can himself use. The advantage we are in quest of is as compared with his state before he produced the article, not with his state while it is lying on hand.

Now as to the *produit consommé ou détruit.* The *débouché* here is a *potential* one; one which *would* or *might* have taken place. Clearly, if any product in the hands of a person, who was going to exchange it for some other, is destroyed or consumed, a market, which would have existed for that other, is prevented or stopped. And though the exchange might have been to the owner of the first mentioned product unprofitable, or have brought him less than the ordinary rate of profits, still he will never be the better for *destroying* it. Its destruction will, probably, raise the profits of the other producers of the same article, and be a benefit to them, but not equal to the injury to the individual producer. Whether it may not be so little conducive to future gain, that he may as well *consume* it for present enjoyment, may sometimes be a question.

M. Say is wrong (note to p. 80 of Lettres à M. Malthus) to say "Je n'ai point dit qu'un produit épargné était un débouché ouvert," he *has.* Mr. Malthus is not attacking the first branch of his maxim " un produit créé," &c., but the second " un produit détruit," &c., and the *converse* of that is,

that if a product which was going to be destroyed
or consumed, is not destroyed or consumed, *i. e.* is
épargné, saved, a *débouché* will exist, which would
not otherwise have existed; the proposition which
M. Say here disclaims.

Suppose the product consumed or destroyed to
be in the hands of óne who did *not* mean to exchange it with another; how is any *débouché
fermé?* A *possible* one, certainly; he *might* have
exchanged it; but if he did he would have stood
in the way of the *débouché* of that particular sort
of article in other people's hands, just as much as
he increased the *débouché* of the sort of article he
exchanged it for. But if it was only a *débouché*
which he *might* have made, had it in his power to
make, but which he was not at all *likely* to have
made, what sense is there in saying, or what practical truth is inculcated by saying, that a *débouché*
is stopped? Suppose, in the last case (as I have
supposed before), he was a *labourer,* and that the
alternative of consuming is keeping a little longer,
and consuming then, and that he is idle during the
interim (the supposition is not very *likely,* I grant,
for a saving labourer is probably a laborious one
too), a *débouché* may rather be said to be stopped
by the effects of his *non*-consumption, according to
the language of M. Say more than any body, as he
talks of the *échange appellé production,* and must
consider the exchange against *labour* as much a
débouché as the exchange against goods.

The consumption or destruction which does

harm is where the article would else have been exchanged for labour, which quantity of labour will not now be performed, or be performed but in a less productive line. But it is very strange to call this exchange for labour a *débouché.* And if it is called a débouché here, it should be so understood in the case of the former proposition, that production opens a débouché; *viz.* a débouché for *labour ;* when it would clearly show how little that proposition has to do with any question of rate of profits to the *capitalist,* or consequently of the inducement to lay out capital.

Though that particular argument, or mode of inference, of Adam Smith, which I have mentioned, is probably erroneous, the question itself, whether increased additions to the capital of a country do or do not tend to lower the rate of profit, is still open. And, with regard to the maxim of M. Say, it does not necessarily follow, that because increased production may be said to find *a market* for itself, it finds *such* a market as affords an undiminished rate of profit to the producers. Mr. Ricardo (p. 359, second edit.), after quoting the doctrine of Smith about the cause of the fall of profits, adds, " M. Say, has, however, most satisfactorily shown, that there is no amount of capital which *may not be employed* in a country, because demand is only limited by production." " There cannot be accumulated (p. 360) in a country any amount of capital which cannot be employed *productively*" (meaning, I presume, " with profit to the owner") " until

wages rise so high *in consequence* of the rise of necessaries, and so little consequently remains for the
profits of stock, that the motive for accumulation
ceases." The latter sentence limits (not to say
contradicts) the former, if " which may not be employed," in the former, means " employed productively," or rather, " profitably :" And if it
means simply " employed," the proposition is useless ; because neither Adam Smith nor any body
else, I presume, denied that it might " *be employed*,"
if you did not care what profits it brought.

That which, according to the passage above
quoted from Mr. Ricardo, would finally annihilate
profits, if the additions to capital should ever go far
enough to bring it into operation, and the fear of
which, therefore, would of course *prevent* additions
to capital from going so far, and would be the
limit to such additions to capital, is " the rise of
wages" above a certain point, " *in consequence* of
the rise of necessaries." And we might infer, that
the same cause, the rise of wages in consequence of
the rise of necessaries, happening in a less degree,
would constitute at every step the cause of the fall
of profits from a higher rate to a lower, and be the
only cause which could possibly occasion such an
event. However, Mr. Ricardo does not mean to
assert this, but thinks that the wages of labour may
rise, and the profits of stock fall, sometimes, *without* that event having been *preceded*, as from the
above sentence taken singly we might have expected,
by a rise in the price of necessaries, but rather

being itself the antecedent cause of a rise in the price of necessaries. But this he considers as a temporary state of things only, as an order of events which is but for a time, and which has a tendency to restore itself; and he thinks the general profits of stock never fall *permanently*, except from the cause referred to above; and which is thus stated in his chapter on Profits, p. 110. " Supposing corn and manufactured goods always to sell at the same price, profits would be high or low in proportion as wages were low or high. But suppose corn to rise in price because more labour is necessary to produce it; that cause will not raise the price of manufactured goods in the production of which no additional quantity of labour is required. If, then, wages continued the same, the profits of manufacturers would remain the same; but if, as is absolutely certain, wages should rise with the price of corn, then their profits would necessarily fall." Except (of course) where this effect is counteracted by improvements, machines, &c., rendering manual labour in manufactures more productive (Note VI).

The immediate market for capital, or *field* for capital, may be said to be labour. The amount of capital which can be invested at a given moment, in a given country, or the world, so as to return not less than a given rate of profits, seems principally to depend on the quantity of labour, which it is possible, by laying out that capital, to induce the then existing number of human beings to perform (Note VII).

Though we generally look on production as effected by capital, that being the first mover, labour, of course, is the immediate agent. Every man who would lay out more capital in production, must call forth more labour, either of people already in some degree employed, or of others, than would else have been called forth. But the portion of the whole mass of possible labour, which has been already selected by other employers, must have been that portion which could be had cheapest; he must, therefore, in determining to employ more labour, determine *ipso facto* to reward it a trifle better than labour was rewarded before. That is, he must make such a bargain with the men he employs, as to exact from them, in return for the whole portion of his capital which he pays them in wages, somewhat less labour than former employers got for the same wages. And that is saying, in other words, that he must expect less *profits*; because less produce: for, as before observed (Note VIII), I am laying out of the question now the case where a new saving is effected, by machinery or otherwise, on the labour in that branch of production; or, what comes to the same thing, where something, which will confer a greater degree of human enjoyment, comes to be produced with a quantity of labour equal to that which would before produce something which would confer only a less degree of human enjoyment.

Then the effect will be, as far as relates to profits, just the reverse of that produced by a saving in labour. But by transferring to the labourers a portion of that command over things in general which he possessed, the man we are speaking of has, probably, caused an increase of demand for necessaries, in proportion to that for superfluities, as compared with what would have been the proportion between those two sorts of demand, if he had exerted that command to procure things for his own consumption. Necessaries will thereby exchange for more of things in general, and superfluities for less : or, in other words, a given quantity of the necessaries of life will exchange for more of the superfluities of life, and vice versâ, than would otherwise have been the case. And, in part, at least, these necessaries will be *food.* Nor will this alteration of relative demand be made up for at the end of the particular act of production, which we are supposing this capitalist to be engaged in, by a corresponding alteration in the relative *supply ;* partly, because it cannot be (from the nature of land), at the same price, and partly because it is probable, that the capitalist or capitalists in question were determined, in their choice of the particular article or articles which they meant to produce, by the state of relative demand when they began, and not by the consideration of the alteration which would be produced in that state, during the course of their production, by the effect of the wages they were going to pay.

The rate of wages then having risen, is, in this case, as we may say, the *same thing* as the fall in the rate of profits ; and the fact of the whole amount paid as wages having increased too, is, by raising the demand for corn above that which was (as compared with the actual rate of supply) the *effectual* demand for it, the *cause* of resorting to inferior soils, or employing more labour with diminished returns, on land.

Now Mr. Ricardo says, that such a fall of profits as I have just described may, indeed, happen; but that, owing to the principle of population, it would be but temporary ; the supply of capital would have outrun for a time that of men ; but the supply of men *would* in time bring things to a level again, *but for* the increased difficulty of raising corn, and consequently increased price of corn, and *consequently* increased wages, which would have taken place in the mean time. At all events, then, the increased price of corn was not the *original* cause of that rise of wages which made profits fall, but, on the contrary, the rise of wages was the cause of the increased price of corn at first, and the nature of land, yielding less and less proportional returns to increased tillage, made part of that increase of price *permanent*, prevented a complete *reaction* from taking place through the principle of population. Because the labourer found that the increase that took place in wages, the increased command over things in general which was afforded him, was continually less and less in proportion a command of necessaries, and more and more in proportion a command of superfluities ; and it is the former only that can constitute an increased inducement to rear a family.

However, we must recollect, that it does not

follow that, even otherwise, the principle of population *would* have brought matters to a level. People are not obliged to take advantage of improved circumstances to increase their numbers to the full extent which the improvement would admit of. The degree, in which they do so, varies continually. The " principle of population" is not a strict, invariable principle, like the laws of motion, by which water finds its level.

In every case the laying out of capital increases the demand for labour, increases the rate of wages, and lowers the rate of profits (if no new saving in labour is effected by it), beyond what *would* have been the case, had that capital not been laid out; but it need not be below what it *was before;* because the supply of labour *may,* just at the same time, be increased as fast or still faster than that of capital: as must happen, for instance, during such a *reaction* of population as was just now supposed.

The rate at which population is increasing at any time, may be considered as in some degree owing to the rate at which additions *have of late* been usually making to capital, and at which they are expected to continue; the addition to capital therefore, at any time, *may* be merely such an addition as was *looked for,* as the rate of increase of population had been framed *in expectation of;* such an addition as, had it *not* come, profits would have *risen,* compared to what they were before. The question will always be, which of the two is at a given time increasing fastest. But owing to the increased disposition of mankind to be frugal and seek for gain, and owing to the length of interval which elapses before the supply of *men* can be increased to meet an increased demand, and owing to the increased prudence and desire of comforts among the poor, preventing the increase of men from being fully in proportion to the demand (Note IX), it seems to me that the demand might be, as it were, *permanently ahead* of the supply, and consequently the profits of stock be permanently falling, from this cause only, over and above the fall which arises from the nature of land. Supposing the degree of inclination to save and gain on the part of the capitalist, and to labour and to increase on the part of the labourer, to remain unaltered, or both to increase in equal proportions, the effect of increased cultivation in raising permanently the price of corn, would be borne partly by the labourer and partly by the employer : the labourer's wages would not be raised in fully equal proportion with the price of corn, nor would they, on the other hand, remain quite stationary : profits would indeed fall, but the amount of the labourer's command of food would also be somewhat abridged. The increased difficulty of procuring food, indeed, would not raise the wages of the labourer at all, except so far as it could be made to influence the relation between the supply of, and demand for, labour. "Common humanity," which Smith refers to, has, as Mr. Malthus justly observes, nothing to do with this.

Besides the effect produced by that part of capital which is spent in *wages*, we may observe that
the other part, which is spent in materials, tends on
the whole, probably, to create a greater demand
for raw produce, in proportion to manufactured
produce, than if the money had been spent in articles of immediate consumption, and not as capital.
Part of this raw produce, may, indeed, be foreign;
but on the whole an increasing disposition to employ capital seems to me to *push demand* (as it
were) more and more in the direction of raw produce, that is, ultimately, of land, away from the
more worked-up sorts of products.

The profits of stock are the remuneration for
the increased productiveness conferred on labour
by capital (Note X). Where you have made an
addition to capital, which in proportion to the
labour and materials, &c., it employs, can produce
more of human enjoyment than the same portion of
capital usually did before, or than the last preceding
addition did (as in the case of some new inventions,
newly-imported foreign commodities, or of a saving
of labour effected in any former branch of production), you may reasonably expect at least *as* high a
rate of profits as was the average rate before.
Where you have made an addition, which, in proportion to the labour, &c., it employs, can produce
only *as much* of human enjoyment as the last additions could, you cannot have a higher rate of profit
than was the average rate before; but you may, as
already observed, have a lower, because you may

be obliged to make such a bargain with your
labourers, &c., to pay them so much higher in proportion than labour, &c., was paid before, as that
your produce may not be so great in proportion to
the *capital* you have laid out, as it is in proportion
to the *labour*, &c., employed with that capital in the
production, and your undertaking, though *equally
productive*, may not be so *profitable*. Lastly, where
you have made an addition to capital, which in
proportion to the labour, &c., it employs, can only
produce *less* of human enjoyment than the same
portion of capital usually did before, or than the
last preceding addition did (which is generally the
case where it is applied to *land*), the profits must
be less than what was the average rate before, as
far as depends on this cause ; *besides* any fall that
they may undergo owing to the bargain made with
the labourer, &c., as in the second case. Additional capital, therefore, is never, naturally, applied
first to land. Production must increase in other
lines ; profits in farming must *rise* beyond what
they were; that is, a given quantity of agricultural
produce command a larger quantity of things in
general, in proportion to what is required for the
labour, &c., that produce it, *before* it will be *equally*
worth while to add to agricultural capital as to add
to capital in other lines.

I repeat, then, that the proposition, that production is only limited by production, finds its own
market, &c., must not be understood as pronouncing
on the actual *degree* of *profits* that increased pro-

duction at any particular time and place will afford. It is nothing to say, that the products will exchange with one another at the same rate as before: the question is, in whose hands are the products? If a larger proportion than before must be put into the hands of the labourers, they may all exchange at the same rate afterwards (if you choose to consider commodities as exchanging with one another), but the *producers*, I mean those who set on foot and direct production, masters, capitalists, will not make so much : or, to put the same thing in another shape, products do *not* all exchange with one another, but some with labour and land. Profits do not depend on price, they depend on price compared with outgoings (Note XI).

The interest of the public is always so far the same with that of the capitalists, that the more capital is employed, and consequently the greater amount of gain made on the whole, though the rate of profits should be less, the better for the public, that is, for consumers. No man, who is not a despot, or a thief, can himself gain unless by conferring some benefit on others in return. But this gain is the gain of *new* capitalists, or of capitalists considered as owners of *added* capital. The interest of the public (I mean, of course, the present interest, that is, considering this as not interfering with the former object), is opposed to that of the *actual* owners of *actual* capital at any given moment, supposing no addition. The *lower* their rate of profits, of course, the better for the public.

A change of profits, owing to a saving of labour, however, is a benefit to both.

The effect of laying out capital seems to be, that where a certain quantity of superfluities would have been consumed this year, a quantity of necessaries nearly equivalent will be consumed, which else would not ; and so on every year while it remains *in :* and that much more than the former quantity of superfluities will be consumed too, but divided among many years. The benefit to the labourer is much *greater* than that to the capitalist (if he could not have got work but by the help of capital), but it is not obtained *at the expense of* that of the capitalist. The *proportion* of necessaries consumed, and consequently demanded and produced, to that of superfluities, may be increasing, and yet the *quantity* of superfluities consumed and produced be increasing too. I say this with reference to the question of Mr. Malthus, who says, that, in increasing production, more and more is devoted to the production of necessaries, and asks, how can that be an *object* or an *inducement* to the rich ? Every body knows that it is not their *object*, but the necessary *incident* to, consequenee of, the attainment of that which *is* their object, gain to themselves.

Wherever an addition is made to capital, which brings, and which is from the first expected to bring, less than what was before the ordinary rate of profits of stock, it is plain, that the absolute amount or degree of disposition to save, in order to

gain, is greater than it was. Before that time
nobody added to capital unless they could make,
say ten per cent.; now they will do it though
they can only expect nine and a half. To say that
people are more disposed to save and gain, *means*
that *more* persons are disposed to lay out capital in
the hope of the former profits ; or else that the same
persons, who laid out capital in the hope of the
former profits, now think it worth while to lay out
more in the hope of somewhat *less* than the former
profits ; probably both. If it is new gains that are
so laid out, it comes to the same thing; if new
gains were formerly laid out, or added to capital,
in the prospect of ten per cent., and now in the
prospect of nine and a half, it is clear that a less
degree of gain is now felt to be a sufficient inducement, that a less degree will now induce people in
general to lay out capital, to save rather than
spend, than formerly (Note XII). Though the
addition were not expected to bring less profits,
still if, after it is found that it does so in fact, the
increased amount of capital on the whole is still
retained in business, it comes to the same thing,
the absolute amount or degree of disposition to
save is clearly greater than it was. It is plain,
therefore, that merely to shew, that an increased
production will lower profits, is not to prove that
it will therefore defeat itself in the end by diminishing its inducement, and cause a *reaction* equal to,
or greater than, the *action*, so as that wealth will
not have been increased, or will be diminished, on

the whole. For, first, the producers must have contemplated, in part at least, this fall of profits, and do not require the same rate of profits, as an inducement, as they did before; and, secondly, if they did not contemplate it, they may yet acquiesce in it when it comes. There is a great deal in habit : a fall of profits, which would have discouraged a man from embarking his capital, may not induce him to withdraw it (Note XIII). Nor does the assertion, that increased production lowers profits, prove that such increased production will *not happen.* For if it be true, that profits have been in modern times gradually falling on the whole, this is what must have been continually taking place. If, owing to the increased cultivation of land, or any other cause, the increase of capital *necessarily* leads to a lower rate of profits, it is clear, if an increase of capital does take place, that the absolute disposition to save is increased in degree and amount.

We often hear of the importance of a taste for employing what is called productive labour rather than unproductive (Note XIV); of the importance of a taste for comforts, and superfluities, and independence, among the labourers; of a greater or less taste for indolence rather than exertion. But frugality is a matter of taste, too; of habit and fashion; of disposition and temper. One man thinks it worth while to save money, or to submit to the labour of managing a concern, for small gains, while another is not tempted by large : and there may certainly be at one time or place more of the former sort of men than of the latter.—See Hume's Essay on Interest (Note XV). There are many things which can only be accounted for by the varying tastes and *habits* of man. Nothing is more dogmatical than the maxim we often hear, that man is always the same. No two men are the same. Why then two nations, or generations? (Note XVI). Mr. Malthus seems to think, that taking the existing rate of profits at any time, the operation of it in encouraging production would, if it had its full swing, increase production so much as to lower profits, and thereby discourage production again. But suppose it to be true, yet (if we are not talking of sudden or partial accidental changes) that would only occasion the withdrawing so much capital as will bring up the rate of profits again. And then it would at least have been useful while it staid in. Nay, capital need not be withdrawn; it would be enough if no more additions were made. It seems an evil, which cures and regulates itself. Indeed, it may be said to prevent itself. For at every step of this process, if it be true, that a certain degree of profit (say ten per cent.) is necessary to induce a continuance of increase of production at the present rate, capital will cease to be invested so fast, at the moment the owner perceives that no more than nine and a half per cent. or nine and three quarters offers itself. Or does *he* imagine that he shall get ten, while we, the philosophers, knowing better, advise him to bold his hand? How do we derive this superior insight into his concerns? Besides, I think, that (*taking one sort of production with another*) a man feels, at *the moment* of *commencing* the production, that he is doing so at less profit, if the fact be so. His less profit, as already observed, *consists in* the worse bargain he makes with the labourer, &c., at setting out. Even if the conclusion be true, then, that receiving less than ten per cent. would discourage production, it only proves that that state of things will never happen; people *will not* produce to such an extent as will bring down profits below ten per cent.: and if they will produce to that extent, it only shews, that they do *not* require so great an amount of profit as an inducement, and therefore will *not* look upon the less amount as a discouragement.

That a " passion for accumulation" should destroy the motive for saving, seems a contradictory apprehension. The meaning of an increased passion for accumulation must be, that people *require less* motive for saving. Why, then, an extreme degree of production must end in a " marked depression of wealth and population permanently" (Malthus, 369), I cannot conceive.

Considering, that an increased employment of capital will not take place unless a rate of profits equal to the former rate, or greater than it, can be ensured, and considering, that the mere addition to capital does not of itself tend to ensure such a rate of profits, but the reverse, Mr. Malthus, and those who rea-

son in the same manner as he does, proceed to
look out for some source, independent of and extrinsic to production itself, whose progressive increase may keep pace with the progressive increase
of capital, and from which continual additional supplies of the requisite rate of profits may be derived.
Such a source is what Mr. Malthus appears to seek
for, under the title of " stimulus to the increase of
wealth ;" and he proposes many, which he afterwards determines to be insufficient. Among these
he introduces accumulation itself, or the addition
to capital ; but that is itself the thing, which we
are seeking to find a stimulus, or motive, for.   If
it has taken place, we have already obtained that
which we are in search of, even though this addition
may not form a stimulus to any further additions.

An extrinsic cause, capable of constantly supplying an undiminished rate of profits to an increasing amount of capital, must be such a cause
as would have *raised* the rate of profits if the
capital had *not* increased.

I have already said, that it does not seem to me
to be necessary, as a motive to the increase of
capital, that the rate of profits upon the existing
capital *should rise*, or that profits upon the
added capital should be the same as they were
on the former; but that to obtain (if it *is* necessary)
as high a rate of profits, in a given country, and in
continual progression, as the nature of things will
admit, considering the exhaustible nature of land,
the requisites are, increased numbers and manual

indnstry, and the application of labour in such a way as to produce a larger proportion of what is desirable to man. Mr. Malthus thinks, that besides all this it is necessary, as part of the fund or source from which profits may be obtained, that there should always be a quantity (and of course it must be an increasing quantity) of the necessaries, &c., of life, placed at the command of those who are not capitalists, nor manual labourers, nor landlords: he calls them *unproductive consumers.*

Mr. Malthus enumerates several different things which have been or might be suggested as causes of the increase of production and of wealth, and successively determines as to each, that it is not, considered separately, a sufficient stimulus to such increase. But he passes rather summarily over the question, why *all united* may not be snfficient.

He denies that increase of numbers can increase wealth. He does not very clearly state what he means. Whether, that it has no tendency to add *at all* to the quantum of products; or, not to add to products in an equal *proportion* to that in which it adds to numbers (see the beginning of this tract); or, not in such a degree as that each individual of the *labouring* class may be as well off as before; or, not in such a degree as that they may be as well off in proportion to the work they do; or, not in such a degree as to add to the *net* produce, &c.; all as different questions as can be. "The increase of population alone, or, more properly speaking, the pressure of the population hard against the limits of subsistence, does not furnish an effective stimulus to the *continued increase of wealth*" (p. 348): " if want alone, &c., were a sufficient stimulus to *production*" (ibid.) : " many writers have been of opinion, that an increase of population is *the sole* stimulus necessary to *the increase of wealth*, because population—must—keep up the demand for an increase of produce, which will naturally be followed by a *continued increase of supply*" (p. 347): " an increase of population will not furnish the required stimulus to an increase of wealth *proportioned to* the power of production" (p. 350): " the *slowest progress* in wealth is made where the stimulus arising from population is the greatest" (ibid.): whether " population alone can create *an effective* demand for wealth" (ibid.): " furnish an *adequate* stimulus to the *increase of wealth*" (p. 351). Scarce any two of these expressions convey distinctly the same meaning.

It is evidently absurd to say, that however different two countries may be, and may always have been, in every respect, the natural tendency to increase of numbers alone will have occasioned the same proportionate increase of wealth in each, reckoning from their first peopling. If *this* is the proposition Mr. Malthus is here answering, it scarce deserves an answer; inasmuch as some countries, as he observes, do not increase their wealth at all, in any sense of the word; do not increase their numbers, nor make those numbers better off. But I should apprehend, that whenever any man asserts, that the tendency to increase numbers is a sufficient stimulus to an increase of wealth, he, at least, means, *supposing* the obstacles from bad government, permitting and committing acts of plunder and oppression, to be removed; and, secondly, I should apprehend, that, having made that supposition, such a person merely means to say, that as to any *positive* stimulus, beyond that of protecting industry, and making it free and equal, you can apply none, but must patiently trust to the effect of the principle of population, which will give in each country that stimulus to increase of wealth, which the natural situation and advantages of every kind will admit. As to which, the plain truth, of course, is, that though it may be true that the *government* can apply no positive stimulus, yet that two countries, equally well governed, equally peopled in proportion to their extent, equally situated as to every natural advantage, may be increasing in wealth at unequal rates, owing to an unequal disposition to gain and frugality, past and present, among the richer portions of their respective inhabitants; and owing to an unequal disposition to work, among the poorer; and unequal skill in both classes; though the natural principle of population, or tendency to increase, may, probably, be the same in both countries. An increasing supply of numbers is not always an increasing supply of *labour* in the same proportion; and if it were, it requires an increasing supply of capital, which it does not necessarily provide, though it may facilitate. Just in the same way as an increased supply of a certain *particular article*, which is not more wanted than formerly, will do more harm than good to the body of producers of that article, and but little good to the world, unless it be matched by an increased supply of certain others, fit to exchange with it; which last supply is encouraged by the former, but not absolutely compelled.

When Mr. Malthus quotes Poland or Turkey, on this question, against his imaginary opponent, one would think he must suppose, that such opponent had asserted, that the tendency to increase would be a *greater* stimulus to wealth in those countries, than in more flourishing ones. For it *would* be a greater stimulus, if it produced *any* increase *there*, where it has so many more obstacles to overcome. One would not have expected this from his observation just before (p. 346, at bottom), that there are countries " *not* essentially different in the *security of property*" or *degree of education*, "which yet, with nearly equal natural capabilities, make a different progress in wealth :" and that it is the reason of *this*, which he intends to inquire into.

The question must be, what effect will an increase of numbers have, as to increase of production, supposing men in other respects to be of the same *dispositions* as before ; which does not mean, to *act in the same manner*, but to act in the same manner *in proportion* to any change, which the supposed event may make in their circumstances.

Mr. Malthus (349) supposes, that the fall of wages, which a fresh increase of numbers would occasion in the first instance, would lead in a little time to a fall of the value of produce, which would *more* than counterbalance it. Of this there is no proof at all. I do not know in what he *estimates* this *fall* in the value of produce. If in labour, it is synonymous with a rise of wages, is *beneficial* to the labourer, and cannot happen, under such circumstances, so as to injure the capitalist, unless he pleases; that is, unless he has increased his capital, and taken lower profits.

In the next section, Mr. Malthus says, that neither is accumulation a sufficient *stimulus* (*cause*, I should have thought; see above) to the increase of wealth. " *It has already been shewn*," he says, " that the consumption and demand occasioned by the persons employed in productive labour, can never alone furnish a motive to the accumulation and employment of capital ; and, with regard to the capitalists themselves, together with the landlords and other rich persons, they have, by the supposition, agreed to be parsimonious," &c., and then he asks, where are purchasers to be found ? But it has not *been shewn*, in the former chapter, that the increased number of productive labourers does not furnish any motive to the accumulation of capital ; it has been shewn, that such a circumstance will not better the condition of the labourers themselves, one with another, that is, will not increase their means in proportion to their numbers, *unless* there is a corresponding increase of capital ; but Mr. Malthus *is* in this chapter *supposing* that such increase of capital *takes place;* he cannot have the benefit of two contradictory and incompatible suppositions at the same time. If these rich people are become more parsimonious, then, even if it be true that there is not so great inducement to accumulate, they do not *want* so great an inducement. Capital and labour may be considered, in some sense, as each the market, mutually, for the other ; they are so treated by Adam Smith. An increase of either, alone, may only stand in more need of a corresponding increase of the other ; but it is strange, if an increase of *both* will not answer every purpose. Mr. Malthus seems to be satisfied with the conclusion, that whenever either gets the start of the other for a time, there will be a reaction, that will depress things even *below* the point they started from ; but there is no proof of this ; the contrary is more conformable to fact : I mean, that it will not even depress it *so far* as to that point. *Semper aliquid hæret,* I apprehend : *habits* of industry and frugality are not implanted by nature, and, when excited by circumstances, or in any way formed at any particular time, they may subsist as habits, and not entirely withdraw themselves again when their immediate cause is withdrawn.

Every step in the course of national improvement is, I believe, the *effect,* and the *cause* in its turn, of an *increased* disposition in the poor to work, and in the rich to save and produce. That is, in the poor man to work more, but for *less* real *wages in proportion* to the *trouble he takes,* though for more in proportion to the number of days he lives as a workman, than before; and in the rich, to save and produce more, but for a *less rate* of *profit* than was before required by him as an inducement. " What good," it may be asked, "results to the community? It should seem by your account as if both branches were, by their own choice, worse off than before." To the rich, that the wealth of many is increased instead of being stationary ; that is, affords an annual produce, on which they may live, instead of eating up the principal sum itself: to the poor, that they may increase; that they may have the pleasure of rearing families, and that *more human beings,* capable of enjoying all that human beings (even poor) are born to, exist. To both, the *moral* felicity occasioned by labour instead of idleness, usefulness instead of prodigality, and waste, and ruin.

In this section of Mr. Malthus, commodities having fallen in exchange for labour is said to check production. In the last section, labour fell in exchange for commodities, and yet that did not encourage production. Production is very hard to be pleased.

When the rich " agreed to be parsimonious," they thereby agreed, that the poor should consume for the present more than they otherwise would have done, in order that they themselves might, at some future time, consume more than *they* otherwise would have done. There seems, therefore, no such difficulty of providing *consumption* enough, as is anticipated by Mr. Malthus. As long as the rich choose to be postponing the period of their own consumption, they are increasing so much the consumption of the labouring poor. If, indeed, they obstinately choose, under these circumstances, to produce for the present more of *those particular* articles of which they have, by the supposition, determined for the present to consume less, they will most likely be losers ; but that is *particular* and *comparative* excess of production; and why is it necessary to suppose they will do any thing so absurd ? Yet this is obviously the supposition which is secretly haunting Mr. Malthus's imagination, when he is arguing against excess of production in *general.*

Of course, we are not allowed, on any account, to take into consideration here, that the addition of capital may reasonably be expected to lead to improvements in the productiveness of labour (Note XVII). We are never, upon Mr. Malthus's plan, to consider more than one thing at a time.

" Upon this principle," he says, " it is supposed, that if the richer portion of society were to forego their accustomed conveniences and luxuries, with a view to accumulation, the only effect would be, a direction of nearly the whole capital of the country to the production of necessaries, which would lead to a great increase of cultivation and population. But, without supposing an entire change in the usual motives to accumulation, this could not possibly happen," p. 360. I have already noticed this. If this be true, it follows, that, 1. It either would not happen at all ; and it seems unnecessary to inquire whether, if it were to happen, it would make a country, which had been " rich and populous" (p. 363), " infallibly become poor, and comparatively unpeopled" (though why it should have that effect, I am unable to conceive ; and here again I must suspect, that the *present state of things*, when the reaction has been *sudden, unexpected*, artificially caused, and aggravated, is running in Mr. Malthus's head) ; 2. Or, if it did happen in any degree, it must be owing to a proportionate " change" (not, I conceive, an *entire* change) " in the usual motives to accumulation ;" that is, by a disposition to save more, and take a less *rate* of profits. And why should it not?

It is certainly absurd to suppose (particularly in a landlord, the case Mr. Malthus here puts) saving pushed permanently to an extreme ; that is, constant saving for the sake of gain, which *never* is to be enjoyed. But why does the proving that that is absurd, and cannot happen, prove at all that it may not be true, that every addition to accumulation, when it *does* happen, will be beneficial?

Mr. Malthus may say, perhaps, that he is reasoning *ad absurdum* ; that he is shewing, that because certain evils would follow, if production were to go beyond a given point at any particular time, therefore it will *not* go beyond that point. But what then ? We know already, that production is always carried to a *certain point* at any particular time, and not beyond: Has *Mr. Malthus* any receipt for carrying it beyond? Will the keeping up a certain number of " unproductive consumers" do it? That is the question.

"No nation," says Mr. Malthus (370), "can possibly grow rich by an accumulation of capital, arising from a permanent diminution of consumption." That means, by the whole nation consuming every year less than they did the last; meaning, by consumption, not destruction, but the final consigning commodities into the hands of those who are to use them for their own enjoyment. Whether the proposition be true or not, it denies that which I apprehend was never asserted. Even those, who most eagerly stand up for accumulation, hold the language of Smith, that " what is saved is as much consumed as what is spent, only consumed by a different set of people" (see Say, " Lettres"). The diminution of consumption by the individual accumulators, means merely, that the commodities are given to be consumed by people, who meanwhile work so much as to produce, after a certain *interval*, a greater quantity of consumable commodities. If, indeed, the *interval* is long (as, if at some particular time a vast quantity of machines were to be made, or land manured, &c.), there will *possibly* be an actual falling off of consumption, in the course of it, as compared to the consumption before it began; but, probably, this never actually happened; and, except in such a case, accumulation and saving does not *in the least* suppose diminution of consumption by the nation at large ; all that it supposes, as to the nation at large, is increase of labour.

If, indeed, a *sudden* extension of saving were to take place at some one moment, and then, *all at once,* some time afterwards, the capital be withdrawn again, in order that its owners might realize their profits, great distress would prevail ; for that supposition means, that at some moment the owners of the subsistence of the labourer withdrew it from him ; told him he had worked long enough, that they now meant to enjoy it themselves, increased as it had been by their long course of production, which was now to stop. This is the sort of case Mr. Malthus seems to have in view; but it is, indeed, morally impossible. Why should all people leave off just together, having previously all carried on saving to the utmost ?

Accumulation, as Mr. Malthus observes, does not require diminution of the *actual* rate of consumption, it may be made by savings out of *increased* means, and .be thus a diminution of *possible* consumption only. By *such* a "diminution of consumption," of course, a nation "*can* grow rich."

" The limits (370) to such an increase of capital from parsimony, as shall not be attended by a very rapid diminution of the motive to accumulate, are very narrow," &c. I cannot conceive, if *increased degree* of parsimony be here meant, how it can

exist, without admitting of a diminution of the
motive to accumulate; or (if you choose to express
it so) of a diminution of the rate of profits (which
is what Mr. Malthus here means), which yet shall
not operate as a diminution of the motive to accumulate.

What is wanted, according to Mr. Malthus
(372), is an increase of effectual demand. How
we are to get this, except by an increase of numbers,
or by an increase of production on the part of the
existing numbers, I cannot conceive. Revenue can
be furnished no other way; and both these Mr.
Malthus denies us.

In page 417, he says, " general wealth, like
particular portions of it, will always follow effective demand. Whenever there is a great demand
for commodities, that is, whenever the exchangeable value of the whole mass will command more
labour than usual at the same price," &c. Now the
demand here spoken of is entirely the demand *of*
labourers; a demand consisting in the offer of *la-*
bour. But the demand created by the labourers, who
are employed in producing any commodity, is, he
says, *not* enough to stimulate to the production of
it; for, taking commodities one with another,
when the labourers had consumed all their shares,
either there would be no surplus, and then what
have the master producers gained? or, if there is
a surplus, no demand has been provided for *it,* and
how then are those who have produced it, to turn it
to account? (Note XVIII). It seems hardly worth

while to start this difficulty, and to ask this question, since he afterwards admits, that the master
producers have nothing to do but to sell the surplus to one another, whereby they consume it all
among themselves. But then the prospect of being
able to do this is not, he thinks, inducement enough
to produce. It will not be mended, then, at any
rate, by making the inducement less, by transferring
part of the surplus to other people.

This argument, he uses against the demand by
the labourers, would be just as good against the
demand by unproductive consumers; when the
demand of *these* has done its best, since it has been
all furnished by the producers, we may still ask,
what are the producers the better if there is no surplus ; and if there is, how are the producers to dispose of it ? This difficulty about disposing of the
surplus arises entirely from confounding the case
of one producer, or perhaps of producers of one
town or country, considered with reference to
others, with that of the whole mass. *One* producer must get rid of his produce; for it is all of
one kind, and he does not want a thousandth part
of it himself. But *the mass* of producers do not
want in the least, *as a mass*, to get rid of their
produce. Each gets rid of his share by exchanging
it with the others. The difference between production and consumption leads us sometimes to
fancy, that those operations must be carried on by
different bodies of men ; but it is quite plain, that
this is not necessary.

In the section on Fertility of Land, Mr. Malthus
observes (376), that a large and fertile country
seldom makes full use of its natural resources,
while small and unfertile countries have sometimes
arrived at wealth far out of proportion to their physical capabilities. He does not here enough include *situation* among " physical capabilities."
For instance, his " fertile country" may be inland,
intersected with mountains, unprovided with rivers,
or not commanding their whole course to the sea ;
his unfertile country, a small tract near the sea,
and centrally situated with regard to those other
countries, whose natural products are of such kinds
as to render exchange profitable to both. Some of
the *small states* he is perhaps alluding to, are little
more than *great towns :* the division into " countries" or " states," for this purpose, is in some
measure arbitrary and nominal (Note XIX).

In countries where, from natural fertility, or the
common use of a cheaply-raised vegetable of food,
habits of industry have not been formed, capital,
Mr. Malthus (400) thinks, is likely to be less beneficial, &c., than a change in the tastes and habits
of the lower classes of people. But, I take it, such
a change generally *follows*, not *leads*, a change in
the tastes, &c., of their betters. Labour does not
go in search of capital, capital goes in search of
labour. Our ancestors, he thinks (377), were
obliged to keep idle retainers, *because* there were
no manufactures brought to market for them to lay
out their money in. The employment of capital,

then, in this case, when it came, must have changed the "habits and tastes" of the rich and poor both; and not been *induced by* a change in those habits and tastes. When he quotes Mr. Ricardo's observation, that he who is rich may easily get labourers to put him in possession of what he wishes, and asks, why, if so, were our ancestors *obliged* to keep idle retainers ?— we must answer, that in part, at least, the reason was, that idle retainers *were* " the objects most useful and desirable to them." Even now, riches are laid out as much in gratifying pride as pleasure. Now what shall be a gratification to pride, is a matter merely of *fashion.* In feudal times, too, every rich man was a sort of king; *defence*, and military strength, was a real " object" to him.

Mr. Malthus winds up (413), by saying, that " accumulation of capital, fertility of soil, and inventions to save labour, all tend to facilitate supply, *without reference to demand,* and that therefore it is not probable they should, either separately or conjointly, afford an adequate stimulus to the continued increase of wealth, which can only be kept up by a continued increase of the demand for commodities." I wish I could even guess what sort of " demand" it is that Mr. Malthus is here looking out for; just before, he has appeared to mean a demand arising from people being induced to *labour* more ; and yet that must add to *supply*, too.

Mr. Malthus sometimes talks as if there were two distinct funds, capital and revenue, supply and demand, production and consumption, which must take care to keep pace with each other, and neither outrun the other. As if, besides the whole mass of commodities produced, there was required another mass, fallen from Heaven, I suppose, to purchase them with. But the fund for purchasing one thing must always be furnished by the supply of another. " But there must be the *will* to consume, as well as the power." Is there any danger that people should not be found, ready enough to consume *something* ?

The fund for consumption, such as he requires, can only be had at the expense of production. It is only attainable by lessening production below what it would else have been. How does it then increase production ? You may wish that production increased faster than it does, that the limit to its increase were removed ; but I want to know, wherever that limit may be at any given time, how can the proposal, that people should produce *less*, remove it any further off ? The limit arising from the labour market, or from land, I can comprehend. We must, in some degree, wait for the former to keep pace with the increased supply of capital. The increased supply of capital promotes, indeed, the increased supply of labour, but not immediately, always; nor always, necessarily, to the same extent : whether we mean, by supply of labour, more people, or increased inclination to work. This part of the demand for capital is, in some degree, independent of it. And the land market cannot be extended at all, and is quite independent. But consumption in general is not a separate fund.

Mr. Malthus thinks, the only fear is of capital being supplied *too fast*: Of mankind being *too* ready to sacrifice the present to the future! *Some* people, with Adam Smith, suppose, that people are always too much *disinclined* to save for future gain. Capital will always be supplied, he says, as fast as it is wanted, without the aid of *patriotism*. If it is supplied as fast as it is wanted, why has it a *price*. So far as "patriotism" is the motive, interest is not; and the service or use of the capital is, *pro tanto*, made a *present* to the consumer. This must surely be a *benefit* to him; and it is difficult to say, *when* such a benefit is not *wanted*. If, indeed, it is conferred *suddenly*, *partially*, and *temporarily*, it may, undoubtedly, do more harm than good in the end.

However, if people *are* so furiously bent on saving, so much the less need must there be of the consumption by the *capitalists themselves*, as an inducement to their increased production. And if the fear is, lest there should not be consumption enough by *any body*, lest people should deny themselves enjoyments to an absurd extent, we may postpone that apprehension till there is the least symptom of its being a reasonable one. Mr. Malthus puts such a case. No doubt, it is *possible*. It is *possible* to conceive a state of things, in which the observation of Smith, "that what is aunually saved is annually consumed, only by a different set of persons," may be no longer true. In the present state of things, saving, by some persons, in order to produce, increases at the moment the means of consumption possessed by landlords and labourers. But *these might* save, too; turning all they got, beyond mere necessaries, into capital: and go on doing so for a long time; and they might be great fools for doing so. *If* they saved and produced, however, that is, laid out their savings as capital, without diminishing the work, if any, which they did before, they certainly would add to their wealth, that is, to their *means* of enjoyment, though they did not choose at present to avail themselves of those means. But if they took advantage of their diminished desires to work less, the public might, probably, not be so rich as they would else have been: but this is not the case Mr. Malthus is here putting; nobody, he says, means, by saving, mere hoarding, nor would it serve at all to meet the real case which it is directed against, which is a case of saving *and producing*.

There are sometimes lumped together, under the name of profits of stock (sometimes by Smith himself, Note XX), two things which are distinct from each other, though it is difficult to draw a line that shall exactly define the limits between them. M. Say calls the one, hire of the productive service of the capital, and the other, wages or reward of the labour of management. Now Mr. Malthus, where he anticipates that when profits

are lowered by competition " pushed to excess,"
people will not, merely for the sake of increasing
their command of luxuries, " submit to the drudgery
of a counting house," considers only the latter of
these. The person, who thus retires from the
counting house, who thus withdraws his *labour*, is
not, on that account, likely to withdraw the assistance of his *capital* from the concern. Now the
more capital there is, the easier can it be borrowed;
and the easier it can be borrowed, the larger share
of a given profit will remain for the salary of the
labour of management, to tempt some other person to come in the place of him who has thus
retired.

Mr. Malthus's object is to discover the means by
which production may be increased, permanently,
to the greatest possible extent. In order to effect
this, he thinks, the point is to keep up an increase
of demand. But demand cannot here mean, as it
does when we speak of a demand for this or that
particular article, a quantity of other goods in the
hands of other people ; because we are now speaking of all the goods that are produced, and there
cannot, therefore, be another universe of goods
forming a demand from without. 1. So far, then,
as demand means an exchange of goods, it is
insured by increased general production ; it is, if it
means any thing, the same with production, supposing the means of *communication* to remain the
same, or, as is probable under such circumstances,
to be increased: the increased demand for one ar-

ticle would be the increased supply of another, and the demand for the *whole* is, in this sense of demand, unmeaning. Then there is, besides goods, nothing in which demand can consist, except land, and labour of all kinds. 2. The demand on the part of land cannot be increased; the land has a certain extent, and no more. " The demand of the landlords for goods, may," it is said, "be increased; if they receive more rent, they are demanders of produce to a greater amount; or, if they keep servants, they are still demanders through the medium of those servants." They are not increased demanders in any sense, which can constitute an increased inducement to produce: to say that they have a greater demand, is only to say that they take more from the producer, and give him no more in return than he had before of them. So, the receivers of taxes (I mean those who spend them, not the *collectors*) are supposed to constitute a demand; but in whatever form, and by whatever medium, this operation of paying and receiving taxes may be carried on, the whole effect and substance of it is, that a portion of the whole mass of things, produced by the whole mass of producers, gets into the hands of people who do nothing, and give nothing in return. You may give a stockholder, or an useless pensioner, money, and he may come back to you, and buy your goods with that money; but the upshot of it is, that you are *minus* so much of your goods, without any return. This is not an increased *demand;* or, call it what you please, it is no increased inducement, from *gain*, to produce. It may be an increased inducement from *necessity*, if that is called an inducement; but no two things can be more distinct than these two motives, confounded and intertwined together by Mr. Malthus. We are continually puzzled, in his speculations, between the object of increasing production and that of checking it.

When a man is in want of a *demand*, does Mr. Malthus recommend him to pay some other person to take off his goods? Probably not. He would say, he should have paid money to unproductive consumers *before* that, and not have produced so much. But does the man himself think so? If his difficulty has not arisen (and we are all along supposing that it has not arisen) from having ill chosen the *particular* article he has produced, or from *sudden, unexpected* changes; if his difficulty would have been equal whatever other article he had chosen, does *he* now wish that he had not produced it at all? He may very probably wish, that some *other person* in the same line had not produced so much. But what does that other person say to it? He has as good a right to be heard Taking the two together, and setting aside (as of course we must) the sacrificing one to the other, is it their *joint* wish that they had not produced *at all* a part of what they have produced? They wished to gain: they find, perhaps, that they have not gained so much as they expected: but do they therefore wish that they had acted so as not

to have gained *at all*? The same argument would
as well have applied to *labour*. It might be said,
" Wages are low : labour then is supplied more
than it is demanded. Can adding to the whole
quantity by working more, or harder, mend the
labourer's situation? It must aggravate it." But
is this *true?* Would the labourers be better off if
they were to agree to work less? If I labour,
where I did not labour before, I produce *something*. Where does it go? Surely, the more is
produced, the more *chance* there is, at least, that
some of it may find its way to the poor labourers
who want it. If it be said, " the labourer has no
alternative *now*, but it would have been better if
labour had not been *supplied* so largely ; that is, if
numbers had not increased so much ; and in the
same way it would be better, in the other case, if
capital had not increased so much"—I answer,
they are quite unlike. Capital brings itself into the
world, as it were. Its increased supply is not like
the increased supply of *labourers :* it is more like
the case of an increased supply of *work*, by people
working harder, without any alteration of numbers. If, by doing so, they *should* find themselves
worse off, *i. e.* that what they got was not enough
to make the additional work worth while, they
could leave off continuing the addition at the same
rate. So could the capitalists. The evil feared by
Mr. Malthus seems to be very well able to cure
itself. " This cure," he may say, " is just what I
am afraid of. The excessive production will occa-

sion, in the end, a permanent reaction." Why *permanent ?* Why will it leave us *worse* than it found us ?

3. Then, as to the demand from *labour;* that is, either the giving labour in exchange for goods, or, if you choose to consider it in another form, but which comes to the same thing, the giving, in exchange for present complete products, a future and accruing addition of value (or usefulness, or desirableness, or whatever you choose to call it), conferred on certain particles of matter entrusted to the labourer. This is the real demand that it is material to the producers to get increased, so far as *any* increased demand is wanted, extrinsic to that which articles furnish for each other when increased. When Mr. Malthus talks of *distribution* (Note XXI), and of the *will* of the owners of articles to exchange them, as important, this is the real point, as it seems to me. Distribute things as you please, people will exchange them till they have got each what he most wishes, and therefore no distribution can alter matters much as to the demand, or supposed demand, on the part of *goods.* But it is very material, with reference to *labour,* whether you distribute them so as to induce a greater supply of labour or a less : whether you distribute them where they will be conditions for labour, or where they will be opportunities for idleness. The inducement to produce more from a prospect of increased gain is diminished, if the producer is obliged to give more, for a quantity of

labour which will not produce more. The increased supply of labour is an important part, therefore, of the increased demand for production; nay, is the only thing which can be considered as extrinsic demand : and that increased supply of labour is promoted by the increased *numbers* of mankind (though Mr. Malthus sets this aside), and by the increased exertions of mankind ; and is *diminished* by any such " distribution" as produces idleness ; such as the maintaining menial servants and other unproductive consumers (Note XXII). If the capitalists are also labourers, their interests in the one capacity may indeed be different from their interests in the other : but their interests as capitalists are the greatest, because they are owners of *all* the capital, but not performers of all the labour. And it certainly never can answer to them to pay people in order to turn them into unproductive consumers, who might otherwise have been clerks, and competed with themselves in the labour of management and superintendence, in order that their own remuneration in that capacity may be higher. However, clerks come under the class of persons whom Mr. Malthus calls unproductive consumers.

Besides this, where the whole object is supposed to be to get consumers who are unproductive, we must consider, that that desirable end is not always attained merely by transferring to them the substance of those who are productive. They *may* obstinately determine to work, or to lay out their money as capital, after all, in spite of you.

You can contract for a man's labour, but you cannot always (or rather do not), in many of the cases put by Mr. Malthus, contract for his idleness. Even your menial servant may privily commit acts of *lèse-consumption*, may lend his savings, or work with his hands at odd times.

Indeed, as the immediate object of the producer is sale, not consumption, it should seem (taking goods all together, that is, without considering the demand for one at the expense of that for another), that it cannot at the time signify to the seller what the buyer means to do with the article when he has got it; whether, if rich, to have it worked up as materials; or, if poor, to work at something else while he is consuming it.

Mr. Malthus may regard the demand on the part of labourers, and the consumption by labourers, as immaterial towards the increase of production, because they add to the supply as fast as they do to the demand. But they do not add to the supply at the *same time* as they do to the demand: they consume first, and then produce. What they have consumed is taken out of the market (if that is so material) *before* what they have produced comes in. In the next place, the very meaning of an increased demand by them is, a disposition to take less themselves, and leave a larger share for their employers; and if it be said that this, by diminishing consumption, increases glut, I can only answer, that glut then is synonymous with high profits; is the very inducement sought, instead of being the check to production. Mr. Malthus, after feeling the difficulty of having to talk of a glut of *all* commodities, defines a glut to be when the commodities will command less *labour*. The cure for, and preventive of, this must be, that increased supply of labour which he elsewhere treats as so unimportant, when he considers it by itself. The not being able to command so much labour as before, too, is only important where that labour would produce no more than before. If labour has been rendered more productive, production will not be checked, though the existing mass of commodities should command less labour than before. But this consideration, too, of the increased productiveness of labour, he neglects, because he takes it *alone*.

The zeal for " encouraging consumption," as supposed necessary for trade in general, springs from the real usefulness of it with regard to the venders of a particular article. The more Mr. Warren can inspire a *taste* for the *consumption* of his blacking, the more he will sell; but by that taste is meant, practically, a disposition on the part of those, who can afford it, to buy his blacking with the money that *would otherwise* have bought other people's, or some other article. But the interests of the producers of *all articles* cannot be any thing like this (Note XXIII). So, it is a good thing for him, that a customer should break his blacking bottle, or spill his blacking, or use it fast (that the *produit* should be " consommé ou detruit"): he will come again to his shop the sooner. But that is only at the expense of some other tradesman. The customer will come with the money that would else have gone to buy something else. Again, I say, the interests of trade *in general* are nothing like this; bear no analogy to it. It is, indeed, the interest of tradesmen in general, that the *means and power* of their customers to buy, should be increased by any means that does not *injure* the tradesmen themselves (not therefore including taxes, anticipation of rent, &c.), and that their customers should not *hoard* their means. And, so far as their customers are *labourers*, it is also an object that they should have the greatest possible taste for the necessaries and comforts of life, as compared to their taste for idleness; because the greater taste for those a labourer has, the more will he increase his *means and power* of buying. *His* means are his labour, which is his own creation, and depends on his own will. A rich man's means are quite different; and are not increased by his having a taste for purchases in *general*, though his means of buying a particular article, as *snuff boxes*, may be said to be increased by his having a taste for snuff boxes, inasmuch as he may save for that purpose what would have gone in other things.

" What we want, are people who buy our goods," it is said, " and do not come in our way by competing with us in the production of them." But they have nothing in the world to give you for

your goods, but what you gave them first. No
property can originate in their hands; it must have
come from your's. Landlords, placemen, stock-
holders, servants, be they what they may, their
whole means of buying your goods was once your
means, and you gave it up to them. A productive
labourer comes with the work of his hands to buy
your goods; he originates that with which he buys,
and the more there are of such the better for you;
the better profits do you make, as I have already
observed. But to talk of its being an increased
gain to you, that people should take part of your
capital, and lay it out in buying your goods, instead
of leaving it in your hands, to do what you pleased
with, would prove, that it would answer to you, if
you heard of a man about to set up in trade, to go
and buy him off, by making him a present of half
your own profits. Would not this be thought
rather insane? We are to consider it, not as the
affair of one person, nor even of the mass of one
trade, but of the whole body of producers. Every
producer is also a consumer, and his *object* is to be
a consumer, the other being only the means.
While they kept this money, then, for their own
use, each might buy with it the goods of the others;
each sold, therefore, to the rest, goods which
amounted in the whole to the full value of this
money. Now, they sell the same goods; but to
strangers. Each loses so much enjoyment, &c., as
that money would purchase, and does not sell more
goods than he might have sold before. And if it

be said, had it remained in the producer's hands, it *would not* have been all laid out in one another's goods, nor in enjoyments, but partly in land and labour ; I answer, first, that you must show, that *none* of it would have been laid out in buying one another's goods, before you can make it appear that it answered better to give away the *whole* of it ; and, secondly, that if they lay it out in hiring land and labour, it is clear they like that way still better than buying one another's goods. The object of selling your goods is to make a certain amount of money; it never can answer to part with that amount of money for nothing, to another person, that he may bring it back to you, and buy your goods with it : you might as well have just burnt your goods at once, and you would have been in the same situation.

The immediate reason why, in Mr. Malthus's opinion (Note XXIV), unproductive consumers are wanted, the desideratum which they are to supply, is stated to be, that "the master producers, from the laudable desire they feel of bettering their condition, &c., do not consume sufficiently to give an adequate stimulus to the increase of wealth." That is, the motive of bettering their condition, urges them on to increase wealth so fast, that they quite forget to provide themselves with another motive. One would think it was not wanted. Surely, if they *will* go on in this course of prodigal parsimony, if they *will* say, we *must* gain, we must make *some* profits, increase our principal, if but a little ; you might let them have their way. *We* are the better for it; and they *like* it. They do *not consume,* only *because* they *produce* instead; which is just what we want them to do. What is the meaning, then, of saying, that they do not consume enough to induce them to produce?

" Consumption is wanted, and you cannot expect it from the capitalists, because they are saving." But by saving, as Mr. Malthus himself observes, nobody means hoarding. You must mean, then, laying out money, to the *extent of their means,* like other people. *How,* if not in buying goods, or enabling others to buy? It is clear, therefore, that the fault must be, not that they do not spend to the extent of their means, but that *their means will not be so great,* unless there are unproductive consumers. Mr. Malthus states it thus : —

" With regard to the capitalists who are so engaged, they have certainly the power of consuming their profits, or the revenue which they make by the employment of their capitals ; and if they were to consume it, with the exception of what could be beneficially added to their capitals, so as to provide, in the best way, both for an increased production, and increased consumption, *there might be little occasion for unproductive consumers.* But such consumption is not consistent with the actual habits of the generality of capitalists. The great object of their lives is to save a fortune ; both because it is their duty to make a provision for their families, and because they cannot spend an income with so much comfort to themselves, while they are obliged, perhaps, to attend a counting-house for seven or eight hours a day."

Production, in the long run, we must remember, is the object he has in view; and if he fears an excess of it at one time, it is only as tending permanently to cripple the future progress of it. Now that which is to interfere with the due progress of production, he seems to think, is, that when a man has got all he can want, he will not go on producing more, and submitting to the drudgery of a counting-house, &c:, unless the rate of profit he can make is great. In order, then, that he should have this inducement, it is desirable that part of his property should be transferred to the hands of unproductive consumers ; because, as he will then not be so well off, he will have greater *stimulus* to exertion, and because, as he will then have less capital, and produce less, there will be less demand for labour, and a higher rate of profits, and he will be *induced* to produce more. Now it is evidently in vain to preach this *to the producers themselves,* because, if you want them to exert themselves more, and produce more, it is as easy to tell them directly to do so, as to tell them to put part of their capital into the hands of unproductive consumers, in order that they themselves may be thereby pinched and screwed up to produce more ; to tell them " the desire of getting more luxuries, &c., for yourselves, is not, as you must feel, a sufficient motive to induce you to exert yourselves so much

as we wish you to do; therefore you had better
substitute for it the desire of producing luxuries for
other people." (The immediate effect of such an
operation too, is, at every moment when it takes
place, to diminish capital and production, though
the professed object is to increase it. The inducement proposed, so far as it is to operate by increasing profits, operates simply by lessening production. And I do not collect how this is to be
counteracted again, much less more than counteracted, which it ought to be, in order to answer its
purpose.) It seems clear, then, after all the talk
about " demand" and consumption," that the real
efficacy of this process is by *constraint*, not *inducement*, and that (though Mr. Malthus, in some
places, says it had better be voluntary) it must be
compulsory on the producers, in order to have its
full effect; that it should be recommended not to
them, but to the *government*; and accordingly we
find, that Mr. Malthus is clearly of opinion, that
the present amount of *taxation* is, in this point of
view, by no means to be lamented over. Now the
fact on which this consideration is founded, I am
by no means disposed to deny. I know, that taxation, especially if (Note XXV) gradually, and, as it
were, insensibly increased, stimulates, by necessity,
persons in business, persons otherwise in comparatively easy circumstances, to increase their exertions, and even their savings, beyond what they
would otherwise have done; and counteracts in this
way, in some degree, the *bad* effects which it has on

production, by extinguishing a vast deal of productive labour, owing to the manner in which the sum raised is applied ; *viz.* to unproductive consumers. But production is surely checked much *more* than it is promoted, by this process. Nor is it quite fair to keep a number of persons idle, in this manner, merely in order to *pinch* those who are likely, from their characters, if you can force them to work, to work to some purpose. That is, to *diminish* that inequality of advantages, which nature makes the reward of unequal industry and talents. This consideration is very well to console us under unavoidable taxation, by showing that the wealth of the country is not *so much* diminished as we should at first have supposed ; but when it professes to warn us against reducing our taxes, gradually at least (Note XXVI), where we can, when it teaches us that idle gentlemen, who live on taxes, are indispensible aids in the raising the annual produce of the country, I, for one, beg to have it a great deal more clearly and fully stated, and a great deal more closely argued, than I can find it stated or argued in the work of Mr. Malthus. Especially when we recollect, that the increase of production always adds to the funds of one great mass of unproductive consumers, the landlords, of itself: it is, therefore, the less necessary to look about for more.

It is an observation which we sometimes hear made, when land is neglected, that " the rent wants raising." But there, the person who is to be *pinched* and *screwed up* to exertion is, by the supposition, some peculiarly inactive person, in whom the desire of bettering himself is not sufficiently strong, and in whom habits of industry have not yet been generated; whereas, in the other case, he is a person peculiarly active and intelligent. For, if we do not suppose him so, and if we suppose him merely like other men, *his exertions* will be no more *quickened,* than those of the unproductive consumer, to whom we are to transfer his property, will be *checked ;* and, if made, will be no more productive, than those of the now unproductive consumer might have been, if he had not been rendered idle by this scheme.

If it be said, " I am not recommending unproductive consumers *de novo,* or the increase of them, I am only stating that the actual existence of them does good :" I answer, 1. An unproductive consumer requires continual supplies, and therefore to recommend that he be continued, is the same thing as recommending that fresh supplies be afforded him out of capital; I say out of capital, because, since the reason for requiring the aid of unproductive consumers is stated to be, that the capitalist, who has the power to consume, will not exert that power, it is clear, that that power of consumption, which is to be transferred to the unproductive consumer, must be out of *that portion* of the power of the capitalist, which the latter would *not* have *spent* in consumption, that is, which he *would* have employed as capital.

2. When you say, that the existence of any thing
is beneficial, you must state what is the *alternative*
with which you compare it. Is it meant, that the
existing unproductive consumers are of more use
than if those individual persons were not in existence, and the society were so much the less? Or,
of more use than if, though they continued in existence, and continued to receive what they now
do, they were to lay out a part of that as capital?
Or, of more use than if those individuals, ceasing
to receive what they now receive, were to become
productive labourers (the unproductive labour, if
any, which they now perform, ceasing, we will suppose, to be any longer desirable). Are we to consider the means of these unproductive consumers as
standing in the place of the means of capitalists
(Malth., p. 465) or of landlords (p. 484)? In one
place, Mr. Malthus includes among his unproductive consumers, overseers of labourers, clerks,
and retail dealers, and enlarges on the necessity of
these classes bearing a due proportion to that of the
manual labourers. But nobody, I presume, was
going to dispute this. It is necessary in order to
production.

Mr. Malthus (p. 481) seems to disclaim any
positive recommendation of the increase of taxation, or of national debt, and merely to be pleased
with them as they are. It is clear, however
(p. 483), that, according to him, if any body had
recommended the creation of the present amount of
national debt, with a view to the promotion of

wealth, it must have been good advice. And even as to the present state of things, he says, " the proportion of capital to revenue is too great" (p. 505) ; therefore, the proportion of revenue to capital is too small, and a conversion desirable (Note XXVII).

All that is intelligible, all that there is of truth, in Mr. Malthus's recommendation of unproductive consumers, seems to me to be the principle (which, however, he never plainly states) of thus exciting the producers, *by necessity*, to *produce more.* It is not easy to disentangle this from the various observations about providing a *demand*, keeping up *consumption*, &c., which, I own, appear to me to be quite unmeaning (Note XXVIII).

But whenever the general reasonings fail, the constant question is, " How, then, do you account for the present state of things? Is the check to trade only partial, and relative ? Is the check in some trades made up for by greater prosperity than usual in others? Must you not, then, admit that it is production *in general* that has become excessive, and overbalanced or outrun consumption? (Note XXIX). And were we not better off during the war, when we paid more taxes, and lent more loans ?

No. The situation in which we now are, is that of *violent*, *sudden*, and *unexpected* changes. It does not at all follow, that where violent and sudden changes in the channels of trade, with sudden cessations of *all* demand (much more of any thing like *effectual* demand), for many sorts of articles, have happened ; it does *not* follow, I say, from the general principle, that others will be proportionably flourishing. Production is not an affair of a moment. There is a stock on hand ; and if that is of goods which are now suddenly become as useless as skaits would be at Calcutta, how can abundance of other things, at once, compensate this ? Of the existing mass of things, a part is, as it were, *destroyed* and *lost* (for it is become utterly useless), without possible benefit to any body. It can only be in the next stage, by transferring production from these branches to others, that the evil could be made up for. But here we must recollect, that when the relative price, which a particular sort of article bears, is suddenly reduced, the check comes upon transactions entered into on the expectation that it would continue, upon operations whose beginning and end are separated, perhaps, by years ; it comes on complicated operations of credit, where men are acting as if they *possessed* what is, in fact, perhaps, to be the remote return of some speculation of another person ; it comes upon vast masses of fixed capital (Note XXX), wedged in one employment, unfit for any other, and whose value, therefore, is turned to a mere cypher, when the demand for their produce fails. Nor can the owner sell his machinery to those (if any), who are carrying on elsewhere the trade which he has lost. It will not answer the carriage of the machine, for the same reason that it ceased to answer to carry the product (or indeed à fortiori); and if his country had a monopoly of the skill and materials for making such machines, he would not have lost the trade; the check would not have happened. Then a portion of capital originally laid out on them, and therefore of wealth, has been annihilated, just the same as if it had been *burnt;* it has been sunk, and the returns which were looked to, now fall. And even the *labour* employed, very likely, partook of the nature of fixed capital in this respect. The habits of the labourers, where division of labour has been carried very far, are applicable only to the particular line they have been used to; they are a sort of machines. Then, there is a long period of idleness, that is, of labour lost; of wealth cut off at its root. It is quite useless to repeat, like a parrot, that things have a tendency to find their level. We must look about us, and see that they *cannot* for a long time find a level; that when they do, it will be a far lower level than they set out from. M. Say may lay the blame of all this on our *customs,* if he likes, whose produce he ingeniously supposes (in his "Lettres"), is employed in paying members of parliament for their votes; *the fault is in war.* The "china-shop," in which we now-a-days " play at cudgels" (according to Hume's metaphor), is not exactly *that* which he looked to. Our public credit (which was the danger he alluded to) stands well enough; and is the only thing that does. But private credit, paper-currency, fixed capitals, in the shape of machinery or improvements sunk in land,—these are frail *play-things*, indeed, for that "*game*,"

> —— which, were their subjects wise,
> Kings would not play at.

The way in which circulating capital can be transferred from one trade to another, without, perhaps, any one manufacturer moving, is pointed out by Mr. Ricardo, p. 80, and it is often very important to bear it in mind. The capital in question, as he observes, is in a great measure borrowed capital, the owner of which is not the manufacturer, but what we call a monied man. This facilitates that transfer of circulating capital, which, when one trade is become bad, brings prices as speedily as possible to the desired level. But the existence of this system (always most prevalent when trade is most cultivated) only *aggravates* the *evil* in any line where the capital is in a great degree *fixed,* or where it is sunk on land. Suppose a change has happened in such a line, the trader is *obliged* to continue to employ, much more nearly (than if there had been less fixed capital) the same amount of circulating capital as he did before, in order not to cease to derive *any* profit from the part that is fixed. The more uncertain is the state of things, and the more there is of lottery in the aspect of affairs, the more likely will he be to do so, in the *hope* that things may come round. Then supposing the fall of profits he thus submits to is from twelve to eight; I say if his capital were all his own, he

would have to make up his expenses to this as well
as he could, it would be a fall of one-third in his
revenue. But if he borrowed it, it is impossible
that the rate of general interest can fall in the same
proportion as the profits of his trade ; if he paid,
for instance, six before, he will pay much more
than four now. If he retained six before, he will
retain much less than four now, for clear profits to
himself. His revenue then will, under this supposition, fall much *more* than one-third. The depreciation in his line may occasion some little fall of
interest, certainly, but others will profit by it rather
than he, because it will be a general fall.

Nothing can be more false than the *metaphorical*
argument of M. Say (vol. i, p. 59, fourth edit.) in
favour of machines ; *viz.* that they bear a revulsion
better, because "elles ne meurent pas de faim."
A revulsion, where there are machines, must diminish the funds for employing labour *as* much as
where there are not. And more. For the interest of
the labourer is, that when there is a check, capital
should *rat* as soon as possible, that he may have
permanent employment of another sort, at good
wages, offered him ; instead of the trade dying by
inches, and the capital in it wasting away to nothing,
which latter is most likely to happen, where there
are machines. And (by the way) the labourers do
not, considered as consumers, derive any benefit
from machines, while flourishing (Say, p. 60), unless the article, which the machines cheapen, is one
that can be brought, by cheapening, within their

use. Threshing-machines, wind-mills, may be a
great thing for them in this view; but the invention of a veneering machine, or a block machine,
or a lace frame, does not mend *their* condition
much.

The principle so often and so well employed by
Smith, that capital is transferable, and that
therefore things will come to a level, mightily assists people who are armed with it, in dismissing
from their minds the very long temporary *interval*
during which the process is going on, and which is
sometimes a much more important consideration to
the happiness of mankind, than the *level* to be
attained at last. Capital is *not* transferable on a
sudden emergency, without much loss by the way.
Local situation, connections, habits of life, talents,
knowledge of the business, knowledge of the
markets which formerly belonged to it, all form
(besides the cause above mentioned) so many rubs
and hitches in the way of the transfer. Like fric-
tion in mechanics, they continually falsify the conclusions of too general theory. The profits of no
two men are exactly equal, and if the average profits of any trade are lowered, that, probably, *quite
cuts up* the profits of *some* individuals. The distress that is occasioned at such times cannot be
estimated in *money*. Even if it *were* true, that
equal gains were making in some other quarter to
compensate for it, the satisfaction of him, who
gains where he did not expect it, is never to be put

into the balance against the suffering of him who is unexpectedly ruined.

Mr. Malthus argues, that there may be such a thing as a *glut* of *all* commodities from excessive production, and that it is seen when they command less *labour*, though the rate at which they exchange with *one another* may be the same as before. But is *this* the sort of glut that prevails *now* ? Labour is then exorbitantly dear! The labourer commands an unusually great quantity of commodities!

It seems, the circumstances of the times do *not* square, after all, with the principles of those who appeal to them as proofs, nay, who have framed principles on purpose to suit them.

It is not true, in the next place, that such mighty prosperity existed during the war (Note XXXI), still less during the time that capital was most largely converted into revenue. If this had been the way to prosperity (si Pergama dextrâ defendi possent), the Waterloo loan ought to have been the making of us. And if we mourn over the abolition of taxation, we must recollect that distress was the *cause* of that abolition, not the effect of it. During a period when large sums are lent to the state, the rate of interest, and the profits of stock, too, so far as they depend on the same causes as the rate of interest, is something *factitious*; it is a sign of the gain of individuals, but it is neither a sign of the increase of capital (just the reverse), nor of the increase of benefits conferred by capital on

the public. The gains made by that portion of
capital, which is lent to spendthrifts, are never
direct additions to the wealth of the community,
as gains made by capital, advanced to labourers in
the process of production, are : they merely drain
by degrees the property of the borrowers into the
pockets of the lenders.

Funded debts are a mode by which a *portion* of
the existing disposition to lay out money, with a
view to gain, may be enabled to vent itself so as
to do no good to production. I admit, that they
also tempt, in some degree, the conversion of
revenue into channels of saving *more* than would
otherwise have been the case, so that the *whole* of
them does not consist of what would otherwise
have been productive capital.

Nor was it the failure of general demand on the
part of the *receivers of taxes*, which was particularly felt soon after peace came, but that on the
part of farmers (owing to their peculiar depression),
and of landlords through them.

It may be said, the destruction of capital diminishes the amount of capital, and consequently
ought to raise the rate of profits ; and therefore, if
after the destruction of capital the rate of profits
is even lower than before, it proves, that capital,
though less in *actual amount*, is still more *redundant*, is greater *in proportion* to the demand for it,
than before. To this I answer, 1. That would
prove, that a still further destruction or conversion
of it into revenue would be desirable. But even

Mr. Malthus does not venture to propose that. 2. The demand for capital, the thing *in proportion to* which capital is at different times more or less redundant, is *labour*, as I conceive, and have already stated. Now that capital is not redundant is, then, I should say, clearly proved by the extreme lowness of wages. It is inconceivable in what sense we can be said to be *producing too much*, when we have been sitting idle for years. 3. Small profits per annum are made now on the whole mass of capital, because it *stands still*, because, for part of the time, part of it is *not* employed *at all*, and therefore is not *in fact* part of capital. All our general reasonings on this subject suppose, that the flow of capital is free : but it is not free. Uncertainty and panic stop its movements, want of credit stops it; a scale of comparative taxation, which suited well enough the former state of things (because the former state of things had been suited *to it*), galls now. New channels are not found in a moment, least of all while things are still fluctuating, and artificial measures, actual or expected, interrupt the settling of the general mass. 4. This distinction between capital and profits is in a great degree merely in terms. Profits depend on the quantity I receive back in return for my whole capital expended. If, at the end of a certain period, that quantity is less than what I expended at first, or greater in but a small degree, am I to say that my capital is less but my profits fair profits, or to say that I have the same capital, or nearly so,

but have made no profits? And *what period* am I
to take for this purpose? It is impossible for the
nation to *take stock* (if I may so express it) till
these fluctuations are over. Many transactions
extend (especially when we consider the capital of
the nation as a mass) over many years. We must
wait to see how they are wound up, before we can
pretend to say what our capital is.

Those, who maintain that production finds a
market for itself, do yet admit, that however true
that may be as a general proposition, it is very
possible so imprudently to select the *particular
article* to be produced, as, with reference to the
existing relative demands for different articles, to
occasion a great loss to the producer, which shall
not be compensated by any gain to any body. Now
exactly the same effect must of course follow,
though without any imputation of imprudence on
the producer, when the relative demands for different articles have been changed by a sudden alteration in the channels of intercourse between
nations, or by other circumstances, such as
arise from the beginning or ending of a war:
and more widely-spreading harm is done in this
case than where the undertaking was imprudent at
the time it was commenced; for then, in all pro-
bability, *other* people took care not to entangle
their interests with it: not so where it becomes
imprudent, as it were, *ex post facto*. Skill and
knowledge in the selection of the particular line
of trade to be pursued, and in the mode of pursuing

it, are for the most part habit and routine, and cannot be formed at once. Experience is wanted: but .that is to be obtained by time, and by losses (Note XXXII).

Not only do sudden changes produce all the same effects as imprudent speculation, but they encourage *actual* imprudence in speculation. We are apt to lump together all persons concerned in trade, and say they know their interest. The prudent ones of course do; but there is another set to be also considered, a set who bear the largest proportion to the others just when they are likely to do the most harm, namely, when there is a general uncertainty in trade, and when trade is more like a lottery than usual; which is the case when there are sudden changes taking place. Yet the others must suffer; the whole of a branch of trade may suffer, for a time, from a few foolish speculations. There is little doubt but that the quantity of new undertakings, which were referred to, during the war, as proofs of wealth, were in some instances proofs of the depressed state of the usual openings for capital. *New* openings were tried, because their unprofitableness was not so obvious.

When Mr. Malthus sighs for unproductive consumers, one cannot help recollecting the increase of *poor rates;* they have furnished, one would think, quite a sufficient drawback on the undue and excessive " conversion of revenue into capital" which he complains of. He seems, too, to forget, what he has elsewhere (Tracts on the Corn Laws) so much insisted on, the *real increase* of the same *nominal* amount of public debt.

If we add to all this, the degree in which all great fluctuations are aggravated by the existence of the system of *credit*, and also, that the public paper credit, or paper money of the nation, has been, up to the moment in which we now are, so dealt with as to increase in an excessive degree even these aggravations, we need hardly resort to any new general doctrines about demand or production, &c., to enable us to account for our present situation.

The credit I mean is not a forbearance of a debt, where the debt so forborne cannot be transferred or negociated by the creditor: for this must be in proportion to actual capital, and is in fact a mere advance.

While a system of credit is extending, and private credit becoming more negotiable by the help of a bank, there is a constant anticipation, as it were, of future profits: what would have been the profits of next year are treated as actually received, and reckoned into the profits of this. When a check to credit happens, and when the power of getting one's private credit transformed into current cash is also diminished (two events not necessarily connected, but which have occasionally come together in our times), the reverse of course happens. Present or immediate gains become as it were thrown off into future: of course then the annual or periodical rate of profits is much less in the latter state than in the former.

All currency or money, considered as money,
independent of the *material*, may be said to be
credit. If two persons exchanged commodities,
land, or labour, directly with one another, that is,
if when A transfers a portion of either of these to B,
B at the same moment transferred something to A,
no such thing as money would ever exist, and no
such thing as credit would ever exist. But it
answers better to A not to take B's goods, &c.,
which, owing to the division of labour, may not
happen to be the sort he wants, but to consider B
as indebted to him, and transfer that debt to other
people, in return for their goods, &c., which he
does want. Money or currency, then, when considered merely as money or currency, may be considered for this purpose as an authentic statement,
which the world gives credit to, that such a trans-
action has happened, that such a debt exists, which
is certain of being paid, or at least that its chance
is worth so much, which they consent to estimate
as high as the creditor does. In one state of society, the world will not consider such a statement
authentic unless backed by the intrinsic value of
the substance to which it is annexed; in another,
they require no such support to its authenticity,
but look to certain *names* affixed to it; and according as these names are more or less known,
the debt can be transferred from hand to hand
through a wider sphere: one piece of paper circu-
lates only among certain merchants of eminence in
the city; another through the whole commercial

world; another through all hands, merchants or not, in a certain town, county, or neighbourhood, another through all hands throughout England. The issuing of notes by a bank, where they originate in discounts, is, as it were, the giving to a bill, by their guarantee, a general currency among those who else would not have taken it.

The more this system prevails, that is, the more disposed the world is to consider such debts as sufficiently secure to induce them to accept them in transfer, the more transactions of production can be carried on in a given time, the more can be produced in a given time, the more rapidly can capitals be turned, and therefore the larger profits can be obtained in a given time upon a given original amount of capital; because the less are the transactions of A impeded by the having to find somebody who wants what he has to give, and who has something to give which he wants. If the debt can be easily transferred, A may transfer his goods, &c., to B, and reap at once the full advantage of the transfer, even though B has not at the time any one thing to give that A wants, and even though he has not at the time any thing whatever to give. The expression of M. Say, that paper does not increase capitals, but only quickens their circulation (vol. ii, p. 142, fourth edit.), and that of Smith, that the effect of it is to prevent capital from lying idle, come to the same thing as what I have been saying: but as to the latter proposition of Smith, it is stock on hand, labour, &c.. that it prevents from lying idle, and not merely gold and silver money. Paper, in Smith's time, was only *encroaching on* gold and silver, and he has confined his speculations on it to the case of there being *some* gold, &c., in circulation *with it,* and to the effects it produces in saving such *gold,* &c. It is more natural and easy to us, now, than it was then to consider currency merely as currency, that is, quite independent of the intrinsically valuable medium to which it may sometimes be attached.

Where expected gains in trade have not been realised, or, what comes to the same thing, where B, in the case put, becomes unable to pay, the possibility of carrying on this system of credit is checked : people, who have been disappointed, will not trust again. But the important point is, that they will in such case almost always carry the reluctance to trust to a *greater* extent than what is commensurate with the actual disappointment. A diminution of wealth, a failure of gains, at the time comparatively small, is by this means followed, if not by a *destruction* of capital, by a destruction of part of what would have been its *circulation,* its *use,* the *turning of* it, and the *profits* made by it in a given time, to an extent comparatively great.

Credit includes not merely expectation of payment, but expectation of punctuality. Any delay, any stagnation, go very far to break it up, and thus create still more delay and stagnation. Now where a change suddenly takes place in the rate at which certain articles exchange with one another throughout the world, and where, consequently, there is a call for a different distribution of capital and labour, some delay will take place, even at the best, before people find out what are the properest new channels. This delay is a dead loss, not compensated by a gain in any other quarter; but, on the contrary, very probably the parent of further loss; since, owing to the existence of credit, a failure in the prospects of one man draws with it a failure of the prospects of another, who might have been in some line which was not at all *originally* affected by the cause which has ruined the former (Note XXXIII). The more credit was previously extended, and the longer credits were given, the more deeply will an adverse change be felt, and the longer will its effects continue to be felt after the change itself has taken place. If, therefore, strict theory would, by considering things as if they directly exchanged with one another, lead us to infer that a check which produced loss in one quarter, would make up for it by producing gain in another, the fact will be continually at variance with those conclusions, owing to the agency of *currency* and *credit*.

Where commerce is at all extensive, facilities of establishing the *credit* system are great, and will be taken advantage of. Such a state, then, the more it prevails, and in the greater degree, is the more liable to suffer from any checks or changes.

There is some consolation in thinking, that such a state preserves the country from a fluctuation of another kind, which is the evil of less advanced ages — famines.

It often happens, that where my debtor's engagement to me is transferred to another person, and by him to another, and so on, each relying on the original credit of my debtor, or else on mine, and not at all on that of the person from whom each immediately received the assigned engagement in question, it happens, I say, that the actual holders of this engagement rely on the disposition of other people to take it from them, and not on any intention or prospect they have of having recourse, in their own persons, to my debtor or to me, at the proper time, for fulfilment of the engagement. They may be so situated, that this would be quite out of their power. But they consider it as actual property, for all that; because, other people (they know), some of whom *can* have recourse to the proper quarter for payment, will treat it as actual property, and will accept it from them as such. If, under these circumstances, I discover that my debtor can pay me only half what he has engaged, and am under the necessity of announcing to the world, that my credit is no longer good to the full extent, the holder of the engagement, if situated as is above supposed, finds it no longer equal to actual property, of course; but he finds it not diminished only to half its value, but

much beyond that; perhaps reduced to no value at
all. For the value of it, in his estimation, depended
on the disposition of some other person to take it
as actual property, and this other person will think
matters much too uncertain to admit of his med-
dling with it at all : or, at least, if he does, he will
make sure as far as he can, and take the chance of
payment at a very low value, below what may turn
out to be the real proceeds. The remainder, the
portion of its value between that which he gives for
it, and that which it turns out to be ultimately
worth, is absolutely lost and destroyed to the
holder; and though it is, on the other hand,
gained for nothing by him who took it of the
holder, there is another loss, that of the *time* during
which my debtor's or my affairs are winding up;
for it may be, that even the half, which he can pay,
can only be got by waiting.

Consider my own situation at the same time.
The same principle applies to it. My credit is not
diminished in proportion to the tangible loss I
have sustained or expect; it is *gone*. At least, it
is diminished in a much greater degree than the
cause : even supposing I have never run it too
hard, never over-presumed on it. But how few
people of extensive credit, especially if rather suddenly acquired, do that! If they scent approach-
ing *danger*, they will use their credit to the utmost,
till the danger becomes *certainty*; they will abuse
the belief, already alluded to, entertained by the

world, that what they promise they can certainly fulfil. They gradually come to promise what they can only *probably* or *possibly* fulfil; but the transition, in the opinion of the public, is not gradual; the change in their credit comes at once. One moment perfect confidence, the next total distrust. What results? I was carrying on business by trusting and being trusted; now, even if I *survive* my embarrassments, I must still trust; I can no more get ready money now than before; but nobody will trust me. I had treated, in my dealings, as actual property, debts due to me in future; I can do so no longer; the debts in question are *really less* sperate, in my own opinion, than they were, and, in the opinion of others, once panic-struck, they are worth *nothing;* at least, as far as depends on my assertion that they are worth any thing, for my assertion will not now pass. I say, then, that in such circumstances, a portion, if not the whole, of my power of anticipation is destroyed; that is as if my capital were extinguished, locked up in a box, *for a year*, or whatever the time is; or, as if the value, or price, of its use for a year, were destroyed *for ever*. And, in either case, the loss in this way, by loss of credit, is *greater* than that loss of my debtor which occasioned me to break. If I should recover my credit hereafter, I may, as it were, *put in* the lapsed year again at some future time, and add so much to my property; but if not, it amounts to the loss of part of my capital for ever ; for if I was able to obtain credit on my name, I coined my name into additional capital.

It is often supposed, indeed, that this capital is a mere non-entity, and can add nothing to wealth, because, though credit means the consent of the world to consider a person as possessing the command of goods to a certain extent, whom they would otherwise not have so considered, yet as the whole mass of goods in the world is not at the same moment increased, the person, so trusted, can only get his share out of the shares of the rest, and the only effect will be, that the nominal prices of goods will rise, and nobody will be the better. But, in fact, it conferred on him a command over *labour* as well as goods, and, if it was obtained in order to be used as *capital*, it was *expended*, in a great degree, in labour. Now the quantity of labour *would* be increased at the same moment, in that case, though that of goods could not have been. And though, as there is no increase at the moment in the quantity of goods, the increased exertions of the labourer are obtained, in great measure, upon *false pretences*, yet they *are* obtained, and more has been produced than would otherwise have been produced in the same time; and thus too there will soon be additional goods to meet, in some degree, the increase of paper. Besides which, the more extended employment of labour increases the chance, at least, of fresh improvements in its productiveness.

These effects, which I have mentioned as tending to shew that the increase of wealth by the increase of paper credit is partly real, depend entirely, it must be observed, upon the circumstance of the accommodation thus afforded, being employed as *capital*, and successfully employed. It is, I believe, only as a means of ensuring *this*, and the payment of the bill, that the distinction between the discounting (at the Bank) of real, and what are called accommodation bills, is important to the public. Every addition to the floating mass of currency, therefore, which is made merely by creating paper for the purpose of advancing to the *government*, who never employ it productively as capital, seems to tend to depreciation without any thing to counteract it. Except that, when there is an increase of taxation, we want more money than before, at certain times, in order to pay it with. The value of money would somewhat rise, therefore, at such times, but for Bank paper; but the Bank paper far more than obviated that particular inconvenience.

The observation of Adam Smith, that "paper credit does not enable you to keep more nominal currency in circulation than there would have been without," is not true (Note XXXIV). Not even where there is gold and silver also in circulation, if the melting and exportation of coin is made difficult and expensive by prohibitory laws. He seems indeed to think that the produce *is* likely to be augmented, *in the end,* by banking operations ; for he merely observes, that it cannot be *immediately* augmented by them.

It seems clear, then, that the contractions of accommodation afforded by a bank cause less work to be done, less produce to be supplied, less real profits to be obtained, and less capital to be in a state of employment within a given time, than would otherwise have been the case ; and that where that contraction is sudden and unexpected, that circumstance will aggravate the evil in a degree which it may be impossible to calculate. A check to private credit will naturally diminish the degree of accommodation which a bank can afford, because there will, in consequence of it, be a smaller number of good bills to discount; but for that very reason such a period is peculiarly unfit to be chosen by such a bank, for a voluntary contraction of their issues, over and above that, which is thus brought upon them by events (Note XXXV).

On the whole, Mr. Malthus, in applying his doctrine to the present state of things in this country, or rather in thinking that it was necessary to frame such a doctrine to account for the present state of things in this country (for that seems to have been the *order* of ideas in his mind), appears to have not sufficiently allowed for the length of time which it takes to recover* from the

* "The necessary changes in the channels of trade would be effected in a year or two." Malthus, p. 499.

effects of sudden changes, or for the complete
loss which is sustained in the process, or for the
general stagnation which may be produced by
checks originally affecting only certain branches, or
for certain peculiar circumstances of our domestic
administration. The events of the times, then, are
not irreconcileable with the general principles he is
opposing, and do *not* render it necessary to look
out for new general principles (Note XXXVI).

When he talks, p. 502, of a diminution of expenditure at the peace, surely there is a diminution
of particular branches of demand, owing to the cessation of war monopoly, &c., rather more material to
our consideration, than any diminution of general
expenditure. If we were "enriched" by the war,
it was not by our expenditure, surely ; there were
other attendant circumstances (not necessarily ac-
companying *all* war) in our favour.

The increased employment of capital, I have
already observed, tends, at the moment, to throw
the current of demand proportionally more on raw
produce, and away from manufactures, than it was
before. Supposing it, therefore, to take place in a
country where the demand for some *manufacture*
had diminished, it might so far do harm. But suppose *corn* is the principal article for which the demand has diminished, which was the case with us,
increased employment of capital, that is, increased
wages given to labour, seems to be just what is
wanted, seems likely to palliate, rather than aggravate the evil.

If it be asked why, upon the principle of accounting for the, distress wholly by sudden interruptions in the channels of trade, did not the war produce as much distress as the peace? two answers shall suffice, though more might be found. 1. Because the changes occasioned by the war, came on gradually ; and those occasioned by the peace, all at once. 2. Because the peace, in a much greater degree than the war, found us with a quantity of capital fixed and sunk in those branches where the demand was checked.

N O T E S.

NOTE I.

MR. RICARDO indeed observes (p. 441, second edit.), that the real interest of a nation by no means requires, that it should contain many rather than few inhabitants ; but is like that of an individual capitalist, whose only concern is what *net* profits he can make. But he is speaking there (as appears in his next page), not of the interest of a nation as synonymous with human happiness, but merely as synonymous with the power of raising taxes, and maintaining fleets and armies. It is plain, that we may sometimes consider how to attain one object, and sometimes how to attain another, without thereby pronouncing which is the more important of the two, without being inconsistent, or falling into error ; unless we confuse the two under one name : which Smith, in the passages Mr. Ricardo is there alluding to, appears to have done.

Nothing, Mr. Ricardo says, can be taken from wages for taxes, because " *if moderate*, they constitute always the necessary expenses of production." It would have been better to have said, nothing can be taken from wages *if* they *are* so moderate as to constitute always the necessary expenses, &c. Because this is by no means always the case : on the contrary, you *can* almost always take something from wages. The confusion, which Mr. Ricardo has pointed out in Smith, between the two objects of having a large taxable fund and of increasing the power of enjoyment among the people, seems to be derived from the French Economistes. An increase of the labourer's consumption, out of the increased production he had occasioned, was an evil, according to their system, instead of being the great end of all the science. They looked at the subject with the eyes of excisemen. They cried up agricultural labour, because, as we happen to be obliged to pay for most part of its produce more than we are for manufactured produce, in proportion to the labour each cost, we can here find a surplus fund to *tax*, in the shape of rent. But this very circumstance, of our being so obliged, is in itself an *evil*. It is a necessary evil; it may be a profitable evil in the end: but, so far, we are worse off. Then they make light of manufactures (compared to corn, as sources of wealth), because, say they, of the price of a piece of lace, one part merely replaces what the labourer consumed, and the other part is only transferred from one man's pocket to another's. (See Mr. Mill's excellent answer, "Commerce defended," p. 25). But substitute "corn" for "lace," the same thing may be said; it would serve just as well against themselves. They say, that a man can produce two or three times as much corn as he can eat. But this does not prove that there must be a surplus. The question is not what he can produce, but what he *will*. The question is not what corn he *can eat*, but what corn and other things he *will expect as wages*. They were very kind in assuming, that a labourer was always to work the most, and consume the least, that nature would allow. Even of slaves, that reasoning would hardly be just: you may reduce your slave's *consumption* as far as you please, but you cannot force him to exert the utmost quantity of *labour* which is naturally in his power.

NOTE II.

That he should get his principal wants supplied with *very little* labour, on the other hand, is probably not conducive to his happiness. See the chapter in Malthus, on the Fertility of Land. Smith is quoted by M. Say (vol. ii, p. 121) to prove, that "une récompense libérale du travail augmente l'industrie de la classe laborieuse, qui semblable à toutes les qualités humaines s'accroît par la valeur des encouragemens qu'elle recoit." I do not know what facts he is here referring to, when he says

" *semblable*," &c. Increase the value of the encouragement of mining labour *compared* to that of farming labour, mining industry will increase at the expense of that of farming. But we are now speaking of *all* sorts, and not of any *alternative :* not of a case where a man says, " Which of two things shall I do?" and determines according to where there is best pay : here it is, " Shall I do any thing or nothing?" and whether the reward of doing something be great or small, it is equally true, in either case, that there is *nothing* to be got by *doing nothing*.

In the purchase of commodities it is continually true, that a man will give *a* for *b*, but will not give 2 *a* for 2 *b*. So it is in the case of labour. He will work *a* for *b* wages ; but not 2 *a* for 2 *b* wages. Then if you give him 2 *b* for 1 *a*, may it not follow, that he will be content with less, and therefore not work even *a ?*

There are two things sometimes confounded, I suspect, in reasonings of this sort, which are often but not necessarily united ; smallness of recompence and uncertainty of it. In countries where tyranny prevails, we are apt to say, cultivation and industry cannot go on, because the cultivator is not allowed to retain more than a very small portion of the produce of his industry. The true reason rather is, partly because he *does not know* that the *whole* may not be taken from him. But I ought to add a more important reason, *viz.*, that it is not any fixed, certain aliquot part of his produce, be it ever so small, that he expects to retain. He does not expect, that the more he produces the more will fall to his share ; but that, if he should increase his produce, he should still be fleeced of all but what would barely keep him alive.

NOTE III.

M. Say puts the case of two articles, in which the difference of durability is very much in favour of the one, and that of usefulness, or desirableness, very much in favour of the other. But that can only prove, that durability is not the *only* recommendation ; which is not denied. He should have compared two articles of nearly equal desirableness, but unequal durability.

NOTE IV.

The reduction of interest of the national debt about the middle of last century (mentioned by Mr. Malthus, page 476, and elsewhere), or rather the rise in the price of stock, which occasioned that reduction, may be partly attributed to the same principle — the security felt, the confidence placed in the funding system; which would naturally not arrive at its height till a good while after the establishment of such a system. Not to mention the uncertainty, which up to that time hung in some degree over the stability of the government itself — of the dynasty.

NOTE V.

M. Say (p. 62) says, " Créer une chose dont le besoin ne se ferait pas sentir, ce serait créer une chose sans valeur : ce ne serait pas produire. Or du moment qu'elle a une valeur, son producteur peut trouver à l'échanger contre celles qu'il veut se procurer." But the question is, how many will " celles" be? What sort of a bargain will he be able to make ? Mr. Mill falls into the same fault when he says (p. 86), that the use of foreign commerce is not to furnish a vent for domestic industry, because that industry always finds *a vent* for itself. " Vent" is comparative, and means not an exchange, but a beneficial or desirable exchange.

Suppose a man, with a very large capital, producing, at a time and place when there is very little capital in the hands of any body else, a great deal of some one commodity. It may be (and I introduce this case because it seems to me, from M. Say's allusions, that it is the case which he has in his mind when he propounds his maxim, and which led him to adopt it) it may be, I say, that he will derive little or no benefit from this great production of one article, because other people have not sufficient desire for it, and at the same time sufficient of other articles, to enable him to get in exchange for it the other ordinary good things of life, to obtain which was his motive in producing it. Unless it is an article of food, it will obviously not procure him any great quantity even of labour; and if it did, that would not mend his situation much, as long as he chooses to employ that labour only in producing still more and more of this same article. Under these circumstances, it would be happy for him if other people were to arise, possessed of wealth, and disposed to employ it in producing various articles different from this which he had been producing, and desirable to him. They would, it is true, injure him by raising the price of labour and land, or raw produce against him; but that would be more than compensated by the *débouché* they would afford. But what general moral can we draw from this, as to the effects of production of commodities *in general?* The additions this man made to produce, opened no débouché, certainly; M. Say's maxim was not true of them. He was either a great fool for laying out all his capital in one way, beyond what the demand would admit of being profitable, or else there must have been some sudden and unforeseen change of circumstances, which made a course, prudent when undertaken, turn out unprofitable to him, till he was relieved by the *produit créé.*

If his product was food, and he had produced twice as much as every body could eat, in this case no new creation of products would open a *débouché* for his stock, till the *numbers* had also increased. Products differ most widely in this respect, happily. Some, a man may well do without; while of some he cannot do without a certain quantity. But, on the other hand, of the former he can generally find room for an unlimited quantity, if he has the means of getting it; while, of the latter, he *cannot* (from "the narrow capacity of the human stomach," as Smith says) consume a great deal *more* than that quantity which he *absolutely wants.* Were it not so, the inequality of fortunes would be much more injurious than it is. We *might* have been so made, that though food, to a certain amount only had, as at present, been *necessary* to us, it might have been a source of pleasure to consume or possess one or two hundred times as much, where we had the power.

NOTE VI.

M. Say himself points out the obstacle to the unlimited placing of capital, arising from the nature of land. Lettre iii.

NOTE VII.

Smith speaks of it as limited by "the business to be trans-acted;" M. Say (as referred to by Mr. Ricardo), by "the extent of employment;" these are vague expressions.

NOTE VIII.

Or (which is saying the same thing in another form) this pro-duce will be divided in a proportion more favourable to the labourer, and less to the employer, than was the case before. Now where a little labour will produce a great deal, especially where it will produce a great deal of *food* in one country, com-pared to what it will in another, it is possible, that the *propor-tion* in which the produce is divided may be, in the former, more favourable to the employer than the latter, and, in that sense, *profits* may be said to be higher; and yet what the labourer gets may be more of absolute subsistence and enjoyment, in propor-tion to the quantity of trouble he takes, in the former than in the latter; and in *that* sense, *wages* may be said to be higher. This is, probably, the case in America. The proposition, therefore, which begins this note, and which may be expressed, if it is *neces-sary* to be brief, by saying that wages are high as profits are low, and vice versâ, is not answered by asking, as the author of "An Essay on the Application of Capital to Land" (p. 22) asks, "How comes it, then, that the wages of labour and profits of stock are high at the same moment in America?" High and low are used in different *senses* in the two propositions. See Malthus, 367.

The author of the Essay just mentioned, observes, with the same view (p. 24), that more will be given for labour when there is most increase of stock, and *that*, if the country is always equally parsimonious, will be when the profits on stock are highest. "The greater the profits of stock," he adds, "the higher will be the wages of labour." The fault of this is, that a word or two is left out. "The greater *have been* the profits of stock" (it should be, to correspond with the reason on which it is founded) "the higher *will be* the wages of labour." And then it does *not* contradict the proposition it is directed against. The high profits and the high wages are not *simultaneous ;* they do not occur in the same *bargain;* the one counteracts the other, and reduces it to a level. It might as well be argued, "the supply of a commodity is most rapid when the price is highest, therefore, large supply and high price go together." It is a mixing up of cause and effect.

NOTE IX.

M. Say (Lettres, p. 60) asks Mr. Malthus, "après avoir écrit trois volumes justement admirés, pour prouver que la population s'élève toujours au niveau des moyens d'existence, avez vous pu admettre le cas d'une grande augmentation de produits, avec un nombre *stationnaire* de consommateurs et des besoins reduits par la parcimonie?" (p. 355). "Tout ce qui peut se produire peut trouver des consommateurs" (Say, Lettres, p. 60). *In time.* But Mr. Malthus says, that the glut he anticipates is *because* this requires time, and the other does not. He expresses it, *in the passage* M. Say has quoted, by the term "*comparatively* stationary number of consumers," which M. Say has *omitted.*

NOTE X.

The profit obtained by capital, or the power of getting something in exchange for the assistance contributed by capital, arises from people's possessing, in unequal degrees, certain things, which give a great *advantage* to labour in the obtaining desirable commodities. If all had these advantages equally, all men would be benefited by it, because each man's labour would produce more than without those advantages ; but that benefit, or the price of it, would not exist in a separate shape, as it now does. Talent, strength, cultivated and habitual acquirements and knowledge, are such advantages ; land is another; and the *unequal* possession of these occasions a price to be given for them ; but that is distinct from *profits,* which I am now considering. Tools and implements, and a stock of materials, such as one man must have to enable him, even singly, to work. Food to maintain a person while he is working, and before the product is completed. But, still more, a stock of the preceding articles enough to assist the labour of many people at once ; for, by this means, combination of labour may be attained, and a certain quantity of labour produce much more than it would otherwise. Implements, also, go further by this means, because they do not lie by. The labour that built a private oven, does not go so far in producing bread, as that which built a baker's oven. If I bake but once a week, I must have an oven, the same as the baker, who bakes always. If there were no capitalists, people would find it their interest to *club* to build a common oven, mill, &c. ; as it is, the capitalist, who has the means by him, builds it, and we pay our club by little and little afterwards, *in the price* of the bread. The capitalist, too, keeps, as it were, an *echo-office* for labour ; he *insures against* the uncertainty of finding a vent for labour, which uncertainty would, but for him, prevent the labour, in many cases, from being undertaken. The trouble of looking for a purchaser, and of going to a market, is reduced, by his means, to a comparatively small compass.

These advantages, of course, are worth paying for. He who does not possess them will, in return for the assistance he derives from them, that is, in return for the means they afford him of working at all, with any prospect of gaining by it, where else he could not have so worked, or of making the work he would else have done produce more, be willing to give back, to the person who affords the advantage, part of his labour ; it will be worth his while to do so, to any extent that does not amount to the whole of the benefit he has derived. He will agree to work part of his time for the capitalist ; or, what comes to the same thing, to consider part of the whole produce, when raised and exchanged, as belonging to the capitalist. He must do so, or the capitalist would not have afforded him this assistance. But as the capitalist's motive was gain, and as these advantages always depend, in a certain degree, on the *will* to save, as well as on the *power*, the capitalist will be disposed to afford an additional portion of these assistances ; and as he will find fewer people in want of this additional portion, than were in want of the original portion, he must expect to have a less share of the benefit to himself ; he must be content to make a *present* (as it were) to the labourer, of part of the benefit his assistance occasions, or else he would not get the other part: the profit is reduced, then, by competition. A man may reduce the rate of his profits by the competition of his capital with itself, independently of that of others; I mean, by adding to his capital in order to gain. He will not gain so much more *in proportion* as he adds. As long as any of these advantages are possessed by some men over others, it does not appear to me, that profits can sink to nothing; unless the owners of those advantages *choose* to make a present of them.

Some of these advantages of superior wealth in production may, of course, be exerted without others. In ancient times, rich men, where slavery prevailed, seem to have sometimes carried on manufactures, &c., in their houses, merely for their own use, to a certain degree. We should hardly call this, now, employing *capital;* especially as it would not produce profits by *exchange*, the way in which we are used to estimate them. But, of course, they had those advantages of wealth which consist in being able to advance tools, materials, and food, though not those which arise from promoting division of employments, and the producing on a large scale for other people. Where the advantage possessed by the owner of capital is more felt in producing one commodity, than it is in producing another, in proportion to the labour employed, of course, when capitalists come to take less remuneration for the assistance of their capital, the former commodity will exchange at a less rate with the latter than before. The advantage possessed by the owner of capital, who can afford to sink it for a long time, that is, by the owner of fixed capital, is greater than that possessed by him who only sinks it for a short time; that is, by the owner of circulating capital, or of fixed capital of less durability. Therefore, when profits fall, commodities will exchange with one another at a new rate, a given quantity of those, which are in a greater degree produced by fixed capital (and which therefore are, in a greater degree, beholden to the assistance of capital on the whole), exchanging now for a less quantity of such as are produced in a less degree by fixed, and in a greater degree by circulating capital. This is what Mr. Ricardo proves with *figures* (p. 30), and makes rather a more important discovery of it than seems necessary, as Mr. Malthus (p. 91), remarks.

Smith considers the payment of the profits of that capital which was employed in building machines, as the payment of the advanced wages of the labour that built the machines, and which labour has concurred in the production of every lot of the article that comes from the machines. This M. Say thinks absurd : but why ? — it is *true*. " Labour would on this supposition be paid after it has ceased." To be sure ; what then ? *all* labour is paid so, *by the buyer*, which is what he is speaking of ; and if he is not, *none* is so paid. *Circulating* capital is equally replaced, with its profit, after the labour, whose pay it had advanced, has ceased. Only the one is replaced in one lump in the price of one lot of the article, the other by *instalments* as it were, and for a long time to come. But this is not true only of machines : in the price of what *particular lot* of *corn* is the *hedger's* labour, the *drainer's*, the *manure fetcher's*, paid ? The profits in fact are always reckoned in *general* on the *whole* capital advanced, not merely with an eye to the particular expense of producing the particular lot sold. In all these cases the wages were advanced : and they are repaid as advanced money is ; sometimes in one sum, soon ; sometimes in instalments ; sometimes by annuity, with or without uncertainty in its duration ; sometimes by perpetual annuity, like the public loans ; — if there is any expenditure of capital whose effects are *for ever*.

But though profits may never be liable to sink to *nothing*, competition may, of course, reduce profits to less than any assignable degree of minuteness, if the owners of capital choose. Wages cannot be so beat down ; there is a minimum in the case of wages, the bare means of subsistence. And when I say there is not in the case of capital, I am supposing the capitalist provided with an independent *subsistence* from rent or labour. A man's advantage over others, in production, may consist in will, as well as in power. This is an advantage over other people equally rich with himself, perhaps, but not *disposed* to make use of the advantage which those riches give them in production. These must be mostly landlords. They cannot be the labourers with whom the capitalist contracts, nor can he, therefore, derive a benefit from this advantage in the bargain he makes with these labourers, directly. But he does so indirectly, by there being less competition with him, so that the benefit he derives, from the assistance he affords to labour, is not *beat down* below the actual amount of the assistance so much in the bargain between him and the labourer as it would otherwise have been.

If each man of a class could never have more than a given share, or aliquot part, of the gains and possessions of the whole, they would readily combine to raise the gains : this is *monopoly*. But where each man thinks that he may any way increase the absolute amount of his own share, though by a process which lessens the *whole* amount, he will often do it : this is *competition*.

Where a man's advantage over other people consists in *land,* he makes the labourer, to whom he gives the land for a time, work for him part of that time ; or, what comes to the same thing, give him part of the produce, or part of what the produce exchanges for. If it is *possible* for him to do this, that is, if the man *can* raise more than what he must himself eat ; if the exacting such a thing would not have simply the effect of preventing the possibility of land being cultivated at all ; this compensation *will* certainly be exacted where the land is appropriated, and unequally appropriated ; however fertile it may be, or however large and thinly peopled. In few countries has rent, I believe, sprung up by nature, and not been originally the effect of appropriation effected by main force. Sometimes it was not the effect of a free bargain even arising out of such an appropriation by force. He, who had got the land by force, sometimes directs by force what shall be paid for it, and collects that by force again ; as in Egypt. In this case it may seem to be rent ; but it is tribute, or plunder : and to reason about it as rent, would but lead to error.

The purchase money exacted from the settlers in the new states of America is, in like manner, owing to artificial appropriation.

The landlord, however, has no choice (as the capitalist has), whether to impart to others the superior advantage which he has over them in production, or to consume, for his own pleasure, that wealth from which he derives this advantage ; for land cannot be consumed, and is of no use if not employed. There is nothing in the case of land answering to the *withdrawing* of capital, to the conversion of capital into revenue, or to saving. No compensation, therefore, is necessary here, answering to that which must be allowed to the capitalist, in order to induce him to save ; *i. e.* to turn his wealth to capital, and to the public good. The landlord can neither add to his land, so as to lower the rate of profits he gets by it, when high ; nor withdraw it, when they are low. In this last respect, machines are like land ; and, owing to it, both must submit to take whatever they can get. Nor do the low profits of land diminish or wear out involuntarily, as it were, the supply of land, as too low wages of labour diminish the numbers of mankind, and supply of labour.

When the landlord lets out the productive service of his land, he is sure, whether he gets more or less of it, to have the land back again. It is different with the capitalist ; he having paid the labourers, &c., in advance, and taken on himself the risk of the success of the project, may, possibly, never see his capital or the whole of it again. It is only by a sort of metaphor, that he can be said to let it out for hire ; he parts with it entirely, and receives, in return, what is not individually the same thing, but quite distinct.

The increase of numbers, or power of the necessaries of life to raise up a demand, does not seem a necessary cause of rent. If a country, even in a natural state, that is, not forcibly appropriated, as above supposed, were once so full of people as to have nearly occasioned the appearance of rent, but not quite ; rent might come into existence, even though the further increase of those people should become, by a change in the laws of nature, impossible. For even if we suppose them all (which we need not) to have at that time as much as they could *eat,* still, if industry and capital increase, the demand for raw produce, as *materials,* will rise, though not the demand for raw produce, as *food.* That land, which raises the former sort of raw produce, will rise then, in time, to an exchangeable value ; and, if the land be convertible, it will encroach on the corn land, and straiten that, and give that an exchangeable value too. But this would extend, of course, but a very little way, compared to the extent to which rent goes now.

Numbers depend immediately on the power of obtaining that necessary of life which is the most difficult to obtain. It will be against *that* part of the " means of subsistence," of course, that population will press. In this country there is generally plenty of *water* for that number of people for whom there is *land* enough to permit them to exist. Water, here, is therefore generally without value. Where it is a little scarcer, it bears a rent; and where it is so much scarcer in proportion to land, that every body who can get enough to drink, may easily get enough to eat, it will form the limit to population, and may bear a rent, while land bears none.

The cause of rent, which is stated last by Mr. Malthus, " the comparative scarcity of the most fertile land," or rather (since " comparative scarcity" means nothing), the unequal fertility of land, is not in any way, that I can even guess at, a condition necessary to the existence of rent. Where unequal fertility exists, high price must have risen to a certain point on the most fertile land, *before* it was worth while to cultivate land of the next degree of fertility, and not in *consequence* of people's happening to cultivate land of the next degree ; nor of " population," or the " progress of society" (Ricardo, 51, 52), except in this way. If, then, land of the next degree had no where existed, the high price and high profits would have continued, and, probably, increased, on the land of the first degree ; and the excess of it above profits in other lines, being an advantage derived not from capital, but ownership of land, would have been separated very soon in the form of rent. Mr. Ricardo says, " as soon as the land, No. 2, was cultivated, rent would begin to appear on the land, No. 1." This is an inversion of cause and effect, like that which he complains of in others, when they consider rent the cause of high price, not the consequence.

In order that rent should exist, it is necessary, certainly, that land should make diminishing returns, in proportion to increased application of labour and capital; that is, that it should at all times be true, whatever be the produce obtained by the existing quantity of labour and capital, that half that quantity, applied in the same manner, would raise more than half that produce, and twice that quantity would raise less than twice that produce ; but it is not necessary that the land should be unequally fertile. And as the less fertile land need not be resorted to, so as to occasion rent, so neither need the additional capital be actually laid out. Rent may arise on the former amount of capital, by an increased demand for corn.

Mr. Ricardo calls rent (p. 47, second edit.), " what is paid for the original and indestructible powers of the soil ;" he, therefore, observes, that the " rent of the forests in Norway" (Adam Smith) is not a proper term, as to so much as was given for the *standing timber*, beyond what would have been given without. The same observation would apply to mines ; here, as in the case of timber, you do not *hire* the use of land, but *buy* so much of an existing thing (wood or ore), as you are able and willing to carry away within the term of the lease. If the forests are primeval, or, at least, natural forests (in that country they sometimes spring up of themselves, according to Mr. Malthus, in the Essay on Population), that payment, to which Mr. Ricardo has denied the title of *rent*, is not *profits* either ; where it is a *planted* forest, part of it *is*.

When Mr. Malthus published his Essay on Rent, it seems to have been partly with a view to *answer* the cry of " No Landlords," which then " stood rubric on the walls," to stand up in defence of that class, and to prove that they were not like *monopolists*. That rent cannot be abolished, that its increase is a natural concomitant, in general, of increasing wealth and numbers, he shewed ; but neither did the vulgar cry of " No Landlords" necessarily mean, that there ought to be *no such thing* as rent, but rather that it ought to be equally divided among the people, according to what was called " Spence's plan." But when he proceeds to vindicate landlords from the odious name of monopolists, from the observation of Smith, " that they love to reap where they never sowed," he seems to be fighting for a *name*. It is with this view, that he places first the property of the land by which more people may live on its produce, than those who raise that produce; and next, that of raising up demanders, by the principle of population; and as these are valuable properties, he thinks rent, being the "indication" of them, must be something respectable.

Of course, however (as Mr. Ricardo observes, p. 507), those qualities are not the better or more advantageous to us, from the circumstance of our being obliged to *pay* for them. Mr. Malthus calls rent a *part* of the surplus produce from land (Essay on Rent, p. 16). But the question is, whose hands that part is in; whether retained by the landlord, or enjoyed for nothing by the public. It is more properly the *price* of a part of the surplus produce. That is a very different thing. To tell us that a thing exists, and is beneficial to us, is not to pronounce a panegyric on the high price we are obliged to pay for it, or on the people who receive that high price, without any exertion or self-denial on their part. There is too much the air of an *advocate* in all these arguments of his. I suppose, the real principle upon which people grumble at rent is, that it is not the compensation to any body for *doing* what costs them any sacrifice to do. A man must be paid for laying out his money as capital; in doing so, he is foregoing the present enjoyment he might have from it: a labourer must be paid for his labour; he foregoes his ease and rest: but a landlord foregoes nothing, in submitting his land to tillage (and even if tilled by himself, rent equally enters into the price of its produce); he gives up nothing.

I do not understand why ground rents of houses in towns are more "a strict monopoly" (Malthus, p. 98) than other rents. They are *higher*, that is all. "That arises from their local situation." So does the rent of all land. Land in the Illinois is not so valuable as equally good land near New York. Ground rents depend on the same causes as all other prices do; the consideration of the degree of advantage or benefit to be derived from the article, combined with that of the difficulty of getting it.

NOTE XI.

He says (p. 46) " Les marchandises, dites-vous, ne s'échangent pas seulement contre des marchandises ; elles s'échangent aussi contre du travail. Si ce travail est un produit que les une vendent, que les autres achètent, et que ces derniers consomment, il m'en coûtera peù de l'appeller une *marchandise*, et il ne vous en coûtera pas beaucoup plus d'assimiler les autres marchandises a celle-là, car elles sont des produits aussi. Les confondant alors les uns et les autres sous le nom générique de *produits*, vous pourrez convenir, peut-être, qu'on n'achète des produits qu'avec des produits."

But he knows perfectly well, that this was not what Mr. Malthus meant by products or commodities (marchandises). I cannot think what is the use of this fencing with *words*. In what sense, too, we may ask, is labour *consumed*, as distinct from consuming the product of it ? What are we the better for calling labour a product, an use directly contrary to the plain common use of the word, and therefore constantly lying open for mis understanding and dispute. These affected *ways of talking* constitute, in great part, what M. Say calls his *doctrine*, which he is so anxious to have taught under the auspices of Mr. Malthus, at Hertford, as, he says, it already is " dans plusieurs parties de l'Europe" (p. 46). " Si vous trouvez (p. 36), une physionomie de paradoxe à toutes ces propositions, voyez les *choses* qu'elles expriment, et j'ose croire qu'elles vous paraîtront fort simples et fort raisonnables ;" doubtless ; and, at the same time, they will very probably appear, by the same process, not at all original or important. " Sans cette analyse," he proceeds, " je vous défie d'expliquer la totalité des *faits;* d'expliquer par exemple comment *le même capital est consommé deux fois ; productivement* par un entrepreneur et improductivement par son ouvrier." It seems to be agreed, " dans plusieurs parties de l'Europe," to call a fantastical mode of expression a *fact*.

If, however, he includes labour, when he says, that production finds a market for itself (the proposition Mr. Malthus resists), then it is plain he will not deny, that there may be a glut

of *that sort of products, which do not comprise labour* (for we must
"speak by the card" now, or "equivocation will undo us"),
measured in labour; in short, that they may exchange with
labour at one rate or at another; just as cotton may with wine;
and that one rate may most encourage labour, and the other most
encourage the production, on the part of a capitalist or master, of
such sort of products. And, consequently, the proposition of
M. Say does not at all prove that *capital* opens a market for
itself, but only that capital and labour open a market for one
another. He has left Mr. Ricardo, then, who quoted his authority (p. 359), quite in the lurch by this explanation. However,
after all, in page 57, we find him talking of "produits," nay of
" toute espéce de produits," as distinct from services prodúctifs,
of which latter labour is one.

M. Say seems to think, that to give a new sense to people's
words, different from that in which they used them, and then
shew that, understood in that new sense, they are no longer true,
is answering them; or rather, is giving "a demonstration"
which "ruins their assertions." Lettres, p. 58, note.

NOTE XII.

"They (commodities) may be exactly equivalent to each other
in exchange, yet why may not both be so plentiful as not to command more labour, or *but very little more* than they have cost;
and, in this case, would the demand for them be effectual?
Would it be such as to encourage their continued production?
Unquestionably not." (Malth. 356). This "very little more,"
is just the difficulty. It is impossible to say *how little* it may be,
and yet be sufficient to "encourage their continued production."
Of course, it can never be *none*, permanently.

M. Say, indeed (Lettres, p. 67), is pleased to observe, that
Mr. Malthus was wrong in supposing "que la production *ne peut*
se continuer si la valeur des marchandises ne paie que peu de
travail au delà de ce qu'elles ont coûté." ("*Would,*" not
"could," is the word in Malthus, p. 356; and so it is in the
other passage, where M. Say chooses to insert "*pourraient*").
"Il n'est nullement nécessaire," he proceeds, "que le produit

vaille *au delà* de ses frais de production, pour que les producteurs soient en état de continuer. Lorsqu'une entreprise commence avec un capital de cent mille francs, il *suffit* que le produit qui en sort, *vaille cent mille francs*, pour qu'elle *puisse* recommencer ses operations." (We might say, " it *can*, certainly, but it will have no inducement to do so." But he seems to mean more). " Et où sont, dites-vous, les profits des producteurs ? Le *capital tout entier a servi à les payer!*" " Les profits," he adds, in a note, " que fait un entrepreneur dans son entreprise, sont le salaire du travail et des talens qu'il a mis dans son affaire." So that, after having been made to stare a sufficient time at the monstrous absurd paradox, which (merely *in order* to make us stare) this grave professor lays before us, after having been duly set to *guess*, like children, we find that he is exactly of the same opinion as Mr. Malthus, whom he contradicts, only he *chooses* to *call* some things " wages of superintendence," which Mr. Malthus did not mean to include when he talked of the labour the article had cost ; and to reckon as part of the " costs of production," what in plain English goes by the name of *profits*. Upon this supposition, we are to understand the assertion, that if a man sets out with a capital, it is enough for him to merely replace it, by considering his expenses of living in the interim, to the extent of what are to be the profits, as paid for with part of his *capital*. This may be a very *convenient* way of talking, I dare say, in itself, but it happens not to be the *language* in which Mr. Malthus has expressed himself, and therefore it cannot serve to contradict *him*.

But M. Say adds, with much complacency, " ce *grand phénomène* de la production, analysé, exposé sous ses *veritables traits*, explique tout" (p. 70).

I cannot tell why M. Say reads his antagonist a lecture (p. 71, 72), on the impropriety of *preaching* dissipation, " point *d'exhortations*," he says " bornons-nous à noter comment les choses se succèdent," &c. M. Say's reflection may be useful to himself, if he is afraid of being run away with by his own feelings on so inflammatory a topic as *saving*; but it is not applicable to Mr. *Malthus*. If M. Say means, that a writer having established a principle, should not draw from it a *practical inference* for the good of his country, I should like to know why? Here in England, strange to say, it is generally the very object we have in view in these speculations. "It is not political economy," says M. Say. It is surely, however, "political economy *considered with a view to its* practical application," and *this* is the very *title* of Mr. Malthus's book.

NOTE XIII.

It is owing to this, principally, that high profits are, as is commonly said, favourable to accumulation of capital. Not merely because there is more to save. For then, high wages and high rent might equally tend to this effect. But that increase, which is in the shape of profits, comes immediately into the hands of those who are already disposed to save, whose habits are already frugal, and who best know, too, how to turn what they save to gain. See an observation of Hume, quoted in Malthus, p. 406.

Another important instance of the effect of habits is the circumstance so much and justly insisted upon by Mr. Malthus (chap. vii, sect. 4), that a certain degree of natural difficulty in raising *food*, is necessary to form habits of industry sufficient to induce people to work for the sake of obtaining *comforts* ; and that it is, often, where people have the most leisure time left after procuring mere subsistence, that they are the least disposed to employ that leisure time to get superfluities.

These observations will apply, I think, to the comparison Mr. Malthus makes (p. 412) between the saving of labour effected by fertile land, and that effected by machines ; the profits made by machines come into hands more capable of employing them in the increase of wealth, and more ready to do so ; and the invention of machines comes upon pre-existing habits of labour, and is sure of producing a profit. But the effect of fertile land *may* be, that no profit at all is gained by it to the owner. It is not a *new* advantage. It always existed, where it exists ; and the consequence may be, a habit of setting such a value on idleness, that the owner of the land cannot make such a bargain with labourers, as to obtain large profits. And then, if he does, he is not the sort of person likely to draw from them further means of increasing wealth, as the owner of machines is.

NOTE XIV.

Which was much less a matter of *taste*, than a change owing to the capitalist having contrived by degrees to bring a greater variety of cheaper or better articles to *tempt demand*. We want to create a "taste" for our manufactures in India. We do not try, then, to *inspire* people with wants, we do not read them lectures in favour of caps and stockings; we put the articles in their way more frequently, and vie with one another in holding out the inducement of cheapness, variety, and goodness.

NOTE XV.

Hume attributes the varying rate of interest primarily to the varying proportion between borrowers and lenders, *or* between prodigality and frugality. It is plain that these two proportions are not *necessarily* the same. More money might be employed as capital in proportion to that spent as revenue, now, than formerly; and yet the proportion of prodigal borrowers be as great, in proportion to the lenders, now, as it was then. There *might*, in those times when profit was higher than now, have been not a single borrower in England; and there *might* now be many. It did not *necessarily* follow, that those who *spend* their fortune should *anticipate* or *outrun* it. But though not necessary it is *natural*, that the two causes above mentioned should exist at the same time : it is natural that an increase in the disposition to save money and make profit by producing, should be accompanied by an increase in the disposition to save money and make profit by lending. And when it was less, than it is now, the fashion for rich men to save, in order to make a profit, it would naturally be more, than it is now, the fashion for *some* of them not merely not to save and increase their fortunes, but to run them out by anticipation.

NOTE XVI.

With regard to the case put by Mr. Malthus, and alluded to in page 51 of this, of *all* consumption beyond bread and water, or mere necessaries, being stopped entirely, I cannot consider that as *illustrating*, by an *extreme case*, the effects of an increasing habit of saving. A *complete stoppage* is not the *extreme degree* of a partial and comparative diminution of it. It is the *contrary*. *None* is not the extreme of *a little*, it is the negation of it. If *any class consume*, the case will be widely different from the chimerical case put by Mr. Malthus, which therefore *illustrates* nothing but itself. Let water be issuing at a hundred holes : what will happen if I stop ninety? To answer this, is it relevant to put a case of stopping *all?*

NOTE XVII.

Inventions to *save labour* form only a part of that which I have elsewhere called increasing the *productiveness* of labour, which will include any invention whereby a given quantity of labour can produce a greater quantity of enjoyment to man, whether in the shape of a new article or an old one. Mr. Malthus (p. 461) makes the like observation as to *foreign* trade, but he is open to it himself as to the question of *internal* improvements in the management of labour ; for he always confines himself to savings effected in the production of some article which was already produced.

NOTE XVIII.

What a producer wants, by way of a demand or market, must be some *increase*. Nothing can provide for an increased demand, that does not provide for an increase of *produce*. He wants to receive more hereafter than what he foregoes now. *One* man may do this, but *all* cannot, without finding some way of *creating* that "*more.*" That *more* is not in the hands of productive labourers. Their means, what they have to purchase with, is part of the already existing stock.

NOTE XIX.

As is the corresponding distinction between foreign and home trade, in a great degree, in principle. The main distinction being only what arises from the reluctance to move capital to a *strange* country, compared to the readiness with which it goes to different parts of the *same* country, wherever there is most demand for it; as is pointed out by Mr. Ricardo.

NOTE XX.

Smith (owing partly to his having confounded these two things, as M. Say observes) considers the profits of stock as if they were a regular percentage. And he argues, that they cannot be considered as the salary of superintendance, because, says he, two capitals of very different amounts may require the same trouble of superintendance, and yet each will make the same rate of profit per cent., which will be two very different sums. It is, as M. Say observes (vol. ii, p. 150, fourth edit.), a mere *assumption*, that they *will* make the same rate of profit per cent. The existing rate of profit means an *average*, not an *universal* rate. Scarce any two capitals make exactly the same rate of profits. The having a legal fixed rate of *interest*, I believe, keeps us from recollecting this always. The very case he has put, if true, would show, that the profit upon the capital is not a percentage. For out of two *unequal* portions of profit, which are, according to him, the same percentage on the amount of the respective capitals, *equal* portions must be deducted for the labour of management, which he supposes to be equal in both. The remainder, therefore, will, after such deduction, no longer be in proportion to the capitals. Or is the labour of management to go unpaid? But he has observed, elsewhere, that it is often transferred to a head clerk or manager, who is directly paid by a salary. Now the *public* cannot care whether it is done by the owner of the capital, or by a head clerk, therefore the price must be the same, and consequently what Smith calls the profits, in both cases. Indeed Smith (in p. 64) says only, that the profit " bears *some proportion* to the stock ;" that is, more stock brings more profit. And the argument he uses, that if it did not, a man would have no motive for laying out the additional quantity, goes no further. This is very different from saying it will be in exact *proportion*.

Besides this difference, which prevents two stocks in two different hands, from bringing the same rates of profit per cent.; it seems clear, that the stock which is in one person's hand, will generally bring a larger *rate* of profit where it is larger, than where it is smaller. The saving, which a large capital effects in labour, must be more than the sum of what would be 'effected by twenty different capitals, separately administered, which twenty capitals would together amount to the larger capital. Besides, there are some employments which large capitals only are fit for, over and above what they have in common with others. The more a man adds to his capital, then, the better profits he is likely to make. This forms a temptation to *go on*. And the prospect of it induces people at first to be content with less profit than they otherwise would.

NOTE XXI.

Mr. Malthus insists on the great importance of what he calls *distribution*. It is not very easy to discover from him exactly what distribution means. At one time it seemed to be something like good roads (p. 414, line 17); at another, to denote the producing more desirable, rather than less desirable things (p. 414, line 13; and 419, line 9, &c.: for distribution cannot include *number* of consumers, I should think). The first sense, *viz.* that which is illustrated by analogy to roads and canals, is exactly answerable to the second head of distribution, according to him (p. 427), " internal and external commerce." But this requisite is itself an employment of *capital*. If too little is employed in transport, and too much in production, I should say the fault is like any other unequal or disproportionate employment of capital in its different lines. So as to the division of land into many hands (p. 428, line 12), you may call this a distribution of produce, if you will; it seems much more obviously to be a distribution of the means of getting it, land, among those who are most likely to use those means.

NOTE XXII.

Converting consumption into capital has a different effect, where your consumption had been partly in keeping unproductive labourers in low stations, and where it had not. In the former case, the cessation of your consumption throws on the world the labourers for whom it creates a demand. But if you had consumed *commodities* it does not; it raises the demand for labourers on the whole. Then it must be true vice versa, *i. e.* when you turn capital into revenue. This seems to prove, that the imposing of taxes is least felt by the poor when it is laid out in keeping soldiers.

NOTE XXIII.

It is the same *source* of confusion (though operating the other way) as that which leads some people to consider all the money raised by taxes, even including that which is simply paid to English stockholders, as lost *to the nation,* because it is lost to the particular people who pay it.

NOTE XXIV.

These gentlemen are sometimes called by Mr. Malthus unproductive *labourers* (p. 477). " They furnish," he thinks, " fresh motives to production, and tend to push the wealth of the country farther than it would go without them ;" *independent* of any good they do by the particular sort of *labour* they perform. It is clear, however, elsewhere, that stockholders, landlords, pensioners, &c., though they perform no labour, may, up to a certain point, produce, in his opinion, the same advantages.

Smith says, " The inhabitants of a large village, it has sometimes been observed, after having made considerable progress in manufactures, have become idle and poor, in consequence of a great lord's having taken up his residence in their neighbourhood." (vol. ii, p. 93.) This *lord*, one would have thought, on Mr. Malthus's system, was just what they stood in need of.

NOTE XXV.

In order to produce any good effect this way, *certainty* is one great object : that is, that the producer should know that he has *so much* to pay, and that all he can make *beyond* that is his own. Such impositions as tithes and poor-rates are, therefore, less calculated to lead to this particular sort of advantage, such as it is.

NOTE XXVI.

" Gradually at least :" of course. Great, sudden changes of almost all sorts, from one state to another, are bad ; but that is not pronouncing which of the two states may be in itself the better. In an article in the Edinburgh Review, in favour of peace (July 1812, p. 223, 224), this consideration was neglected.

It may be extremely true, besides, that now is not the best time to attempt to reduce our taxes *by sinking funds :* that is work for sunshine. Its *immediate* effect is to *increase* taxation at the expense of private capital : my objection to it therefore is just the reverse of Mr. Malthus's.

It may be doubted whether opening, by new arrangements, or the demolition of old and absurd ones, fresh channels of trade, the advantages of which may probably be over-rated, or which will require a sacrifice of any existing interests (see Malth. 509), is well-timed *now.* I should be inclined to say, do nothing now, which will *ruin any* branch of trade. Stand still, at least, and do not go any farther in the work of *partial* destruction. Open no great new markets. You have the experience of the India trade in your eyes. Bear in mind the lessons of distress, and in more easy times make such careful alterations as may prevent that distress from being so great another time.

NOTE XXVII.

" When profits are *low* and *uncertain,*" says Mr. Malthus, " when capitalists are quite at a loss where they can safely employ their capitals, and when, on these accounts, capital is flowing out of the country ; in short, when all the evidence, which the nature of the subject admits, distinctly proves, that there is no effective demand for capital at home, is it not contrary to the general principles of political economy, is it not a vain, fruitless opposition to that first, greatest, and most universal of all its principles, the principle of supply and demand, to recommend saving, and the conversion of more revenue into capital?" In such a situation the misfortune to the public is the falling off of production, the misfortune to the numerical *majority* of the public is the diminished demand for labour. Persons who would invest capital without wishing for more than very moderate profits, but endeavouring at the same time to keep as much as possible out of the way of uncertainty, would be most useful, I should think, at such a time. To advise them rather to convert capital into revenue, to withdraw actually invested capital in order to spend it, is surely like burning your house down for fear it should take fire.

"Low and uncertain", we must observe, are two very different things. Lowness of profits has not the effect of causing money to be hoarded ; or, what comes to the same thing, reluctantly and hesitatingly circulated ; as uncertainty has. This amounts to an *annihilation* of part of the capital; that is, of part of its "productive service," or use.

NOTE XXVIII.

These arguments of Mr. Malthus have been answered by M. Say. But his " Lettres" are a little too much confined to what regards himself personally, to be of so much use as might have been wished in removing the difficulties raised by Mr. Malthus with regard to the subject in general. There is an asperity, too, about them, which seems quite unnecessary. To be sure, Mr. Malthus has dared to question the expediency of the French laws for the division of property ; a system, which is called in the Traité de l'Economie Politique, " la marche bienfaisante de la nature," and set forth by an elegant metaphor. M. Say adorns his " Lettres," too, with angry and eloquent sarcasms (also adorned by metaphors) against the English system of government ; which are doubtless very grateful to the ears of those for whom they are in a more especial manner intended.

NOTE XXIX.

We often hear our distresses attributed to the excess of production, and in the same breath *particular articles* mentioned, of which the demand has fallen off from the peace : it is quite clear, then, that such persons do not *mean* that production is too great, that we have produced *too much*, but that we have produced *the wrong things.*

We are apt to hear of certain countries, as *Holland,* brought as examples to prove that production, carried to a great extent, causes an actual *diminution* of people and a withdrawing of capital. But great wealth is apt to be *abused.* So is strength of constitution ; and as some people fancy gout to be a *natural* appendage to robustness ; and excess in drinking, &c., to be rather conducive to strength than not ; so they fancy excessive taxation (which can only be in rich states, because rich states alone can bear it) to be in some way a *cause* of wealth, and lay the blame of the *decay* on the excess of production and accumulation.

Mere exportation of *capital,* too, from such a country, is not decay ; it is the natural course of things ; there must be diminution, or at least stoppage, of *numbers,* in order to constitute a positive symptom of *decay.*

Small states, such as are little more than *towns,* may sometimes decay, just as one town decays and another springs up in a large country : that is, where their original advantages were *peculiar,* and *depended on* the want of similar advantages possessed at the same time elsewhere. Whether a town shall stand in this place or in that is, besides, partly accidental, and so therefore is the change of it from one place to another.

NOTE XXX.

See the excellent observations of M. Say, " Lettres a M. Malthus," p. 120, 121.

NOTE XXXI.

Mr. Malthus describes the increase of wealth as having been " rapid and astonishing," " during the *last thirty or forty years*"

(p. 422). We have not been at war *quite* all that time. *Some* part of the increase, I apprehend, is owing to the parallel increase carrying on in *America* all the time. The political *separation* of the two countries only increased the advantages to be derived from their *commercial connection*. A country, such as America, cannot make a full use of its own advantages but through means, which increase the prosperity of the rest of the world. That is the very nature of voluntary exchange -- mutual benefit.

NOTE XXXII.

The observations of M. Say are excellent on these points. "Lettres," p. 115, 123, &c. I do not understand page 113, about America.

NOTE XXXIII.

" C'est l'*entrepreneur* que tous les risques atteignent," says M. Say, " Lettres," p. 29 ; but if the risk is great it extends to others, and affects others through him.

NOTE XXXIV.

Adam Smith (vol. ii, p. 44, edit. 1806) says, that when a bank discounts a real bill for a merchant, it only advances a part of the value, which he would otherwise have been obliged to keep by him for answering occasional demands ; and that this is all that it ought to do ; and that while it does so no greater amount of currency will, on the whole, be in circulation than was before. I cannot conceive why any of these conclusions follow.

The encroachment of paper money on gold and silver, while it drives out those metals from their employment as money into their employment as metals, must greatly diminish their price on the whole. They were wanted for two purposes, and they are now wanted only for one. Though it were true, then, that the paper must still be at par with the metals, and that their market and mint prices must still be equal, *both* prices have fallen, estimated in things in general; and, for this reason, a far larger amount of nominal currency may be expected to be in circulation, owing to this introduction of paper.

NOTE XXXV.

It is singular, that Mr. Malthus, in p. 445, reasons of the affairs of 1815 and 1816, as if money price meant the same thing all that time.

Among the artificial measures, which kept up the distress, due regard must be paid to the Corn Bill, which came just *after* all the worst part of the *evil*, which it professed to prevent, was done irrecoverably; and served principally to prevent the countervailing good, which the healing process of nature, if allowed to *settle*, was about to extract from it. It may turn out, in case of some future *war*, to have been a very useful measure of national security, for aught I know. I am only speaking of the *present*. Of course, however we may *talk* of " prosecuting war with a view to a safe and honourable *peace*," we all know, that, even in the high state of civilization which Europe boasts to have obtained, peace is in fact always to be considered as a state which exists and is tolerated principally with a view to war, and in which, of course, the great point is to make all things *idonea bello*, as much as possible.

It is supposed by some persons, that though freedom from restriction is a very good thing for the generality of trades, yet that the external trade in corn forms an exception, and that restrictions ought to be applied to this trade, even if banished from every other. Whatever may be the reason for this opinion, it is not difficult to give a reason for asserting the direct *contrary;* namely, that even if every other trade were under restrictions, the corn trade ought to be free : the reason I mean is, that Nature has made the success of that species of production much more *fluctuating*, from one year to another, than that of trades in general; and that therefore it stands more than trades in general, in need of that equalization and means of finding a level, which can only be produced by free intercourse.

Some of the advocates of the Corn Bill were admirers of the

principle upon which the old Bounty system was founded, and rested their support of the Corn Bill upon that principle ; and accordingly they considered it an advisable measure, even without any reference to our existing situation, and even without any reference to the question of making ourselves independent of foreign supply in case of war. They told us, that the measure would indeed at first make provisions rise, but (like the Morning Post in the *Rejected Addresses*) " pledged themselves that they would soon *fall* again," and be permanently cheaper than if no such regulation were adopted. But here they confounded two measures and two principles, totally unlike and opposite. A bounty on exportation (laying aside the question whether it is *worth while* to pay it for the sake of the object) does certainly tend to encourage cultivation, and probably to lower the ultimate permanent price of corn (notwithstanding the arguments of Smith) ; but it does so by affording a readier *vent in cheap years* than would naturally have existed, and by thus relieving the farmer from part of his uncertainty, from part of the chances against him, which form the discouragement to till. But a restriction on importation has a directly contrary effect : if it prevails in a country where there would otherwise be importation in average years ; the consequence of it must be, that the average price of corn is higher, and that therefore it is *less easy* for the farmers, when there comes a year of plenty, to relieve the glut by exportation. It is pretty clearly now perceived, accordingly, that the bill was by no means a measure of protection to the farmers, as it was meant to be ; but a cause of ruin to them.

> Evertere domos totas optantibus ipsis
> Dii faciles.

Now, when distress is owing to a war expenditure and taxation, however much it may be the fashion to lay all the blame on the government or legislature, they may at least say, that they *never supposed* the war would *promote* prosperity, that the taxes were not laid on for *that purpose*, that they were only meant as the " least of two evils." But when, after a strong measure of a very artificial kind has been adopted professedly for the relief of distress, distress of the same identical kind still continues, we have surely a right to complain and to find fault.

At the time when the bill passed, we were told by some, that it was mere incendiary talk to pretend that 80*s.* would be a *minimum* price, for, said they, "it will be a *maximum.* It never can exceed 80*s.*; for at that point foreign corn will come in and keep it down: it may, and will, often be below it." How then was the measure to be consistent with the reason on which it was founded, *viz.* that 80*s.* was the *lowest price that would remunerate* the farmer, or be such an inducement to him as to enable us to grow all our corn at home? How then would it be consistent with the object of keeping up rents? — an object always disclaimed directly, but always maintained indirectly, as for instance when it is observed, that if something is not done the land will become bankrupt, and furnish nothing to its owners!

The expression, "the landed interest," is very well adapted to lump together the interests of two different classes, interests which are by no means exactly the same in themselves, or of the same concern to the public; that of the farmers, and that of their landlords; of those who pay rent, and of those who receive it. It *may* be important that a farmer should be enabled (even by some sacrifice on the part of the rest of the public) to get reasonable profits; because that will enable him to employ labourers and raise corn: but that the landlords should keep up their rents to any given amount, can concern nobody but themselves.

" But the interest of one class is the same with that of another. Each class is interested in the prosperity of the others. It is an obsolete, barbarous prejudice then, that treats them as opposed." Is it not an obsolete, barbarous prejudice, too, to support any branch of trade or production by permanent protecting duties? The interests of all classes are certainly the same, generally speaking, by *nature;* but that does not prove that an *artificial* protection or benefit to one is a good to the rest; and it does prove the contrary; for if the interests of all classes are the same, it will follow, that a tax on one class for the benefit of another (and such is the Corn Bill, professedly, *if it operates*) cannot benefit either.

The truth is, that this general maxim about the interest of one class being the same with that of others is very well in a *speech*, where you are obliged to express things in a short manner, and where you are tempted to express them in a decisive and striking manner, especially if it has an air of liberality and candour into the bargain; but, for the purpose of reasoning and reflection, it, like most other *short maxims*, does harm, because it is sometimes true and sometimes false; it is true in some cases, and not true in others. It is very true that the contrary proposition is at least equally erroneous, and more hurtful, and till lately was more generally received, and therefore was more necessary to be guarded against: but one extreme is not cured by running into the other.

In order to make the bill complete it should have included a *Bounty on exportation;* and such a provision should even now be incorporated with it while it continues, which at present it must do, probably.

The other great evil of the measure (I mean instance in which it defeats and counteracts its own objects, supposing them to be proper and permanent ones) is, that at 80*s*. it *at once* lets in the foreign corn, which may be at 30*s*., instead of operating by means of a *duty*. This discourages farming as much as any measure that can be well devised. How can the farmer inquire what is the price of corn, and means of supplying it, in some distant part of Europe? Yet on that his interest in a given year may directly depend. That which at this moment is behind a curtain, as it were, with regard to him, may the next dispose entirely of his fate. Naturally, his consolation in a scarce year is high price, in a year of plenty, exportation. The Corn Bill denies him both. It makes the progress of price in scarcity be 60, 70, 80 — 50. If the restriction operated by way of a duty, the influx of foreign corn would be gradual, the farmer would feel his way, and be able to judge what was coming. But on the present plan it comes in a sudden rush, of which it is *impossible* for any body to calculate (especially too when combined with the warehousing system) the effect or price. A duty, too, might afford us the means of paying (what we *must pay* if we mean to protect the farmer at all by a restrictive system) the bounty on exportation. Though indeed the restriction, on importation is just as completely a *tax* as any that might be raised to pay a bounty with.

As to the policy of the measure at all, I cannot help thinking the consideration of it would be rather simplified by stating the question to be (what it really *is*), What we ought to do when, owing to peculiar temporary circumstances during about ten years, price had been excessively raised and cultivation excessively pushed ; and when, on those temporary circumstances having suddenly ceased, corn, far less than half as dear as it was here during the existence of those temporary circumstances, at once flowed in upon us? I say this is the real question ; because, however we may have been treated with *general* reasonings on it, I take it to be quite clear, that restriction would never have been proposed in 1814, if it had not been for the existence of such a particular state of circumstances.

Nothing can be more laudable in itself than the feeling expressed by Lord Liverpool, not to *change* continually in matters of this sort ; to let the producer *know* what he is to look to, instead of keeping him in constant uncertainty. But, in this instance, he *is* in constant uncertainty, *now*. The measure itself has placed him in a situation where he does not know what to reckon upon ; nay worse, where having been led to believe that he was *protected*, he feels distress and difficulty besetting him, he knows not from what source. *Perseverance*, in *such* a measure, produces, then, the very evils, and worse than the very evils, attributed by Lord Liverpool, so justly in general, to *change*.

People say, " We went on very well during the war, and why should we not be prosperous if we could keep up to a like state of things ?" But we *cannot* have a state of things in all respects like that ; and then to make it like in some only, may obviously make us worse instead of better. The particular sort of advantages the war gave us in some parts of our foreign commerce we *cannot* by any laws of ours perpetuate. To perpetuate by laws the advantage the war gave our farmers, since we cannot perpetuate the other, is only doing harm. Because this not only has no tendency to *perpetuate* the commercial advantages alluded to, but brings them to an end *sooner* than they otherwise would have been brought.

We are much too ready to suppose, that with a view to *war* the Corn Bill is necessary. The stoppage of all foreign supply of corn is not a necessary consequence of being at war. Was the late war one of a common, every-day kind? Is there a " continental system" in all wars which we are engaged in? Did even the continental system entirely stop our supplies? And might we not, even if it *had* been in practice a complete stoppage of intercourse with the continent, still have got corn from America, if we had not *chosen* to quarrel with that power?

The first point, in order to meet a war, is surely to increase our wealth and population as much as we can. The Corn Bill clogs and checks the progress of both. It is a perpetual drag to our wheel; while those of other nations are free to run forward.

NOTE XXXVI.

M. Sismondi declares, that with the principle, that a producer becomes consumer of his own products or of other people's, " il devient absolument impossible de comprendre ou d'expliquer *le fait le plus demontré de tous dans l'histoire* de commerce, c'est l'engorgement des marchés" (quoted by M. Say, " Lettres," 15). *Is* any such fact proved by history, as to *all* commodities, *except* when there have been great checks and changes?

Mr. Ricardo, one of the advocates of the principle here attacked by M. Sismondi, has written a chapter on Sudden Changes in the Channels of Trade, on purpose to disencumber the general principle from the argument that is drawn from such periods of stagnation as the present

THE END.